MASTING AND RIGGING

SHIP "MOUNT STEWART"   [*Frontispiece*

From a Pencil Drawing by the Author

MASTING and RIGGING

THE

CLIPPER SHIP & OCEAN CARRIER

*With Authentic plans, working drawings and
details of the nineteenth and twentieth
century sailing ship*

BY

HAROLD A. UNDERHILL

M.C., A.M.I.E.S.

*Author of "Sailing Ship Rigs and Rigging"
and "Deep-Water Sail"*

Plans, Drawings and Details by the Author

GLASGOW

BROWN, SON AND FERGUSON, LTD., NAUTICAL PUBLISHERS

52 TO 58 DARNLEY STREET

First Edition 1946
Reprinted - 1949
Reprinted - 1953

---

*Made and Printed in Great Britain by
Brown, Son & Ferguson, Ltd.,
Glasgow*

PREFACE

In *Sailing Ship Rigs and Rigging* I forecast a future volume, covering in detail the subject I then treated in outline. Early 1939 saw a start made on drawings and text, then came the threat of the second world war and I found myself back serving with H.M. forces.

The next four years provided neither time nor opportunity for proceeding with the work, but at the end of 1943 I was fortunate enough to be stationed on the coast of Scotland, and being within a few hours journey of my office, decided to resume work during periods off duty and at such times as I could get leave. It is under these circumstances that the book has been completed.

It may perhaps be suggested that in starting with the iron and steel sailing ship and working back, I have placed the cart before the horse, for this however I make no apology. In the first place we do know where sailing ship design ended, but who can say just where it began? Secondly, to the best of my knowledge no text books were ever published covering the iron and steel period, whereas for the earlier ships we have such works as Steel's *Mastmaking, Sailmaking & Rigging* of 1794; *Souvenir de Marine* by Admiral Paris; and *Plans ou Dessins de Navires* to mention just those which have been reprinted within the last few years. There are of course others, not easy to obtain perhaps, but available for reference in many libraries. There are also many fine collections of contemporary models from which one can gain a wealth of information.

I have confined this volume to what I have called the clipper and carrier period, representing the final development of commercial sail, and I am satisfied that this was a very clearly defined era. The advent of the type we now know as the clipper ship was a very important milestone, and to attempt to go back to the next one would require a volume much too cumbersone to handle in comfort.

GLASGOW,   HAROLD A. UNDERHILL.
1946.

CONTENTS

vii

LIST OF PLATES

ix

MASTING AND RIGGING

MASTING AND RIGGING

CHAPTER I.

PRINCIPLES OF RIG AND RIGGING.

THE windjammer has often been described as the most beautiful of all man's creations, and few, even those who experienced the hardships of life in sail, will dispute this; but surely she has other claims too, for is she not also an outstanding example of engineering skill? Yet one rarely hears any reference to this side of her character, although it is an important one and certainly deserves more notice. Consider some of the larger vessels such as *Pruessen* or *Potosi* for example, ships having 50,000 sq. ft. of canvas aloft and 137,727 ft. of running gear, all of which could be handled and controlled in all kinds of weather by a relatively small number of men; remember also that some of the lighter sails were as much as 200 ft. above the deck. Think of the strain exerted by this enormous area of canvas, to say nothing of its actual dead weight with spars and gear, yet, thanks to the well designed arrangement of stays and rigging, it was all supported by very lofty and comparatively light masts. Can there be any doubt as to her claim to more than mere beauty?

There is still another angle, the orderly arrangement of all her gear. For the uninitiated to stand on the deck of a deep water sailing ship and gaze at the mass of chain and cordage aloft, is to gain an impression of tangle and confusion, yet in actual fact the direct opposite is the case. The sailing ship's gear is a model of order and system, with a place for everything and everything in its place. Every rope and line has its purpose and allotted place on belaying pin or bitts, and that place will be in the same relation to the surrounding gear on all ships, irrespective of size or nationality. The lead of the gear follows a clearly defined principle, and any sail trained seaman can go straight to the pin he wants no matter how dark the night, whether he is familiar with that particular vessel or not.

At first sight, to understand the function and lead of all the gear of a square rigger may well appear to require life-long study, but when once the basic principle has been grasped the whole intricate network becomes easy to follow. Like most things which have developed out of years of practical experience, the basis of it all is just sound common sense, and I hope that by the time the reader has reached the last chapter he will have

1

sufficient knowledge to understand all he sees on sail and rigging plans, or for that matter the actual ships should one of the few remaining square-riggers come his way, and that the model builder will have been steered clear of the pit-falls into which many seem to slide. How frequently one sees models, otherwise excellent examples of craftsmanship and skill, spoiled by small faults which if reproduced in the full size ship would make it impossible to work her. For example, reef-tackles so close in that they could not possibly stretch the reef band taut; or more common still, yards hoisted so close up under the fore and aft stays that they would jamb before they could be swung in either direction. Small points perhaps, but to anyone with any knowledge of the sailing ship, sufficient to spoil what might otherwise have been a very interesting model.

I do not propose to go very closely into the description of the various rigs, as I assume that anyone sufficiently interested in rigging details to read this book will already have a working knowledge of sailing ship types. In any case the subject has been fully covered in *Sailing Ship Rigs and Rigging*, and to do so here would be needless repetition. However a few brief notes will be given before going on to the masting and rigging details but such notes will be restricted to the use of the gear and rigs in general.

A craft is said to be square-rigged when she carries sails spread on yards whose position when at rest is thwartships, i.e. at right angles to the centre line of the vessel. Fore and aft rig consists of sails set on gaffs, booms or stays parallel to the centre line, and a certain amount of fore and aft canvas is always included in the rig of any square-rigger. A mast is said to be *fully* square-rigged when it carries square sails on all its components including the lower-mast. Thus the square-rigged masts of a barque are *fully* square-rigged, as is the fore-mast of a brigantine or barquentine, but not the foremast of a topsail-schooner where square sails are carried only on the topmast.

Originally all ships masts and spars were built up of timber, and their length was to a large extent governed by the material available. The required diameter could always be obtained, either from a single tree when one large enough was to be had, or by building together the hearts of several trees as will be described in the chapter on timber spars. Additional height was obtained by fitting extra masts above the lower one, the first addition being the topmast, then the topgallant, followed by the royal and in some cases skysail mast (Fig. 1A). As time went on the multiplicity of units was reduced and the royal and topgallant masts were constructed as one spar, although they retained their individual rigging and names. The skysail mast when carried, also formed part of this one spar (Fig. 1B). With the larger iron and steel craft came the introduction of the lower and topmast as one, known as a pole mast, although here again the two sections were functionally quite independent and still retained the names of lower and topmast respectively, and carried tops and cross-trees as in the case of separate fidded topmasts. (Fig. 1c). A fidded mast is one which can be lowered down along the fore side of the mast immediately below, and is supported in position by a fid, or short bar of wood or iron, passing through the heel of the mast and resting on the trestle-trees on either side.

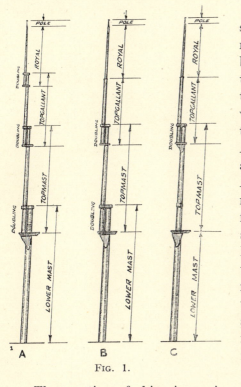

FIG. 1.

The upper masts were, as already stated, fitted on the fore side of the mast below; the topmast being kept up by the trestle-trees of the lower top; the topgallant by the trestle-trees of the topmast cross-trees, and so on. There were however two well known exceptions to this. The four-mast barque *Lawhill* had her topgallant masts fitted abaft the topmasts, and the clipper *Patriarch* was built with telescopic masts, the topgallants and royals being fitted in the tubular topmasts, and when struck slid down inside the mast itself. I have no details of the construction of these masts, but as the experiment was never repeated it seems safe to assume that it did not prove an unqualified success, although the vessel made a name for herself as a clipper. When aloft these masts had the appearance of single poles from keel to truck.

The masting of ships is a science developed from long experience and there is little doubt that in the early days it was largely a matter of guess work, each builder rigging by rule of thumb and putting in what he thought best. Sail plans were increased until experience pointed out the limits to which masting could safely be carried; successful ships were watched and compared one with the other; their dimensions noted and passages recorded, not forgetting the question of freedom from trouble, and as the result of all this there materialized tables of general proportions to form the basis of new designs. These tables apply not only to the lengths of masts and spars in relation to the hull, but also the proportions of the spars themselves so that adequate strength can be obtained without unnecessary weight, and so we have definite proportions for all spars. To enable these tables to be of practical use it was necessary to standardise the points at which the spars should be measured, and also to establish just how the ships should be measured to provide the basic length from which the length of the spar could be calculated.

By the period in which we are interested, not only were these tables in more or less general use as the basis of all spar design, but, in the case of iron and steel craft, vessels were being built to the rules and specifications of such societies as Lloyd's, which include tables of minimum spar proportions for vessels of given size. Spar tables for both wood and iron or steel vessels will be found in chapter IX.

Incidentally, these matters of spar proportion, together with that of rake, are two very common faults in model construction, and perhaps the worst offenders are the sailor built models. Models made by seamen on long passages, or for that matter retirement ashore, are often perfect in the lead of the gear and other rigging details but hopelessly out of proportion, with the length of their spars grossly exaggerated. This tendency is quite natural, as anyone who has looked down from the royal yard, or up from the deck of a large sailing ship will agree. The distance seems immense. So it was to the sailor serving in a windjammer, his normal view point was either looking down at a deck much reduced by the distance from which he saw it, or along individual spars, which by their very nearness impressed him with their great size. He rarely saw his ship from a distance and so had no chance of estimating the true proportions, therefore, the magnitude of the spars compared with the smallness of the hull as seen from aloft were fixed in his mind, and reproduced in his models.

The idea that great rake on a mast is the hall-mark of speed is no doubt a legacy of the old sea story, where the pirate brig always had lofty raking masts. It is true that many of the early ships did have considerable rake, particularly the small brigs, schooners, and naval cutters. But rake in itself is not necessarily a factor of speed, it needs a well balanced combination of rake, hull design, and mast spacing to produce a good fast ship, for the model builder to exaggerate the rake of a vessel's masts with the misguided idea that by so doing he is making her a clipper, is about as foolish as adding an extra funnel to a "three-island tramp" and calling her an ocean greyhound! A certain amount of rake aft is both normal and advantageous, it gives the backstays a better set and greater strength to resist the forward momentum of the mast when the ship is plunging into a head sea. The average rake on the masts of vessels of the later day type is in the neighbourhood of from 5° to 6° at the main mast, and it is customary to increase the rake slightly on each mast from bow to stern. Thus the main would have about 1° more than the fore, the mizzen 1° more than the main and so on, making the masts "fan-out" as it were. This applies to square-rigged craft, but not as a rule to the ore and aft rig.

To return to spar proportions. The basic length on which mast and spar lengths are calculated is the length between perpendiculars, which is from the inside of the stem—the rabbet—to the rabbet of the stern post, both measured at the level of the upper *continuous* deck; this in a sailing ship is normally the main deck (**Fig. 2**). In vessels where the stem forms a long sweeping cut-water, as with the iron or steel ships, the length is measured from the point

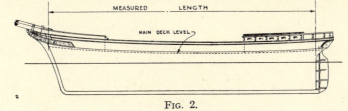

FIG. 2.

where the main deck line would intersect the after edge of the stem if the latter were continued in a straight line with the part below the cutwater, (**Fig. 3**).

In wooden masts the diameters are given at seven points along the length,

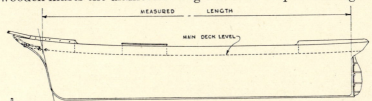

FIG. 3.

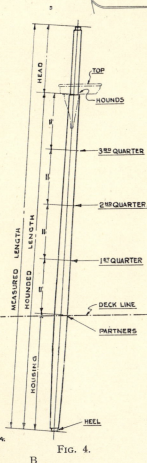

FIG. 4.

B

namely heel, partners, 1st, 2nd and 3rd quarters, hounds and head, (**Fig. 4.**) The partners is the point where the mast projects through the main deck, and this forms the "given" or basic diameter from which all other diameters are calculated. For example, 1st quarter is 60/61 of the given diameter, the 2nd, 14/15, the 3rd 6/7, the hounds 3/4, the head 5/8 and the heel 6/7. Full details of these various proportions will be found in chapter IX.

The hounded length of a mast is the distance from heel to hounds, the housing from heel to partners, and the headed length, or mast-head, from the hounds to the upper surface of the mast head cap. The overlap of two masts, such as the lower-mast and topmast, or topmast and topgallant, is known as the doubling. (**Fig. 1.**)

Topmasts, topgallants and royals are measured in the same way, although slight modification is necessary in the case of combined topgallants and royals, but all this will be covered in detail in the chapter on the use of tables.

Bowsprits are measured at six points: the bed—which forms the given diameter, 1st, 2nd and 3rd quarters, cap and heel. That part of the bowsprit which is inside the hull is known as the housing.

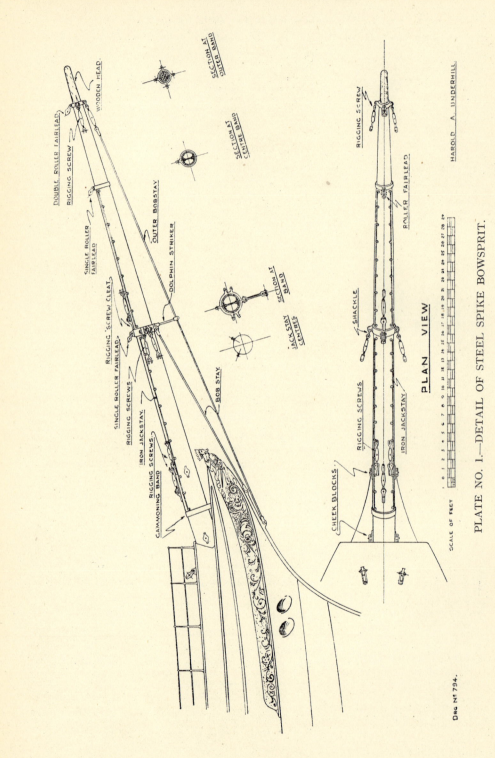

PLATE NO. 1.—DETAIL OF STEEL SPIKE BOWSPRIT.

HAROLD A. UNDERHILL

DRG. NO 794.

Yards are measured at five points: the slings or centre of the yard, 1st, 2nd and 3rd quarters on either side and the yard-arm. Jib-booms, booms and gaffs are also measured in much the same way. The tables of iron and steel masts and spars give diameters at fewer points than is the case with wooden spars; this is due to the fact that metal masts are to a large extent parallel sided, or where there is taper it is more or less regular throughout the length.

Tops are semi-circular platforms of wood or iron built round the hounds of the lower masts where they serve the dual purpose of extending the topmast rigging and forming a working space for men aloft. They are supported by cheeks, trestle-trees and cross-trees (Fig. 5). Cheeks are flat timbers or iron plates bolted on each side of the mast and projecting forward to form a bracket supporting the topmast above. Trestle-trees are timbers or angle-irons fitted along on top of the cheeks in a fore and aft direction. Cross-trees are light spars of wood or iron running thwart-ships across the trestle-trees to support and stiffen the top against the crushing strain of the topmast rigging. In wooden ships the trestle-trees are made at least twice the depth of the cross-trees, so that the latter can be let into them until the upper faces are flush, making a level surface on which the decking of the top can be spiked. In iron or steel tops cross-trees are not usually necessary, as the tops are stiff enough without them. The decking is kept clear of the sides of the mast to allow the

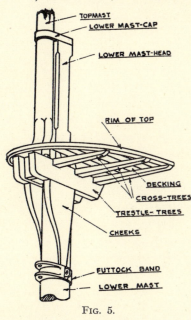

FIG. 5.

standing-rigging to pass round the lower mast head at the hounds, and the opening so formed is known as the lubbers-hole. Hard wood blocks, termed bolsters, are fitted on top of the trestle-trees on either side of the lower-mast, their upper faces are rounded off and their purpose is to form a seating for the lower rigging and prevent it being cut by the sharp edges of the trestle-trees.

The top-mast cross-trees—here the term is applied to the complete assembly and not merely to the thwart-ship spars—are made up of trestle-trees, cross-trees and bolsters as in the case of the tops, but, except in iron or steel vessels, cheeks are omitted and decking never used. Light spars or spreaders extend from the cross-trees in line with the back-stays of the topgallant and royal masts, and are provided with thumb cleats in which the stays rest, so stiffening the rigging of these masts. (Fig. 6.)

Tops and topmast cross-trees are usually fitted parallel to the water line, although in the case of some of the later steel vessels they are made square with the mast as this simplifies construction. Generally speaking, the design of timber and metal tops is much the same, differing only in constructional details.

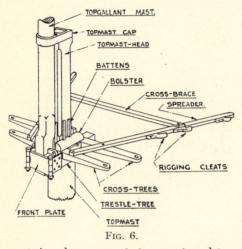

FIG. 6.

Spars may be roughly classified as follows; yards, spars set thwartships to carry square sails; gaffs, spars which extend the heads of fore and aft sails; and booms spreading the foot of fore and aft sails. This classification is not entirely correct, one exception being the studding-sail boom, for this is undoubtedly a square sail spar.

The masts are supported by the standing rigging which may be grouped under three general headings, (a) the shrouds, which are confined to each individual section of the mast, i.e., lower-mast, topmast and topgallant, and support it in a thwart-ship direction, (b) back-stays, in which one may include the cap-stays, to resist the forward pull of the mast, and (c) fore and aft stays which lead forward and brace the mast against any strain in the direction of the stern. The lower shrouds extend from the hounds of the lower-mast down to the bulwarks, and are usually from four to six in number according to the size of the ship. The topmast shrouds, more commonly known as the topmast rigging, extend from the topmast cross-trees—hounds—to the rim of the top. Topgallant shrouds or topgallant rigging, extends from the topgallant hounds down to the ends of the topmast cross-trees. Futtock shrouds are short shrouds from the rim of the top or cross-trees, down to a band on the mast a short distance below it. The purpose of the futtock shrouds is to counteract the upward pull of the topmast or topgallant rigging. (Fig. 7.)

The lower cap-stays are set up between the lower cap and the bulwarks. Cap-stays are found in most iron or steel vessels, but rarely in wooden craft. Then come the

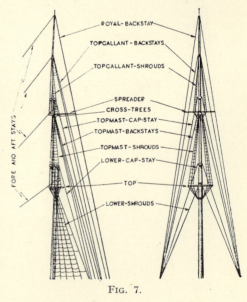

FIG. 7.

topmast back-stays which are set up between the topmast cross-trees and the bulwarks, they vary in number from one to three per side according to the size of the vessel. These are followed by the topmast cap-stay which extends between the topmast cap and the bulwarks. The topgallant and royal back-stays are rigged between their respective hounds and the bulwarks. The manner in which these back-stays lead varies slightly in different ships and will be covered fully in the chapter on standing rigging.

Fore and aft stays are set up between their respective hounds and the deck, or between hounds and a lower point on the mast forward of the one to which they belong. There are various methods of leading these stays, but these can be left to the appropriate chapter, it being sufficient at this stage to merely outline the salient points. Generally speaking a stay takes its name from the mast to which its upper end is attached, thus the fore-royal stay extends from the head of the fore royal mast down to the jib-boom: it will be noted by the way, that its opposite number leading aft is the fore royal *back*-stay. Where several fore and aft stays lead off the same mast head, as in the case of the fore topmast, the inner one takes its name from the mast, i.e. the fore topmast-stay, and the remainder from the sails they carry; jib-stay, outer jib-stay and so on. This is not always quite as simple as it may seem, for stay-sails, like many other items of a sailing ship's gear, frequently had several alternative names, a fact which is apt to be very confusing to the beginner. In modern wire rigged ships the lower fore and aft stays are often double, that is two wires side by side and seized together to form a single stay.

As there is no downward pull on the bowsprit or jib-boom, they are stayed against stress in three directions only; the bobstay and martingale stays to oppose the upward pull of the head-stays, and the guys or shrouds to counter-act the lateral strain on either side. The martingale—or dolphin-striker, to give it its older name—is a spar projecting down from the underside of the bowsprit, and acting as a strut to increase the downward pull of the martingale rigging and the head stays which pass through the jib-boom and so back to the hull. The martingale rigging is in two parts, that between the jib-boom and the fore side of the martingale being the martingale stays, and between the martingale and the hull the martingale back-stays, sometimes called back-ropes. These latter not only balanced the forward pull of the stays, but, by spreading to the hull on either bow, checked any tendency for the martingale to cant over to either side. In vessels rigged with bowsprit and jib-boom the martingale rigging is usually chain, although there are of course, exceptions. The martingale stays are of fixed length, shackled to the jib-boom at one end, and the martingale at the other, but martingale back-stays have either hearts and lanyards or rigging screws for setting the gear up taut.

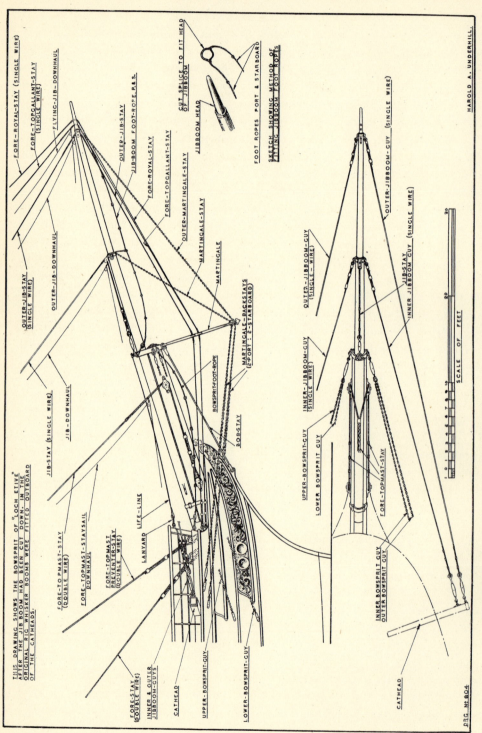

THIS DRAWING SHOWS THE BOWSPRIT OF "LOCH ETIVE" AFTER THE JIB BOOM HAD BEEN CUT DOWN. IN THE ORIGINAL RIG WHISKER BOOMS WERE FITTED OUTBOARD OF THE CATHEADS.

SKETCH SHOWING METHOD OF FITTING JIBBOOM FOOT ROPES.

FOOT ROPES PORT & STARBOARD

CUT SPLICE TO FIT HEAD OF JIBBOOM

JIBBOOM HEAD

FORE-ROYAL-STAY (SINGLE WIRE)

FORE-TOPGALLANT-STAY (SINGLE WIRE)

FLYING-JIB-DOWNHAUL

OUTER-JIB-STAY

JIB-BOOM FOOT-ROPE P&S.

FORE-ROYAL-STAY

FORE-TOPGALLANT-STAY

OUTER-MARTINGALE-STAY

MARTINGALE-STAY

MARTINGALE

MARTINGALE-BACKSTAYS (2 PORT : 2 STARBOARD)

BOWSPRIT-FOOT-ROPE

BOB-STAY

OUTER-JIB-STAY (SINGLE WIRE)

OUTER-JIB-DOWNHAUL

JIB-STAY (SINGLE WIRE)

JIB-DOWNHAUL

FORE-TOPMAST-STAY (DOUBLE WIRE)

FORE-TOPMAST-STAYSAIL DOWNHAUL

FORE-TOPMAST PREVENTER-STAY (DOUBLE WIRE)

LANYARD

LIFE-LINE

FORE-STAY (DOUBLE WIRE)

INNER & OUTER JIBBOOM-GUYS

CATHEAD

UPPER-BOWSPRIT-GUY

LOWER-BOWSPRIT-GUY

OUTER-JIBBOOM-GUY (SINGLE WIRE)

OUTER-JIBBOOM-GUY (SINGLE WIRE)

INNER-JIBBOOM-GUY (SINGLE WIRE)

JIB-STAY (SINGLE WIRE)

INNER JIBBOOM GUY (SINGLE WIRE)

FORE-TOPMAST-STAY

UPPER-BOWSPRIT-GUY

LOWER BOWSPRIT GUY

INNER BOWSPRIT GUY

OUTER BOWSPRIT GUY

CATHEAD

SCALE OF FEET

HAROLD A. UNDERHILL.

PLATE No. 2.—RIGGING PLAN FOR BOWSPRIT AND JIBBOOM OF AN IRON VESSEL.

DRG N° 804

Bobstays are rigged between the stem and the bowsprit at or near the cap, and take the upward pull of the head stays which set up on the bowsprit. Bobstays may be either chain or solid iron bar, the latter being most commonly used in the later day ships. Iron or steel vessels with single spar—spike— bowsprits may have a modified form of martingale, or it may be omitted altogether and an additional bobstay taken out to the end of the spar. This reduction in head gear is possible owing to the fact that the spike bowsprit is relatively short and of great strength, the tubular construction being strengthened with internal stiffening webs as shown in the sections on Plate 1.

The bowsprit and jib-boom guys are equivalent to the shrouds and back-stays of the masts, and are led as follows. The bowsprit guys extend from a point at or near the bowsprit cap, and are set up at the bows on either side, while the jib-boom and flying jib-boom guys run from their respective stops to the bows, or in some cases the cat-heads. Older vessels with long jib-booms have spars of either wood or iron projecting from the bows at either cat-head, these serve the dual purpose of giving the maximum spread to the rigging, and at the same time keeping it clear of the anchor gear. These spars are known as whisker booms. (Fig. 8.)

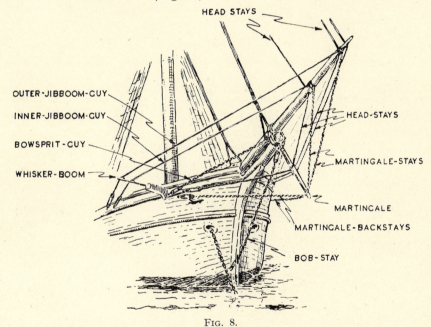

HEAD STAYS

OUTER-JIBBOOM-GUY

INNER-JIBBOOM-GUY

BOWSPRIT-GUY

WHISKER-BOOM

HEAD-STAYS

MARTINGALE-STAYS

MARTINGALE

MARTINGALE-BACKSTAYS

BOB-STAY

FIG. 8.

Generally speaking, sails take their names from the mast or stay on which they are carried. Thus the square sail carried on the fore royal mast is the fore-royal; on the fore topgallant mast, the fore topgallant; on the fore-topmast, the fore topsail. The sails on the lower masts are the exception, for collectively they are termed courses, and individually fore-sail, main-sail, and cro'jack (cross-jack), the latter being the lower sail on the mizzen-mast, a gaff sail set on aftermost mast of a square-rigger is always the driver or spanker, while gaff sails on any other square-rigged mast are known as spencers. Fore and aft sails set on stays are either stay-sails or jibs according to their position.

Running rigging is largely named after the particular portion of the sail it serves, and if its name is to readily suggest to the reader, as it should, its use and location, it is necessary to be conversant with the parts of a sail. Stay-sails are as a rule triangular in shape, although there are exceptions as we will see in Chapter V. The fore, or leading edge is the luff, sometimes

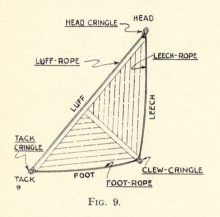

FIG. 9.

called the fore-leech; the after edge, the leech, and the lower edge the foot. The upper corner is the head, the forward lower corner, the tack; and the after lower corner, the clew. Eyes or cringles are worked into each of the corners for the purpose of bending the sail. (Fig. 9.)

The top of a square sail is of course the head; the two sides are the leeches; and the lower edge the foot. Cringles are fitted in each corner and known by the positions they occupy, thus those at the head are head-earing-cringles,

—"earing" because the lashing which is reeved through them is known by that name; and the lower ones, clew-cringles. Cringles are also worked into the leeches opposite the reef-bands, (Fig. 10.) The parts of a gaff sail are, head; luff-edge nearest the mast; leech—after edge; and foot, and the four corners are peak; throat; tack; and clew respectively, as shewn in Fig. 11. Cringles and reef bands are fitted on gaff sails which are lowered down the mast when taken in.

All sails are edged with rope, which again takes its name from the position it occupies, i.e. head-rope; luff-rope;

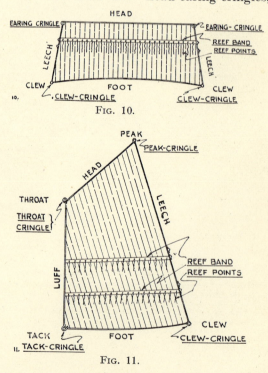

FIG. 10.

FIG. 11.

leech-rope; and so on. Collectively round the whole sail these ropes become the bolt-rope.

At one time square sails were laced direct to the yards and of course hung below them. (Fig. 12A.) This however was before the period in which we are now interested, I believe the jack-stay came into general use in the early part of the nineteenth century, before 1820, I think, but I have no knowledge of the actual date. The jack-stay, which continued in use right up to the end of square-rig, consists of a wire or iron stay carried on short iron stanchions fitted along the top of the yard (Fig. 12B), and to this the sail is tied—or "bent"—with what are known as "rovings". The act of attaching

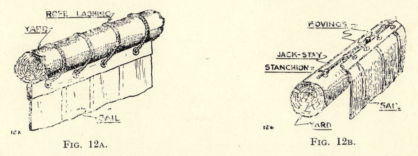

FIG. 12A.   FIG. 12B.

any sail to a spar or stay is termed "bending" the sail. When loosed a square sail hangs down the fore side of the yard, and in furling is gathered up on *top* of it. Stay-sails are bent to their respective stays by means of hanks, or metal rings, which enable the sail to slide freely up and down the stay.

The method of bending square sails is a point the small scale modeller would do well to watch. It is quite common on small scenic models to see the sails stuck along the underside of the yard. To be able to see the yard at all from the fore-side of a square sail is all wrong, it should be visible only from the after, or windward side. This again is a small point perhaps, but an important one, for the projecting yard casts a shadow on the sail where no shadow should be, and that is very noticeable.

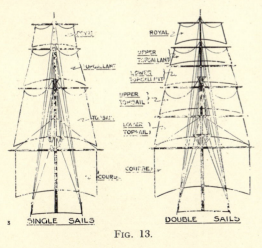

FIG. 13.

Originally all square sails extended the full height of their respective masts, but as the size of ships increased, and perhaps more important still, crews were reduced, these sails became too large to be handled by the smaller number of men, and the topsails and topgallants were divided into two parts; upper and lower topsails and topgallants respectively, (Fig. 13). When this is done the lower yard in each case is made a fixture to

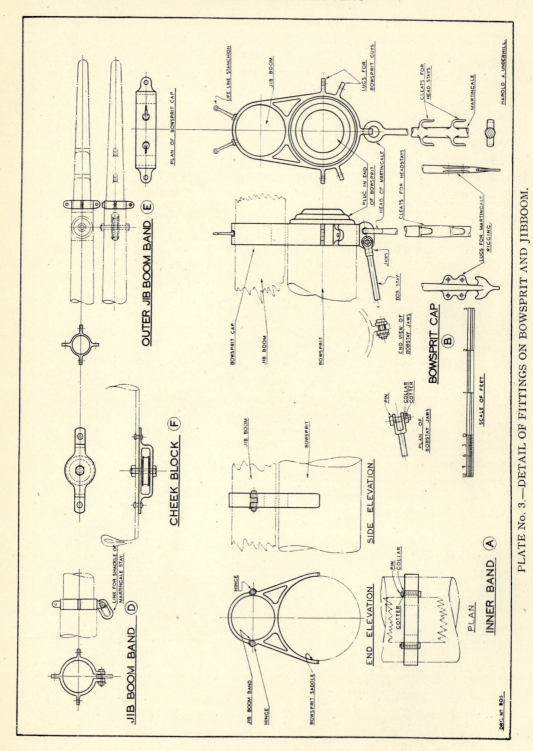

PLATE No. 3.—DETAIL OF FITTINGS ON BOWSPRIT AND JIBBOOM.

the cap of the mast below, while the upper yard travels on parrals sliding on its own mast. Thus the lower topsail yard is supported by the lower mast cap, and the lower topgallant yard by the topmast cap, while the upper topsail and upper topgallant yards are attached to parrals sliding on the topmast and topgallant mast respectively.

This division of topsails and topgallants did not come about all at once, nor was it entirely a matter of size, for as we shall see later, the idea seems to have developed out of Howe's patent close-reefing topsail. However the increase in the size of sails undoubtedly led to its general adoption. Topsails were first divided, leaving single topgallants above them, then as ships became larger the practice spread to the topgallants. Double topsails became the established rig for all sizes and types of craft, but both double and single topgallants continued in use right up to the end of sail, and only during the last few years of sailing ship construction did single topgallants disappear from the ranks of newly launched ships, even then they were still well represented among the ships afloat. In some ships double topgallants were carried on the fore and main, and single on the mizzen.

When it becomes neccessary to reduce the area of individual sails, it is done by reefing, although in modern ships with double top and topgallant yards it is more usual to take in the whole sail, and many such vessels have no reef points on their upper square sails. However just now we are interested in reefing. Across the width of the sail are re-inforcing bands to which the reef points—short lengths of cordage—are attached, while on the leeches are two cringles per side, one directly in line with the reef band, and the other a little distance below it. Reef-tackles (Fig. 14) are rigged from the yard-arms,

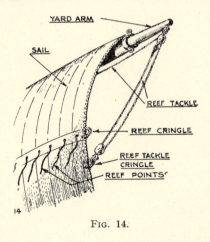

FIG. 14.

and have their lower blocks hooked into the lower of the two cringles. When it is desired to take in a reef, the tackles on either side are hauled taut, so bringing up and stretching the reef-band tightly below the yard. The tackles being in the lower cringles, leaves those on the band free to be lashed out to the yard-arms, after which the reef-points are passed up on either side of the yard and tied off on top, so that the reef-band now becomes the head of the sail, and all the slack canvas is confined and held to the yard by the reef-points. The yard is of course lowered down to suit the reduced size of the sail.

A brief general description at this point of the running gear, its names and various duties, will no doubt help the beginner to a quicker understanding of the leads to be detailed in Chapter VI. The principal items of running rigging are—the halliards, which hoist the sails; sheets, which are attached to the clews, or in the case of gaff sails, the booms, and serve to control the foot of the sail; down-hauls, which as their name suggests, are used to haul down a sail or yard when taking it in; and clew lines, used to haul up the clews of such sails as are hauled up to the yard when being taken in. There are of course many others, such as bunt-lines, slab-lines, leech-lines, etc., but these latter are rather in the nature of a secondary battery, whose function is to assist the primary gear in its work. All this may sound a very formidable list, but as already stated, if you know the parts of the sail, the very names suggest the location and function of the gear and it is in fact all very simple.

As we have already seen, certain yards remain in a fixed position, or at least at a fixed level, while others travel up and down their respective masts. This may be said to divide square sails into roughly two groups; those which when being taken in clew up to a fixed yard, and the second group where the clew of the sail remains at a constant level and the yard comes down. This is not really quite true, for with some sails, the royals for example, the yard cannot come all the way down owing to the standing rigging, and therefore the clews must go part of the way to meet it, but the division into two groups is near enough for general description. In the first group we have the courses, lower topsails, and lower topgallants, while the second group covers all other square sails, including all *single* topsails and topgallants. If we take the function of the gear on one or two sails as examples, that should be sufficient to explain the broad principle of all.

For our first example we will take one of the courses, (Figs. 15 and 16). The courses, being bent to fixed yards, do not require halliards. All lower yards are however fitted with lifts which extend from the yard-arms, through a block at the lower mast cap and so down to the deck. The purpose of the lifts is to trim the yard to the horizontal position, or cant one side up out of the way when alongside in dock. At the yard-arms and extending aft are the brace pendants, each having a block at the outer end. Through these blocks the braces, which swing the yards in fore and aft direction, are led. At the extreme end of the yard-arms are the reef-tackles.

On the fore side of the sail, we have the leech-lines leading from

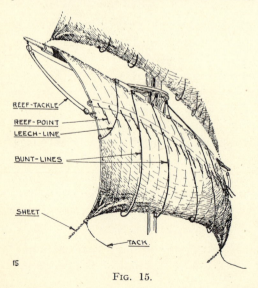

REEF-TACKLE

REEF-POINT

LEECH-LINE

BUNT-LINES

SHEET

TACK

15

FIG. 15.

the leech, through blocks on the yard and so down to the deck as will be detailed later; and buntlines, which are similar in every respect except that they lead from the foot of the sail. The number of buntlines will depend upon the size and cut of the sail. (Fig. 15.) On the after side are the clew-garnets—although why they should be *garnets* on the courses when on all other sails, where they occupy the same position and serve the same purpose, they are clew-*lines*, I do not know. It is just another of those incongruities of the windjammer, like the cro'jack on the mizzen for instance. However to return to the clew-garnets. They lead from the clew of the sail, through blocks at the bunt—centre—of the yard and down to the deck. Slab-lines correspond with the buntlines except that they are on the after side of the sail. (Fig. 16.)

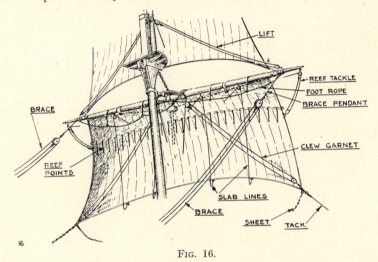

Fig. 16.

Before going on to the sheets and tacks let us see just what happens when the gear already described is used. If we haul on bunt-lines, leech-lines, clew-garnets, and slab-lines, the sheets being eased away of course, it is obvious that the clews of the sail will be hauled up to the bunt; the leeches drawn along the yard by the clew-garnets and leech-lines, and the rest of the sail gathered up by the bunt-lines and slab-lines (when rigged). By this we will have spilled the wind out of the sail and bunched it along the yard ready for furling. In actual fact it was not quite as easy as it sounds, and often meant a good hard fight to get the sail in, but we are only concerned with the function of the gear, not the man power necessary to operate it. In many of the large steel barques of later vintage, the upper clew-garnet blocks are fitted at the yard-arms instead of the bunt, and the leech-line becomes a bunt-line by being bent to the foot instead of the leech of the sail. The advantage of this arrangement is that it distributes the sail more evenly along the yard and gives less canvas to pack at the bunt. However, all this will be dealt with more fully in chapter VI.

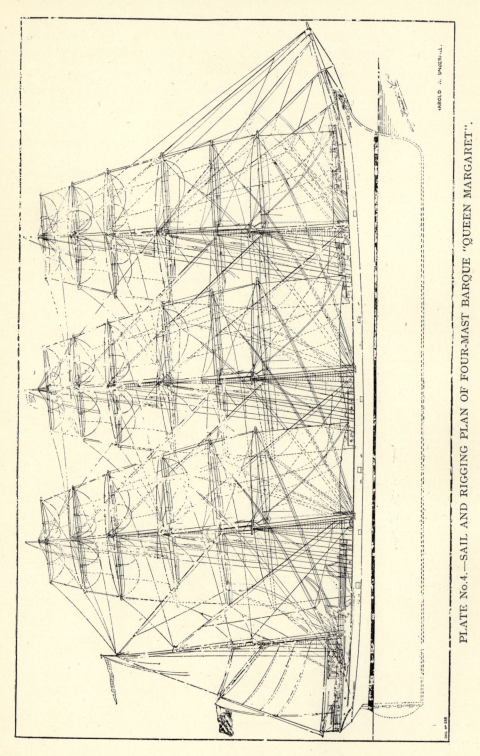

PLATE No. 4.—SAIL AND RIGGING PLAN OF FOUR-MAST BARQUE "QUEEN MARGARET".

Sheets and tacks are provided to control the foot of the sail and transmit its pull to the hull. They are both bent to the clew cringle. There is also a third line which is known variously as the tail-rope, lazy-tack or lazy-sheet, and its purpose is to control the clew of the sail when transferring from tack to sheet, or vice versa. Also, when clewing up the sail, the tacks and sheets are often unbent from the clew-cringles and the lazy tack controls the foot until the sail is up to the yard.

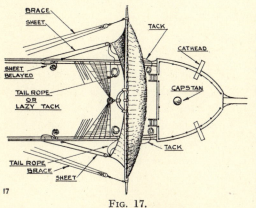

FIG. 17.

When a ship is dead before the wind the yard will be square across the hull, and the pull of the sail taken by the sheets on either side, with the tacks doing little more than steady the clews. (Fig. 17.) But should the ship be "on a wind", i.e. with the wind a point or so before the beam, the yards will be braced up sharp and the weather—windward—clew must be taken forward, otherwise the sail would be aback. When the yards are braced up in this way the tack on the lee side and the sheet on the weather are unbent. This is where the tail-rope comes into operation, it is hauled taut and made fast while the sheets are transferred, the lee sheet is then hauled aft and the weather tack forward. (Fig. 18.)

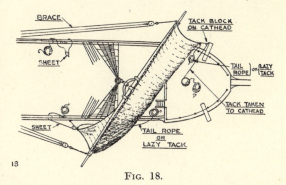

FIG. 18.

There is one more item we must mention before going any further, and that is the gasket. Gaskets are lengths of line used to lash the rolled up sail on top of the yard when furled. They are attached to the yard, and in furling are passed down abaft the yard, up on the fore side, and so on round the yard. When not in use they are coiled and left hanging from the yard, and can be seen in many photographs of ships under sail, as in Fig. 19. For our example of sails bent to hoisting yards we will take an upper-topsail, (Figs. 20 and 21). The upper-topsail is parraled to the topmast and hoisted by means of the topsail halliards. It will be sufficient at this

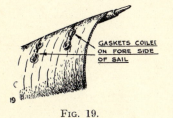

FIG. 19.

point to say that the halliard is divided into two sections; First the tye, which extends from the yard, over a sheave let into the mast head just below the cross-trees, and down a short distance on the after side; secondly the halliard

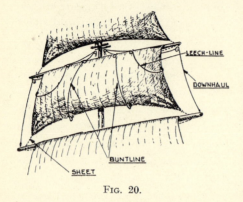

FIG. 20.

proper which continues from the end of the tye down to the deck, and embodies the purchase tackle. This latter may be rigged in various ways, all of which will be covered in detail later on. The lifts of the upper-topsail are standing-lifts, that is to say they are fixed at both ends and do not lead down to the deck. They support the outer ends of the yard when it is down, and when it is in the hoisted position they hang in a bight abaft the yard. (Fig. 21A.)

The upper ends of these lifts are attached to the mast at the cross-trees. Owing to the great length and weight of the yards in some modern ships, it became a common practice to fit double lifts, known as inner and outer lifts respectively

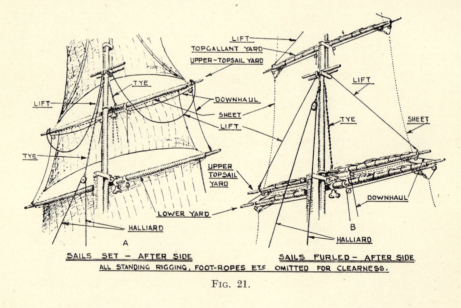

FIG. 21.

The outer ones were rigged to the yard-arms as above, and the inner lifts came down to a point about half way along the yard.

We have already seen that upper-topsails and upper-topgallants are bent to yards which are lowered when taking in sail, and as these yards can travel right down to the yard below, obviously there is no need to haul up the clews of the sail, and of course no clew lines are necessary. In place of these, however, we have down-hauls which lead from the arm of the yard below the sail, up and through a block at its own yard-arm, in to the bunt and so down to the deck. When the sail is full of wind the forward pull, combined with the heel of the vessel, could be sufficient to cause the parral to jamb on the mast, and if it were not for the down-hauls, which exert a downward pull at both yard-arms and the slings, the yard would not come down. In calm weather and the ship on an even keel the yard will of course come down by its own weight. On upper-topsail and upper-topgallant yards the sheets remain fixed, as will be explained in due course.

Single topsails, single topgallants, royals, and skysails all have yards which come down when taking in sail, but owing to the doublings and standing rigging they do not reach the yard below, therefore these sails have halliards, lifts, bunt-lines and clew-lines, and of course, leech-lines when carried.

The rigging on a stay-sail is very simple. The halliard leads from the head of the sail, through a block at the head of the stay, and so down to the deck. The down-haul is also attached to the head of the sail and led down the stay to a block at the foot, from which point it goes away to its belaying pin. To prevent the down-haul hanging or blowing about in a large bight, it is led through the outer eyes of short strops called lizards, these are seized to hanks at intervals down the luff of the sail. The sheets are attached to the clew of the sail and led aft to their belaying points. Head-sails and lower stay-sails have double sheets, this saves passing it over the stay next abaft every time the ship goes on to the other tack; the weather sheet is paid out and the lee sheet hauled in (Fig. 22).

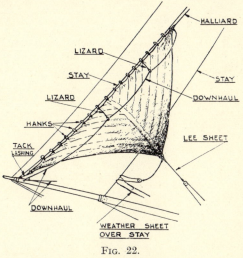

FIG. 22.

Gaff sails may be divided into two groups, those which hoist up and down the mast, and the second group where the gaff remains at a fixed level and the sail is taken in by being brailed in to the mast. In the first type the gaff is provided with two separate halliards; the peak halliards which control the peak or outer end of the gaff; and the throat halliards which are attached to the inner end at the gaff-jaws. These twin halliards are necessary in view of the fact that the gaff is lowered horizontally every time the sail is furled, and has to be hoisted to its correct angle when making sail. The two halliards enable the angle of the gaff to be adjusted to make the sail set properly. By the way, this term "peak" is frequently used by writers of fiction to describe

C

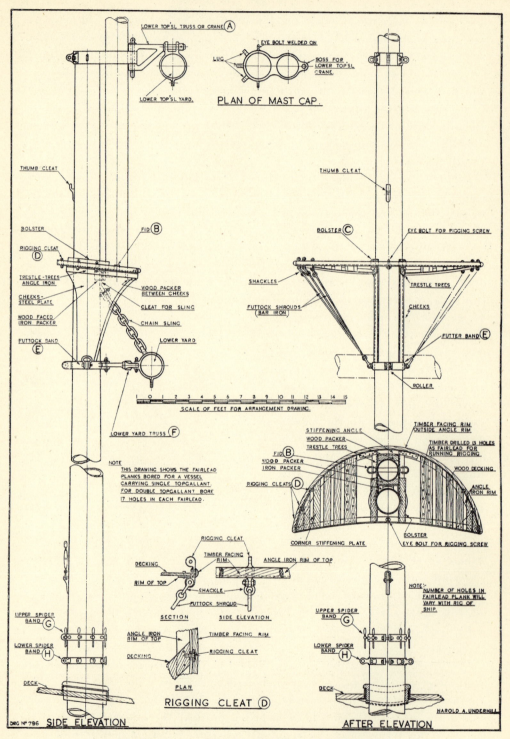

PLAN OF MAST CAP.

LOWER TOP'SL TRUSS OR CRANE (A)
LOWER TOP'SL YARD.
EYE BOLT WELDED ON
LUG
BOSS FOR LOWER TOP'SL CRANE.

THUMB CLEAT
THUMB CLEAT

BOLSTER
RIGGING CLEAT (D)
FID (B)
TRESTLE-TREES ANGLE IRON.
CHEEKS-STEEL PLATE
WOOD FACED IRON PACKER
FUTTOCK BAND (E)
WOOD PACKER BETWEEN CHEEKS
CLEAT FOR SLING
CHAIN SLING
LOWER YARD

BOLSTER (C)
EYE BOLT FOR RIGGING SCREW
SHACKLES
TRESTLE TREES
FUTTOCK SHROUDS (BAR IRON)
CHEEKS
FUTTER BAND (E)
ROLLER

LOWER YARD TRUSS (F)

SCALE OF FEET FOR ARRANGEMENT DRAWING.
0 1 2 3 4 5 6 7 8 9 10 11 12 13 14 15

NOTE
THIS DRAWING SHOWS THE FAIRLEAD PLANKS BORED FOR A VESSEL CARRYING SINGLE TOPGALLANT. FOR DOUBLE TOPGALLANT BORE 17 HOLES IN EACH FAIRLEAD.

STIFFENING ANGLE
WOOD PACKER TRESTLE TREES
FID (B)
WOOD PACKER IRON PACKER
RIGGING CLEATS (D)
TIMBER FACING RIM OUTSIDE ANGLE RIM
TIMBER DRILLED 13 HOLES AS FAIRLEAD FOR RUNNING RIGGING
WOOD DECKING
ANGLE IRON RIM
CORNER STIFFENING PLATE
BOLSTER
EYE BOLT FOR RIGGING SCREW

RIGGING CLEAT
TIMBER FACING RIM
DECKING
RIM OF TOP
SHACKLE
FUTTOCK SHROUD
SECTION
ANGLE IRON RIM OF TOP
SIDE ELEVATION

ANGLE IRON RIM OF TOP
TIMBER FACING RIM
DECKING
RIGGING CLEAT
PLAN
RIGGING CLEAT (D)

UPPER SPIDER BAND (G)
LOWER SPIDER BAND (H)
DECK

UPPER SPIDER BAND (G)
LOWER SPIDER BAND (H)
DECK

NOTE:- NUMBER OF HOLES IN FAIRLEAD PLANK WILL VARY WITH RIG OF SHIP.

HAROLD A. UNDERHILL

DRG N° 796   **SIDE ELEVATION**   **AFTER ELEVATION**

PLATE No. 5.— DETAIL OF STEEL LOWER MAST.

the head of the upper mast. This of course is entirely wrong, the peak is the outer end of the gaff, the cap or "bun" at the top of a mast is the "truck". However, to revert to our hoisting gaff. Lines known as vangs extend from the peak down to the bulwarks on either side, and serve to steady the gaff and prevent it sagging away to leeward, In the same way tackles called boom-guys are rigged between the boom and the rail. The luff of the sail may either be seized to hoops round the mast, or to runners in a metal track on the after side of the mast. The tack and clew are seized to the inner and outer ends of the boom respectively, and the sheet, which takes the form of a heavy tackle, is attached to the outer end and belayed on deck. The boom-topping lifts lead from the end of the boom, through a block above the gaff-jaws and down to the deck. They are as a rule double, one on either side of the sail, and by acting as "guides" help to control the gaff when it is being lowered for furling or reefing the sail. The object of the topping lifts is to support the end of the boom when the sail is furled, or during the process of reefing, and they are so rigged as to take the weight of the boom as soon as the halliards are eased away, although while sail is set they are left sufficiently slack not to chafe the sail. (Fig. 23.)

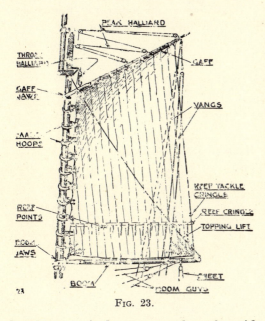

FIG. 23.

The second example, the standing gaff, remains aloft at all times and for this reason does not need both peak and throat halliards, in fact in most cases it has no real halliards at all. The inner end of the gaff is attached to the mast by means of a goose-neck, which is a kind of universal joint, and the peak is supported by a wire span which takes the place of the peak-halliards. Vangs are rigged as in the case of the hoisting gaff. The head of the sail runs in and out along the gaff, either on hoops round the spar, or in a track fitted along the under-side of it. The luff of the sail is laced to a jack-stay on the after-side of the mast. The head out-haul which as its name implies hauls the head of the sail out to the peak of the gaff, is attached to the peak of the sail and passes over a sheave in the end of the gaff; back to the mast and down to the deck. The head down-haul is also attached to the peak of the sail, and leads down to the deck via a block below the goose-neck of the gaff. The foot of the sail is controlled in the same way by means of out-haul and in-haul rigged along the boom. In place of the topping lift, the boom is supported by means of a wire span extending from the peak of the gaff down to its

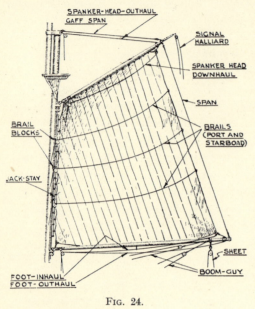

outer end. This type of sail is taken in by being gathered or "brailed" in to the mast, and across the body of the sail are several lines or "brails". These reeve through cringles on the leech of the sail, are taken forward to blocks on the mast, and so down to the deck (Fig. 24).

We have made no mention of that important item of gear, the foot-rope below a yard or jib-boom. This is not to be confused with the bolt-rope along the foot of a sail, although this also is known as the foot-rope. Foot-ropes are rigged below yards and certain booms to give men a foothold when working along the spar. On spars

FIG. 24.

of considerable length the foot-ropes are supported at intervals by means of short wire strops known as stirrups, which are seized to the jack-stays and hang down abaft the yard. The lower end of the stirrup has an eye-splice to which the foot-rope is seized.

To conclude this brief resume of rigging, which I fear many will find very elementary and tedious, I will summarize the various combinations of double and single square sails. First of all we have the vessel with single topsails, and of course single topgallants, for you never see double topgallants above single topsails. Incidentally, except for the naval training brigs, native built Indian craft, and perhaps an odd ship left over from the last century, this rig is not likely to come within our period. (Fig. 25) shows the rig with sails set, and also yards down and sails furled. The next pair of sketches (Fig. 26) show double topsails with single topgallant

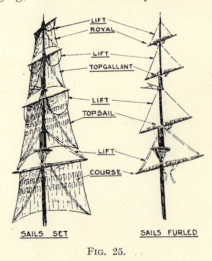

FIG. 25.

and royal above. The third arrangement (Fig. 27) has double topsails, double topgallants and royal, while lastly Fig. 28 illustrates the stump-topgallant or bald-headed rig, which consists of double topsails, double topgallants, and nothing above. This rig was the last frantic effort to economise in both men and materials, at the time of the sailing ship's final fight against the competition of steam.

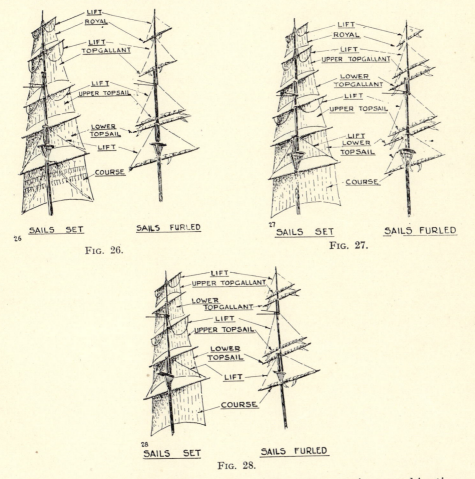

FIG. 26.

FIG. 27.

FIG. 28.

At a little distance it is quite easy to confuse these various combinations, particularly with the modern ships where both double and single-topgallants are cut with great width and relatively little hoist. For example, a vessel rigged with shallow single topgallants, and royals above, can easily be mistaken for a stump-topgallant ship; both have a total of five yards on each mast. The famous *Queen Margaret* had very shallow single topgallants, with royals and skysails above, and at first glance it was easy to mistake her for a ship rigged with double topgallants and royals. Of course when the yards are down and sail furled it is quite impossible to make any mistake, but under sail is a different matter.

CHAPTER II.

MASTS AND SPARS OF IRON AND STEEL VESSELS.

THE subject of masting and rigging is a large one even when, as in the present case, it is limited to one definite period, and if it is to be covered in detail, one must follow through the stages employed in actual shipbuilding practice, and which the model builder would do well to follow in his own work. In the shipyard the first spar to go in is the bowsprit, followed by the lower-masts with their standing rigging and yards. The topmasts, topgallant and royal masts then go into position in that order, their respective yards being sent aloft and crossed as the standing rigging progresses on each mast. The final job is the running rigging and bending of sails. It is my intention to keep to that sequence except that I will fully detail all spars before going on to the standing and running rigging. In the same way I will group all sails into one chapter, so that when we start the lead of the running gear we can continue right through without interruption or break. There is considerable difference between the masts and spars of iron or steel vessels and those of wooden craft, and for that reason I am devoting a chapter to each. The spar construction on composite built vessels is usually a combination of both iron and wood, in that it is common practice to use iron lower-masts and, in some cases yards, with wooden topmasts, topsail yards, and all lighter spars above these. For details of such ships the reader will have to work from both chapters, taking the metal spars from this and all timber spars from the next. Just what spars are wood and what are iron must be taken from the plans and specifications of the ship in question, or if this information is not available, it is safe to assume that the bowsprit and all lower-masts will be iron, while the jib-boom and everything above the lower-masts will be of timber.

It may be as well at this point to mention one rather obvious fact, namely that no one drawing of any individual spar can be said to be true to all ships, or for that matter all ships of that one class. Designers had their own ideas on matters of small detail, and, to a limited degree, general rig. For example some ships have five head-stays, others only four. Then again, the size of the vessel also affected the design, the number of topmast backstays for instance, may vary from three to one per side. These points must be ascertained from the sail and rigging plan of the particular ship under consideration. To give fully detailed drawings of all possible combinations is of course quite impossible, what can, and has been done in this book, is to give drawings and descriptions of typical examples for both metal and timber, the constructional details of which can be said to apply in general to all vessels of the class, and only require minor adjustment in spacing or assembly of components to bring them into line with any specific vessel.

Incidentally, the publishers can supply large scale fully detailed drawings of many well known ships of the clipper and carrier period, and it will be surprising if they are unable to furnish plans suitable for almost any rig belonging to that period. However, should the reader wish to design his own sail and rigging plan, he will find the tables and data in Chapter IX, of considerable assistance, and, providing the main dimensions are known, will have no difficulty in producing accurate spar details.

After that digression I will proceed with the subject of this chapter. The bowsprit has undergone many changes during the evolution of the sailing vessel, and even the short period in which we are concerned can show considerable modification. Originating as a steeply steeved single spar, rather like a pole mast with an exaggerated forward rake, it gradually flattened out and a sprit-topmast was added at the outer end. The steeve—or angle between bowsprit and water line—decreased still further, and the sprit-topmast, now laid along the spar, became the jib-boom. To this was added the flying jib-boom, and in some cases a further extension known as the jib-of-jib-boom. Below these spars were hung the sprit-sail and sprit-topsail yards, these latter of course belong to the period of the bluff apple-bowed craft and as such were out of use before the time we have under consideration, although isolated cases are on record of clippers rigging such sails below their bowsprits.

As design advanced, ships bows became finer and unable to carry the great weight of masts and spars right forward. The masts moved aft, resulting in a corresponding reduction in the length of headgear outboard, until by the end of the clipper era it had shrunk back to a bowsprit and jib-boom. With the advent of the iron and steel vessels it returned to its original single spar in the form of the spike bowsprit, or spike boom as it is more usually called.

The spike boom in larger British deep water craft, may be regarded as a spar carried only by the later and larger steel vessels of the carrier type, although it was common enough in many of the smaller wooden vessels of the coasting fleet, and was used by the Americans in several of their large wood built square riggers.

The measured length of a steel bowsprit is its outboard length, and in this it differs from the timber spar. Spike booms are measured outboard as far as the cap-band, this however will be described in detail in Chapter IX. The given diameter is taken at the bed, which of course is its point of greatest dimension, and from which the spar tapers in both directions. There are of course exceptions to every rule, and there are cases where the spar continues

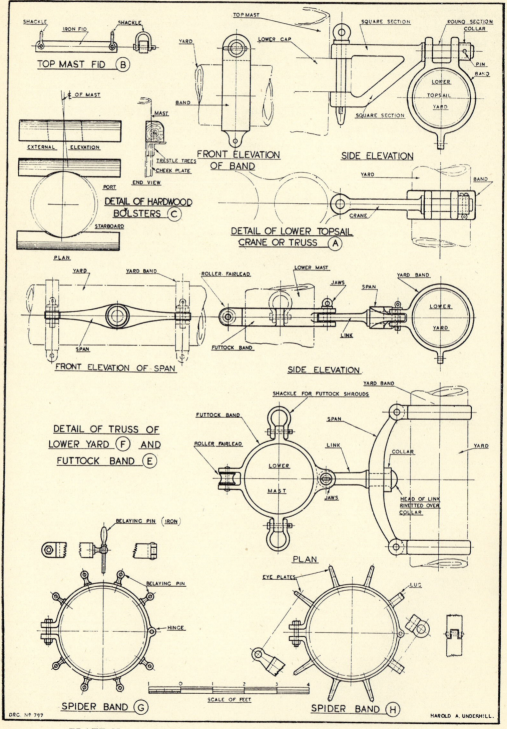

PLATE No. 6.—DETAIL OF FITTINGS ON STEEL LOWER MAST.

to increase in diameter right back to the heel. However the rule is laid down in all tables and should be accepted as standard practice, although in most models this part of the spar will not be seen in any case.

The plating of spars is of little use to the model enthusiast, but it may be of interest to give just one or two brief notes on the way plating is arranged. After all, one knows of several cases where modellers have coppered the bottoms of $\frac{1}{4}''$ scale models, using hundreds of scale copper foil sheets pinned on. I myself always construct models of wooden vessels by building with planks on frames, following both internal as well as external work as closely

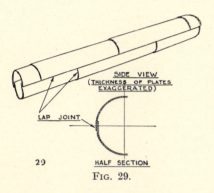

SIDE VIEW
(THICKNESS OF PLATES EXAGGERATED)

LAP JOINT

29   HALF SECTION

FIG. 29.

as possible, and reproducing all iron work on the spars as a matter of course. So why not at least suggest the plating on major spars of a large scale model of a steel ship? Fig. 29 shows the plating on a bowsprit, from which it will be seen that the overlapping plate is always on the upper side like the slates of a roof, so that there are no ledges in which moisture can lodge and form rust.

There are two common methods of building the bowsprit into the hull of an iron or steel vessel, the most usual being that shown in Fig. 30A where the spar projects through the forward end of the fo'castle. In this type the bed of the spar is riveted direct to the main deck beams, with suitable web plating to distribute the load. The second method is for the spar to project through the deck of the fo'castle as in Fig. 30B. There were many well known examples of this arrangement, *Preussen*, *Mozart* and *Pommern* to mention but a few. However the constructional details are much the same in both and the drawing on Plate 1 will serve equally well for either type. There was one well known vessel which did not fall into either of these two categories, that

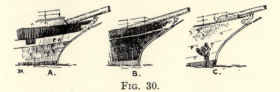

30.   A.   B.   C.

FIG. 30.

was the auxiliary five-mast barque *France II*, for her bowsprit was bedded flush on the fo'castle deck (Fig. 30c) which to my mind made a very unsightly job.

The fittings on a spike bowsprit are clearly shown on Plate 1 but it will be as well to give a brief description of them, starting at the point where the spar leaves the hull. The junction between the bowsprit and the bulkhead is made with an angle iron ring riveted to both bulkhead and spar. Just clear of the bulkhead an iron cheek-block (Fig. 32) is riveted on either side of the spar, these for the inner ends of the fore-topmast-stay. These blocks are

not always used, as we will see when we come to the standing rigging, but that of course may apply to any of the gear shown on the plate. Next comes the gammoning band, an iron or steel band round the bowsprit, bolted on the underside to the stem head structure. This band is the modern equivalent of the gammoning rope

FIG. 32.

of the old wooden ship. On top and a little further outboard are three cleats with rigging-screws attached. There are several ways of making these cleats, two of which are shown in Fig. 33. On the bowsprit shown in the plate the centre cleat is for the jib-stay; the one on the port side for the fore-topgallant-stay; and the starboard one for the fore-royal stay. A detail of this spar complete with rigging will be found on Plate 19. The arrangement of these cleats is of course subject to considerable variation, one alternative for example, would be to fit the cleats for the fore-topgallant

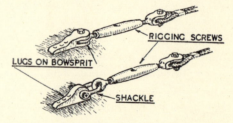

FIG. 33.

and fore-royal stays just forward of the third band, so saving the length of wire along the spar. On either side of the bowsprit at this point is a second cheek-block, these act as fairleads for two parts of the double fore-topmast stay.

Out board of the cheek-blocks mentioned above is the cap-band, which gets its name from the fact that it is situated in the position where the bowsprit cap would be if a separate jib-boom had been carried. On the top of this band is a lug to which the roller fairlead, which is really rather like a small iron block of substantial construction, is bolted. On each side of the band are two lugs to which are shackled the rigging-screws of the upper

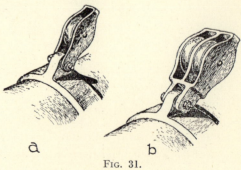

FIG. 31.

and lower bowsprit guys, while a large lug on the underside takes the jaws of the martingale and iron bob-stay. On top of the spar and just forward of the cap-band is the cleat and rigging-screw for the outer-jib stay. The next band has a single lug and fairlead on top for the outer-jib stay. (Fig. 31.)

The last, or outer-band, has a single lug on top for the double roller fairlead serving the fore-topgallant and fore-royal stays. A single lug is formed on either side of this band for the outer bowsprit-guys, and one below for the outer bob-stay. This last band forms the end of the metal spar, and beyond it is the head or pole, which is a wooden terminal driven into the end of the tubular spar.

Along either side of the centre line and extending about two-thirds the length of the spar, is an iron jack-stay supported on short iron stanchions. This provides a hand grip for men working on the foot-ropes, or a foot hold when walking on top of the spar. The exact location of this stay will be seen in the sections on Plate 1.

Our next consideration will be the bowsprits of iron or steel vessels rigged with timber jib-booms. Here we have greater variety, both in proportion, construction and actual rigging details. The relative length of the jib-boom outboard of the cap, ranged from about three times the length of the bowsprit in some ships, down to equal length in others. However about two to one was perhaps the most common in ships of the iron and steel period.

For our detailed example I have selected the famous wool clipper *Loch Etive*. She was an iron ship of 1288 tons, built in 1877 for the Loch Line, by A. & J. Inglis of Glasgow and may be said to be typical of the Clyde-built clipper of the period. The detailed drawing on Plate 2 shows the *Loch Etive's* headgear as it was after the jib-boom had been shortened some 10 ft. 0 ins., and with the fore-royal and fore-topgallant stays leading through the spar just forward of the outer-jib stay. The original rig is shown on her sail and rigging plan published in *Sailing Ship Rigs and Rigging*.

As is usual with iron ships, the *Loch Etive* had an iron bowsprit and long timber jib-boom, which, as already stated, was later cut down to the length shown on Plate 2. The martingale was an iron forging, as were the whisker-booms on the cat-heads. These booms were very common on the iron clippers, but not so prevalent in ships of later date.

The construction of an iron bowsprit follows very closely that of the spike boom, at least as far as the cap-band, and it will be sufficient to simply enumerate the fittings shown on our example; always bearing in mind that it *is* only one example. At the inboard end and close against the bulkhead is the heel-chock of the jib-boom. This is a timber stop bolted on top of the bowsprit to prevent the heel of the boom coming too far inboard. Its upper surface is the same as that of the jib-boom, so that when the latter is butted

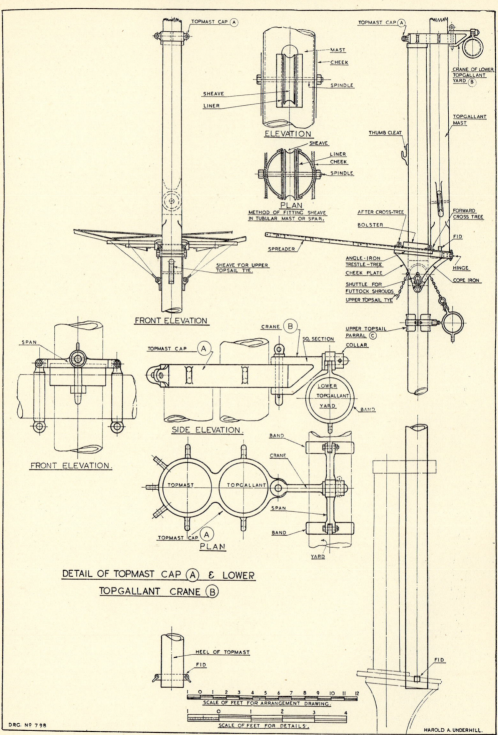

TOPMAST CAP (A)

MAST
CHEEK
SPINDLE

SHEAVE
LINER

ELEVATION

SHEAVE
LINER
CHEEK
SPINDLE

PLAN
METHOD OF FITTING SHEAVE
IN TUBULAR MAST OR SPAR.

TOPMAST CAP (A)

CRANE OF LOWER
TOPGALLANT
YARD (B)

TOPGALLANT
MAST

THUMB CLEAT

AFTER CROSS-TREE
BOLSTER

SPREADER

FORWARD
CROSS TREE

FID

ANGLE-IRON
TRESTLE-TREE
CHEEK PLATE

HINGE
COPE IRON

SHUTTLE FOR
FUTTOCK SHROUDS
UPPER TOPSAIL TYE

SHEAVE FOR UPPER
TOPSAIL TYE.

FRONT ELEVATION

UPPER TOPSAIL
PARRAL (C)
COLLAR

SPAN

FRONT ELEVATION.

CRANE (B)

TOPMAST CAP (A)

SQ. SECTION

LOWER
TOPGALLANT
YARD

BAND

SIDE ELEVATION.

BAND

CRANE

TOPMAST   TOPGALLANT

SPAN

BAND

TOPMAST CAP (A)
PLAN

YARD

DETAIL OF TOPMAST CAP (A) & LOWER
TOPGALLANT CRANE (B)

HEEL OF TOPMAST
FID

FID

SCALE OF FEET FOR ARRANGEMENT DRAWING.

SCALE OF FEET FOR DETAILS.

DRG. No 79B

HAROLD A. UNDERHILL.

PLATE No. 7.—IRON OR STEEL TOPMAST AND CROSS-TREES.

against it, it forms a continuous spar. There are several ways of cutting the face of the chock where it meets the jib-boom, sometimes it is square as in our example, at others it forms either a scarfed or stepped joint with the boom as shown in Fig. 34.

Just outboard of the heel-chock is the inner jib-boom band. This is

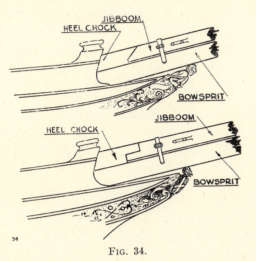

FIG. 34.

riveted on to the bowsprit and serves to confine the heel of the boom to the top of the spar. When docking or moored in a crowded anchorage, the jib-boom was hauled inboard until the outer stays came against the bowsprit cap. This was known as "rigging in" or "striking" the jib-boom. To enable the heel to be lifted high enough to clear the chock and come in on deck, it is necessary to raise it out of the inner band, and for this purpose the top of the band is hinged to open. Fig. 35 shows two methods of making inner jib-boom bands. On either side of the bowsprit are two cheek-blocks, one close inboard and the other just abaft the bowsprit-cap. These are for setting up the fore-topmast stay. The outer cap takes the form of twin bands, the lower and larger one encircling the bowsprit, and the upper and smaller one supporting the jib-boom. The cap is fitted at the end of the bowsprit, which

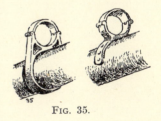

FIG. 35.

is closed by an iron plug, decorated on its outer face with raised circular bosses. In some ships this plug was made of wood and decorated with some form of symmetrical carving. Typical bowsprit caps are shown in Fig. 36.

To turn to Plate 2. On top of the bowsprit cap are two light iron stanchions set at an angle of about 40° to the vertical, these are for the life-lines, or hand-lines which extend between these stanchions and the knight-heads

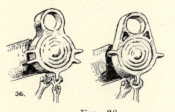

FIG. 36.

and form a hand grip for men working on the spar. The upper-band of the bowsprit cap is made an inch or so larger than the actual diameter of the jib-boom, and should be lined with leather to prevent undue chafe on the timber spar. This clearance also provides sufficient play to allow the boom to cant up clear of the heel chock when being hauled inboard. On each side of the lower part of the cap are two lugs for the upper and lower bowsprit guys, while on the underside is one large lug drilled for the martingale and the jaws of the iron bob-stay.

The martingale is a forged bar tapering to either end. The upper end has an eye forged into the lug on the under side of the bowsprit cap, which leaves it free to move in any direction, so that its actual angle is fixed by the setting up of the martingale rigging. In the centre of the martingale are four thumb cleats arranged in pairs on either side, these are for the head-stays, which lead through the jib-boom; over the cleats and back to the bows. At the foot are lugs or eyes in a fore and aft direction, those on the after side for the port and starboard martingale back-stays, and on the fore side for the martingale-stays. The foot of the martingale is finished off with an ornamental spear head.

An alternative method of attaching the martingale to the bowsprit cap is by means of a double hinged joint as shown in Fig. 37.   There are also cases where the martingale is attached to the lug of the cap by means of simple jaws like those of the short martingale of the spike boom, this however is not a common practice with the long spar used below a bowsprit and jib-boom, as should the rigging not be set up equally on either side, it would impose a bad twisting strain on the jaws and the lug of the cap. A form of universal joint, no matter how simple, is the best attachment for a martingale set up with flexible rigging.

FIG. 37.

The jib-boom is of course a timber spar, and in the example shown in Plate 2 it is of the same diameter from cap to heel, although in some cases, examples of which will be given later, the heel was made rather smaller.   Outboard the spar tapers from cap to head, with stops or shoulders at intervals along its length. The heel-chock is roughly "D" shaped in section, the flat side of the "D" being slightly hollowed to saddle the upper surface of the bowsprit, and the round of the "D" conforming to the section of the jib-boom, so that the top and two sides make a continuous spar with it.

The jib-boom of the *Loch Etive* was round in section throughout its entire length, but in some cases the heel is hexagonal or square, in which case the heel-chock will of course be made to match. However, to return to Plate 2.   Just forward of the inner jib-boom band is a sheave hole for the heel-rope. This line is rigged when required for hauling out the jib-boom, and is not in position under normal circumstances. The sheave hole is cut in the horizontal plane and the forward edges on either side are grooved to allow the heel-rope to lead fair on to the sheave. (Fig. 38.)

The next fitting is an iron band at the first rigging stop. The stop is a square check or shoulder, equal in depth to the thickness of the metal forming the band, so that the surface of the spar on the inboard side is flush with the outer diameter of the band, and the spar forward of this point is of the

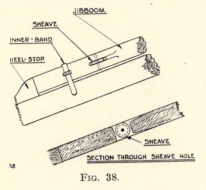

same diameter as the inside of the band. On top of the band is a pair of lugs with a roller between them forming a fairlead for the stay, while a single lug on either side receives the inner jib-boom guys. The band does not completely encircle the timber spar, but has a gap of some two inches on the underside and the ends flanged down. These flanges are drilled for a bolt, which serves to draw the band tightly round the spar, or alternatively

FIG. 38.

be slacked off and moved forward when rigging in the jib-boom.   A link is fitted on the bolt and between the flanges, and to this is shackled the head of the inner martingale stay. (Fig. 39.)

It will be noted that in this case the roller fair-lead forms an integral part of the band, instead of being a separate block bolted on; however, this is quite optional. From the centre band the jib-boom tapers down to the next stop, which is formed in the same way, although here the metal band is a driving

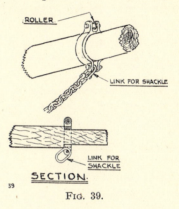

FIG. 39.

fit or shrunk on the spar and has no tightening gap on the underside. It is provided with three lugs, one on either side for the outer jib-boom guys, and one below for the outer martingale-stay. Just inboard of this band is the sheave hole for the outer jib-stay, this of course is cut in the vertical plane. Outboard of this last band is the head or pole of the jib-boom, which is pierced with two holes for the fore topgallant-stay and fore-royal stay respectively. The inner lips of these holes are rounded off on their upper and lower edges; this is to prevent "nipping" the stay where it enters and leaves the hole.

Plate 5 is the general arrangement drawing of a lower-mast for iron or steel construction, and Plate 6 detailed drawings of each component. I have not included any drawings of the mast partners as this comes under the heading of hull construction. Just above the deck is the first spider-band "H". This has six welded eyes arranged three on either side, and two heavy lugs on the fore side of the mast. The eyes are for sundry lead and purchase blocks, while the heavy lugs take the lead blocks of the lower topsail sheets.

The band is in two halves, hinged together on the fore side and drawn tightly round the mast by means of a nut and bolt passing through a pair of lugs on the after side. The next spider-band is constructed in the same way, but carries eight iron belaying pins in short iron brackets or stanchions.

On the after side of the mast is a cleat and rigging-screw for the lower end of the topgallant stay of the mast next abaft. This of course would not be required on the aftermost mast of any vessel, where provision is made for the boom goose-neck, spanker jack-stay, etc. I would also again remind the reader that, as will be explained when we come to the standing rigging, the position of any fitting used as an anchorage for standing rigging will vary from ship to ship. and therefore it must always be remembered that I am merely describing one example.

Next comes the futtock-band "E", the principal function of which is to anchor the truss of the lower yard, although it also serves to hold down the futtock-shrouds and provides a fairlead for the topgallant-stay of the mast next abaft. This fairlead consists of two lugs and a roller on the after side of the band. On the port and starboard sides of the band are lugs to which are shackled the forged eyes in the lower ends of the iron futtock-shrouds, and on the fore side are the jaws to receive the lower truss "F".

The object of the truss is to support and keep the yard at the correct distance from the mast, and of course, in so doing it transmits the pull of the sail through the yard to the mast. The truss forms a universal joint giving the yard free movement in almost any direction except out from or in to the mast. The actual weight of the yard is carried by the chain sling. The perspective sketch (Fig. 40) will help those who have difficulty in reading working drawings, and from this it will be seen that the futtock-band has

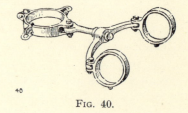

FIG. 40.

jaws fitted in the horizontal plane, into which is hinged a short link which passes through a bow shaped bar attached to the yard by means of two bands. This bar can rotate on the forward end of the link, so allowing the yard to be canted up as required, while the jaws at the futtock-band permit free movement from side to side.

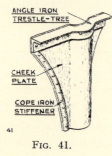

ANGLE IRON
TRESTLE-TREE

CHEEK
PLATE

COPE IRON
STIFFENER

FIG. 41.

We now come to the construction of the top. The cheeks are metal plates curved in the centre to sit snugly on the mast, to which they are riveted. A cope iron—half round section—is riveted on the outside of the leading edge to stiffen it, while the angle iron trestle-trees are riveted along the top edge. (Fig. 41). The rim of the top is an angle iron bar forming its outer perimeter and supporting the decking. Bolted outside the vertical face of this angle is a timber facing, half-round in section. This facing is carried round the front and sides, but not across the after end of the top, and its object is to prevent the sails and gear chafing on the iron-work. Riveted to the rim are

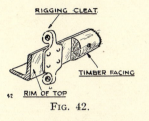

FIG. 42.

six rigging cleats "D" (Fig 42). These are fitted three on each side in the positions shown and serve as anchorages for the standing rigging; their upper lugs taking the rigging-screws of the topmast shrouds, and the lower ones the shackles of the futtock-shrouds. The futtock-shrouds are iron bars with eyes forged in either end, and must be made exactly to size for their respective positions, as there is no means of adjusting them when once they are in place. On top of and bolted to the trestle-trees are the bolsters "C". These are hard-wood blocks on which the eyes of the lower rigging rest, as will be described in a later chapter.

The heel of the topmast is held in position by the trestle-trees on either side, and wooden packers fore and aft. That on the after side is bolted to a metal plate welded to the lower-mast (Fig 43), while the one on the fore side is carried by the cheek plates. The topmast is supported by a metal fid "B" passing through the heel and resting on the trestle-trees on either side. The fid has a shackle in either end, and these serve to prevent it working out of place.

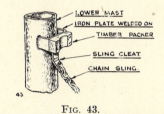

FIG. 43.

Timber decking is provided on the top and is bolted to the lower flange of the rim. The two inner spars, which are kept well clear of the mast to allow plenty of room for the lower rigging, are of hard wood and have a number of holes bored through them to form fairleads for the running rigging. A detail of the arrangement of these will be found on Plate 39.

The rim of the top is stiffened by metal corner plates at the junction of side and rear members, also an additional angle is riveted inside the main rim where it crosses the fore ends of the trestle-trees. The timber packer on the fore side of the topmast will come forward to this point. Eye-bolts are provided below the forward edge of the top for the bunt-line blocks of the courses. These have been omitted from the drawing on Plate 5 as they were found to rather complicate and obscure some other details, however, their positions can be seen clearly in the sketch (Fig 44) where they are shown with the blocks attached. This sketch also shows most of the other details of a metal top. On the after side of the mast above the top is the thumb-cleat which supports the eye of the double lower-stay.

At the head of the mast is the mast cap, which like the futtock-band, is a solid forging shrunk and riveted to the plating of the mast. On the

D

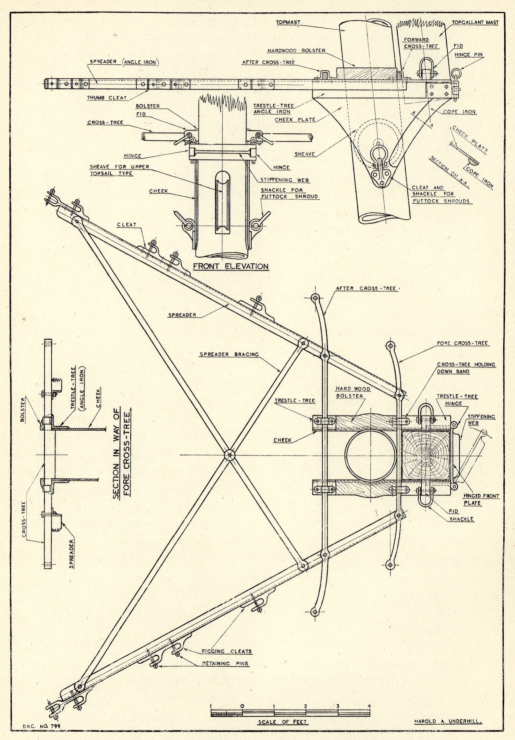

PLATE No. 8.—DETAIL OF STEEL CROSS-TREES.

after side of the cap is a lug for the fairlead of the royal-stay of the mast next abaft; on each after quarter, a lug for the lower cap-stay shackle and on each side of the lower mast head, a lug for the lower yard lift blocks. On the fore side of the cap is the boss for the crane—truss—of the lower-topsail yard "A". It will be seen that the inner end of this crane pivots on the cap, allowing

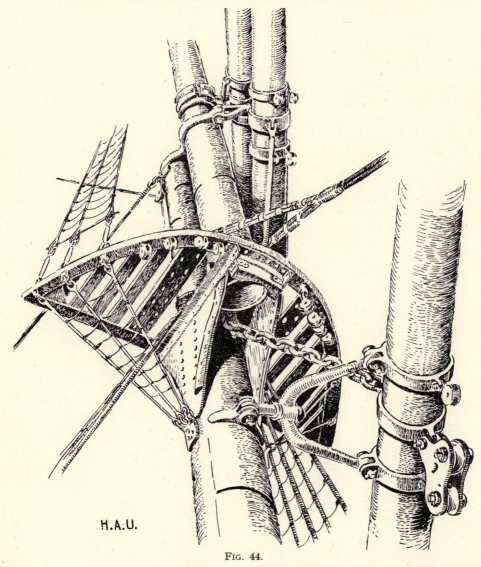

H.A.U.

FIG. 44.

the yard to swing from side to side, while the outer end pivots horizontally in lugs on the yard-band, leaving the yard free to cant at will. The whole assembly forming a universal joint like that of the lower-truss. Between the cheeks on the fore side of the lower-mast immediately below the top, a plate cleat is riveted (Fig. 43) and to this the chain sling of the lower-yard is shackled.

Fig. 44 is a sketch looking up at the underside of a steel top, and examination of this together with the detailed drawing on Plate 5 will reveal several alternative arrangements. In the vessel shown in the sketch the futtock-band has been omitted and the mast jaws of the lower-truss are formed in a saddle riveted on; the futtock-shrouds shackle to cleats riveted direct to the mast; the cheek-plates and trestle-trees are straight, not curved to fit the mast; there is a metal strut between the foreside of the top and the underside of the lower topsail yard, this serves the same purpose as the chain sling of the lower yard and takes the weight of the lower topsail yard off the crane and lower-cap. This was quite common practice in large ships, and also was often added to composite and wooden vessels when they were getting on in years and showing signs of strain. Finally the cap-stays are shown shackled to cleats riveted to the mast instead of to lugs on the side of the cap. This sketch is included to show some of the variations possible in one short section of the mast, and even then it does not by any means cover all. Fig 45 is an alternative construction for lower mast cap.

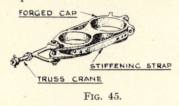

FIG. 45.

Some ships have ventilated lower masts, these are formed by substituting a mushroom ventilator for the usual filling plate or plug in the mast head (Fig. 46). This mushroom head was of the normal type, consisting of an inverted dished plate supported on short struts, leaving an air space at the top of the tubular spar.

Fig. 47 shows another arrangement for the lower-truss, the principal difference being that this type has an additional hinged joint in the link member. This joint allows

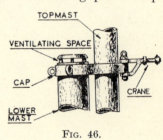

FIG. 46.

for movement in a vertical direction and compensates for any little inaccuracy in the length of the chain sling. The span is also different in shape and round in section, this type of span was commonly found in the trusses of wooden vessels.

Plate 7 illustrates a typical iron or steel topmast, the heel of which is stepped in the top and supported by the fid as already described. As the parral of the upper-topsail yard has to travel up and down the mast, it will be obvious that there can be little or no taper between the lower-mast cap and the topmast cross-trees. If the topmast were tapered

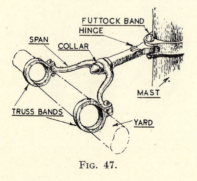

FIG. 47.

to any great extent the parral would be too slack when the yard was hoisted, or so tight on the mast when the yard was down that it would tend to jamb.

Plate 8 is a large scale detail of the topmast cross-trees, which are built up as follows. Cheek-plates are fitted, curved to fit snugly on the mast, with the distance between their parallel faces equal to the diameter—or breadth— of the heel of the topgallant mast, and their leading edges are reinforced with cope iron as in the case of the cheeks on the lower-mast. Along the top of the cheeks are riveted the angle iron trestle-trees, and across these the two iron cross-trees; one of which passes between the head of the topmast and the heel of the topgallant, and the other across the after ends of the trestle-trees. The cross-trees are iron forgings, roughly square in section, but it will be noticed that their depth is increased between trestle-trees, which not only locates their own positions, but also forms distance pieces and stiffeners for the cheeks and trestle-trees. The cross-trees are held in a fore and aft direction by holding-down straps bolted or riveted to the trestle-trees. The front of the trestle-trees are closed by a plate—or gate—so attached that either end can form a hinge, and the removal of the locking pin from either side allows the plate to swing open on the other, thus facilitating the hoisting in or removal of the topgallant mast. Hard wood bolsters are fitted on top of the trestle-trees in way of the topmast head.

Bolted on the underside of the cross-trees and extending aft are the angle iron spreaders, which are stiffened by diagonal bracing forged from flat bar iron. On the outer faces of the spreaders are bolted the rigging cleats, these are forged rather like double and single thumb-cleats with longer tails. Locking pins are fitted through the tails of the cleats to prevent the back-stays being thrown out should the lee rigging slacken off when the ship is braced up sharp. By the way it is quite common practice for the spreaders to be bolted on top of the cross-trees, the only difference being that the angle must be turned up the other way, that is to say with the horizontal flange down. Either method is correct.

Owing to differences in rake and height, the length and angle of the spreaders may vary on each mast, and it is not possible to lay down anything in the nature of a standard design. Nothing looks worse than spreaders which distort the direct lead of the back-stays, and should they be too wide and cause the stays to bulge out in a thwart-ship direction, they would produce a bad twisting strain on the topmast head when the weather stays became really taut. The spreaders must be so fitted that they just rest alongside the back-stays when the mast is properly set up, and the length and angle for each mast must be worked out separately.

In model work there are two ways of arriving at the proper set for the spreaders, the best being to work it out on paper, as this allows the cross-trees and spreaders to be fully assembled before the masts go into position. If the model builder is at all handy with the drawing board this will offer no difficulty. The way to go about it is as follows.—First make a drawing of the side elevation and thwart-ship elevation of the mast, full size for the actual model, and taking great care that the rake and *diameters* are accurately set out. On these views draw the back-stays, or such stays as will come on the spreaders, and here again great care must be taken that the exact point of contact with the bulwarks is set off in both views. Another point to watch is that allowance be made for the thickness of any stops or shoulders which may increase the diameter of the mast at the point of contact with the rigging, for any such projections will of course alter, even though very slightly, the angle of your rigging. In fact, the main point is accuracy in draughtsmanship.

Having accurately set out these two views you now have a true picture of the angles your rigging will really take, and you now have to make a plan view shewing the exact positions of the various stays *at the level of the spreaders.* On one corner of your sheet produce a straight line A B (Fig. 48) which represents the centre line of the ship, and across one end of this line draw C D at right angles to it. The intersection of these two lines—point E—represents the centre of the topmast at the level of the spreaders. Now with a pair of dividers measure from the side elevation the distance from the centre of the topmast to the first back-stay—all measurements must of course be taken at the level of the spreaders—and mark this off from point E along A B, which gives you point F, and through this point produce line G H at right angles to A B. Now from your thwart-ship elevation measure the distance from the centre of the mast out to the point where the first stay crosses the level of the spreaders, this distance is then set off on either side of A B along line G H. The points thus found, namely X and Y, are the exact position the first stay port and starboard will occupy in relation to the topmast at the level of the cross-trees. Repeat this for all other stays which contact the spreaders, and you will have a range of dots or points as shown in the sketch (Fig. 48). When all are located, draw lines through these points representing the angles of the spreaders, complete the detail of the topmast cross-trees round point E and you have a full size template on which you can build your complete cross-tree assembly including spreaders, with the comforting knowledge that providing your drawings have been carefully made, your cross-trees will go into position without throwing the back-stays out of line. All this looks rather complicated and startling in print, but as a matter of fact it is nothing more than our old geometrical friend of elementary school days, the truncated pyramid. The only point, and I make no apology for stressing this, is that you must be accurate in setting out your two elevations.

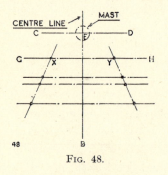

FIG. 48.

Don't just use the original sail and rigging plan;   the bulwarks on your model may be just a shade thicker than true scale proportions, which, if the stays set up inboard, would make your rigging angle a little steeper;   or your masts being a shade over size would produce the same effect. So forget all about your original design and measure everything from the actual work, then you will be sure to have the correct angles, which of course is the basis of it all.

The alternative method is to completely rig your masts without spreaders, then lay the spreaders along the stays and from them mark the cross-trees for the points of intersection, at the same time marking the spreaders themselves for the position of the rigging-cleats. The topmast and topgallant will then have to be unrigged so that the cross-trees and spreaders can be finally assembled. In using this method it is very necessary that the masts and rigging be properly set up and checked for rake and thwart-ship plumb, also that the rigging is properly attached, for rigging just knotted in place will probably run at a different angle to the same gear when finally set up. This method gives a lot of additional work and may not be satisfactory in the end, so I strongly advise the modeller to use the drawing board. I need hardly say that in writing the above I have had in mind the large scale model, where mast fittings will be built up in metal. In small scale work, where wood is largely used and the model builder has no strong objections to adhesive material, the vessel can be completely rigged and the spreaders added after all the standing rigging is set up, although if possible they should go in before the yards are rigged, otherwise the braces may cause a little undignified language.

To return to Plate 8. At the heel of the cheek-plate there is a cleat and shackle for the futtock-shrouds, while built into the mast between the cheek-plates is a sheave for the upper-topsail tye. On Plate 7 will be found a detail showing how sheaves are boxed into tubular spars, and this will apply to either masts, yards or booms. The heel of the topgallant mast is confined by the cheeks and trestle-trees on either side; the forward cross-tree on the after side, and the hinged gate on the fore side. It will be noted that the fid extends to the full width of the trestle trees and is provided with shackles, which in this case serve the double purpose of keeping the fid in place and also providing attachments for the upper ends of the standing lifts (see Plate 23). The topmast cap is similar to that of the lower-mast, as is the crane for the lower-topgallant yard, although this yard has twin bands and a span between them in place of the single band with double lugs.

Although these drawings illustrate masts fitted for double topsails and double topgallants, they will of course apply equally well to the single topgallant rig, the only difference being that the lower topgallant crane and the boss which carries it will be omitted from the topmast cap. The parral of the upper topsail yard has been included in this drawing of the topmast, but I will leave its description until we come to the yards.

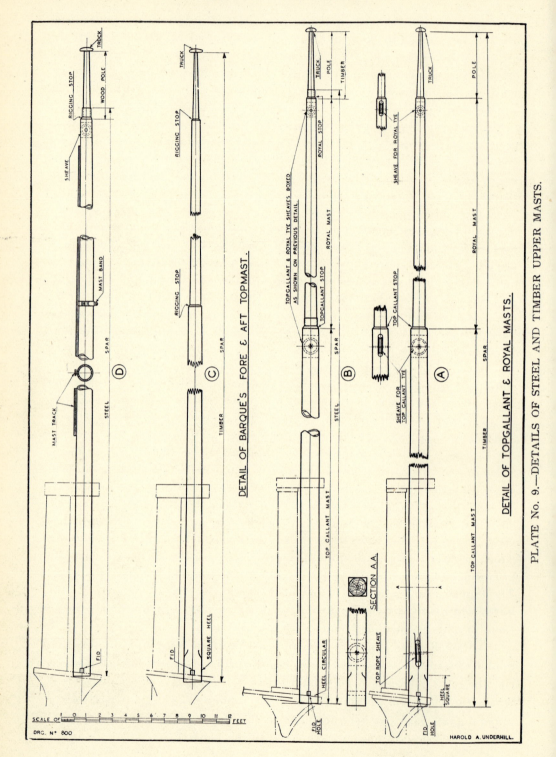

DETAIL OF BARQUE'S FORE & AFT TOPMAST.

DETAIL OF TOPGALLANT & ROYAL MASTS.

PLATE No. 9.—DETAILS OF STEEL AND TIMBER UPPER MASTS.

HAROLD A. UNDERHILL.

The remarks already made regarding possible alternatives for the lower-top apply to the cross-trees, which, as mentioned in chapter I is a term used to cover the whole assembly of cheeks, trestle-trees, cross-trees and spreaders. I have already mentioned that some of the later steel carriers had tops which were built square with the mast instead of parallel to the water line, this was just a matter of economy, and anyone accustomed to costing iron and steel work will appreciate the saving resulting from cutting out all those awkward skew sweeps, such as where the trestle-trees are curved at an angle round the mast. Right angle work is always cheaper to produce than jobs containing difficult bevels. All wood and composite ships, and the big majority of iron and steel vessels too for that matter, were however fitted with tops parallel to the water line.

All masts and spars above the topmast head are as a rule made of timber, even in the modern steel ships. The steel ship *Mount Stewart* for example, whose spar and rigging plan appears in Plate 25 had red pine topgallant and royal masts above steel lower and topmasts. This ship, together with her sister *Cromdale* were fine vessels of 1903 tons register and built by Barclay, Curle, of Glasgow, in 1891, when iron and steel sailing ship construction was at its highest level. They were owned by D. Rose of Aberdeen, and the *Mount Stewart* had the distinction of being one of the last large square riggers to be owned in Great Britain. However some of the large steel carriers were masted in steel throughout, and I have therefore included drawings of steel topgallant and royal masts.

To take the timber spar first. (A) Plate 9 shows a typical timber topgallant and royal mast such as would be carried by an iron or steel vessel, although except for a possible difference at the heel to suit the metal cross-trees, the spar would be the same for either metal or wood vessels. The heel is square in section and fully occupies the space in the cross-trees forward of the topmast head. Through the heel in a thwart-ships direction is the square fid hole. A short distance above this is the inclined sheave hole for the heel-rope, used when getting the mast aloft from the deck. Stops are formed for the topgallant and royal rigging; these stops are shoulders made by the reduction in the diameter of the mast, and on them the eyes of the standing rigging are bedded. Metal funnels are fitted over these shoulders, but they can be left until we come to detail the standing rigging. Immediately below their respective stops are the sheaves for the topgallant and royal tyes, these of course are fitted in the fore and aft plane. Above the royal stops is the pole, or mast-head, which is fitted with the truck—or bun shaped disc—on top. The truck has two sheave holes diametrically opposite, these are for the signal halliards. (Fig. 49). This completes the mast.

The all steel mast (B) is similar in design, but the heel is of course circular instead of square, as the advantage gained would not justify the extra cost for forming the square heel on a cylindrical spar. The stops are formed by a tapered reduction as in the case of the wooden spar, and the next section of the mast is inserted in the "neck" of the stop. One or two ships were built with the steel masts formed without stops, rigging bands being shrunk and riveted on instead. These bands had lugs to which the rigging was shackled, this however was a very uncommon arrangement and should not be copied in model work unless the builder is quite certain that his prototype was so rigged. At the head of the mast a wooden pole is made a driving fit in the neck of the royal stops, and this is finished off with the usual truck. Stump-topgallant masts were built in the same way, except of course, that the pole head was fitted in the topgallant stops.

FIG. 49.

Drawings (C) and (D) are the topmasts for a barque's fore and aft rigged mast, and really require no further description.

Regarding the plating of metal masts one very common practice is to build them with all horizontal joints as laps with the edges looking down, as described for the bowsprit. These horizontal joints are staggered, but the vertical joints are continuous for the length of the spar. Another method is to make all horizontal joints as butt joints with external butt-straps. Figs. 50 and 51 give some idea of the general appearance of these masts, but the thickness of the plating has been slightly exaggerated to show the construction more clearly. The plating of upper masts on which parrals have to slide is different. Here all joints are butted and all straps inside the spar leaving a flush surface outside on which the parral can travel freely. All masts are stiffened with internal angles running vertically up the spar.

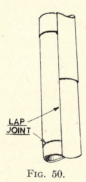

LAP JOINT

FIG. 50.

Plate 10 shows the construction of the mizzen mast of a three-mast barque—or of course the jigger of a four-poster. Four feet up from the deck is a spider-band of normal construction, and above this on the after side of the mast is the goose-neck of the spanker boom. This is carried on two saddles riveted to the mast, and it will be noted that the upper one has a vertical tongue running up and down the mas immediately below the fulcrum boss. The object of this is to give additional support against the weight of the boom, and so prevent any tendency for the boss to sag downwards. Fig. 52 shows another type of goose-neck. Here the boom is carried between the two saddles, and as the lower one has to carry the weight it is provided with the vertical tongue. The sketch shows the boom disconnected for the sake of clarity.

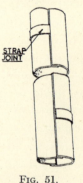

STRAP JOINT

FIG. 51.

On the after side of the mast and extending between the boom and the gaff, is the iron jackstay to which the luff of the sail is bent. This stay consists of an iron bar, round in section, carried on short iron stanchions riveted to the mast. At intervals up the mast are the eyes for the brail blocks, these are arranged in pairs on either side of the jack-stay, the usual number being three pairs along the length of the stay, but this and the actual location will require to be obtained from the sail and rigging plan.

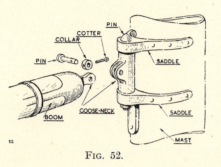

FIG. 52.

Next comes a mast-band for the goose-neck of the gaff, and it will be noted that this also has a vertical tongue below the boss. Saddles like those supporting the boom may of course be used in place of this band, either method being perfectly correct.

There are two alternative methods of supporting the mizzen or jigger topmast of a steel barque. For larger vessels the usual arrangement is a top as shown on Plate 10. This is simply a small edition of the tops fitted on the square rigged masts, except that only two rigging-cleats are provided instead of three, and the half-round timber chafing strip can be omitted from the outer edge of the rim as there are no square sails to chafe on the iron work. In this drawing I have shown a steel topmast, but should a wooden mast be carried, the only structural difference would be to arrange the packers to suit the square heel instead of the circular one.

Small steel barques often carry cross-trees (Fig. 53) on their fore and aft masts instead of the top described

FIG. 53.

above, and these are the same as the topmast cross-trees of the square rigged mast except that the spreaders are omitted.

A thumb cleat is provided abaft the mast for the lower stay, or, and this applies to the square rigged mast also, several cleats may be fitted round the head of the mast as shown in the sketch Fig. 54. The mast cap is of the same design as used for the other masts, although the number and position of the eye-bolts will of course have to be decided from the sail and rigging plan. This is a matter which will always vary in different ships, and before starting work on a mast

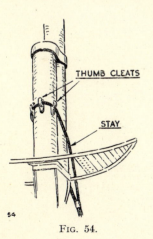

FIG. 54.

cap, the rigging plans must be consulted and the cap designed with sufficient lugs to carry all the rigging and blocks which have to be attached to it. Time spent in working out details on paper is never wasted, but is in fact absolutely necessary if the model is to be a first class job and free from those little "make do" items, which are usually the result of having overlooked some point of attachment.

The boom shown in the drawing is a timber spar, but should a metal one be carried the external appearance will be much the same. The function of the goose-neck is to provide a universal joint between the boom and the mast, and its construction will be perfectly clear from the various drawings and sketches. On a timber spar the side straps are let in flush with the surface of the wood and through riveted. After this is in position an iron band is passed over the goose-neck and shrunk on the spar, keeping everything nice and tight. The next fitting is the band for the boom-guys, this has a lug on either side for the shackles of the wire pendants. At the extreme end of the boom is the outer-band or sheet-band. This has an eye on top for the shackle of the boom-topping span, and a "U" shaped bar forged on the under side for

Fig. 55.

the upper blocks of the spanker-sheet. An alternative construction is shown in Fig. 55. Just inside the outer band is a sheave hole cut in the vertical plane, this is for the spanker foot-outhaul.

The goose-neck of the gaff is the same as that on the boom. About the middle of the gaff is a band for the inner end of the peak-span. Next comes a combined band and cheek-block. The band has four eyes; the upper one for the outer end of the peak-span; one on either side for the vangs, and the lower one for the top of the boom-topping span. The cheek-block is for the topsail sheet. Outside the band is a sheave hole—cut in the vertical plane—for the spanker-head outhaul, while at the end of the spar there is a metal ferrule to prevent splitting, and screwed into the very end is the eye for the shackle of the signal-halliard block. Along the underside of the spar is the mast track, in which the shoes carrying the head of the sail travel when being hauled in or out. Fig 56 shows an alternative type of gaff goose-neck. In this case the main fitting takes the form of a traveller on the jack-stay and requires a short standing halliard to support it. This type of construction seems to be relatively weak, and the only possible advantage is that it can be adjusted for height by lengthening or shortening the chain.

The topmast may be either wood or

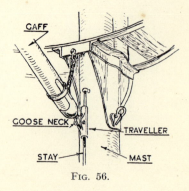

Fig. 56.

metal and the details are shown on Plate 9. The steel mast has a track on the after side, metal shoes fit this track and are attached to the luff of the jib-headed topsail. Alternatively the sail may be bent to hoops encircling the mast between the lower cap and the topmast hounds; above this point the sail will be set flying.

In the case of the full rigged ship the spanker fittings are of course the same, but will be in addition to those already described for the square rigged mast. The top will be the normal size, and not reduced as for the fore and aft mast, if the mast, either square rigged or fore and aft, carries a futtock-band, the boss of the gaff goose-neck will either be incorporated in it or carried on a separate saddle immediately below it.

Quite a number of the large carriers are built with pole masts, i.e. topmast and lower mast in one piece. This makes very little difference to the fittings beyond the fact that a mast band takes the place of the lower-cap, and the top may be set a little further aft as there is no topmast heel to clear. The construction of the top will remain the same, but it must be remembered that the forward topmast shroud should be on, or a little abaft, the mast centre line, never forward of it, which may mean moving the rigging cleats a little further aft than shown on the drawings where they have been made to line up with a fidded topmast. As pointed out in Chapter I, the section of the mast above the lower-topsail yard is still known as the topmast, even though it is in fact continuous with the lower mast. The band fitted in the

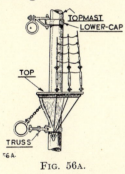

FIG. 56A.

position normally occupied by the lower-mast cap, carries the lower topsail crane and all the lugs the cap would have. Above this point the spar is identical with the normal steel topmast. (Fig. 56A.)

Now just a word about the big steel barquentine before we leave the subject of metal masts. The fore and aft masts of these vessels were huge spars, those of the *Mozart* for example were 178 ft. from heel to truck, with the lower-masts of steel and the topmasts timber. *Mozart* had a very simple form of cross-trees (Fig. 57) on her fore and aft masts, but this should not be taken as a representative type, the more usual method being cross-trees as described for the barques mizzen, or alternatively a miniature top such as was carried by the big German five-mast two-topsail auxiliary schooners of the Vinnen fleet. (Plate 50). These vessels were unique in rig and will be dealt with under that heading in Chapter VIII.

FIG. 57.

These big barquentines usually carry timber gaffs fitted with jaws to slide up and down the mast when making or taking in sail, and in many vessels

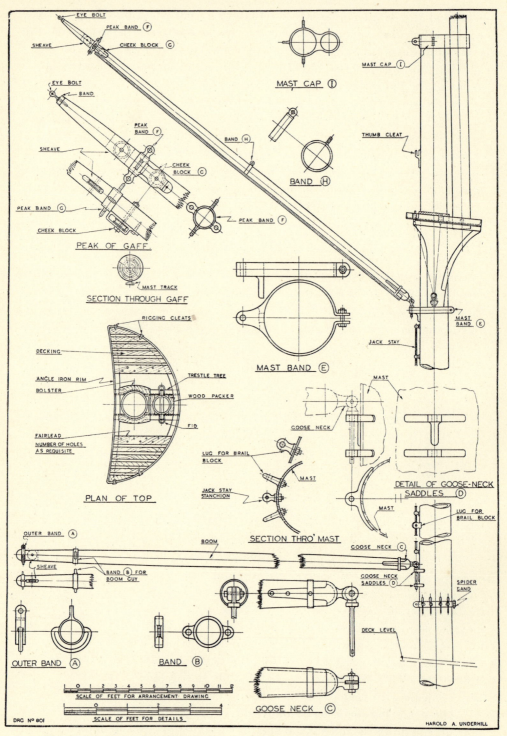

EYE BOLT
PEAK BAND (F)
SHEAVE
CHEEK BLOCK (G)

MAST CAP (I)

MAST CAP (I)

THUMB CLEAT

EYE BOLT
BAND

PEAK BAND (F)
BAND (H)

SHEAVE

BAND (H)

CHEEK BLOCK (C)

PEAK BAND (C)

CHEEK BLOCK

PEAK BAND (F)

PEAK OF GAFF.

MAST TRACK

SECTION THROUGH GAFF

MAST BAND (E)

JACK STAY

RIGGING CLEATS

DECKING

MAST BAND (E)

ANGLE IRON RIM
BOLSTER

TRESTLE TREE

WOOD PACKER

MAST

FAIRLEAD
NUMBER OF HOLES
AS REQUISITE

FID

GOOSE NECK

DETAIL OF GOOSE-NECK
SADDLES (D)

PLAN OF TOP

LUG FOR BRAIL
BLOCK

MAST

MAST

JACK STAY
STANCHION

SECTION THRO' MAST

GOOSE NECK (C)

LUG FOR
BRAIL BLOCK

OUTER BAND (A)

BOOM

GOOSE NECK (C)

SHEAVE

BAND (B) FOR
BOOM GUY

GOOSE NECK
SADDLES (D)

SPIDER
BAND

DECK LEVEL

OUTER BAND (A)

BAND (B)

GOOSE NECK (C)

SCALE OF FEET FOR ARRANGEMENT DRAWING
0 1 2 3 4 5 6 7 8 9 10 11 12

SCALE OF FEET FOR DETAILS
0 1 2 3 4

HAROLD A. UNDERHILL

PLATE No. 10.—BARQUE'S IRON OR STEEL LOWER FORE AND AFT MAST.

jaws replaced the goose-neck on the boom too. When the boom is fitted in this way, a timber collar encircles the mast immediately below it and carries the weight of the boom and jaws. However this type of gaff and boom is simply a slightly larger edition of that carried by the wooden schooners, and will be covered in more detail under that section.

Plate 11 shows a range of steel yards from lower to upper-topgallant, although in all but the largest of modern carriers the lighter yards are of timber. However even with the timber yards, modern vessels usually carry the type of trusses and parrals shown in this drawing, and it is only in the smaller wooden ship that the older type of timber parral, which will be described in detail in the next chapter, is used.

Starting at the bottom of the sheet we begin with the lower yard. In the centre is a band (A) having a lug placed at about 20° abaft the top centre line, this is for the chain sling, the upper end of which shackles to the sling-cleat below the top. On the underside of the band is the lug to which the iron sheet-block is bolted. Plate 12 is a series of large scale details including this band and other components of the yards. The iron sheet block consists of two triangular plates held together by a central bolt passing through a tubular spacer; the upper corner forms the attachment to the yard and the two lower ones are occupied by the sheaves. On either side of the centre-band are the quarter bands—or truss-bands—to which the span of the truss is bolted. Detail (F) on Plate 6 is a large scale drawing of the truss assembly which is made up as follows. The inner end of the link hinges in the jaws of the futtock-band, while the outer end, which has a shoulder formed on it, passes through the centre of the span and is riveted over a collar on the inside, leaving sufficient clearance to allow the span to rotate freely. The ends of the span are bolted between the twin lugs on the after side of the truss-bands, while below these bands are lugs for the shackles of the clew-garnet blocks.

Below the yard are two circular fairleads for the lower-topsail sheets, while at the outer ends are the iron sheet blocks (E) through which the sheets are reeved. These blocks are on the after side of the yard. Outside the cheek-blocks are the yard-arm bands which have three lugs; one on top for the lift; one on the after side for the brace pendant; and one below for the clew-garnet block, or, in the case of upper yards, clew-line or down-haul blocks. In ship or brig rigged vessels the yards on the aftermost mast would of course have the brace-pendant lugs on the fore side of the band.

In large ships steel yards have two jack-stays as shown on the drawing. The one to which the sail is bent being at about 40° on the forward side of the top centre line, and the other, which was the result of the large diameter of the yards of some of the big craft, is fitted along the top where it serves as a hand grip for the men working on the yard. This stay is sometimes used for tying off reef points when they are carried in pairs on the fore side of the sail, but this is a point to be covered later in Chapter V. By the end of the sailing ship era, the big carriers had yards of such diameter that lying across them was rather like trying to get a grip on the side of a cylindrical boiler, and it is not surprising that the extra jack-stay came into being. The exact position of these two stays will be found in the sectional view on Plate 11. At the outer ends of the yard are short jack-stays for lashing the head-earing. In the example from which I have taken these drawings, this stay is on the centre line of the yard and fitted with a hook, but in many ships the latter is not included and the stay is further forward, say at 20° from the centre line, i.e. midway between the other two jack-stays.

The next yard, that of the lower-topsail, is much the same, the principal difference being that the eye of the centre-band is double and bored to take the head of the crane as shown in the detailed drawing. This yard also has an additional band (H) for the inner lift, which of course would not be required if single lifts were carried. One or two of the later carriers had a short chain sling to take the weight of the lower-topsail yard. This was rigged exactly as for the lower yard except that the angle of the chain was much flatter; the sling-cleat (Fig. 43) was riveted to the fore side of the topmast, but kept down fairly close to the cap-band to allow the maximum travel for the upper-topsail yard, and the lower end of the chain sling shackled to a lug provided for that purpose on the centre band. This rig was of course only used in vessels having pole masts, as the cleat would prevent the topmast passing through the lower mast cap.

On the upper topsail yard the centre-band has no eye on top as this yard is fitted with a parral as shown in the detail on Plate 12. The construction of this parral is as follows. A split band passes round the mast and is joined on the thwart-ship centre line by bolts passing through flanges formed for that purpose. Broad metal liners are riveted inside each half of the band, and where timber topmasts are carried these liners are themselves lined with leather to prevent damage to the spar. The object of these broad liners is to increase the bearing surface and prevent the parral canting, which would of course result in jambing on the mast. The forward half of the ring has a shank which passes through the centre of the parral-span and is riveted over a collar on the inside, but left sufficiently slack to allow the span to rotate. Jaws are formed in the outer ends of the span and bolted to lugs on the after side of the parral-bands—or quarter-bands. Just abaft the top centre line another span connects the two bands, this has a hole in the centre to which the chain tye is shackled.

The remaining yards follow much the same lines as those already described except for a few minor differences; for example, the crane of the lower-top-gallant is attached to a span connecting two bands, instead of to the centre-band; the upper-topgallant has only one jack-stay as the yard is too small to justify two; and so on, but all these details should be perfectly clear from the drawings, and it is only a waste of space to describe them all. I have shown the plating in this drawing and it will be seen that it is arranged exactly as for the spike bowsprit.

Another feature, which having come in at the very end of the sailing ship period was only used on a few ships, is the mast track in place of parrals on the hoisting yards. This track is "H" section bar of heavy weight riveted up the fore side of the mast; on this track is a large shoe or runner which will slide freely up and down, and is connected to the after side of the yard by means of a link and span, much like that used with the normal parral. This arrangement came too late to have a chance of getting over its teething troubles, and there were several cases of failure under stress of weather, resulting in the loss of spars. No doubt experience would have found the cause and corrected this weakness which presumably was one of inadequate strength of shoe, but the days of sail were almost at an end and there was no opportunity for further experiment on large ships. Not that all ships so rigged were failures, the second *Magdalene Vinnen*, a four-mast barque built in 1921, was one which, to the best of my knowledge, had no trouble with the rig.

In ship model work the construction of iron and steel masts and spars provides the metal craftsman with a good outlet for his skill, and on such scales as 3/16 in. or 1/4 in. to the foot it is possible to reproduce faithfully all constructional detail. Many ship modellers do not seem to be aware of the fact that brass angle, cope, and many other sections can be obtained in extremely small sizes, from most of the larger dealers in model supplies—particularly those catering for the model locomotive man—and that these sections are ideal for ship model work. One stock section which can be of the greatest interest is a round brass bar with a fine hole running through the centre, this can be obtained in a range of diameters and is grand stuff for turning out brass sheaves for blocks.

In the same way, box and many other kinds of wood suitable for model work, can be obtained in lengths of about 30 in. and all sections down to about 1/16 in. square. It is always advisable to lay in a stock of any material you are likely to require *before* you start work on the model, for if you take this precaution you will not be held up during the progress of work, or tempted to make something "do" because you have not got the proper material at hand just when you need it. Not that I advocate the use of ready made fittings, far from it, for to my mind that reduces model work to mere assembly, and would, for me, kill all interest in the model either during building or after completion. On the other hand I do like to have a good supply of "raw material" to draw on.

E

CHAPTER III.

MASTS AND SPARS OF WOODEN VESSELS.

Timber masts and spars can be divided into two classes. Firstly those made from a single tree, and secondly the "made mast" constructed from the soundest portions of several trees. The governing factor in deciding which method should be used was of course, the size of the required spar. If small enough it was got out of a single tree, but if too large for this it had to be built up.

Yards were rarely so large that their diameter could not be got out of the trees available, but it was not always possible to provide sound trunks of sufficient length to make the spar in one. The original method of getting over this difficulty was to splice a short length on each end of the yard, but round about **1780/90** the practice of making yards in two pieces with a joint in the centre came into vogue, and as it was found to be stronger it soon replaced the older method of construction.

We are not particularly concerned with the actual practice of mast making any more than we were with the bending, rolling and riveting of the plates forming the steel mast, but I cannot refrain from a brief mention of the old built mast, which in my personal opinion was an outstanding example of craftsmanship.

Fig. 58 is a section through a large built mast such as would be carried by a man-of-war, and shows how the hearts of several trees were built together

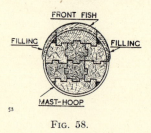

FIG. 58.

to form a single spar. The dovetailing seen in this view would appear quite complicated enough even if the intersections shown ran straight up and down the mast, but in addition to all this, all faces of each of the components had a series of rectangular projections and recesses formed from the solid. The projections, termed "coaks", on the face of one member interlocked into the recesses in the face of the member adjoining, and vice versa. Marking out and cutting these coaks and recesses called for very accurate workmanship, as it was necessary that they should interlock with good surface contact, without either straining the spar, leaving spaces for the accumulation of moisture, or gaps which would weaken the spar. Fig. 59 shows one of the mast components as it would appear when ready for assembly into the mast. Coaking was not restricted

54

to the construction of masts, but when yards were made in two pieces the central joint was in the form of a long scarf which was coaked along the adjoining faces. (Fig. 60).

When the mast had been assembled and dressed smooth it was hooped, that is fitted with iron bands at about five feet intervals. These bands were

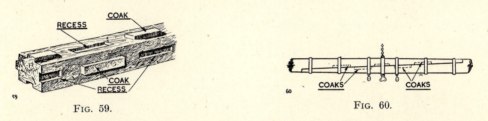

FIG. 59.   FIG. 60.

forged to the required diameter, then heated to almost red heat and driven along the spar to their respective positions. As each ring reached its allotted place it was dowsed with cold water, which caused it to contract and so compress all the mast sections tightly together. This is what is meant by a band being "shrunk" on. By the way, the mast was prevented from burning by being suitably greased for the whole length along which the hoops had to travel to reach their appointed places.

To prevent the sails being chafed by the hoops, a timber facing was fitted all round the forward half of the mast on top of them. This coating was laid in three sections running up and down the mast, the centre one being the "front-fish", and the pieces on either side the "fillings". (Fig. 58). The underside of this coating was recessed to fit snugly over the hoops and so make good contact with the mast the whole way. Naval vessels had rope lashings termed "woldings" between each of the iron hoops and laid on outside

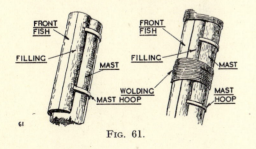

FIG. 61.

the fish and fillings. The wolding consisted of thirteen turns of rope nailed with wolding nails, which had leather washers under their heads. Fig. 61 shows the appearance of a mast with front fish, fillings and wolding in position.

These large built masts were chiefly used in naval construction, but they were necessary in some of the larger merchant craft. Quite a number of vessels with masts out of single trees were hooped as a matter of additional strength and the question of whether a model should be fitted with hooped or plain masts, is one which must be settled from the plans used to build it. Now to proceed with the timber bowsprit. I have devoted rather a lot of space to drawings of the bowsprit, both in iron and wood, but I think this is quite justifiable. To me, the bowsprit seems to disclose more character and indivi-

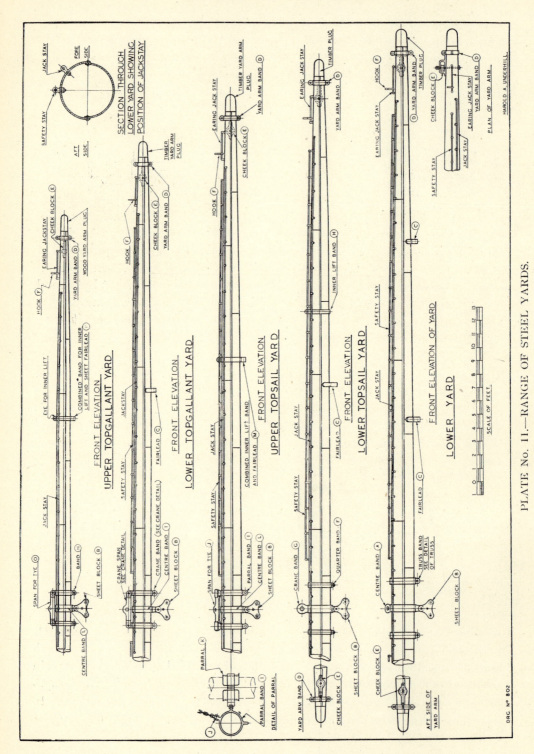

PLATE No. 11.—RANGE OF STEEL YARDS.

duality than any other spar, perhaps this is because it is always exposed to view, no matter whether sail is set or furled. Other spars may have their characteristics and special features, differing in different ships, but these are always clothed in a web of rigging and often completely hidden by the sails they carry, and it is only by the cut of the sails themselves that they offer much help in identification.

In the case of models this is particularly noticeable, the bowsprit seems to take on additional prominence and is the natural starting point for close inspection. It is laid out at a convenient angle for examination, and thanks to the fact that there is very little rigging on top of it, its fittings can be scrutinized without having to peer round back-stays or through shrouds as in the case of masts and yards. Any fault in rig, or poor workmanship in the construction of the bowsprit, will be seen immediately and therefore I feel that a little extra space given to it will not be space wasted.

Plates 13 and 14 illustrate three different examples of the timber bowsprit as found in deep water vessels, while further examples will be found in chapter VII. under the heading of COASTERS. However, before going on to the plates mentioned above, let us turn to Plate 17 which includes a detail of the inboard portion of the bowsprit. This drawing shows a bowsprit built into a vessel having a topgallant-fo'castle, but, except for the fact that the deck above would be merely a light anchor deck or omitted altogether, the arrangement would be the same for a flush decked ship.

The tenon on the heel of the bowsprit fits into a mortice cut in the fore side of a heavy post extending from the keelson up through the uppermost deck, this in most cases will be the pawl-bitt post of the windlass. Forward of the heel is the housing, which may be either square, octagonal or round in section, and extends to the inboard face of the stem. Resting on top of, and strapped down to, the stem head, is the bed, which will of course be square in section, while outboard of this is the hounding. The knightheads, or timbers on either side of the actual stem, come up on each side of the bowsprit at the bed and hold it snugly in position.

Plate 13 illustrates the outboard features of two typical timber bowsprits, and to follow our practice of working backwards, we will take the upper drawing first as being the more modern of the two. This is an example of one of the last representative types of wooden deepwaterman, the barques and barquentines of the timber trade. These vessels were built round about the end of the nineteenth and the beginning of the twentieth centuries, by which time the elaborate figure-head and trail-boards had in most cases disappeared, and the rabbet line of the planking followed the outer curve of the stem instead of running straight from forefoot to knight-head. However all this is rather by the way, we are only supposed to be interested in the spars.

The hounding of this bowsprit is round in section and fitted with an

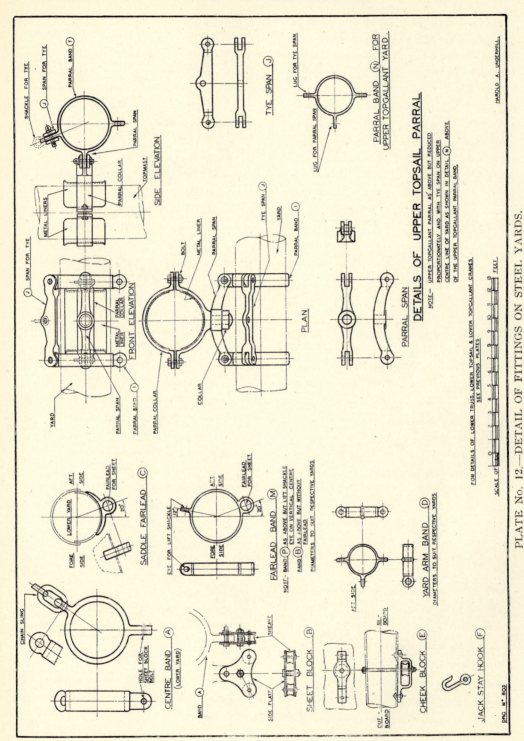

PLATE No. 12.—DETAIL OF FITTINGS ON STEEL YARDS.

iron cap similar to that detailed on Plate 3 for the iron spar. Below the
cap is the martingale, which is a timber spar with metal head and fittings.
In the example shown the head has a double knuckle joint, this however
is quite optional and may be substituted by either an eye in the top of the
spar and forged into the hole in the lug of the cap; or simple jaws on to the
lug, although as mentioned in the previous chapter, the latter arrangement
is not very suitable. If the simple eye is used it may be forged as part of the
metal head, or alternatively simply driven into the top of the martingale
with a metal ferrule shrunk on to prevent splitting. However to revert to
the type illustrated. The skirt of the head forms a socket into which the
wooden spar is driven, while the rigging cleats on either side are metal forgings
let in flush with the surface of the wood and through riveted from side to
side. The lower end of the spar is fitted with an iron ferrule having eyes fore
and aft for the martingale-stays and back-stays. This ferrule is driven hard
against a stop formed in the end of the martingale, in fact all metal work
finishes flush with the wood.

On the underside of the bowsprit is a thumb-cleat for the fore-topmast
stay. This of course is only required when the stay is set up as shown, and
it may be substituted by either cheek-blocks, or battens as illustrated in
the next example. The jib-boom requires no special attention as it is just
a repeat of that described for the iron bowsprit.

The lower illustration is the bowsprit of a slightly larger and earlier
type of ship. In this case the spar is shown hooped for its entire length, the
two outer ones having lugs for the double bob-stays and bowsprit-guys.
Along either side of the bowsprit is a batten or bees, which is of course just
the modern development of the bees of the old timer. In their original form

FIG. 62.

bees were short flat timbers fitted immediately behind the
bowsprit cap, where they served as fairleads for the head-
stays, (Fig. 62), but in later ships they have become battens
extending the full length of the bowsprit, and finally
disappeared altogether. In all other constructional details
this spar is the same as the first example, differences in rig
will of course be dealt with in the appropriate chapter.

The third example, Plate 14 illustrates the bowsprit of one of the "Frigate
built" ships, which, compared with the modern carrier, or even the later
clippers, may appear rather exaggerated in length. It is however quite correct
and its prototype will be found in almost any of the well known "frigates"
such as *Kent*, *True Briton*, *Renown*, *Shannon* and many others.

These frigate built ships, the majority of which were turned out by the
Blackwall yard, were fine craft designed on the model of the naval frigate;
rather short, very little sheer and plenty of freeboard, with typical man-of-war
ends having sweeping cutwaters and stern windows complete with dummy

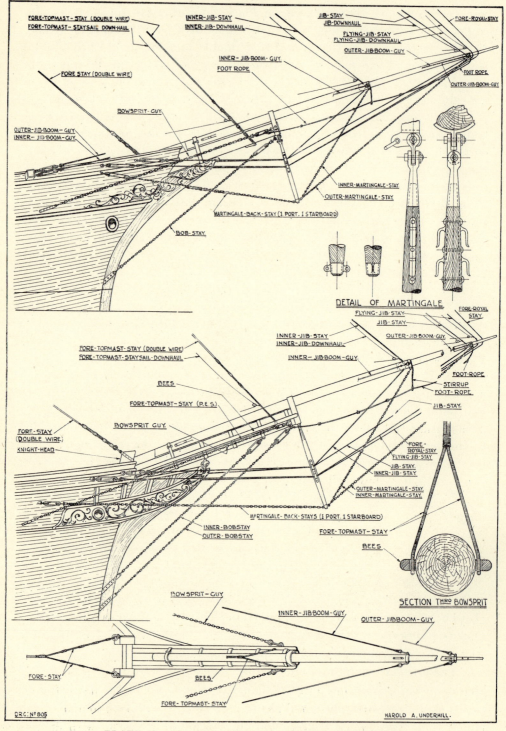

PLATE No. 13.—TWO TYPICAL TIMBER BOWSPRITS.

quarter galleries. These characteristics were retained right up to the end of wooden construction, and as far as the stern is concerned were even reproduced in the iron Blackwallers *Superb, Carlisle Castle* and the famous *Melbourne*, which is perhaps better remembered as the *Macquarie*. However all this is rather beside the point.

Their spar plans were very lofty, with high, steeved bowsprits and long jib-booms and flying-jib-booms, the latter being rigged naval fashion as a separate spar on the starboard side of the jib-boom. Another feature of the earlier ships was the relatively small mizzen mast, often placed rather close abaft the main. The tops were large and "square", and up to about 1866 all ships carried single topsails, after which date new ships came out with double yards and older vessels were converted.

Naval design in the days of sail was very conservative, and men-of-war, both sailing and auxiliary, continued to fit their jib-booms with a short

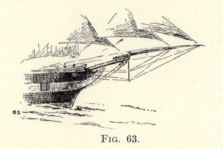

FIG. 63.

doubling on top of the bowsprit until mast and sail disappeared from H.M. ships (Fig. 63). This practice was followed by the early frigate built ships, whether Blackwallers or not, and examination of old prints, paintings, etc., seems to suggest that the short doubling was common to all ships of this class until about 1851, after which the jib-boom housing gradually extended aft until it ultimately reached the heel-chock at the knightheads as shown in the drawing. Evidence based solely on prints and the like cannot be regarded as conclusive, but it gives us at least some idea as to when the change began.

The actual bowsprit and jib-boom follow very closely the previous examples, and therefore require no detailed description, but one point which does deserve mention is the setting of the bowsprit-cap, which in this instance is fitted perpendicular to the water line instead of at right angles to the spar. This is not necessarily a feature of the frigate built ships, as examples of both types of cap will be found, nor was its use confined to craft of this class. As far as my own records of frigate built ships are concerned, the first example I can find of the cap being fitted square with the spar was the *Kent* of 1852; she was followed in this rig by a number of famous ships including *La Hogue*. In 1857 the *Windsor Castle* was launched with the old perpendicular cap, as were *Renown* (1860), *Star of India* and *True Briton* (1861) and *Shannon* (1862). Other ships of this period—1857 to 1862—came out with their caps at right angles to the spar, and from this it seems safe to assume that both types of cap were in common use from 1857 onwards, possibly the square fitted cap was the result of the introduction of iron for this purpose.

64

FIG. 64.

The flying-jib-boom is placed suffiiciently over to starboard to clear the head-stays setting up on the jib-boom, this means about 45° to 50° off the centre line, although I have seen examples of it right over to starboard in the same horizontal plane as the jib-boom itself. The outer-band of the jib-boom is a double one, rather like a small bowsprit-cap set at an angle; the lower ring is a driving fit on the jib-boom end, and the upper one just large enough for the flying-jib-boom to slide through. The heel of the flying-jib-boom rests in a small socket provided on the bowsprit cap for that purpose, and the spar is secured in position by means of a lashing passed round both booms and finished off with frapping turns round its own part and between the two spars. A similar lashing, known as the "belly-lashing", is passed at a point midway between the bowsprit-cap and the jib-boom band. Some ships dispensed with the flying-jib-boom socket on the bowsprit cap, depending on the heel lashing to prevent the spar from sliding inboard. The outer end of the flying-jib-boom has a sheave hole and holes as required for the head-stays.

Mention has been made of the spritsail yard, but this is of no interest to us in its true form as the spritsail was out of use long before our period, however quite a number of the old ships used this yard as a spreader for the jib-boom rigging, (Fig. 64). There are several ways of fitting and rigging

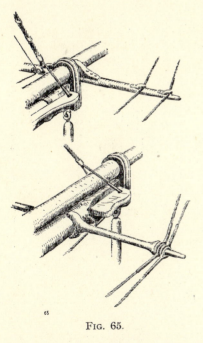

this spar, two of which are illustrated in Fig. 65. The upper sketch shows the spar carried forward of the bowsprit-cap and supported by two timber cleats shaped to fit the jib-boom; thumb-cleats are fitted on the outer ends to receive the jib-boom rigging. The lower sketch is of the spritsail yard fitted abaft the cap. Here the yard is in two sections, each having jaws which fit snugly against the bowsprit, while their outer ends are provided with stops for the jib-boom-guys. There are several other ways of fitting these spars, but the two examples shown are quite typical and may safely be used should the model builder be lacking details for his own particular vessel.

By the way there have been examples of the martingale being made like the spritsail yard in the lower sketch; the top of the spar had jaws to fit the underside of

FIG. 65.

the bowsprit, and the lower end stops against which eyes formed in the martingale rigging rested. The head-stays either passed over thumb

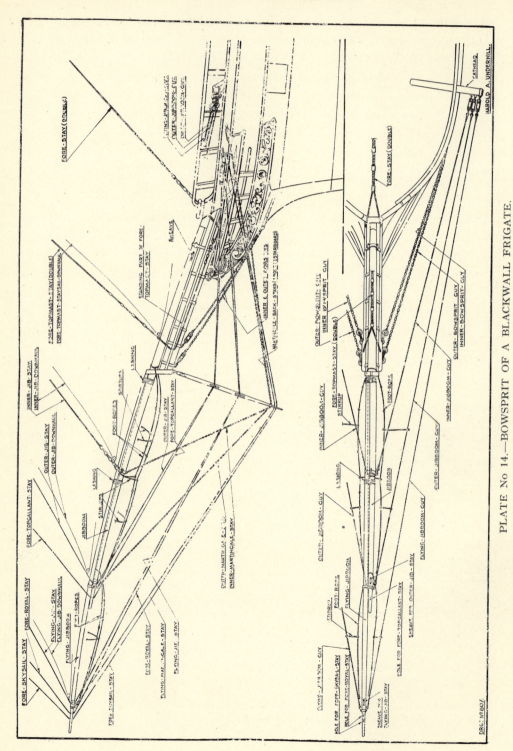

PLATE No 14.—BOWSPRIT OF A BLACKWALL FRIGATE.

cleats in the usual way, or through holes in hard wood battens bolted on to
the side of the spar. However I do not know of any case of this rig which
comes within our period, although there may of course be many.

The drawing on Plate 15 shows two masts, one square rigged and the
other a barque's mizzen. These are not shown hooped, but this is optional
and the model builder must be guided by his knowledge of the vessel he is
copying.

We will take the square rigged mast as the basis of our description as
this contains the most detail. It will be seen that the heel has a square tenon
which sits in the mast-step on the keelson. A band is shrunk on immediately
above the tenon, and further bands are placed between the heel and the deck.
From the heel the mast increases in diameter up to the partners, or point
where it passes through the deck, then reduces again until it reaches the
required diameter at the hounds. Immediately above the deck are two spider-
bands; one with eyes for the lead or purchase blocks and the other fitted with
belaying pins. These bands are as detailed on Plate 6.

On Plate 16 we have large scale details showing the head of the mast as
formed to receive the top, and also after the complete top assembly has been
built on to it. The port and starboard sides of the spar are dressed down to
make a flat seating and stop for the cheeks, while across the fore and aft sides
at the level of the hounds, stops are formed on which the cross-trees rest.

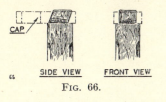

CAP

SIDE VIEW   FRONT VIEW

FIG. 66.

Above the hounds the mast head is squared with
the corners chamfered off as shown, and at the
extreme top of the head a square tenon is cut to
take the lower-mast cap. When timber mast caps
are used the tenon is inclined aft to prevent the
cap drooping forward. (Fig. 66).

The cheeks—sometimes called bibs—are brackets of elm, fir, or oak,
fitted on either side of the mast to support the weight of the topmast. The
top edges of the cheeks are from four to six inches in thickness according
to the size of the vessel, this tapers off towards the heel, where it finishes
equal to the depth of the stop and is "washed" away into the round of the
mast, the joint being covered by the futtock-band. The top edges of the
cheeks are parallel to the water line and not square with the mast. The cheeks
are well supported for not only do the heels rest on the stops formed in the
mast, but the inner surfaces of both mast and cheeks are coaked and through
bolted with five or six bolts.

The trestle-trees are timbers an inch or so thicker than the top of the
cheeks and resting on them, where they are held in position by bolts through
the mast. The distance between the trestle-trees is equal to the thickness
of the mast head, while between their fore ends is a spacer which also serves
to confine the fore side of the topmast heel. The three cross-trees run thwart-

ships; one on either side of the lower mast-head and the third across the after end of the trestle-trees where it forms the rear edge of the top. They are let in flush with the upper face of the trestle-trees, and taper to their outer ends which are checked to receive the rim of the top. The two forward cross-trees rest on the seats formed in the mast as already described.

On top of the trestle-trees are the hard wood bolsters on which the eyes of the rigging rest, while on each face of the mast immediately above the bolsters are vertical battens of hard wood which prevent the rigging cutting into it, and at the same time convert its square section into one more suitable to receive the rigging. The timber decking is laid fore and aft, leaving the usual lubbers-hole round the mast and providing the hard wood fairleads for the running rigging.

The top shown in Plate 16 is that of the modern wooden vessel and is very different in shape to the old massive tops from which it descended, although the constructional details are essentially the same. The old top as carried by ships of the Royal Navy and early merchantmen was large and very "square," with considerable projection on the fore side of the mast. (Fig. 67A.) This type of top obviously restricted the angle to which the yards could be braced, not perhaps so much when the yards were at full hoist, for being single topsails they would be well up the mast, but under reefed canvas the forward shrouds must have been very much in the way. In trying to improve the sailing qualities of their vessels the designers of merchant craft started reducing the size and weight of the tops, and the first move in this direction was to give greater sweep to the forward edge. (Fig. 67B.) This not only cut down weight and reduced the spread of the forward shroud, but also caused less chafe on the topsails. Incidentally, this latter point was not of such great importance in naval vessels, for with their large crews they could hand or take in sail as often as necessary and it was not likely to be left slatting about if it was not doing useful work. Further it must be remembered that the tops were part of the fighting equipment of naval vessels, being used as platforms from which rifle could be directed.

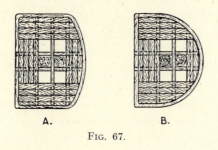

A.   B.

Fig. 67.

The change from the shape shown in the second sketch to that of the detailed drawing was not made in a single step, and examples of all intermediate forms will be found in ships of various dates; nor was the change solely a matter of saving weight, although it did of course produce that result. The final development of the "triangular" form of top was really due to the introduction of the double topsail, where the lower-topsail yard is at the level of the lower-mast cap. The single topsail yard hoisted up to a point just below the cross-trees, where the rigging is very narrow and offers little obstruction; but the lower yard of the double rig is only a few feet above the widest part of the topmast rigging, and with the old type of top the forward shrouds would be almost hard up against the yard the whole time. The obvious solution was to reduce the spread of the two forward shrouds in the topmast rigging, and, as it would serve no useful purpose to have a lot of timber outside the rigging, the tapering form of top came into being.

The rim of the top is let into the fore ends of the trestle-trees and the outer ends of the cross-trees, making a flush upper surface on which the timber decking is laid. Slotted holes, just large enough to pass the flattened ends of the iron futtock-shrouds, are bored through the outer ends of the cross-trees and the planking above as shown in the large detail on Plate 15. The outer edge of the top is faced with cope iron.

The construction of the barque's mizzen shown on the plate follows the square-rigger just described, except that the top is slightly smaller and has only two cross-trees.

Like their iron sisters, many of the smaller wooden barques carry simple cross-trees in place of the top on the mizzen, or in some few cases even a single thwart-ship spreader like the small schooner, this however is not common practice.

Snows, and a few small ships and barques also, set their spankers on a small trysail-mast abaft the lower-mast. The heel of this mast is stepped in a hard wood block on deck, while the head projects a foot or more up through the top, which in the case of the barque is increased in size to take it. This arrangement is shown in the chain-dot line on the drawing. In Plate 15 I have shown the gaff fitted with timber jaws, but most modern wooden ships have their gaffs rigged with the normal iron goose-neck. When the trysail mast is carried both gaff and boom are made with small timber jaws to fit it. To keep the jaws in place, whether on lower or trysail mast, they are fitted with a parral or necklace passing round the mast.

The topmast heel is square and fills the space between the cross-trees, if its own section is not large enough to do this it is faced with timber to build it out to the required size. It is pierced for the iron or hard wood fid which passes through it and extends the full width of the trestle-trees. The topmast shown in the drawing is offset in a fore and aft direction to clear the cross-tree, this is done by cutting away the after side and making up the fore. If the heel were not offset in this way it would mean leaving excessive clearance between the two masts for the whole length of the doubling; or alternatively, reducing the thickness of the cross-tree in way of the two masts and so weakening it, therefore it is common practice to offset the heel, so providing a neat doubling without weakening the cross-tree. In ships fitted with the old type of heavy timber mast cap, the wider spaced doubling had often to be accepted if sufficient material was to be left between the holes, for mast-head tenon and topmast, and in this case there was no need to off-set the topmast heel. Above the heel the topmast may be dressed down octagonal and then round, or alternatively reduced directly from the square to the round; in either case it will be round in section by the time it reaches the lower-mast cap. Just above the heel is the sheave hole for the top-rope, which is used to hoist the mast into position.

The topmast head is detailed on Plate 17, showing the futtock-band with shackles for the topgallant rigging, and above this the sheave for the upper-topsail tye. Next, the cross-trees assembly which consists of trestle-trees, cross-trees, and spreaders; the latter being timber spars bolted to the cross-trees and having a timber cross-brace half-checked into them. An alternative bracing was to use light iron bar arranged diagonally as shown in the detail for iron or steel vessels. The front of the trestle-trees are closed by a hinged iron plate. Above the cross-trees the mast-head closely resembles that of the lower mast, being square in section with chamfered corners, and having battens nailed on in way of the rigging immediately above the bolsters. A square tenon is cut in the head to take the iron mast cap, which is much like the lower one except that the boss for the lower-topsail crane will of course be omitted, and the number and position of the various eyes may vary.

The combined topgallant and royal mast is quite simple. The square heel is off-set like that of the topmast and is provided with the usual fid and sheave hole for the top-rope. Next is the sheave for the topgallant tye, and above this the topgallant hounds, or stops for the topgallant rigging. The royal mast continues from this point, and is provided with a sheave for the tye and royal stops above. Above all is the tapered head or pole, finishing with the circular truck in which are the sheaves for the signal halliards.

The lower truss on Plate 17 is the same as that already described except for minor differences in design. In the first place it incorporates the additional hinged joint shown in Fig. 47, and secondly it has greater sweep, giving much more clearance from the yard. The lower-topsail yard also has a feature not included in the details of iron and steel vessels, that is the iron strut between the yard and the top. By taking the weight off the lower-topsail crane, this strut serves the same purpose as the chain sling already mentioned.

Plate 18 illustrates a complete range of timber yards and is I think self explanatory, although I would again mention that while the majority of the fittings shown would apply equally well to wood or iron ships, this type of parral is not likely to be used on a modern iron vessel, where even the wooden yards would have the all metal parrals detailed in the previous chapter. Two types of jack-stay stanchion are shown, one for screwing and the other driving into the spar, but in either case the spar is bored before insertion. The parrals of the hoisting yards are formed of timber truss or parral battens coaked and bolted to the yard, and shaped to fit the mast with sufficient clearance to slide freely after the leather liners have been fitted. The after side of the parral is closed with a hinged iron strap, which is leather lined like the fore side. This type of parral is used in all wooden craft. It will be noticed that the relative length of the yard-arm varies considerably, this is due to the fact that some yards require sufficient length to stretch the reef-band, which is of course some way down the sail and therefore longer than the normal head; sails which do not reef have no need for any extension beyond the head, so the arms can be kept short.

The stun'sls carried by the clippers as additional fair weather canvas will be covered in a later chapter, but some mention must be made of the fittings necessary to rig them. I do not propose to detail the stun'sl booms or yards at this point, for they are just plain spars and will be better taken with the rest of the rigging. Each boom was carried in a pair of boom irons on the yard, one at the extreme end of the yard-arm and the other at the quarter; the yard-arm iron consisted of a cranked arm welded into a cup shaped ferrule on the tip of the yard, while at the outer end was the band which encircled the boom, (Fig. 68). This outer end could either be plain or, as was more usual, have a small lignum vitae roller inserted in the underside to make the boom slide freely in and out.

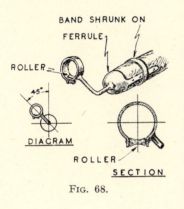

FIG. 68.

The quarter iron is made up of two bands connected by a small bar or neck welded between them; the lower and larger band goes round the yard at the quarters, while the smaller one, which is made to hinge open, holds the inner end of the boom, (Fig. 69). Both these irons are set on the yard so that the boom lies at an angle of about 45° on the fore side.

FIG. 69.

Before leaving the subject of timber spars there are one or two points which may be mentioned. In Plate 18 I have shown all yards circular in section throughout, but quite a number of ships have their yards formed octagonal at the bunt and extending as far as the first quarter. Another point is the fitting of sheaves at the yard arms. In the drawing the sheaves are inserted in the circular yards, but there are several alternatives to this; the yard may be left square at this point, with the sheave in the centre; or the sheaves may be fitted as cheek-blocks of either wood or iron on the after side of the yard. Lastly there is the question of hooping the yards; this may vary

F

between the yard which has no iron work other than that necessary to carry the fittings, and one which is hooped at every few feet of its length. This, like so many other points, is one which the model maker must settle for himself, either from his knowledge of his own particular ship, or if he has no actual knowledge, as fancy dictates. I think it safe to assume that this question of hooping is largely a matter of the material available at the time of the ship's construction; if really good timber is available then there is no need for it, certainly not on the lighter spars, but if it is of poor quality, then hooping will no doubt go a long way to check the extension of shakes or cracks. These remarks do not of course apply to the large built spar, here the idea of hooping is to bind the components tightly together.

In model work the selection of good material for spars is also important, for poor or faulty timber is apt to warp badly in large scale models. Another point, models of timber spars should never be varnished, but very lightly french polished, just enough to give them the appearance of having been oiled.

CHAPTER IV.

STANDING RIGGING.

I HAVE already said that the rigging of ships developed over a long period of time, and it is therefore to be expected that the arrangement of her gear should be a good indication of the period to which she belongs. Conversely, the model builder must know how his ship should be rigged to portray the particular period he has in mind. One does at times come across a model with a hull of one period and rigging of another, but this is usually the result of an old hull having been re-rigged or "restored", possibly by someone who, from lack of knowledge, takes as his guide a rig which is current at the time of "restoration".

We are not concerned with the historical facts of how or when the various changes took place, for most of them were before our period, but it may be of interest to mention why development followed the line it did, and at the same time give the reader some idea of what does and what does not belong to the time of the clipper and carrier.

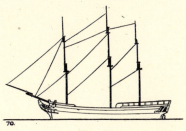

FIG. 70.

Fig. 70 is taken from the 1794 edition of Steel's "Elements of Mastmaking,

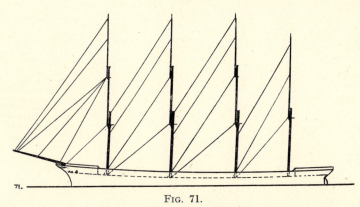

FIG. 71.

Sailmaking and Rigging," and may be said to represent the end of the eighteenth and beginning of the nineteenth centuries, while Fig. 71 shows the same

71

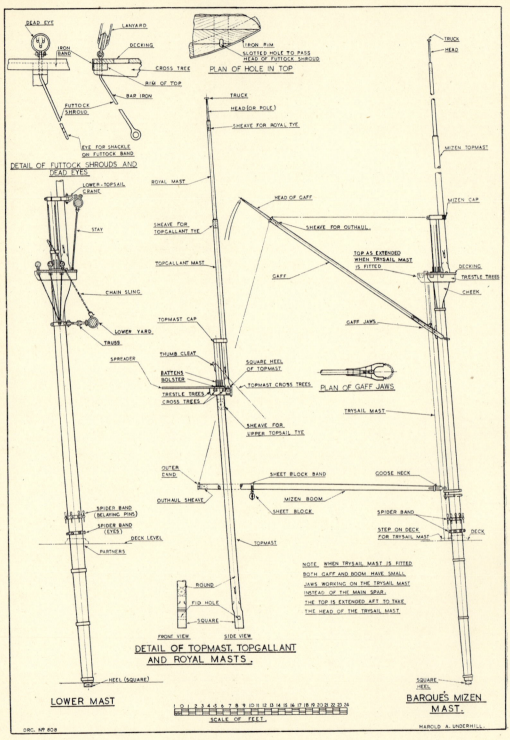

DEAD EYE
LANYARD
IRON BAND
DECKING
CROSS TREE
RIM OF TOP
BAR IRON
FUTTOCK SHROUD
EYE FOR SHACKLE ON FUTTOCK BAND

DETAIL OF FUTTOCK SHROUDS AND DEAD EYES

IRON RIM
SLOTTED HOLE TO PASS HEAD OF FUTTOCK SHROUD
PLAN OF HOLE IN TOP

LOWER TOPSAIL CRANE
STAY
CHAIN SLING
LOWER YARD
TRUSS
SPREADER

SPIDER BAND (BELAYING PINS)
SPIDER BAND (EYES)
DECK LEVEL
PARTNERS

HEEL (SQUARE)

LOWER MAST

TRUCK
HEAD (OR POLE)
SHEAVE FOR ROYAL TYE
ROYAL MAST
SHEAVE FOR TOPGALLANT TYE
TOPGALLANT MAST

TOPMAST CAP
THUMB CLEAT
SQUARE HEEL OF TOPMAST
BATTENS
BOLSTER
TOPMAST CROSS TREES
TRESTLE TREES
CROSS TREES
SHEAVE FOR UPPER TOPSAIL TYE

OUTER BAND
OUTHAUL SHEAVE

ROUND
FID HOLE
SQUARE
FRONT VIEW
SIDE VIEW

DETAIL OF TOPMAST, TOPGALLANT AND ROYAL MASTS.

HEAD OF GAFF
SHEAVE FOR OUTHAUL.
TOP AS EXTENDED WHEN TRYSAIL MAST IS FITTED
GAFF
GAFF JAWS

PLAN OF GAFF JAWS

TRYSAIL MAST

SHEET BLOCK BAND
GOOSE NECK
MIZEN BOOM
SHEET BLOCK

TOPMAST

NOTE WHEN TRYSAIL MAST IS FITTED BOTH GAFF AND BOOM HAVE SMALL JAWS WORKING ON THE TRYSAIL MAST INSTEAD OF THE MAIN SPAR. THE TOP IS EXTENDED AFT TO TAKE THE HEAD OF THE TRYSAIL MAST

TRUCK
HEAD
MIZEN TOPMAST
MIZEN CAP
DECKING
TRESTLE TREES
CHEEK

SPIDER BAND
STEP ON DECK FOR TRYSAIL MAST
DECK

SQUARE HEEL

BARQUE'S MIZEN MAST.

DRG. Nº 808

0 1 2 3 4 5 6 7 8 9 10 11 12 13 14 15 16 17 18 19 20 21 22 23 24
SCALE OF FEET.

HAROLD A. UNDERHILL.

PLATE No. 15.—TIMBER MASTS.

rigging on a vessel of the twentieth century; the difference is very obvious. In the first example the fore and aft stays on main and mizzen lead to points high up on the mast in front, while all those of the fore mast go well out on the bowsprit; the result being that each spar is to a large extent dependent on its neighbour. In the event of the fore-topmast being carried away most of the tophamper on the main would go too, followed in all probability by the mizzen, while should the bowsprit go there would be a good chance of losing everything, including the lower-masts. In the modern ship all lower and topmast stays lead either right down to the deck, or at least to points very near it, while the topgallant and royal stays are set up at the head of the lower-mast instead of the topmast cross-trees. With this rig the whole of the fore topmast above the lower cap could go, and still leave the rigging on the main intact. In fact the modern design aims at making each mast as independent as possible.

Generally speaking one may say that the earlier the period the higher will be the fore end of the respective fore and aft stays. A very sketchy definition perhaps, but quite sufficient to call the model builder's attention to a point which is well worth watching. It is not my intention to swamp the beginner with dates and periods, and if he is designing his own rigging plan the best advice I can give him is to study carefully all available drawings, pictures, or authentic models of the period before putting a pencil to paper.

Another word for the modeller. The relative size of standing rigging is most important, yet it rarely receives the attention it deserves, so many model builders being content to rig a model with only one or two sizes. It is perhaps difficult to obtain the range of sizes required, but it can be done and is well worth the effort, and the realism of the result will more than repay the trouble involved. If you look at a ship or ship photographs, particularly with sails furled, the masts and spars dominate the whole picture even though all the rigging may be perfectly visible. But in a large percentage of models the opposite is the case, the masts are seen dimly through a forest of heavy rigging; the general effect is that of a lattice construction, instead of a few main spars clothed in a mere gossamer of delicate rigging. If the correct size cannot be obtained then it is always better to err on the small side, and generally speaking this applies to all model work. Plate 25 shows the standing rigging of the ship *Mount Stewart* in outline and indicates all the sizes used, which are really relatively few and should be easily obtained for a moderately large scale model, while in chapter IX, I have given tables of actual sizes for various types of craft and also the relative proportions of one stay to another, so there should be no excuse for badly proportioned rigging.

Frequent reference will be made in this chapter to rigging-screws, worming, parcelling, serving, etc., and no doubt most readers will be familiar with them, but perhaps not all, so a few brief notes at this point may save a lot of time for the beginner who otherwise might be left in doubt. The function of a rigging-screw is to draw taut the particular item of gear to which it is attached. It consists of a cylindrical shell or barrel screwed internally with right and left hand threads at opposite ends, into these are screwed short members having either eyes or jaws at their outer ends. The shell may be circular throughout its length, and tapering slightly to either end; or have a hexagonal portion in the centre for the use of a large spanner. (Fig. 33). In either case there will be a hole through the centre of the shell at right angles to the centre line, this is for use of a tommy-bar. If the shell is rotated by means of the tommy-bar or spanner, the two outer members will be drawn together or forced apart according to the direction of rotation.

Worming a rope is to fill the spaces between the strands by winding spun-yarn or small cordage into them, the object being to make a smooth

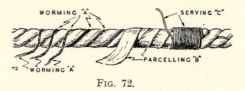

FIG. 72.

and fair surface for parcelling, (Fig. 72A). Parcelling is to wind narrow strips of canvas round the wormed rope, (Fig. 72B), the canvas is then well tarred before serving. The rope is served by winding spun-yarn or small cordage tightly on top of the parcelling in the opposite direction to the lay of the rope, (Fig. 72c), or as the old rhyme has it:—

"Worm and parcel *with* the lay,
Turn and serve the *other* way".

The object of serving is to protect the rope from chafing, and it is put on with a serving mallet, which closely resembles an ordinary tent mallet with the top hollowed out to saddle the rope. The rope to be served is first stretched taut between two fixed objects, then, at the point where the serving is to start the serving material is tucked under three strands of the rope—like the tucks of a splice—and taken twice round both rope and mallet, one turn being on either side of the handle, (Fig. 73). The mallet is then rotated in the opposite direction to the lay of the rope, keeping the serving material taut all the time. As this is being done a helper passes the ball of serving material round and round the rope, keeping pace with the turns of the mallet, until the required length has been served and is finished off with three tucks under the strands as in the case of the start.

FIG. 73.

For the model maker serving is undoubtedly the most tedious job of all, and one to which there is no royal road or short cut; but no model of any size should be allowed to pass without it, and no model maker who aims at first class results would think of omitting it on account of its tedious nature.

I think we can now pass to the actual rigging of ships, starting with the bowsprit. I will in each case base my description on the modern steel ship equipped with rigging-screws, etc., then continue with details of the same unit as carried by a wooden ship rigged with dead-eyes and lanyards. It would be extremely cumbersome and quite unnecessary to entirely separate the two classes, as in the main the lead of the gear will be much the same, the principal difference being in the manner of setting up. The only standing rigging in which there is any major difference are the head-stays, which on the spike bowsprit terminate on the spar, whereas when a jib-boom is carried they continue through it back to the bows of the ship—this however will be clearly explained in its proper place.

Rigging the Bowsprit.

Our first example will be the steel spike bowsprit shown on Plate 19.

Bob-Stays.—There are two bob-stays, inner and outer, both of which are of round iron bar with jaws forged at either end. To receive the lower jaws lugs are formed on the forward edge of the stem member and drilled for the bob-stay bolts. (Fig. 74.)

Inner Bob-Stay.—No provision is made on this stay for adjustment of length, the inner jaws are bolted to the stem immediately below the figure head, and the outer jaws to the lug below the cap-band on the bowsprit. One point to watch when designing a rigging plan, is that the lug on

FIG. 74.

the stem is so placed that the stay can take a straight line to the bowsprit cap without fouling the figure-head. I know there are examples of the bob-stay having to be curved to clear the head gear, but this is usually the result of damage, or alteration, for such a stay has little or no strength until it straightens out, by which time the bowsprit would be away.

Outer Bob-Stay.—This is of sufficient length to allow for the insertion of a rigging-screw between the outer jaws and the bowsprit. The inner jaws are bolted to the lower lug on the stem, while the outer ones engage the eye of the rigging screw on the bowsprit band. An alternative method of tensioning this stay, is to make the rigging-screw an integral part of it by screwing it directly into a shell having right and left hand threads at opposite ends, into the upper end of which is screwed a short member to bolt on to the bowsprit band, (Fig. 75). The stay passes through the jaws on the bottom of the martingale and is held in position by a cotter pin below it. In some vessels chain is used for the outer bob-stay.

LEFT-HAND THREAD

TENSIONER
RIGHT HAND THREAD

BOB-STAY

FIG. 75.

Single Bob-Stay.—The next example is of the iron bowsprit with jib-boom Plate 2. This has a single bob-stay which is rigged like the inner bob-stay on the spike boom.

Bob-Stays: Wooden Vessels.—Plates 13 and 14 illustrate the wooden ship which may have either single or double bob-stays, but a description of the single stay will suffice, as unlike the spike boom they are both alike. The lower end of the stay shackles to the bob-stay plate on the stem; while the upper end of the chain shackles to the iron strop of a lignum vitae heart, and is set up with a lanyard to a similar heart below the bowsprit. The method of reeving the lanyard and a general description of the form of dead-eyes, hearts, and bulls-eyes will be given at the end of this chapter. There are several forms of stem plate, three of which are shown in Fig. 76. The first

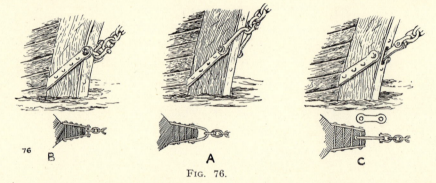

FIG. 76.

two are perfectly simple and should, I think, be quite clear from the sketches. The third and perhaps most common type has, like the others, a plate on either side of the stem and through riveted, but in this case a slot or mortice is cut in the fore side of the stem between the plates and extending in depth to beyond the first rivet. A short link-plate is inserted in the mortice before the outer rivet is driven home, and to the outer end of this link the chain bob-stay is shackled. This type of plate is also very largely used by schooners of the coasting fleet.

Bowsprit-Guys.—These may be either chain or wire, both of which are shown on Plate 19; wire to port and chain to starboard; these are of course alternatives and would not be used together in the same ship. They may also be either double or single according to the size of the ship. The outer ends of the guys are set up to the bowsprit with either rigging-screws or hearts and lanyards according to the type of rig. If wire guys are used the ends would be "turned" on metal thimbles for shackling to the rigging-screws and chain-plates, these thimbles would be of the solid type as on Plate 24. Where wire is used in conjunction with hearts it would be turned in the score of the heart. The inboard end is shackled to a chain-plate on the bows, which should be so placed that the upper guy follows the steeve of the spar. If for any constructional reason the guy cannot be arranged on the line of the spar, it should be as near as possible below it, not above, for as explained in Chapter I the strain on the bowsprit is always upwards and to one side. In the case of single guys, they will of course be placed on this line. Another point to watch is that all bowsprit gear is kept clear of the anchors and ground tackle although it must be as far aft as possible with a view to obtaining the maximum spread.

Jib-Boom-Guys.—In the case of the spike bowsprit these are at times termed outer-bowsprit-guys owing to the fact that this type of spar really has no jib-boom, however their rig and purpose is the same in either case. In ships carrying jib-booms the number of guys will vary with the length of the spar; the frigate built ship for example has three per side, consisting of inner, outer, and flying-jib-boom-guys respectively. The method of setting up may also vary considerably; on the spike boom they are shown going to chain-plates on the bows, while in the other plates they set up to the cat-heads, an arrangement which may include the use of a spritsail yard in some of the older ships. Another method is to set them up abaft the cat-head and give them additional spread by the use of whisker-booms, (Fig. 77). The question of whether rigging-screws or hearts and lanyards are used will of course depend on what is used throughout the ship; if the standing rigging on the masts is set up with screws, then screws will be used on the bowsprit, or if dead-eyes are used on the masts, hearts will be used for the bowsprit.

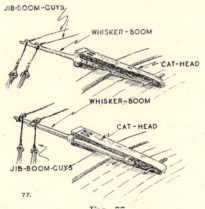

JIB-BOOM-GUYS
WHISKER-BOOM
CAT-HEAD
WHISKER-BOOM
CAT-HEAD
JIB-BOOM-GUYS
77.

FIG. 77.

It will be noticed that on the spike boom the rigging-screws are shown at the bowsprit end, while on the timber ships the hearts and lanyards are at the cat-heads; there is no hard and fast rule governing this, except that they should always be in the most accessible place. In the case of the spike boom illustrated the inboard ends are well down the ship's side and difficult to get at, so the screws are at the spar; but on the wooden ships the inboard ends are at the cat-heads which are even more accessible than out on the jib-boom, which explains the position of the hearts and lanyards.

In most ships of our period the guys will be of wire, although a few early ones may have carried rope, in which case it would be cable laid. This perhaps calls for a little explanation. If when you hold a piece of rope horizontally in front of you, the lay runs downwards from left to right—like a normal right hand screw thread—that is "ordinary-laid" rope, (Fig. 78A); but should the lay run in

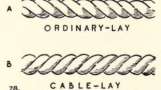

A   ORDINARY-LAY

B   CABLE-LAY
78.
FIG. 78.

the opposite direction, i.e., downwards from right to left, then it is "cable-laid", (Fig. 78ʙ). Wire, by which is meant wire rope of course, is ordinary-lay.

Many of the big steel ships, particularly those run largely by young cadets, rigged triangular life-nets below their bowsprits from one jib-boom-guy to the other on the opposite side.

Foot-Ropes.—These are made of well stretched rope and rigged on either side of the bowsprit, where they are supported by stirrups. To provide a good foot-hold over-hand knots or turks-heads are worked on the rope at about four feet intervals.

In the case of the spike boom the foot-ropes extend from the outer band to within about three feet of the fo'castle head, this distance being left for setting up with lanyards. An eye-splice is worked in either end, the outer one having a normal thimble and the inner a lanyard-thimble, see Plate 24; the outer eye is seized to a convenient shackle at the outer-band, while the inboard end is set up by lanyard to a ring-bolt at the knight-heads. The stirrups are short wire or rope spans with an eye-splice in each end, the upper eye is seized to the jack-stay on the boom and the lower one to the foot-rope. Short spans made in the same way are rigged between the foot-rope and the jib-boom guys to steady the former.

Where bowsprit and jib-boom are carried it is usual to rig separate foot-ropes on each spar. They are made up in the same way, except that those on the jib-boom may have their forward ends joined in a cut-splice just large enough to fit snugly round the jib-boom head and rest against the outer-band —see sketch on Plate 2. A cut-splice is formed by overlapping two ropes and splicing them into each other, so making an eye of the required size, (Fig. 79). The inner ends of the foot-ropes are usually seized to a convenient point on the bowsprit cap, such as the shackle of the bowsprit guy, or an eye-bolt provided for the purpose. Another method is to take a turn of the inner end round the jib-boom and seize it back to its own standing part as shown

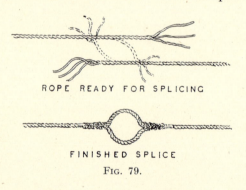

ROPE READY FOR SPLICING

FINISHED SPLICE

Fɪɢ. 79.

on Plate 14. The jib-boom stirrups have the usual eye-splices at the lower ends, and are joined in a cut-splice to fit snugly round the spar. Flying-jib-booms are rigged in the same way. All cut-splices should be wormed and served all round the eye; this also applies to the eye-splices in the lower ends.

Hand-Lines or Life-Lines.—These are shown in Plate 2 of the iron bowsprit and are rigged in pairs, one on either side of the spar. Their forward ends are passed through the eyes of the small stanchions on the bowsprit cap, where they are finished off with stopper or wall and crown knots on the outboard side. The inner ends are spliced round lanyard thimbles and set up to the knight-heads or convenient stanchion with a lanyard.

Martingale-Stays.—These are of chain and usually two in number, although on long spars three may be carried. The upper ends shackle to their respective jib-boom bands, and the lower to the lugs on the fore side of the martingale. In the frigate built ship on Plate 14 the flying-martingale-stay is shackled to the outer band of the flying-jib-boom, brought aft through a hole in the foot of the martingale; up to the ships bows, and inboard through a circular fair-lead in the bulwarks, to be set up on deck to a convenient cleat.

Martingale-Back-Stays or Martingale-Back-Ropes.—Made of chain and usually one per side, although occasionally rigged in pairs as shown in Plate 2. Their forward ends shackle to the after side of the martingale, and the after ends are set up at the bows with either rigging-screws or hearts and lanyards. Like the bowsprit-guys they should be given the maximum possible spread without fouling the ground tackle.

Setting up the Standing Rigging.

The standing rigging leading down to the ship's side must not only have a strong anchorage to the hull, but also a means of being set up taut. The former provision is catered for in a variety of ways, particularly in the case of timber or composite ships, and it must be understood that the arrangements described here do not necessarily cover all. On Plate 20 there is a drawing showing the inside of the bulwarks of a modern iron or steel ship, together with a section through the ship's side at the rail. From the latter it will be seen that the main plating of the hull is carried a short distance above the deck level, and to the inside of this plating the flanges of the chain-plates are riveted, thus connecting the rigging to the hull proper and not the lighter bulwark plating. The chain-plates are of round bar iron with flanges forged on their lower ends; the upper ends are brought up through the teak main-rail, immediately above which they are forged in a close fitting eye round the bow of a large shackle, which in turn bolts to the lower end of the rigging-screw. The set of these chain-plates is very important and they must line up with their respective stays—in both fore and aft and thwart-ship directions—otherwise they will put undue stress on the main-rail and bulwarks. The rigging-screws are of normal design although large and heavy on account of the load they have to carry. The method of attachment will vary in different ships, and one alternative is shown in Fig. 80 where the shackle is

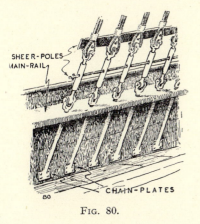

SHEER-POLES
MAIN-RAIL
CHAIN-PLATES
80
FIG. 80.

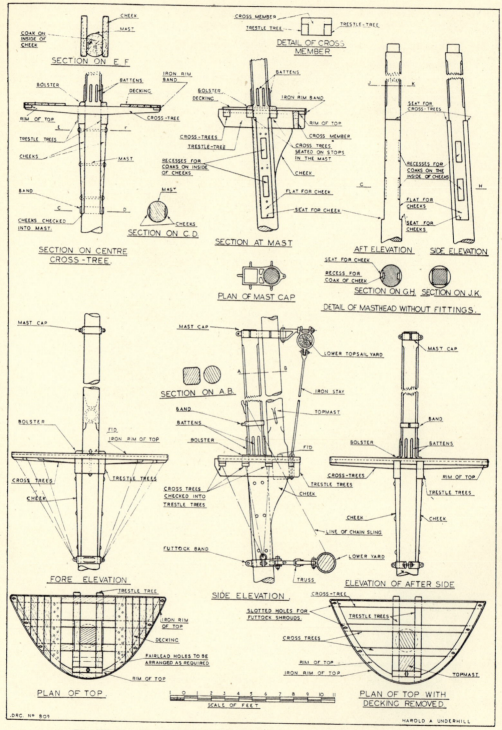

PLATE No. 16.—CONSTRUCTION DETAIL OF WOODEN TOP.

dispensed with; it will also be noted that the solid thimbles in the rigging are parallel to the ship's side, instead of at right angles as is more common. The method of turning the rigging on the thimbles will be dealt with later. Fig. 81 shows the position of the rigging screws on "half-round" and vertical sided poops respectively.

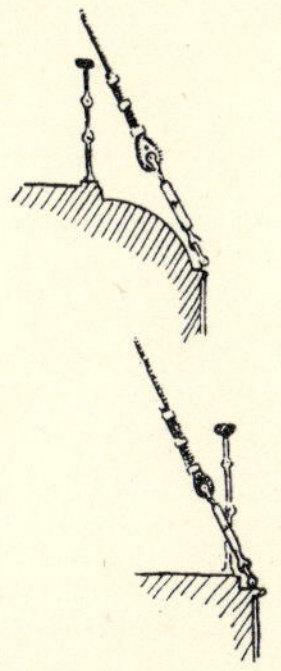

What is perhaps the most common arrangement for the modern wooden ship is shown on Plate 21. Here the chain-plates are made of flat bar iron and fitted outside the hull below the deck lines; they extend to the level of the topgallant-rail where they bolt to the strap of the lower dead-eye. Various other arrangements are shown on Plate 21 including the old fashioned channels as carried by the frigate built ship *True Briton*. Composite craft may follow any of the types shown; *Cutty Sark* for example had chain-plates like those of a steel ship, except that dead-eyes were fitted instead of screws; while *Torrens* was rigged as detail (C) on Plate 21 although she was originally designed with plates as (D).

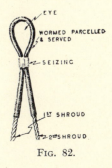

FIG. 81.

There are only two methods of setting up the rigging in common use; the rigging-screw—sometimes called a bottle-screw—and dead-eyes and lanyards, or in the case of bowsprits, hearts and lanyards. The former has already been described in detail, while the construction and proper way to reeve the lanyards of the latter will be given at the end of this chapter.

Rigging the Lower Fore-Mast.

By the beginning of our period wire had to a large extent superseded hemp for all forms of standing rigging, although this does not mean that rigging-screws were in common use, they really came into vogue with the larger iron or steel vessel. Wire rigging with dead-eyes and lanyards was in general use with the wood, composite, and many of the iron clippers, and was in fact favoured by builders of wooden ships to the very end. There were a few twentieth century wood built craft turned out with screws, but they were the exception rather than the rule. I have shown wire rigging in all the drawings reproduced here, but if hemp is required, tables giving the relative sizes, together with the proportions of dead-eyes, etc., will be found in chapter IX.

Shrouds.—Wire—in all descriptions of standing rigging I shall assume that wire is used, it being understood that hemp can be substituted in ships so rigged. Shrouds are made in pairs, formed by a single length extending from the bulwarks, round the mast, and back to the bulwarks on the same side. They are seized together to form an eye round the mast (Fig. 82) and the full compliment of shrouds for one side of any mast is known as a "gang".

EYE
WORMED PARCELLED & SERVED
SEIZING
1ST SHROUD
2ND SHROUD

FIG. 82.

To make the first pair of shrouds, the required length is cut, including an allowance for seizing back when turning in the thimbles or dead-eyes; the length of the first shroud is then marked off from one end—each shroud will be progressively longer as they extend further aft—and with this mark as centre the wire is wormed, parcelled and served for six or seven feet on either side.   This length is sufficient to cover the eye and far enough down each shroud to protect it from chafing by its neighbours or the futtock-shrouds. Wire rigging was sometimes only parcelled and served, but with hemp, worming was always done before parcelling.   It is customary to add riding turns—additional serving on top of the first service—in way of the eye, as in bending the shroud round the mast-head, the serving on the outside opens up and the riding turns fall into the spaces left, so keeping out moisture.

When the centres of the double shroud length have been served, the two sides are brought together and seized with seven turns, on top of which are six riding turns and the whole seizing finished off with two frapping turns between the two parts.   The seizing of the first pair of shrouds is so placed that when the eye is in position over the mast and beaten down, the seizing will be just below and not on top of the bolster. Before being placed over the mast the whole eye is parcelled again on top of the serving, starting from the legs and working back to the centre, each turn overlapping the one below like the weather-boarding on a roof. After this final parcelling the eye is given several coats of paint and is ready to go over the mast-head.

When the eye is complete the position of the dead-eye or rigging-screw thimble is marked off on each leg, which is then wormed, parcelled and served on either side of this mark for a distance equal to that seized back when the thimble or dead-eye is turned in.   The distance between the mast-head and the dead-eye is known as the "warp" of the shroud. The thimbles or dead-eyes can now be turned in and the first pair of shrouds is complete. The first shroud on either side should be served for its entire length as a precaution against chafe by the courses, this of course does not apply to fore and aft rigged masts or the mizzen of ships which do not cross a cro'jack.

The remaining pairs of shrouds to complete the gang are made in the same way.   Should there be an odd number of shrouds on each side, the last

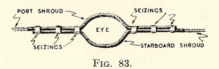

FIG. 83.

one can either be taken round the mast and seized back to its own part, or seized to its opposite number in what might be termed a cut splice, except that the junction is by seizing instead of splicing.   (Fig. 83).

When the complete gang is ready they are put over the mast-head in the following order. First the most forward pair on the starboard side, then the forward pair on the port side: followed by the second pair to starboard, and the second pair to port and so on until the whole gang is in position. Fig. 84 is a diagrammatic illustration of the sequence. As each pair is put over the mast, it is well bedded down on the bolster or rigging already in position before placing the next pair. When all shrouds are in place they are set up by rigging-screws or dead-eyes. The last or aftermost-shroud on each side of the fore and main masts is known as a "swifter".

It may be of interest to mention how shrouds were cut for length in the old days. Detailed drawings were few, and it is doubtful if many practical riggers could have read them anyway, so a rule of thumb method was used to arrive at the additional length necessary for each shroud further aft. Two bolts were driven in the rigging loft floor, the distance between them being equal to the estimated length of the forward shroud, including the allowance for seizing back. The rope for the shrouds was then wound round outside these two bolts, one complete turn representing a pair of shrouds; each turn was then passed outside the previous one until the necessary number for the gang had been passed. When all turns were on and flat on the floor, they were cut in a straight line opposite one of the bolts, and the inside coils formed the first pair of shrouds; the additional circumference on the turn at each end of the coil provided the extra material required in each successive pair.

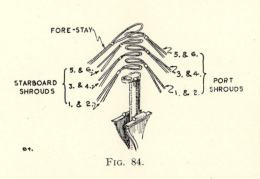

FIG. 84.

Sheer-Pole.—The sheer pole is a timber or metal spar running across the foot of the standing rigging. Where rigging-screws are used the metal thimble is provided with two holes, the lower one for attachment to the screw and the upper one free. In Plate 20 the sheer-pole is of bar iron about 1″ in diameter and passed through the free holes in the metal thimbles; the ends may either be seized in position, or the ends of the bar drilled and cotter pins fitted to prevent the pole working along. The sheer-pole serves as a lower ratline and at the same time prevents the rigging twisting when tightening up the screws. Another method, not so commonly used, is shown in Fig. 80. Here the sheer-pole is a flat iron bar bolted to the free holes in the thimbles, which are turned in a fore and aft direction for that purpose. Where dead-eyes are used the sheer-pole is seized to the outside of the rigging just at the throat-seizing of the dead-eye.

Ratlines.—These are run parallel to the water line and about 15 inches apart starting from the sheer-pole; they may be made from cordage, timber battens, or round iron bar. When the shrouds exceed three or four in number, it is usual for only every fith or sixth ratline to go right across, the remainder stopping one shroud short fore and aft. There are variations of course, one being to take all ratlines to the forward shroud and only stop them short on the after side. For the last ten feet or so near the mast head all ratlines go right across, for by this time the whole gang of shrouds has become very narrow.

Fig. 85 shows the correct way to rig rope ratlines. They start with an eye-splice seized to the shroud with spun-yarn, they are then clove-hitched (Fig. 86) to all intermediate shrouds and finished off with another eye-splice seized to the last shroud to be covered. Timber and iron ratlines usually only cover three shrouds, and are made a few inches longer than the actual span to provide room for a square seizing at either end, a similar seizing is of course passed on the centre shroud too.

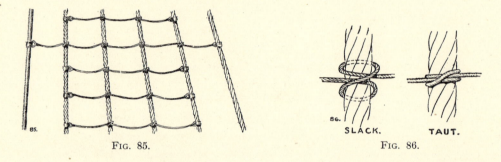

FIG. 85.   SLACK.   TAUT.   FIG. 86.

It has been stated that the foremost shroud on all masts carrying courses should be served for its entire length, but in the interests of economy some of the big carriers dispensed with this and encased the shroud in chafing mats or puddening, a serviceable if unsightly arrangement.

Fairleads are fitted inside the shrouds in the positions described in chapter VI, and through them the running rigging is lead down to the pin-rail. The most usual arrangement is a small circular bulls-eye having one large or three small holes. They have a vertical groove on one side to saddle the shroud, and a score round the circumference by means of which they are seized to the rigging. Another form of fairlead is a continuous batten running across the inside of the rigging and bored out as required; both these types are of course made from hard wood. (Fig. 87).

A wooden hook-cleat—Fig. 88—is seized to No. 2 shroud on each square rigged mast, this is to catch the braces should they be slacked away and allowed to slide down the face of the rigging. Some ships rove their lower braces through wire pendants for the same purpose.

No mention has been made of tackle or burton-pendants on the lower mast, for they were obsolete before the period covered by this book.

Fore-Stay.—Double wire.   There are two ways of making this stay; one from a single wire, middled and doubled back on itself to form an eye for the mast-head (Fig. 89A); or alternatively using two lengths of wire by passing them round the mast-head from opposite sides and seizing the end of each to the standing part of the other, then seizing the two main parts together to form an eye (Fig. 89B).   In either case the eye will be wormed, parcelled and served all round, for sufficient length to reach a short way down the two legs as with a pair of shrouds; on top of the serving the eye is leathered—i.e., encased in leather—for such distance as may be in contact with the mast.

FIG. 87.   FIG. 88.   FIG. 89.

The stay may go over the mast in one of two ways; the first is to bed the eye hard down on top of the last shroud on the bolsters, in which case it must come down through the lubbers-hole as in Fig. 90A and not over the rim of the top as sketch "B".   The second and modern way is to put the eye round the doubling, just sufficiently high up to clear the rim of the top when the stay is set up taut, and to support it on thumb cleats round the spar, (Fig.54).

The lower end of the fore-stay may be set up in various ways; on deck

FIG. 90.   FIG. 91.

as in Plates 2 and 19; at the knight-heads as Plate 13; or round the bow-sprit as in Plate 14.   For the two former, deck plates and solid thimbles as Fig. 91 will be provided in the required position and at such angles as will enable the "V" of the stay to lead fair on.   To set up the stay the eye is passed over the mast-head and bedded down on either thumb cleats or rigging: the

G

two lower ends are then marked for the position of the thimbles and parcelled and served on either side of it as described for the shrouds. It will then be leathered in way of the actual thimble. When all is ready, each leg is passed through its respective deck plate and hove taut round the thimble, the ends are then brought back against their own standing parts and each seized in three places. The two parts having been properly set up they are brought together about ten feet above the deck and seized. The exact position of this seizing will be governed by the tension of the double stay before the seizing is made, and also the location and angle of the deck-plates. The third method mentioned is one more frequently used on the fore-topmast stay, and will be described in detail under that heading.

Lower-Cap-Stays.—Single wire. May be one or more in number according to the size of vessel. Both ends are parcelled and served, the upper one being turned on a solid thimble which shackles to a lug or cleat at the lower-cap; the bottom end being turned on a similar thimble for shackling to the rigging-screw, or alternatively on to the dead-eye. The usual rigging practice is for the cap-stays to set up immediately abaft the last shroud, but there are exceptions, as for instance the *Mount Stewart*, Plate 25, where the cap-stay sets up between the fourth and fifth shrouds, while the first topmast-back-stay is between the fifth and sixth shrouds. It may be repeated here that cap-stays are not usually found in older ships or the smaller wooden craft.

Crane-Lines.—When the main and mizzen topgallant-staysails are furled they rest up and down the after side of the fore and main masts respectively, in a position which is out of reach of the shrouds. Obviously men must get at these sails to pass the gaskets when furling, and one way is to "ride" down the sail from the stay, but lines are also rigged between the fore-most shroud on either side and the mast, (Fig. 92A). In rigging these lines an eye-splice is formed in one end and seized to the inside of the forward shroud at the required level, the line is then passed across to the mast and clove-hitched to the vertical part of the stay abaft it; the line then continues over to the foremost shroud on the other side where another eye-splice is formed and seized in position. The number and position of these lines will be governed by the location and depth of the sail when furled. On the fore and aft masts of barques these lines are rigged in the same way except that the centre is of course hitched to the jack-stay abaft the mast. These lines must not be confused with the fairlead pendants sometimes rigged between the shrouds

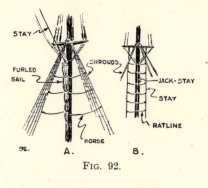

FIG. 92.

to prevent blocks and gear from slatting against the mast; these latter will be further mentioned under the heading of running rigging.

One or two of the big four-posters rigged a vertical stay close on either side of the jigger-mast, between the top and the deck. Ratlines were provided between these stays and the jack-stay abaft the mast, so making a jacob's ladder on either side for easy access to the sail when furling. (Fig. 92B).

The use of the term "crane-lines" will probably raise a small storm, for everyone seems to have their own ideas on the subject, and I have heard them called stays'l-horses, swifters, hand-lines and man-ropes, but as the last three are already in common use for other gear, I have decided to use the only one which seems to be "to let".

Rigging the Lower Main-Mast.

Shrouds.—As for fore mast.

Main-Stay.—Double wire. This is made up exactly as the fore-stay but the method of setting up on deck may vary slightly.   The most usual practice is to provide deck-plates and thimbles on either side of the fore-mast to which the stay is set up as for the fore-stay, the two parts being brought abaft the mast and seized.   The ship *Acamas* had a pair of short steel samson posts projecting through the deck about five or six feet forward of the fore mast, each post was provided with a pair of thimbles on the after side for one leg of the main and main-topmast stays respectively (Fig. 93).   Another arrangement is to set the stay up to a roller riveted on the after side of the mast just

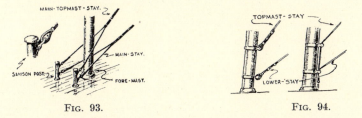

FIG. 93.   FIG. 94.

above the deck, or alternatively to use the roller as a fairlead and seize the stay to a thimble in deck-plates.   When this latter method is used the roller and deck-plate would be slightly off the centre line to allow the main topmast-stay to come down alongside it.   (Fig. 94).

Lower-Cap-Stays.—As on fore-mast.

Crane-Lines.—As requisite and rigged as on fore-mast.

Rigging Lower Mizzen-Mast.

Shrouds.—As on fore-mast but number according to rigging plan.

Mizzen-Stay.—As fore-stay, but in small vessels, particularly barques, will be single instead of double wire.

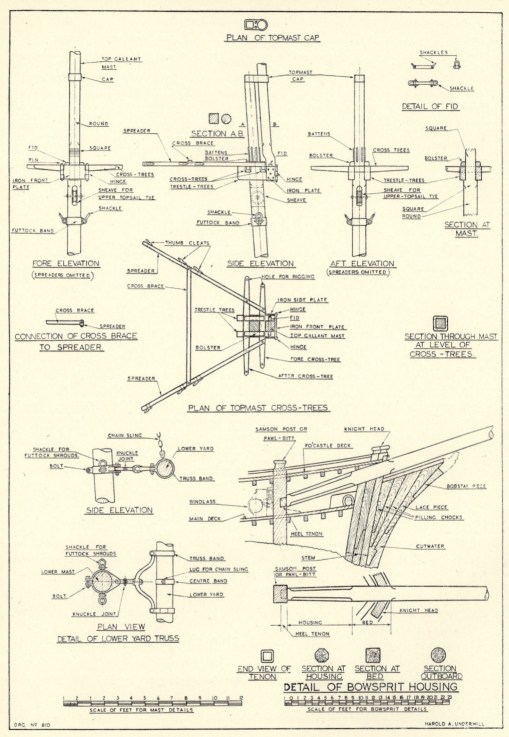

PLAN OF TOPMAST CAP

DETAIL OF FID

SECTION A.B.

FORE ELEVATION
(SPREADERS OMITTED)

SIDE ELEVATION

AFT ELEVATION
(SPREADERS OMITTED)

SECTION AT MAST.

CONNECTION OF CROSS BRACE TO SPREADER.

SECTION THROUGH MAST AT LEVEL OF CROSS-TREES.

PLAN OF TOPMAST CROSS-TREES

SIDE ELEVATION

PLAN VIEW
DETAIL OF LOWER YARD TRUSS

END VIEW OF TENON

SECTION AT HOUSING

SECTION AT BED

SECTION OUTBOARD

DETAIL OF BOWSPRIT HOUSING

SCALE OF FEET FOR MAST DETAILS

SCALE OF FEET FOR BOWSPRIT DETAILS

DRG. Nº 810

HAROLD A. UNDERHILL

PLATE No. 17.—DETAILS OF WOODEN CROSS-TREES AND BOWSPRIT.

Lower Cap-Stay.—As on fore, but where multi stays are carried the mizzen will as a rule rig one less than the fore and main.

Staysail-Horses.—As requisite and rigged as fore-mast.

NOTE.—Rigging-screws were at times fitted on the lower ends of fore and aft stays as shown in Plate 5, but this was not the general rule.

Rigging the Fore-Topmast.

Fish-Tackle-Burton or *Fish-Tackle-Pendant.*—This may also be known as the fore-topmast-burton.

The fish-tackle-burton is used in all ships not provided with anchor cranes or davits on their fo'castle heads, which broadly speaking may be said to mean all except the larger iron or steel craft. The purpose of the burton is to carry the fish-tackle used for getting the anchors over the bows, either for stowing on deck when she got out of soundings, or putting them over again when approaching land. When not in use it is set up between the cross-trees and the knight-heads, either by hooking the lower block to a convenient ring-bolt, or more commonly, seizing it ot the fork of the fore-stay. The fall is then hauled taut and clove hitched to the stay; the slack is wound tightly round one leg of the stay until expended, when the end is seized in position.

The burton—or pendant—is single wire, and when set up should reach about two-thirds of the distance to the knight-heads. An eye, large enough to give plenty of clearance round both top and topgallant masts, is formed in the head, either by splicing or seizing back, and well parcelled and served. The lower end may be spliced or seized back on a large metal thimble.

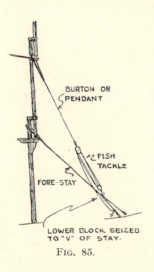

BURTON OR PENDANT

FISH TACKLE

FORE-STAY

LOWER BLOCK SEIZED TO "V" OF STAY.

FIG. 85.

The fish-tackle consists of double and treble blocks, the former being provided with a large hook on the crown and a thimble on the heel; the treble block shackles to the lower eye of the burton. The fall is spliced round the thimble of the double block; reeved through the treble block on the burton; down and through the double block, and so on until all sheaves are expended. This leaves the fall leading off the upper block. (Fig. 95). When in use the fall is taken to the capstan via a single lead block shackled to a convenient ring-bolt in the deck.

The fish-tackle-burton is the first unit of rigging to go over the topmast head and is bedded down on the bolsters with the "V" of the eye well on the fore side of the mast.

Fore-Topmast-Shrouds or *Fore-Topmast-Rigging.*—In ships of our period the topmasts usually carry three shrouds per side, although an isolated old-stager with four may have survived into the early part of it. The shrouds are made up in pairs and singles as in the case of the lower mast, and the order of rigging is also the same. The forward pair starboard go first over the mast-head and are bedded down on the eye of the fish-burton; then follows the first pair port, and lastly the singles. If the odd shroud on either side is formed with a separate eye, then the starboard one will go first, but if they are joined by what we will call a cut-seizing—Fig. 83—then of course they must go on together. When four shrouds are carried the order will be exactly as for the first four shrouds of the lower rigging.

The heads of the shrouds are made like those of the mast below, being middled, parcelled and served, and then seized together to form an eye. The method of setting up varies, but the majority of ships use either rigging-screws or dead-eyes and lanyards; whichever it is, the method of turning them into the bottom of the shrouds will be as given at the end of this chapter. The lower shackle of the rigging-screw, or the strop of the lower dead-eye, is bolted to the head of the futtock-shroud where it projects up through the top. A small sheer-pole of the type used on the lower rigging is now fitted, and the shrouds are ready for setting up by screw or lanyard. In some small vessels lanyard thimbles are used in place of dead-eyes, but this is not a very common practice on the topmast rigging. Another arrangement occasionally seen in very small craft such as the smaller brigantine, is to make the shrouds and futtocks in one; the shrouds are carried down through holes in the rim of the top and finish about three feet short of the futtock band by being spliced round lanyard thimbles. Lanyards are then reeved between the shackle on the futtock-band and the thimbles in the ends of the shrouds. The shrouds

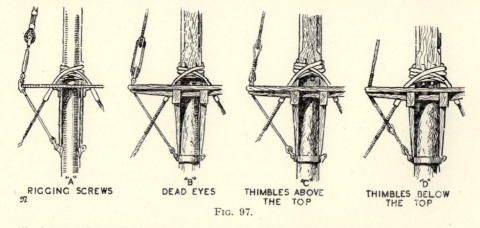

"A"
RIGGING SCREWS   "B"   "C"   "D"
DEAD EYES   THIMBLES ABOVE   THIMBLES BELOW
THE TOP   THE TOP

Fig. 97.

will of course be well parcelled and served at the point where they pass through the rim of the top. Fig. 97 illustrates various ways of setting up top-mast shrouds.

Ratlines.—These are carried right across, the eye-splices being seized to the outer shrouds, and the centre clove-hitched to the middle one. At the head of the rigging, say the last eight or ten feet, the ratlines are carried across to the aftermost topmast-backstay, (Fig. 96). This is to make up for the restricted width of the shrouds at this level.

FIG. 96.

Fore-Topmast-Backstays.—Single wire. There may be one, two or three topmast-backstays per side according to the size of the vessel, and the actual number must be ascertained from the sail and rigging plans. The backstays go over the mast immediately after the shrouds, on top of which they are bedded. If there are two or more per side they are made up like the lower shrouds, being middled, parcelled and served, and seized together to form an eye for the mast-head. The odd numbers are treated like the single topmast shrouds and either furnished with individual eyes, or crossed and seized to their opposite numbers in a "cut-seizing". The rigging sequence follows the same rule; first pair starboard, first pair port, followed by single starboard and single port, or if joined by seizing then the two singles together. The lower ends are parcelled, served and turned on rigging-screws or dead-eyes in the usual way.

Fore-Topmast-Preventer-Stay or *Inner-Fore-Topmast-Stay.*—Double wire. This stay is not in common use but is peculiar to a few of the larger clippers, which owing to their lofty rig were given an extra stay between the fore-stay and the normal fore-topmast-stay. The names I have used above may cause some comment, for like the naming of the masts of a six-mast barquentine, it is always good bait to throw out if you wish to start a really hot wordy battle! It has always been the accepted practice that the innermost stay from the fore-topmast head is the fore-topmast-stay; but it is equally well established that the innermost stay-sail from the topmast head shall be the fore-topmast-staysail, and further, in ninety-nine cases out of a hundred the fore-topmast-stay sets up on the bowsprit, not on deck. The stay now under consideration complies with the first of these rules but not with the two latter, so you have the choice of changing the name of either the stay or the sail, and as these ships carry another stay rigged exactly as the normal fore-topmast-stay, I prefer to change the name of the stay. However one could fill a whole chapter on the pros and cons of the various schools of thought so for the purpose of this book, *fore-topmast-preventer-stay* it is going to be.

As the term "preventer-stay" is not in the normal vocabulary of the modern ship, it may be of interest to explain its origin. In the good old days when ships more or less took pot shots at each other on sight, leaving all questions until afterwards, it was the practice to duplicate all the principal stays by running them in pairs with a space between them.   Thus the fore-stay had the fore-preventer-stay running parallel to it a foot or so below; the fore-topmast-stay had its fore-topmast-preventer-stay immediately below it; the main-stay with the main-preventer-stay below and so on; the object being that should one be shot away its partner would carry on the good work. In men-of-war a diagonal lacing ran between the two stays, so that either or both could be shot through in several places yet still continue to function.

Now to return to our modern fore-topmast-preventer-stay.   It is rigged and set up exactly as the fore-stay, except that the head is at the topmast-cross trees instead of the lower-mast.   The eye is made by either of the methods already described, but it is large enough to go round topmast and topgallant with the "V" well forward of the cross-trees; the length of this eye will be from 9 ft. 0 ins. to 12 ft. 0 ins. according to the size of the ship.   In older wooden ships it was customary for the fore-topmast-stay and all jib-stays to be bedded down hard on the rest of the topmast rigging, their eyes coming out below the leading cross-tree, much as the fore-stay does in Fig. 90A; but later—again like the fore-stay—the practice of supporting all head-stays on thumb-cleats—Fig. 54—on the after side of the topmast-head became general.   This point however will always be clearly shown on the rigging plan. The lower ends of the stay, after each part has been parcelled, served and leathered, are set up round the solid thimbles in the deck-plates and seized back to their own respective standing parts, Plate 2.   The two legs of the stay are then brought together and seized as in the case of the fore-stay.

Fore-Topmast-Stay.—Double wire.   This is usually the first stay to go over the topmast-head, the only exceptions being ships provided with the preventer-stay already described.   The eye in the head of the stay will be made as detailed for the fore-stay and will be from 9 ft. 0 ins. to 12 ft. 0 ins. long according to the size of the vessel.   It is passed over the mast head and bedded down on the topmast rigging already in place, or on thumb-cleats on the doubling; if the former it will pass outside the trestle-trees and under the forward cross-tree, with the "V" well on the fore side of the mast.   If seated round the doubling, the thumb-cleats must be sufficiently high to allow the stay to take a straight line to its lower anchorage without fouling the forward edge of the cross-trees.   The lower end may be set up in various ways.   In Plate 19 of the spike boom, the two parts of the stay come down on either side of the bowsprit; are reeved through the outer cheek-block on their respective sides; up through the inner cheek-blocks; set up taut and seized back to their own standing parts with three seizings.   When all is taut the two parts of the stay are brought together a few feet above the spar and seized.   Both legs of the stay will be parcelled and served for the whole length between the points where they are seized above the spar, and their extremities, this is of course done before reeving through the cheek-blocks, in way of which the stays should also be leathered. Plate 2 of the *Loch Etive* also shows this method. Plate 14 and the lower drawing on Plate 13 are the same in principle, although they differ in detail. In the first place both ships have battens instead of cheek-blocks, and in Plate 14 the stay is set up with hearts and lanyards on either side of the bowsprit, while in the lower drawing on Plate 13 each part of the stay passes through circular fairleads in the bulwarks and is set up to bitts on deck.

The upper drawing on Plate 13 illustrates another fairly common method used in both wood and iron ships. In this case the two parts of the stay are passed under the bowsprit from opposite sides, and each brought up on the other side and seized to its opposite number with three seizings. This is perhaps more clearly shown in Fig. 98 where it is applied to an iron vessel. The two parts of the stay are seized together just above the spar as already described, and will of course be parcelled and served for their entire length from this point to the ends, they will also be leathered where they are in contact with the spar. Thumb-cleats are provided to prevent the stay sliding inboard along the spar.

FIG. 98.

Jib-Stay.—Single wire. The stay is cut off to the required length allowing for the eye and method of setting up. The upper end is parcelled and served for sufficient length to form an eye equal to that of the fore-topmast-stay. The length served is then middled and turned back on its own part and the seizings put on, (Fig. 99). The lower end is marked at a point about three feet above the jib-boom, and the stay is then parcelled and served from this point to its extremity. The eye is placed over the topmast-head and bedded down on that of the fore-topmast-stay. The stay will be set up according to the rigging plan; on the modern spike boom it reeves through a roller fairlead on the cap-band and is set up taut by a rigging-screw cleated on the bowsprit, Plate 19. The next example is the same rig applied to a bowsprit and jib-boom. The two drawings on Plate 13 represent what is perhaps the most usual way of setting up this

FIG. 99.

stay when a jib-boom is carried.   Here the stay passes down through the inner sheave-hole in the jib-boom;   over the port upper thumb-cleat on the martingale, and is set up at the bows with hearts and lanyards. The end of the stay may either be turned directly on the score round the heart, or on a thimble and shackled to a metal strop round the heart.   The last example Plate 14 is not much used.   In this case the stay is reeved round a roller fairlead on the inner-jib-boom-band; set up taut, and seized back to its own standing part. All stays will of course be parcelled and served from a few feet above the bowsprit. Note when only two jib-stays are rigged the first one, which I have just described, is usually known as the *jib-stay*, but if three are carried then it becomes the *inner-jib-stay*.

Outer-Jib-Stay.—Single wire. This is made just the same as the jib-stay, except of course for length. The eye is passed over the mast-head and bedded down on that of the jib-stay, and the lower end parcelled and served from a point about three feet above the boom to its extremity. On the spike boom the end is reeved through the roller fairlead on the outer band, and set up by rigging-screw on top of the spar, Plate 19. In all ships carrying timber jib-booms it reeves down through the outer sheave-hole; over the starboard upper thumb-cleat on the martingale and is set up at the starboard bow, Plates 2, 13 and 14.

Some ships have chain inserts in their head-stays where they pass through the jib-boom, or even right back to the bows; this however is usually the result of repairs. If on examination, the stay is found to be sound except for signs of chafe or wear at the jib-boom and martingale, the doubtful end may be cut off and replaced by chain, which has the advantage of being cheap and requiring neither parcelling nor serving.

Fore-Topmast-Cap-Stay.—Single wire.   Number as shown on rigging plan. This stay—or stays—is made up exactly as that of the lower mast.

Rigging the Main-Topmast.

The fish-tackle-burton is of course not carried on either main or mizzen topmasts.

Main-Topmast-Shrouds.—As on fore-mast.

Main-Topmast-Backstays.—As on fore-mast.

Main-Topmast-Stay.—Double wire. The head of the stay is made up and put over the mast as described for the fore-topmast-stay. The foot, after each leg has been parcelled and served for the required distance, is usually set up to deck-plates and thimbles on either side of the fore-mast and immediately ahead of those of the main-stay. The two parts of the stay are then brought together and seized abaft the fore-mast, keeping far enough aft to ensure an acute angle in the "V" of the stay. One alternative is to set the stay up to samson posts as in the case of the ship *Acamas*, (Fig. 93); while another is to reeve the double stay through a roller fairlead on the after side of the fore-mast, where it is either seized back to its own standing part, or may be continued to the deck and set up with a rigging screw.

Main-Topmast-Cap-Stay.—Single wire. As on fore-mast. Number according to rigging plan.

Rigging the Mizzen-Topmast.

Mizzen-Topmast-Shrouds.—As on fore-mast.

Mizzen-Topmast-Backstays.—As on fore-mast but frequently less in number, this will be shown on rigging plan.

Mizzen-Topmast-Stay.—May be either double or single wire according to the size of the ship, but will certainly be single in the case of a barque. Made up and rigged as for main-topmast-stay.

Mizzen-Topmast-Cap-Stay.—Single wire. As on fore-mast. This stay is frequently omitted.

Rigging the Fore-Topgallant-Mast.

The topgallant and royal masts partly reverse the usual order of rigging, in that the fore and aft stays go over the mast first, or below the shrouds and backstays instead of on top of them as in the case of lower and topmasts.

Topgallant-Funnel.—This is a metal sleeve—Fig. 100—made a good fit on the topgallant hounds or stop, and is intended to prevent the rigging cutting into the mast; it is made sufficiently long to project above the eyes of the rigging when all are in position.

Mast-Head-Strop.—This is a grommet or endless rope ring into which two metal thimbles are seized at diametrically opposite sides. The grommet is wormed, parcelled and served before seizing in the thimbles, and when finished must be a tight fit on the mast above the stop. In forming the strop it is advisable to make the grommet on the large side and start seizing from the thimbles, working in towards the centre; the seizings can then be continued until the internal diameter of the strop is slightly less than the measured

FIG. 100.

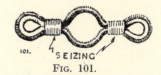

SEIZING

FIG. 101.

diameter of the mast, which will make a good snug fit on top of the funnel, (Fig. 101). The mast-head-strop is usually the first item of rigging to go over the mast, but there are several examples of modern steel craft having it put on after the shrouds. This arrangement has several advantages, one being

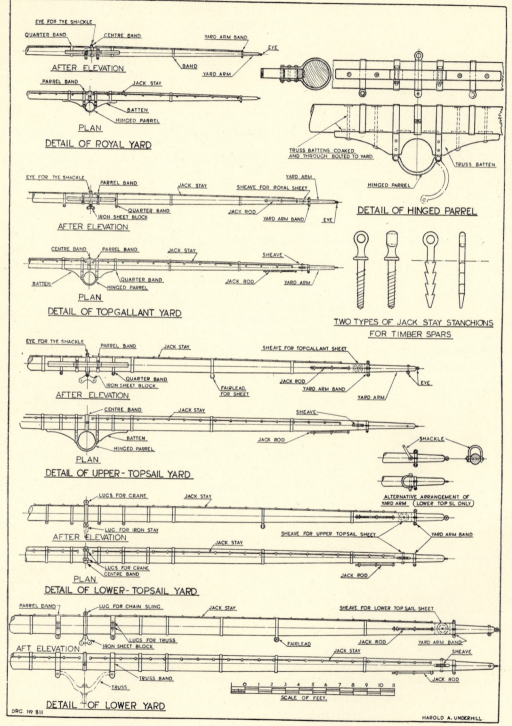

PLATE No. 18.—RANGE OF TIMBER YARDS.

greater freedom for the upper-topgallant-lifts which are shackled into the thimbles. Where double topgallant-lifts are carried they may either both be shackled into the thimbles of one strop—placed in either of the positions already mentioned; or alternatively two strops may be used, one above and one below the shrouds, and to these the outer and inner lifts respectively may be shackled.

Fore-Topgallant-Stay or *Flying-Jib-Stay.*—Single wire. The head of this stay is parcelled, served and turned to form an eye to fit snugly round the mast at the topgallant stops. When complete the eye is over parcelled and painted as in the case of the shrouds and must finish a tight fit round the mast above the stops. The eye is then got over the mast and bedded down on top of the mast-head-strop, or if the latter is to be fitted above the shrouds, on to the base of the stop. The stay is then marked at a point about three feet above the boom and parcelled and served from that point to its extremity. On the spike-boom the stay reeves through the port fairlead on the bowsprit end and is set up by a rigging-screw as shown in the drawing. In ships with timber jib-booms the stay reeves down through the innermost hole in the jib-boom head; back over the lower port cleat on the martingale, and sets up on the bow with lanyards and hearts, or may be taken through a fairlead in the bulwarks and set up on deck.

Fore-Topgallant-Shrouds.—Wire, two per side. The topgallant shrouds are made up in pairs as in the case of the lower and topmasts, except that the eye in each pair must be a snug fit round the mast above the stops. The starboard pair go on first and are bedded down on top of the fore-topgallant-stay, they are then followed by the pair on the port side. The usual method of setting up is to reeve the lower ends of the shrouds through holes in the arms of the cross-trees; turn in lanyard thimbles about three feet from the futtock band, and set them up with lanyards between the thimble and the shackle on the band, as shown in Fig. 97D for the lower rigging. In this arrangement the shrouds and futtocks are of course all in one length. The shrouds will require to be served and leathered in way of the cross-tree arms, and the serving may continue to the thimbles. Some vessels, particularly among the big steel carriers, have iron futtock shrouds at the cross-trees, in which case the topgallant shrouds are set up with rigging-screws.

Ratlines.—Rigged as on the topmast shrouds except that there is no middle shroud. At the head of the rigging they extend across the backstays and are clove-hitched to the after shroud and intermediate stays.

Fore-Topgallant-Backstays.—Single wire. The number carried will vary according to the size of the vessel and must be taken from the rigging plan. If there are an even number per side they will be made in pairs, with eyes as for the topgallant-shrouds; if single the opposite sides may either be joined in a "cut-seizing" or provided with separate eyes. In either case the eyes

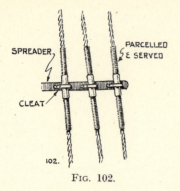

FIG. 102.

must be made a good tight fit round the funnel above the stops. Whether in pairs or single the order of fitting will be as usual, i.e. starboard side first followed by port etc. The backstays will be marked for the point of contact with the spreaders, and with this as centre will be parcelled and served for a distance of three feet on either side, the actual point of contact will then be leathered in way of the cleat, (Fig. 102). The lower ends will be finished off as other backstays and set up immediately abaft the topmast-cap-stays.

Rigging the Main-Topgallant-Mast.

Topgallant Funnel.—As on fore-mast.

Mast-Strop.—As on fore-mast.

Main-Topgallant-Stay.—Single wire. The head of this stay is made up as for the fore-topgallant-stay. The lower end will be parcelled and served from a point about three feet short of its contact with the fore-mast down to its extremity. The stay will reeve through a fairlead on the after side of the fore mast in a position to be obtained from the rigging plan, this in modern vessels will most probably be about the futtock-band of the fore lower mast; from the fairlead it is taken down abaft the mast and is either set up on deck, or to cleat on the mast itself. In older ships the fairlead may be rather higher up, say on the after side of the lower cap, in which case the stay will set up in the top with either screw, or hearts and lanyard.

Main-Topgallant-Shrouds.—As on fore-mast.

Ratlines.—As on fore-mast.

Main-Topgallant-Backstays.—As on fore-mast.

Rigging the Mizzen-Topgallant-Mast.

Topgallant Funnel.—As on fore-mast.

Mast-Strop.—As on fore-mast.

Mizzen-Topgallant-Stay.—As on main-mast.

Mizzen-Topgallant-Shrouds.—As on fore-mast.

Ratlines.—As on fore-mast.

Mizzen-Topgallant-Backstays.—As on fore-mast but probably less in number, this to be checked from rigging plan.

Rigging on Fore-Royal-Mast.

The royal rigging sets up at the royal stops. The shrouds and ratlines are not provided, it being usual to have to shin up the mast to reach the head of the rigging; however in some of the later ships, particularly those carrying cadets, jacob's ladders were rigged abaft the royal mast, (Fig. 103).

Royal Funnel.—As topgallant funnel.

FIG. 103.*Mast-Head-Strop.*—As topgallant mast-head-strop.

Fore-Royal-Stay.—Single wire. This stay is made up exactly as the fore-topgallant-stay; and the eye, which must be a snug fit round the royal stops, is bedded down on the mast-head-strop. The lower end, after being parcelled and served from three feet above the boom, reeves through the outer hole in the jib-boom head; back over the lower starboard cleat on the martingale, and sets up on the starboard bow as in the case of the other head-stays.

Fore-Royal-Backstays.—Single wire. One per side, joined in a "cut-seizing" which is parcelled and served and fitted tightly round the mast. The stay will be parcelled, served and leathered in way of the spreaders as was done with the other backstays, and the lower ends set up in the usual way abaft the topgallant-backstays.

Unless a skysail mast is carried this will be the last standing rigging to go over the mast and the truck can now go into position, the truck should not be fitted at an earlier stage, as owing to the smallness of the eyes in the royal rigging it would hamper the work.

If a skysail-mast is fitted as a standing spar, the rigging will be as described for the royal-mast.

Rigging the Main-Royal-Mast.

Royal Funnel.—As topgallant funnel.

Mast-Head-Strop.—As topgallant mast-head-strop.

Main-Royal-Stay.—Single wire. Except for the matter of length this stay is made up as the fore-royal-stay. The lower end is reeved through a fairlead on the after side of the fore-mast, usually at the lower mast-cap, and is set up with screws or hearts and lanyards in the top.

Main-Royal-Backstays.—As on fore-mast.

Skysail-mast when carried is rigged as on the fore.

Rigging the Mizzen-Royal-Mast.

Royal Funnel.—As topgallant funnel.

Mast-Head-Strop.—As on fore-mast.

Mizzen-Royal-Stay.—As on main mast.

Mizzen-Royal-Backstays.—As on fore-mast.

There is no need to describe the rigging on the fore and aft mast of a barque, beyond pointing out that the lower mast will be as a normal square rigged mast, except that the number of shrouds will be reduced and a single instead of double lower stay is carried. The rigging on the topmast is really that of the topgallant and royal of the other masts.

When ships carry a flying jib-boom the fore-topgallant-stay, fore-royal-stay, and fore-skysail-stay will occupy the positions shown on Plate 14. Otherwise the rig will be as just described.

Barquentine Fore and Aft Masts.

Perhaps a brief mention of the standing rigging on one of the big barquentines such as *Mozart* may be of interest, although except for the matter of proportion, there really is no difference from that already covered in this chapter. The fore-mast certainly requires no mention, it is just a normal square rigged mast; stump to'gallant rigged in the case of *Mozart*, but that is only one example. At first glance the standing gear on the fore and aft masts seems extremely light, but that is more apparent than real due no doubt to the very lofty nature of her lower-masts.

Lower Shrouds.—Five per side, made up and put over the mast head as already described; lower ends set up with rigging screws to chain plates inside the bulwarks in the usual way. All rigging was of course wire. It should be noted that, unlike the square rigged mast, the second shroud is opposite the mast, the first shroud being before it. The reason for this is that with the square rigged mast the normal load is always forward, while with the fore and after the *weight* of all the spars tends to load the mast aft; another point is that by moving the shrouds forward greater freedom is given to the boom.

Ratlines.—In *Mozart* these were rigged across the three aftermost shrouds, with every sixth running across the whole gang.

Cap-Stays.—One per side; upper ends turned on solid thimbles and shackled to lugs on the cap; lower ends set up as shrouds.

Triatic-Stay or *Spring-Stay.*—Single wire. This stay runs horizontally between main, mizzen and jigger mast caps, and is set up to lugs provided on the fore and aft sides for that purpose.

Topmast Shrouds.—Two per side. The heads were bedded on the topmast hounds in the usual way; while the lower ends, after being parcelled and served, passed over the boxed ends of the cross-trees and were held in position by straps bolted on (Figs. 57 and 104). The ends were turned on lanyard thimbles and set up to shackles on the futtock-band with lanyards.

Topmast-Backstays.—Single wire. Two per side, made in pairs in the usual way; parcelled and served in way of spreaders and set up with rigging-screws.

Topmast-Stays.—Single wire. Eye formed in head to fit mast, lower ends set up with screws on the crown of the lower-mast cap. (Fig. 105).

Between the fore and main masts were three stays, set up in the usual way, except that the head of the main-topmast-stay was shackled to a lug on the fore side of the cap instead of having an eye round the mast.

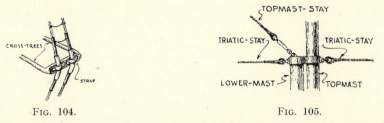

FIG. 104.   FIG. 105.

I do not propose to make any mention of the small wooden barquentines at this point, as they will be described in detail under the heading of small craft in chapter VII.

Rigging the Yards.
Lower-Yards.

Slings.—Chain. Except for one or two isolated cases slings are always of chain. In ships having iron or steel masts the upper end of the sling is shackled to a cleat immediately below the top, (Fig. 43) and the lower end to the lug on the centre yard-band. The steel four-mast barque *Peking*, now the training ship *Arethusa*, is one of the exceptions, for her trusses are in the form of large rigging-screws with one or two links of chain at the end. As a matter of fact there are one or two rather unusual features about the rigging details of this ship.

In wooden ships it is usual to pass the chain up through the lubbers-hole; round the back of the lower-mast head; down through the lubbers-hole on the opposite side, bringing the two ends together in one shackle on the lug of the centre yard-band. Abaft the mast the sling may either sit in a thumb cleat on the doubling (Fig. 106A), or down near the bolsters, (Fig. 106B).

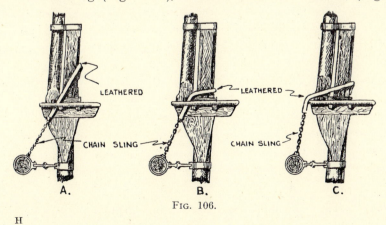

FIG. 106.

H

In either case it will be well parcelled and leathered where it rides on the mast and passes outside the standing rigging. A few ships brought the slings out over the lip of the top, (Fig. 106c), but this is a very bad arrangement as it puts an unnecessary load on the forward end of the trestle-trees.

Foot-Ropes.—Wire or hemp. These are made in two sections, one on each half of the yard and crossing at the mast. In modern ships the foot-rope is made up with thimbles spliced in either end; the outer ones being shackled or seized to some convenient point at the yard-arm—the brace-pendant shackle for example; while the inner ends are passed in front of the mast and set up with lanyards to the jack-stay on the opposite half of the yard— see detail of upper-topsail-yard on Plate 23. An alternative was to seize the inner ends to the span of the truss instead of to the jack-stay; they are still taken across the mast of course, the starboard foot-rope being seized to the port-side of the truss and vice versa. The foot-ropes are parcelled and served in the way of the stirrups and at the ends for such length as may chafe on the yard. The foot-ropes may either reeve through the eyes of the stirrups and be seized in place, or alternatively they may merely be seized below the eyes.

FIG. 107.

In many of the older ships the foot-rope has an eye, large enough to fit the yard arm and sit snugly against the stop, spliced in the outer end, (Fig. 107), this however, rather dates back to the time when iron bands were still something of an innovation.

Stirrups.—These are made to finish at about three feet six inches long with a thimble spliced in each end, and are parcelled and served for their entire length. The stirrup hangs down the after side of the yard, the upper eye being seized to the jack-stay and the lower to the foot-rope. The number of stirrups will depend upon the length of the yard.

Flemish-Horses.—This is really a small additional foot-rope, rigged on all yards which carried reefing sails to enable a man to sit well out on the yard-arm when passing the earing. It was very necessary on the old type of yard with long arms, but on the modern yard which has little or no yard-arm, the outer band to which the normal foot-rope is bent is so near the end that no advantage would be gained by rigging flemish horses, although I have an idea that I have seen them on the yards of one of the big steel carriers. Another point against the flemish-horse in the modern ship is the fact that some of them dispense with reefing on most sails.

The horse is made with a thimble spliced in either end; the outer one being shackled or seized to an eye screwed into the end of the yard-arm, and the inner one seized to the jack-stay some little distance in board. When rigged the horse forms a bight of about the same depth as the foot-rope. Plate 23.

Beckets.—These are short lengths of cordage attached in bights at interval

along the jack-stay. When working on the yard a man can pass his arm through
the bight of the becket as a safety measure, and so have both hands free for
the job to be done. This is illustrated in Fig. 108 which shows a becket in

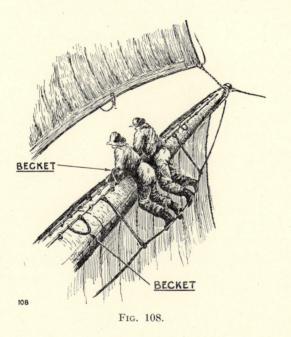

BECKET

BECKET

108

FIG. 108.

use. Each end of the line is clove-hitched to the jack-stay and seized back to
its own part as shown in the details and sketches on Plate 23.

Lower-Topsail-Yards.

Slings.—Chain. Normally slings are only carried on lower yards, but
there are exceptions in the case of some of the big steel barques, of which
Peking is one. When carried the sling is rigged as described in Chapter II.,
which may be repeated briefly as consisting of a short chain extending between
a cleat on the pole topmast and a lug on the yard. When additional support
was considered necessary, the more usual method was to fit a stay or strut
between the underside of the yard and the forward edge of the top; however
in the greater majority of ships the lower-topsail-crane was strong enough
to support the yard without assistance.

Foot-Ropes.—As for lower-yards.

Stirrups.—As for lower-yards.

Flemish-Horses.—Not carried on lower-topsail-yards.

Beckets.—As for lower-yards.

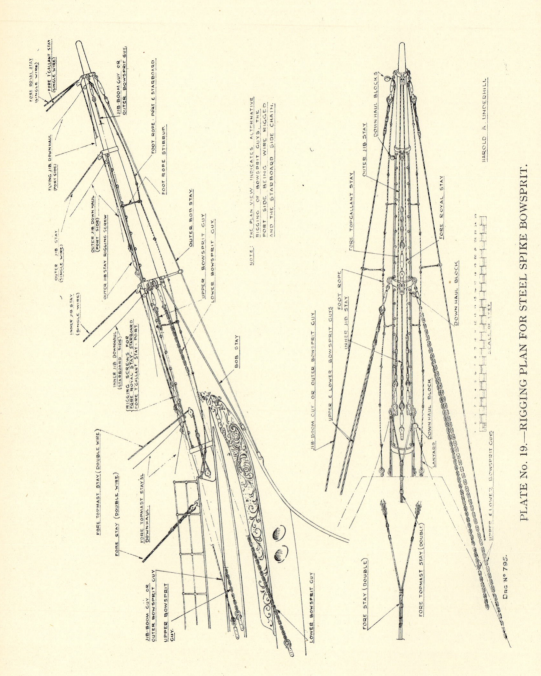

FORE ROYAL STAY (SINGLE WIRE)
FORE T'GALLANT STAY (SINGLE WIRE)
JIB BOOM GUY OR OUTER BOWSPRIT GUY
FOOT ROPE - PORT & STARBOARD
FLYING JIB DOWNHAUL (PORT SIDE)
FOOT ROPE STIRRUP.
OUTER JIB STAY (SINGLE WIRE)
OUTER JIB DOWN HAUL (PORT SIDE)
OUTER JIB STAY RIGGING SCREW
OUTER BOB STAY
INNER JIB STAY (SINGLE WIRE)
UPPER BOWSPRIT GUY
LOWER BOWSPRIT GUY
INNER JIB DOWNHAUL (STARBOARD SIDE)
RIGGING SCREWS FOR FORE ROYAL STAY, STARBOARD FORE T'GALLANT STAY - PORT
BOB STAY
FORE TOPMAST STAY (DOUBLE WIRE)
FORE STAY (DOUBLE WIRE)
FORE TOPMAST STAYSL DOWNHAUL
JIB-BOOM GUY OR OUTER BOWSPRIT GUY
UPPER BOWSPRIT GUY
LOWER BOWSPRIT GUY

NOTE: THE PLAN VIEW INDICATES ALTERNATIVE RIGGING OF BOWSPRIT GUYS, THE PORT SIDE BEING WIRE RIGGED AND THE STARBOARD SIDE CHAIN.

FORE TOPGALLANT STAY
OUTER JIB STAY
DOWN HAUL BLOCKS
FORE ROYAL STAY
JIB BOOM GUY OR OUTER BOWSPRIT GUY
UPPER & LOWER BOWSPRIT GUYS
FOOT ROPE
INNER JIB STAY
DOWN HAUL BLOCK
LANYARD DOWNHAUL BLOCK
UPPER & LOWER BOWSPRIT GUYS
SCALE OF FEET
HAROLD A UNDERHILL

FORE STAY (DOUBLE)
FORE TOPMAST STAY (DOUBLE)
DRG Nº 795.

PLATE No. 19.—RIGGING PLAN FOR STEEL SPIKE BOWSPRIT.

Upper-Topsail-Yards.

A detailed drawing of the rigging on a modern upper-topsail-yard will be found on Plate 23, this will of course apply to a large extent to the complete range of yards.

Standing-Lifts.—Single wire. One or two lifts may be rigged according to the length and weight of the yard. The length of each lift must be such that it just takes the weight of its own particular part of the yard when the latter is in the lowered position. Both ends of the lift are turned on metal thimbles and seized back to their own standing parts; they are also parcelled and served for some distance in from each thimble as a protection against being chafed by the rigging, or the yard when hoisted. The upper thimbles —of both inner and outer lifts when they are fitted—go on to the shackles at either end of the topgallant-mast fid, and come down on the fore side of the cross-trees. The lower ends shackle to lugs provided on the yard; the outer to the yard-arm band and the inner to a special band for the purpose. Plate 23.

Foot-Ropes.—As for lower-yard.

Stirrups.—As for lower-yard, but number as required.

Flemish-Horses.—As for lower-yard. (If required.)

Beckets.—As for lower-yards.

Lower-Topgallant-Yards.

Foot-Ropes.—As for lower-yards.

Stirrups.—As for lower-yards, but number as required.

Flemish-Horses.—Not carried on lower-topgallant-yards.

Beckets.—As for lower-yards.

Upper-Topgallant-Yards.

Standing-Lifts.—Single wire. Usually one per side, but some of the big steel vessels rigged two as on the upper-topsail. These lifts are made up just as those for the upper-topsail-yard. The upper ends shackle to the eyes of the mast-head-strops at the topgallant hounds; the lower ends to the yard as shown in Plate 23. The lifts must of course be kept on the fore side of the shrouds. If double lifts are carried the outer one may be taken to a second mast-head-strop as already described.

Foot-Ropes.—As for lower-yards.

Stirrups.—As for lower-yards, number according to length of yard.

Flemish-Horses.—As for lower-yards. (If required.)

Beckets.—As for lower-yards.

Royal-Yards.

Standing-Lifts.—Single wire. Usually one per side, although a few of the big ships carried double lifts right up to the royals. They are made up as for the upper topsails-yard, with the upper thimbles shackled to the royal mast-head-strop, and the lower ones to the yard. The lifts will of course be on the fore side of the rigging.

Foot-Ropes.—As for lower-yards.

Stirrups.—As for lower-yards, number according to length of yard.

Flemish-Horses.—Not usually carried on royal-yards.

Beckets.—As for lower-yards.

Skysail Yards.

When carried these are rigged as described for the royal-yard.

Standing Spanker Gaffs.

With very few exceptions, such as Fig. 56, the throat of a standing gaff is supported by a goose-neck on the mast. and the following description is based on this rig.

Peak-Span.—Single wire, or in some cases chain. The span is made to the required length with a thimble turned or spliced into each end. The inner end shackles to a lug on the after side of the mast-cap, or in some ships to a mast-head-strop at the topmast hounds; the outer end is shackled to the eye on top of the outer band of the gaff.

FIG. 109.

Boom-Topping-Span.—Single wire. This may at times be termed boom-topping-lift, although that is more usually applied to a lift leading in to the throat of the sail, as on a hoisting gaff. With the standing gaff the boom is supported by a span extending between the outer ends of both gaff and boom, and that is the rig now described. The lift has a thimble at either end; the top being shackled to the lower lug of the outer band on the gaff, and the bottom to the upper side of the outer band on the boom.

Vang-Pendants.—These will be covered with the vangs under the heading of running rigging.

Monkey-Gaff.—This is a small signal gaff, rigged from the topmast cross-trees to give the signal halliards greater elevation than when rigged in the usual way at the spanker gaff, (Fig. 109). It is rigged as a standing gaff with a wire peak-span and single wire vangs, which are usually seized to the backstays a little distance below the gaff.

Fittings Used on the Standing Rigging.

I expect that most readers will be familiar with the various fittings used with wire and rope rigging, or at least have a very good idea as to what they should look like, but not everyone will know just how these should be proportioned.   Plate 24 is a sheet of scale drawings covering most of them and showing their construction, while in chapter IX there are tables which give the relative proportions of dead-eyes and the diameter of eye to use for any size of rigging.   On this latter point I need hardly mention that the various fittings will not necessarily bear the same relation to each other as shown in the drawing, for the simple reason that all items are available in a wide range of sizes according to the particular duty for which they are intended.   Metal thimbles for example may range in size from $1\frac{1}{8}$ ins. long to nine or ten inches, and dead-eyes from 3 ins. to 16 ins. in diameter.   However generally speaking their proportions will remain constant and can be scaled up or down as required.

Solid Metal Thimble.—Sometimes referred to as a cringle.   Drawing (A on the plate referred to illustrate the type of solid thimble used with rigging screws, deck-plates, etc.   The lower and larger hole is for the bolt passing through rigging-screw jaws or the sides of the deck-plates; while the smaller one takes the sheer-pole of the shrouds and backstays, or may be used for a tommy bar to prevent the stay twisting when tightening up the screw on a single stay.

Metal Thimble.—Detail (B) is an ordinary metal thimble as used in eye-splices, ends of pendants, and a hundred and one other jobs.

Metal Lanyard-Thimble.—Detail (C).   This is used in place of a heart on small stays, hand-lines, etc., etc., which are set up with lanyards.   It is spliced into the end of the gear like an ordinary thimble, but the flat top allows the turns of the lanyard to lie side by side without over-riding.

Metal Deck-Thimble or *Deck-Cringle.*—Detail (D).   This consists of a sheave, contained in a metal shell attached to a lug projecting up through the deck, and is largely used for the lower ends of fore and aft stays.

Dead-Eyes.   (Upper).—Detail (E).   Dead-eyes are made of hard wood such as lignum vitae.   The lanyard holes are rounded off in the direction of the lead so that the cordage follows a curve through the eye, thus avoiding sharp corners which would chafe or nip the lanyard.   This rounding forms grooves or scores in the face of the dead-eye as shown.   One hole, the left hand one on the inboard side, is not rounded off on this side, the reason for this will be explained later.   Round the circumference of the dead-eye a score is made to suit the size of standing rigging to be used.

Dead-Eyes.   (Lower).—Detail (F).   These are made in the same way as the upper eyes except that all lanyard holes are rounded on both sides, and

the score round the outer circumference is made to suit the flat metal band
—or strop—by means of which the dead-eye is bolted to the head of the
chain-plate,

Circular Heart.—Detail (G).   This is a circular block of lignum vitae
with a score round the circumference for turning into the end of the standing
rigging, or to take a wire or metal strop.   The centre is cut out in the form of
a "D" lying on its side, and along the straight side of this are three rounded
scores for the lanyards, which in section resemble the tops of three fixed
sheaves.   Hearts are used in place of dead-eyes for setting up bowsprit rigging
and fore and aft stays.

Oval-Heart.—Detail (H).   Except for external shape, the principle and
construction of this heart is the same as the circular one.   The oval heart
belongs to an earlier period, and except perhaps for one or two of the older
frigate built ships will not be found in any of the craft we are now considering.

Turning in Dead-Eyes, Thimbles Etc.

The act of seizing the standing rigging round the outer score of a dead-eye
is termed "turning-in" the dead-eye, and this of course applies equally well
to hearts, thimbles, or any other fitting which is fixed in the same way.

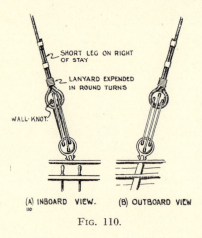

SHORT LEG ON RIGHT
OF STAY

LANYARD EXPENDED
IN ROUND TURNS

WALL-KNOT.

(A) INBOARD VIEW.   (B) OUTBOARD VIEW

FIG. 110.

When turning in thimbles on wire
standing rigging which is at an incline,
the short leg is always brought up under
the standing part; that is to say, on all
fore and aft stays the short leg will be
nearest the deck, and on shrouds and
backstays it will be on the inboard side
of the standing part.

In turning in dead-eyes, whether the
rigging be wire or hemp, the short leg is
always on the right of the standing part
when seen from the deck, (Fig. 110).   Thus
the short legs will be on the after side of the
starboard rigging, and fore side of the port.

It is usual to use three seizings when turning dead-eyes or thimbles into
standing rigging; a throat seizing immediately above the dead-eye, followed
by one half way up the short leg, and the third an inch or so from the end of
the leg.   However there is no hard and fast rule on this, for some riggers put
on four or even five seizings. The end of the stay should be capped and whipped
before being turned on the dead-eye, the capping being intended to prevent
moisture working its way down the lay of the rope.   A temporary whipping
is always put on either side of the point where it is proposed to cut a rope,
this is to prevent unlaying when the cut is made.

Reeving Dead-Eyes.

There are two rules which are always observed when reeving dead-eyes.—

1st. The lanyard reeves *outwards* through the holes in the upper dead-eye, and *inwards* through the holes of the lower.

2nd. Assuming that you are standing on deck and looking outwards, the lanyard always starts at the left-hand hole of the upper dead-eye, which of course is the one which has no score on the inner face.

The lanyard is prepared by whipping one end to prevent unlaying, and forming a wall knot in the other. The lanyard and the holes in the dead-eyes are then well greased and all is ready to start reeving.

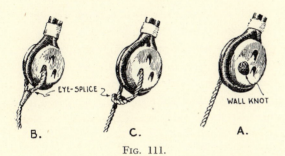

FIG. 111.
FIG. 112.

Order of Reeving.—(As viewed from the deck and looking outwards.)

1st. Pass the lanyard outwards through the left hand hole of the upper dead-eye, and haul through until the wall knot is bedded against the plain face, of the hole (Fig. 111A and Fig. 112).

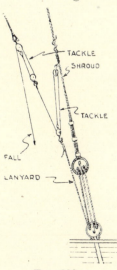

FIG. 113.

2nd. Pass the lanyard inwards through the left hand hole of the lower dead-eye.

3rd. Reeve outwards through the centre hole of the upper dead-eye.

4th Reeve inwards through the centre hole of the lower dead-eye.

5th. Reeve outwards through the right hand hole of the upper dead-eye.

6th. Reeve inwards through the right hand hole of the lower dead-eye. The lanyard is then set up taut by attaching a tackle to the shroud with a selvagee-strop well above the upper dead-eye, (Fig. 113). When the lanyard has been set up full due, it is temporarily seized to its own part while the end is passed between the throat seizing and the deadeye-with a hitch, (Fig. 112). The remainder of the lanyard is expended in round turns round the shroud and the end seized; the temporary seizing is then removed.   When finally set up the result should appear as in Fig. 110.   Seen from the inboard side the lanyard inclines upward from the lower left hand hole to the upper centre hole; from the lower centre hole to the upper right hand hole, and from the lower right to the throat seizing.   On the outboard side the lanyard passes between corresponding holes in upper and lower dead-eyes.   As the wall-knot is always at the left hand hole when seen from the deck, it follows that it will be forward on the starboard side of the ship and aft on the port.

The practice of starting the lanyard with a wall-knot is most commonly used, but there are alternatives.   One is to eye-splice the lanyard into the upper left hand hole as shown in Fig. 111B; another to form a small eye-splice in the end of the lanyard in place of the wall-knot, the lanyard is then reeved outwards through the hole in the dead-eye and down through its own eye, (Fig. 111c).   Two well known ships used these methods, *Macquarie* being rigged as Fig. 111B., and *Loch Tay* as Fig. 111c.   In both these methods the order of reeving will be as already described, but all holes in the upper dead-eye will be scored on both sides instead of having one plain on the inner face for the wall-knot.

Reeving Hearts.

There are several ways of reeving hearts.   One is to eye-splice the lanyard round the first score in one of the hearts, then pass it over the scores in each heart in turn until all are taken up.   It is then set up with a tackle, and when taut enough, the running end is seized to its neighbour, whipped, and the spare cut off, (Fig. 114).   Alternatively the end may be passed between the heart and the throat seizing with a hitch and finished off as in the case of the dead-eye lanyard.

FIG. 114.   FIG. 115.

Another method is to temporarily seize one end of the lanyard to the standing rigging beyond the heart;   then reeve through both hearts until all scores are taken up; set up with a tackle on the free end, and when sufficiently taut seize both standing and running parts to their neighbours, cut off spare lanyard and whip the ends, (Fig. 115).

Reeving Thimbles and Lanyards.

These are only used for light stuff such as hand-lines, foot-ropes etc. The lanyard is eye-spliced into one of the thimbles; reeved through both until enough turns are passed; the remainder of the lanyard is then expended in round turns round its own parts and finished off with half-hitches and the end seized back. See sketch of foot-ropes lanyard on Plate 23.

Order of Setting up Standing Rigging.

Before finally leaving the subject of standing rigging it may be helpful to tabulate for easy reference the order of placing the rigging over the masts.

Lower-Masts.

1st. *Shrouds.*—Starting with the first pair starboard side, followed by first pair port, and so on alternately until all are on.

2nd. *Fore and Aft Stays.*

3rd. *Cap-Stays.* (When carried.)

Topmasts.

ON FOREMAST ONLY.

1st. *Fish-Tackle-Burton.* (If carried.)

ON ALL OTHER MASTS.

1st. *Shrouds.*—Starting with the starboard pair, followed by the port pair, and finishing with the singles.

2nd. *Topmast-Backstays.*—Starting with the starboard pair and following on as with shrouds for as many as requisite.

3rd. *Fore and Aft Stay(s).*—In the case of the fore-mast where there are several fore and aft stays at the topmast head, the innermost one goes on immediately following the backstays, the remainder go on in progressive order outboard. On the remaining masts there will be only one stay, and this will follow the backstays.

4th. *Topmast Cap-Stay(s).*—(If carried.)

Topgallant-Mast.

1st. *Mast-Funnel.*

2nd. *Mast-Head-Strop.*—This position is optional and the strop may be put on over the shrouds if desired.

3rd. *Fore and Aft Stay.*

4th. *Shrouds.*—Starboard pair, then port.

5th. *Backstays.*

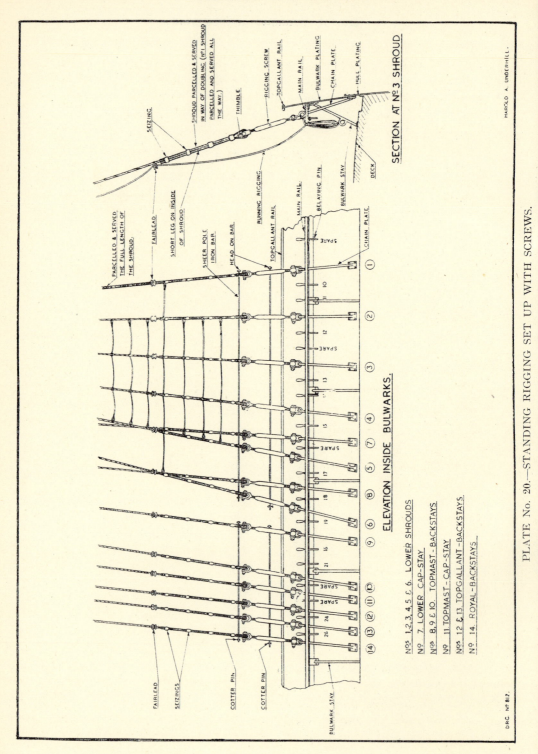

SECTION AT Nº 3 SHROUD

ELEVATION INSIDE BULWARKS.

Nºs 1, 2, 3, 4, 5 & 6. LOWER SHROUDS
Nº 7 LOWER CAP-STAY
Nºs 8, 9 & 10. TOPMAST - BACKSTAYS
Nº 11 TOPMAST - CAP-STAY
Nºs 12 & 13 TOPGALLANT - BACKSTAYS
Nº 14 ROYAL - BACKSTAYS

PLATE No. 20.—STANDING RIGGING SET UP WITH SCREWS.

Royal-Mast.

1st. *Mast-Funnel.*

2nd. *Mast-Head-Strop.*

3rd. *Fore and aft Stay.*

4th. *Backstays.*

Skysail-mast—when carried—is rigged as royal.

Plate 22 shows the standing rigging in place on the various masts and should be consulted in conjunction with the above table.

CHAPTER V.

SAILS.

I CANNOT attempt to describe the art of sailmaking, but will have to content myself with the finished product as used by merchant vessels at the end of the sailing ship era. Sailmaking is not merely a question of filling a given shape and area with canvas, that would be comparatively simple, but to droduce a sail that will set well in spite of the heavy drag on two or more corners is another matter, and depends entirely upon the skill and experience of the craftsmen. The great billowing sail, flying high on fathoms of slack sheet, may be a joy to the decorative artist, but would hardly satisfy the master of a modern windjammer.

In model work the sail is just as important as any other component, and badly proportioned cloths, or cloths running in the wrong direction is enough to spoil any model. For this reason printed sail cloth as sold for model work is rarely satisfactory; either the seams will be out of scale, or if alright in this, they will be running in one direction across the sail instead of being arranged to give maximum strength.

The canvas generally used in the British merchant service is 24 ins. wide, and made in six or eight different weights, which are known by numbers starting with the strongest. Thus numbers 1 to 5 weigh 1·15 lbs; 1·08 lbs. 1·0 lbs; 0·93 lbs. and 0·85 lbs. per yard respectively. Canvas is made up in bolts—i.e. rolls—of 40 yards. Canvas 18 ins. wide is available and occasionally used for jibs and spankers, but this is not common practice.

Cloths.—The cloths of a sail are the widths of canvas which are sewn together to form it. The direction of the cloths is arranged to give the maximum strength to the sail.

Seams.—The cloths are joined by overlapped seams sewn down each side. On some sails the seams may vary in width betweeen $1\frac{1}{4}$ ins. to $3\frac{1}{2}$ ins. at different points along their own length. These variations, or taper in the seam, will not apply equally throughout the whole sail, but will gradually increase or decrease in adjoining seams and so "mould" the sail to the sail-maker's requirements. The average distance centre to centre of seams will be 22 ins. for the 24 ins. canvas and 16 ins. for that 18 ins. wide although these will of course vary slightly in sails where seams are tapered.

Tabling.—The edges of sails are tabled—or hemmed as it would be termed in domestic life—by being turned over and sewn down. The width of the tabling is varied according to its position and the size of the sail, and, like the seams, may in some cases vary along its own length for the purpose of shaping the sail. For example the tabling on the leech of a spanker is wider at the peak and clew than in the centre, thus giving the leech a slight outward curve, which straightens out under load. If the leech were made dead straight in the first instance, it would curve inwards when fully stretched.

Linings.—Linings are additional cloths sewn on the fore side of the sail to strengthen it, and take their names from the positions they occupy. Thus the head-linings are along the head of the sail; leech-linings along the leech; foot-linings along the foot, and so on.

Bunt Line Cloths.—These are additional cloths sewn on the fore side of the sail to prevent chafing by the bunt-lines.

Leech-Line-Cloths.—Chafing cloths below the leech-lines.

Mast-Cloths.—Additional cloths on the after side of the sail to prevent it being chafed by the mast.

Top-Cloths.—Chafing patches on the after side of topsails and topgallants to prevent them being chafed by the tops and topmast cross-trees respectively.

Middle-Band or Belly-Band.—An additional cloth running horizontally across the sail to strengthen it.

Reef-Tackle-Pieces or *Reef-Tackle-Patches.*—Strengthening cloths running diagonally down from the reef-tackle-cringle to distribute the pull.

Reef-Bands.—Cloths sewn across the fore side of the sail in way of the reef points.

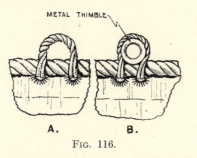

FIG. 116.

Reef-Cringles.—These are formed on the leech of the sail and used to haul out the head when reefed. They may either be plain as Fig. 116A or have a metal thimble inserted as Fig. 116B. To form a cringle two holes are made in the sail at the required distance apart, close against the leech-rope and eyeletted. A single strand is taken from a piece of rope of the size of the required cringle. About one-third of this strand is then passed through the left hand eyelet; brought back against its own part and laid up again following the original lay of the rope; this is continued for a distance equal to the length of the finished cringle, (Fig. 117A).

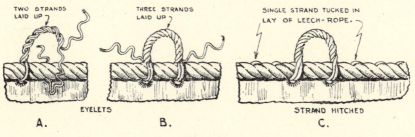

FIG. 117.

The longer of the two ends is then passed through the right hand eyelet and laid up in the space left between the two strands already laid up, thus making a complete three strand cringle, (Fig. 117B). We have now a single strand at each end of the rope cringle, these are hitched through their respective eyelets and the ends worked along the leech-rope by tucking them over and under alternate strands as in splicing, (Fig. 117c). An alternative method of finishing off, is to work the ends up towards the end of the cringle by tucking them over and under its own strands, and cutting off the surplus when the centre is reached.

Reef-Points.—The lengths of reef-points are usually twice the greatest circumference of the yard or boom. If more than one row of points are fitted, each row nearer the yard can be reduced by 3 ins. on either side of the sail, or a total of 6 ins. in the point. The sail is pierced through the reef-band and seam, making a hole just large enough for the reef-points to pass through. The hole is eyeletted with yarn and strengthened by a small rope grommet of the same size as the hole, sewn on the after side. After whipping the ends, the reef-point is thrust through the hole until it hangs down on either side of the sail, one third on the fore side, and two-thirds aft, or alternatively the after leg may be made 12 ins. longer than the fore, see detail on Plate 28. The exception to this last rule are fore and aft sails and a square sail having more than one reef-band. In both these cases the reef-points are put through with both legs of equal length. The points are held in position by being sewn to the upper part of the grommet on square sails, and the lower part on fore and afters. In other words, they are sewn on the side nearest to the spar round which they are intended to tie.

Jack-Line-Reef or *French-Reef.*—A detail of this type of reef will be found on Plate 26. The reef-band is pierced and the holes protected by grommets sewn on as for reef-points. One end of the jack-line is eye-spliced round the leech-rope and carried across the face of the reef-band, with a small bight or loop passed back through each of the holes in the sail. Each bight is seized to its own part to prevent pulling out straight, (Fig. 118). The other end of the jack-line is spliced round the leech-rope on the opposite side of the sail. The after jack-line passes across the after side of the sail; through the bights in the jack-line and is eye-spliced to the leech-rope at either end.

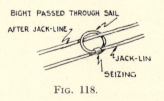

FIG. 118.

Reefing Beckets.—These are used in conjunction with the jack-line reef and consist of plaited or braided strops, each having a toggle and two loops, (Fig. 119A) and attached to the iron jack-stay on the yard. In reefing the looped strop is passed under the jack-line on the fore side of the sail and put over its own toggle on the yard, (Fig. 119B).

Grab-Lines.—These run vertically up the sail and are used to haul the reef-band up to the yard when reefing. The lower end is spliced or seized to one of the bights of the jack-line, and the upper end eye-spliced into the nearest head-hole above it. If more than one line of reefs are fitted, the grab-line is seized to all intermediate jack-lines. Grab-lines are not always

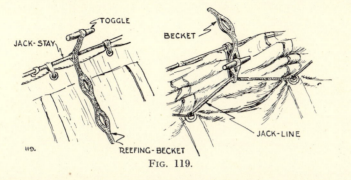

Fig. 119.

fitted, particularly in the case of single reefs, but when used there are generally four or five lines in the width of the sail. Another method of reeving the grab-line is to eye-splice one end to the head-hole; pass the line down the fore side of the sail; through the hole in the reef-band; up the after side of the sail and eye-splice it into its own eye at the head.

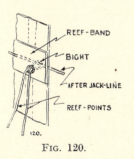

Fig. 120.

Double-Reef-Points.—Another form of reefing occasionally used on courses is to have the points in pairs on the fore side of the sail, and when reefing tie off round the iron jack-stay instead of round the yard. In this case the reef-point is middled and the bight pushed through the hole in the sail, a jack-line is then reeved through all the bights on the after side of the sail and eye-spliced to the leech-rope at either end, (Fig. 120). The points are then pulled taut on the fore side of the sail and sewn to the grommets as before.

Bolt-Ropes.—These are sewn on the after side of square sails and usually the port side of fore and afters. The head-rope of a sail is several sizes smaller than the leech and foot-ropes. For example, a sail having a $5\frac{1}{4}$ ins. circumference—by the way, all rope is measured by its circumference and not by diameter—leech and foot ropes, has a head rope of only $2\frac{1}{2}$ ins. On fore and aft sails the bolt-rope may either be the same size all round, or the luff-rope may be larger. Thus a jib having 3 ins. leech and foot-ropes may have a luff-rope of $3\frac{1}{4}$ ins.

Where sails are subject to chafe from spars of rigging they are leathered over the edge of the canvas and the bolt-rope.

Earing-Cringle.—To form the head-earing-cringle the leech-rope is carried about 18 ins up beyond the head of the sail; turned back and spliced into

I

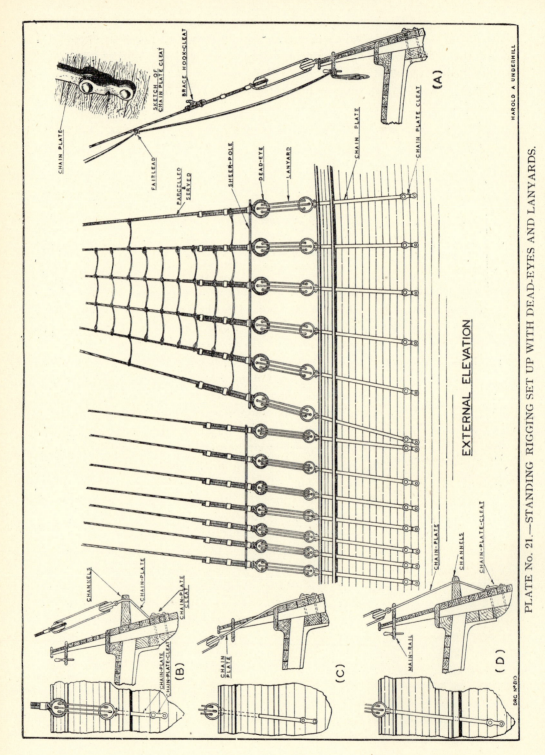

PLATE No. 21.—STANDING RIGGING SET UP WITH DEAD-EYES AND LANYARDS.

its own standing part to form an eye. The splice is tapered, and when completed is cross sewn for additional strength. The head rope, which has also been left longer than the nett required length, is then spliced into the crown of the eye. See detail on Plate 26.

Spectacle-Clew-Irons, Clew-Rings and Clew-Cringles.—The spectacle-clew-iron—Fig. 121A—is almost universally used in modern vessels. The leech-rope and foot-rope are eye-spliced round the thimbles of the outer spectacle eyes, and the sheet shackled to the large centre eye. On courses which have their clew-garnets rigged to the bunt of the yard the lower clew-garnet block shackles to the small inner eye. Another form of metal clew is the plain iron ring with thimbles, round which the leech and foot ropes are spliced, (Fig. 121B). Old time merchant craft used rope cringles stuck in the clew, (Fig. 121C), while the sailing man-of-war had clew-cringles formed as part of the bolt-rope, (Fig. 121D). However we are only concerned with iron clews, which, while there are several shapes, are all identical in the method of fitting. The leech rope and foot-rope are spliced round the thimbles on the spectacle-iron, with the eyes leathered in way of the thimbles and the rest of the splice tapered, parcelled and served. The bolt ropes are then marled to the sail over the parcelling and serving.

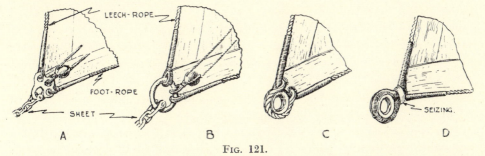

FIG. 121.

Holes.—Sails are pierced with a number of holes for various purposes. These holes are strengthened either with rope grommets sewn to the sail, metal thimbles, or in the case of small holes as for forming rope cringles, eyeletted with yarn. The *head-holes* are immediately below the head-rope and are for the robands used in bending the sail to the iron jack-stay. They are arranged singly and in pairs in alternate cloths thus; one cloth has a single hole in the centre, the next has two holes near the seams, the next a single hole and so on across the sail as shown in the detail sketch on Plate 26. Staysails have holes up the luff for the attachment of the hanks, these are arranged on an even pitch of from 27 ins. to 36 ins. Gaff sails have holes up the luff at about 27 ins. pitch, and one hole in the centre of each cloth along the head. *Bunt-line-holes* and *leech-line-holes* are provided for their respective lines, and *reef-point-holes* are pierced in the reef-band for the reef-points or jack-line as already described.

Earings and Reef-Earings.—These are short lines used to lash out the head of the sail to the yard-arm. The reef-earing being used when the sail is reefed.

Bunt-line Fairleads.—These are circular thimbles or small lignum vitae bulls-eyes on the fore side of modern sails, as fairleads for the bunt-lines. A short length of line is middled and put round the fairleads and the two parts

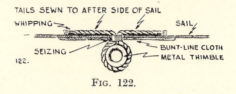

FIG. 122.

seized together behind it. After being whipped the two ends are passed through an eyeletted hole in the sail, separated on the after side like the two legs of a split pin and sewn down on the after side, (Fig. 122).

Sails.

Plate 26 shows the fore and aft sides of a range of modern square sails. In this detail I have taken a course having vertical leeches, but the relative length of foot and head may vary in different ships. The foot of a course is governed by the beam of the ship and the distance between the sheaves for the sheet and tack on opposite sides, so that when the yard is braced up sharp, both sheet and tack can be hauled taut without the clew cringles coming chock-a-block to the sheaves in the bulwarks. However the shape of the sail will be taken from the sail and rigging plan.

On the fore side of the sail is a single reef-band which is one-third of a cloth wide. The middle-band is a full cloth wide and is put on midway between the reef-band and the foot. The leech-linings are one cloth wide and the foot-lining half a cloth. The six bunt-line-cloths are a full cloth wide and are shown extending from the foot to the middle-band, but they may be carried right up to the head of the sail. Small circular thimbles are put on as already described, as fairleads for the bunt-lines. Reef-points are shown as these are most commonly used on courses, but some of the modern carriers have jack-line reefs on all reefing sails. Reef, reef-tackle and bowline cringles are shown in their respective positions. It may perhaps be mentioned here that the width of linings, reef-bands, bunt-line-cloths etc., are the same on all square sails shown, and therefore will not be specified in the descriptions of the remaining sails on this plate.

The lower-topsail is shown as having four bunt-line-cloths, as in fact have all sails above the course. This is the most common arrangement in modern vessels, but must of course be checked from the sail plan of the vessel under consideration; further, although these cloths are shown running vertically as for a sail clewing up to the yard arms, they will of course always follow the lead of the bunt-line, and should that run diagonally across the sail the cloths must do the same.

The upper topsail is much the same as the lower except for the addition of the reef-band and cringles. In this example I have shown jack-line reefing and grab-lines, this however is optional. Some vessels have reef-points on all sails, others reef-points on courses and jack-lines on the topsails, while the third group, which includes a number of modern vessels, have jack-line reefs throughout. All other sails on this plate are just smaller editions of the lower topsail.

Plate 27 illustrates staysails, spankers and a triangular course. During the last forty years of sailing ship design, various methods of making staysails were tried out with a view to improving efficiency, but the examples shown in this plate represent the most common practice. Generally speaking it may be said that where the foot and leech make a wide angle at the clew, the cloths are arranged running parallel to both and joined by a seam running from clew to luff and at right angles to the latter, as shown on the jib in the plate. In cases where the foot and leech are at or near a right angle, the cloths run parallel to the leech for the whole depth of the sail, as illustrated by the top-

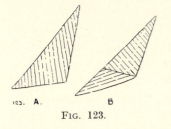

FIG. 123.

mast staysail. The methods tried include all cloths running perpendicular to the foot, (Fig. 123A); lower cloths running parallel to the foot and upper ones perpendicular to the luff, (Fig. 123B); while the present day yacht practice is to make the lower cloths perpendicular to the foot, and the upper ones perpendicular to the leech. However unless the reader has definite knowledge to the contrary he will be well advised to follow the general principles laid down above for any model he may have in hand.

Taking the jib as the first example, it will be seen that the luff has an outward curve, or roach as it is called, and that the maximum roach is directly opposite the clew. In model work, except perhaps those intended for actual sailing, all sails would be made without roach except on the foot of gaff and staysails, as this curve is really intended to compensate for stretching on the edges of the sails. The jib requires little in the way of description, the drawing being self explanatory. It will be seen that strengthening cloths are put on at the head, tack, and clew, while in some cases a band is also run on top of the seam from clew to luff; when this is done it should be one cloth wide at the clew, tapering to two-thirds at the luff. The example shown has rope cringles, but this is optional, and circular metal cringles may be inserted in place of these, as shown for the jib-headed topsail on Plate 28. The tabling on the jib should be about 3 ins. wide. Except for difference in shape, the details of the topmast-staysail will be the same as for the jib.

The standing spanker has a mast-lining—or luff-lining—half a cloth wide running from tack to throat, also short leech-lining and strengthening patches at both peak and clew; these are a full cloth in width. The luff has holes at about 27 ins. centres for the robands, used in bending the sail to the iron jack-stay abaft the mast. The leech has a slight roach formed by making the tabling 6 ins. wide at peak and clew, and only 3 ins. wide in the centre. Circular metal cringles are inserted in peak, throat, tack and clew, while rope cringles are provided along the leech for the brails; the number and position of these must be taken from the sail plan. The foot is roached as shown. The hoisting spanker is much the same in general construction, the principal difference being that two reef-bands one-third of a cloth wide run across the sail, and the usual reef and reef-tackle cringles are added. The brail cringles will of course not be required.

Triangular courses save considerable work when going about, and were carried by quite a number of the later carriers. There are no tacks or sheets to tend when the yard comes round, as the sail has a single sheet set up to a ring bolt in the deck, or to the lower spider-band. The cloths run parallel to the leeches and are joined in a vertical seam up the centre of the sail. The head of the sail is made the same as a normal square course with the usual head-holes and earing-cringle, but the lower ends of the leech-ropes are spliced on to a single clew-iron. The fore side of the sail has a middle-band and leech-line-cloths, but no reef-band is carried.

Our next examples are on Plate 28 and are the sails of a ship carrying single topsails and topgallants. The course is as already described except for proportion, and the number and position of the bunt-line-cloths. The linings are one cloth wide on the leeches and half a cloth on the foot.

The topsail has three reef-bands, each one-third of a cloth wide; the reef-points on the first and second reefs from the head have short legs on the fore side and long on the after side of the sail, while the points of the third reef have both sides equal. Rope reef-cringles are stuck in either end of the reef-band; and three feet below the lowest reef-band are the reef-tackle-cringles. While below these again are three bowline-cringles per side. The middle-band is one cloth wide and put on midway between the third reef-band and the foot of the sail, the ends being sewn down under the linings. Reef-tackle-patches run diagonally from the reef-tackle-cringles down to the middle-band; they are two-thirds of a cloth wide at the cringle and one-half at the band. This sail is rigged with one bunt-line per side, and the cloths run diagonally up from the foot of the third reef-band. Linings are one cloth wide on the leeches and half a cloth wide on the foot. On the after side of the sail is a top-cloth eleven cloths wide, and having its upper edge level with the top of the middle-band on the other side of the sail. The mast-cloth, which extends from the upper edge of the top-cloth, to the head of the sail, is five cloths wide. For the sake of clarity I have shown the top-cloths as though they were single sheets covering the whole area, in practice they are of course, made up of a number of normal cloths sewn on top of those forming the sail.

The fore side of the topgallant is plain except for the bunt-line cloths. The linings are one-half cloth wide on both foot and leeches. On the after side of the sail is a top-cloth nine cloths wide and two and a half deep, with a mast cloth of single width running to the head. The royal is perfectly plain, with linings as on the topgallant.

The jib-headed topsail requires no description beyond calling attention to the slight roach on the leech, this is obtained by tabling 6 ins. at peak and clew, and 3 ins. in the middle of the leech.

The spanker of the modern sailing ship appears in many guises, all with the idea of doing away with the necessity for reefing a large sail, it being easier to take in a relatively small sail than to reef a large one.

The introduction of double topsails and topgallants led to taking in complete square sails instead of reefing, and the practice spread to the spanker, which was divided into two by various means. One arrangement was to divide the spanker diagonally from throat to clew, or in other words setting a trysail on the boom, with what might be termed an inverted triangular ring-tail from the gaff, (Fig. 124). Sometimes this trysail had a short head equal to about one-third the length of the gaff, this was laced to a small spar and hauled up to two blocks on the under side of the gaff. In some cases the gaff

Fig. 124.   Fig. 125.

was dispensed with altogether and only the trysail carried, which led to the introduction of a form of jib-headed topsail extending down the leech of the trysail, (Fig. 125), an arrangement much favoured in small brigantines, barquentines and schooners. All these rigs are in the nature of labour saving modifications carried out by the masters themselves, rather than part of the original design.

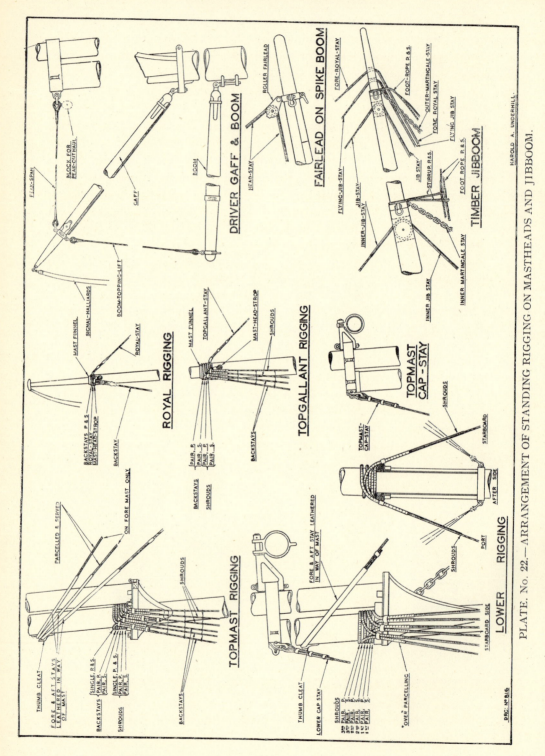

PLATE. No. 22.—ARRANGEMENT OF STANDING RIGGING ON MASTHEADS AND JIBBOOM.

The designed double spanker is provided with two gaffs, (Fig. 126) and was introduced by the Germans. The only vessel I can think of which was so designed and built outside Germany, was the auxiliary five-mast barque *Kobenhavn*, built by Ramage and Ferguson, at Leith in 1921, and I believe that she later removed the middle gaff. There is nothing out of the ordinary in the way these spars are rigged, they are normal gaffs except that the lower one serves the dual purpose of both gaff and boom.

The sister ships *Mount Stewart* and *Cromdale* were designed with very small loose footed spankers; the gaff was very short and the foot, which of course had no boom, ended about twenty feet short of the taffrail.

Some of the older ships had an additional reef-band across the spanker from throat to clew, which when the reef was tied down converted the sail into a trysail. This however is rather before our period. I have made no mention of the spencers carried on the fore and main masts of many clippers, but these were in fact just loose-footed spankers.

FIG. 126.   FIG. 127.

The jib-headed topsail also joined the ranks of the divided sails, and A. D. Bordes' famous fleet of big four-mast barques were rigged with the jigger topsail divided along the line of the peak-halliards, (Fig. 127). This small sail seemed to be carried under most conditions, and was in fact often the only canvas on the jigger.

Two other interesting sails are the bentinck-foresail and the nock-staysail both of which I have incorporated in the sketch of the brigantine, Fig. 125. The former was chiefly found in the collier brigs of the Tyne—Thames coal trade, although a few other coasters and some whalers were also rigged in this way. The rig consists of a course cut rather narrow at the foot, which was extended by bentinck-boom stretching from clew to clew. The centre of the boom is held down by a sheet set up to the deck just forward of the mast, which allows the foot of the sail to pivot as in the case of the triangular course. The ends of the boom have light braces to steady it, but as there are no tacks or sheets, considerable labour is saved when going about; a very important factor to vessels in a trade which called for regular beating up and down the busy London river. The boom is permanently attached to the sail, and when the latter is furled it hangs immediately below the lower yard.

The nock of a staysail is the vertical luff laced to the mast. This type of staysail, in various shapes and sizes, is largely used between the fore and main masts of brigantines and barquentines.

Studding-sails will be dealt with more fully when we come to the running rigging, for as sails they are simply a number of cloths sewn together to form a quadrilateral, without any additional cloths beyond small linings in each of the four corners. The chief interest in studding-sails lies in the rigging and that will be fully dealt with under the appropriate chapter. However on Plate 30 I have shown small scale drawings of lower and topmast stun'sls, which clearly indicate the run of the cloths and position of linings. The top-gallant stun'sl will be much the same as that of the topsail except for a slight difference in angles.

Bending Sails.—Square sails are bent to the yards by means of robands passed through the head-holes and tied off round the iron jack-stay. The earing-cringles are lashed out to the yard-arms by the head-earing as shown in Fig. 128, although on modern vessels the earing is usually passed round the short earing-jack-stay described in chapter II., instead of the yard-arm

Fig. 128.   Fig. 129.

Spankers. The luff of the standing spanker is bent to the iron jack-stay on the after side of the mast, and the head to the slides or shoes of the mast-track on the underside of the gaff. Wooden ships sometimes use hoops along the gaff in place of the mast-track, (Fig. 129). The peak and clew cringles are shackled to the outhauls and downhauls on gaff and boom respectively. The throat is bent to an eye-bolt below the goose-neck, and the tack to the jack-stay at the boom goose-neck.

Hoisting spankers have their luffs seized to wooden hoops round the mast or trysail mast, while their heads are laced to the gaff. Peak, throat, tack and crew are all bent to their respective points with earings.

Staysails. The hanks are reeved on the stay and seized to the holes in the luff of the sail, (Fig. 130). The tack is seized to the foot of the stay in the most convenient manner. Fig. 131 shows one method; here the tack is held down by a short wire strop passed round the boom, the length of this strop is of course made to suit the required position of the sail. The halliards and downhaul are shackled to the head, and the sheets to the clew.

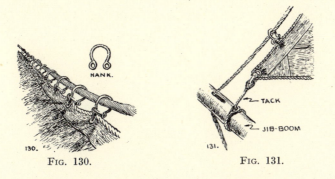

FIG. 130.   FIG. 131.

Jib-headed topsail. Some of the modern steel ships have a mast track up the after side of the topmast and the luff of the sail is seized to the shoes of this, but the more usual method is to provide wooden hoops on the mast between the lower-cap and the topmast hounds, like those on the luff of the hoisting spanker. That portion of the sail extending above the topmast-hounds is set flying.

Stun'sls have the outer part of their heads laced to their respective yards.

Special Sails.

Cunningham's Self-Reefing Topsails.—The aim of this patent is to provide a sail which can be reefed quickly and without sending men aloft. The inventor claims that two men can reef a topsail from the deck in less than three seconds, an operation which with normal reefs would take many men aloft for at least half an hour, and under some conditions may even run into hours. Just how accurate this estimate of time proved to be I do not know, but the rig became popular and owners soon discovered that it enabled them to reduce the size of crews. The self-reefing topsail had a comparatively short reign owing to the introduction of the double topsail, or to be more exact, Howe's close-reefing topsail, which really was the forerunner of the double topsail. This rig, while not entirely workable from the deck, had many advantages and no complicated gear aloft to go wrong or jamb, and it soon won favour, gradually replacing the single topsail, self-reefing or otherwise.

However to return to Cunningham's patent. The operation of the rig is based on two general principles. Firstly, the sail is rolled round its own yard in reefing, and secondly, the rotation of the yard is on the principle of par-buckling a barrel down the face of a wall. The yard hangs in the bight of

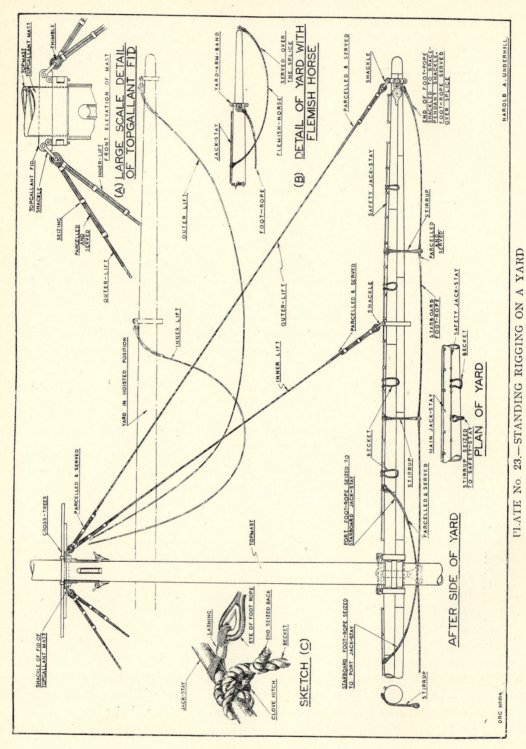

(A) LARGE SCALE DETAIL OF TOPGALLANT FID

(B) DETAIL OF YARD WITH FLEMISH HORSE

SKETCH (C)

PLATE No. 23.—STANDING RIGGING ON A YARD

HAROLD A. UNDERHILL.

DRG. No. 814.

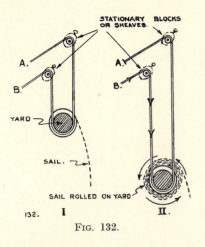

STATIONARY BLOCKS OR SHEAVES.

A.

B.

A.

B.

YARD

SAIL.

SAIL ROLLED ON YARD

132. I II.

FIG. 132.

double halliards as shown diagrammatically in Fig. 132. Sketch I shows the yard at full hoist and suspended in the bight of the halliard; if part "A" of the halliard be kept fast and part "B" paid out, the yard will descend, rotating in the direction of the arrows and rolling the sail round itself as it does so, sketch II. Conversely, if part "B" is hauled in—"A" still remaining fast— the yard will ascend and the sail unroll from it. If on the other hand both "A" and "B" are hauled in or paid out together, the yard will ascend or descend without rotating, in fact be hoisted or lowered like a normal yard. This is used when making or taking in sail, for, as will be understood later, this rig can only be used for reefing and *not* for furling the sail, that has to be done in the usual way.

So much for the general principle, now for detail. Plate 29 shows the construction and rig of Cunningham's patent. The chain tye (Part A) is shackled to the purchase block of the halliard (Part A); then reeved over the sheave in the topmast below the cross-trees; down the fore side of the mast and round the whelped boss (N) on the centre of the yard; under the jockey-roller (C); up over the lead blocks on the underside of the cross-trees, and shackled to the purchase block of the halliard (part B). The inventor claims that it is better for the tye (part B) to be led up under the heel of the top-gallant mast and over a sheave in the head of the topmast as shown in sketch VI. This however weakens the topgallant mast, as it is necessary to fit a sheave in the heel of the mast, and provide a slot long and deep enough to allow the tye to pass on the fore side of the cross-tree, and up between the two masts to the upper sheave.

The topmast is encircled by a parral of normal type, but the fore side of the parral strap (Q) is provided with arms to which the fixed bunt-straps (K) are bolted. The bunt-straps (K) encircle the yard and form the bearings in which it can rotate.

In the centre of the yard is a metal sleeve as shown in sketch IV. This is firmly fixed to the yard and consists of a central grooved boss (N) with whelps to grip the links of the chain tye which passes round it. On either side are rectangular grooves forming the bunt-strap seatings. On top of the bunt-straps are the lugs which form the bearings for the jockey-roller (C). The purpose of this roller is to keep the tye in contact with the whelped boss for about three-quarters of its circumference. On the fore side of the bunt-straps are lugs for the bonnet-link (W); and on the under side are lugs to which is bolted the metal span of the upper downhaul block.

Along the yard are timber jack-stays to which the sail is bent. To prevent the rolled sail being chafed by the lee rigging when the yard is braced up sharp, a small chafing-spar (D) is carried abaft the yard. This spar is supported in the centre by short slings (S) from the parral strap, and at the ends by jaws which engage on arms extending aft from the yard-arm-straps (O).

The yard-arm fitting consists of a grooved boss (T) driven firmly on to the yard and fixed, but free to rotate in the strap (O). On top of this strap is the iron block (H) for the topgallant sheet, this block also provides the attachment for the standing lift (M). The arm extending aft from the yard-arm-strap carries the jaws of the chafing-spar as already mentioned; the shackle (P) for the brace block, and the outer studding sail boom iron (R), the shank of which forms the bolt for attaching the jaws for the chafing-spar. The inner studding-sail boom irons are also carried by the chafing-spar.

The centre cloth of the sail is omitted for about two-thirds of the depth down from the head as shown in sketch III., this enables the sail to roll round the yard on either side of the centre fittings. Incidentally it will now be seen why this rig cannot be used for furling, obviously the sail can only be rolled to the depth of the opening. When the sail is set the gap is closed by the bonnet (V), which consists of two cloths of canvas, one on either side of the sail and fixed to battens or travellers. The sail is roped on either side of the central gap, and the travellers, which are spaced about 14 ins. apart, are made to slide freely up and down this gap, but at the same time prevent the sail pulling out from between the two bonnet cloths. These wooden travellers are shown diagrammatically in sketch V. The lower ends of the bonnet cloths are sewn to the sail at the foot of the gap, and the top traveller is attached to the fixed bunt-straps by means of the link (W) which keeps it in position just below the level of the yard.

In operation the bonnet works rather like a venetian blind. When the sail is rolled up in reefing, the lower end of the bonnet being sewn to the sail, rises with it, pushing up each traveller in turn as it reaches it and bunching the canvas bonnet cloths as it does so. On the other hand, when a reef is being let out, the bonnet, being fixed at the top to the link and at the foot to the sail, expands as the foot of the sail goes down, and so keeps the gap fully covered at all times.

The downhaul (L) is used to get the yard down should it tend to jamb when reefing or furling. All foot-ropes, stirrups, etc., are attached to the chafing-spar and not to the yard itself.

Colling and Pinkney's Patent Self Reefing and Furling Topsails.

This patent has several advantages over Cunningham's topsail, the greatest being that the sail can be either reefed or completely furled from the deck, and any amount of canvas between the whole sail and nothing, can be exposed at will. Other points in its favour are that there is no need for the open panel and its somewhat cumbersome bonnet in the centre of the sail; the gear is less complicated, and lastly the actual yard does not rotate and can therefore be slung and rigged in the usual way. On the opposite side of the balance sheet, Cunningham's patent is perhaps more positive in operation.

The principle of Colling and Pinkney's rig is extremely simple, and can be seen in a large number of domestic window blinds. On the fore side of the topsail yard is a revolving yard or roller, to which the sail is bent. At either end of the roller are small metal drums, to which the reefing-halliards are attached. When the sail is furled—completely rolled on the spar—there are only three turns of the reefing-halliards round their respective drums, but when the sail is being set by hoisting the yard and hauling on the sheets, it unwinds the roller, causing it to rotate and wind an equal number of turns of the reefing-halliards on to the drums. When it is desired to reef or furl the sail, hauling on the reefing halliards makes the roller rotate and wind the sail back on again.

Plate 30 shows the rig in detail. The topsail yard (A) is fitted, and parralled to the mast in the usual way. The yard-arm-bands have a bracket (B) on the fore side to carry the rotating spar (C), and projecting upward from the band is a curved arm (D) which has a ring or bulls-eye in the top to act as a fairlead for the reefing-halliard (E). On large yards this arm may be fitted with a sheave in place of the fairlead. Supporting crutches (F) are placed on either side of the centre of the yard, the distance between them usually equals about one-fifth the length of the roller. On the ends of the roller are the reefing-halliard drums (G). Four or more timber battens are fixed longitudinally on the rotating spar, one being slotted to form a jack-stay to which the sail is bent. The length of these battens is equal to the head of the sail measured *inside* the bolt-ropes, and their depth the same as the *diameter* of the leech-rope.   In furling the canvas rolls on the battens, while

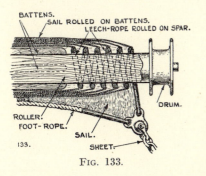

FIG. 133.

the leech-rope winds itself in a spiral along the actual spar outside the battens, making a neat flat roll, (Fig. 133).

The topsail yard has a tye and halliard rigged in the normal way, together with the usual foot-ropes, stirrups, lifts, brace-pendants etc. The reefing-halliards, one on each side, are reeved when the sail is furled; the ends are attached to their respective drums, and wound round three times in such a way that their running ends lead upward off the *fore* side of the drums, see end view. From the drums the reefing-halliards lead up through the fairlead (E); down

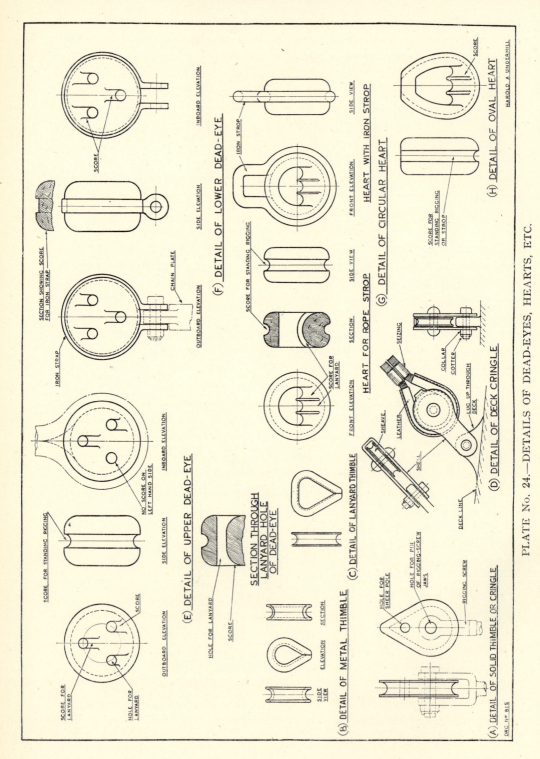

PLATE No. 24.—DETAILS OF DEAD-EYES, HEARTS, ETC.

through the lead blocks (I) at the topmast cap; and shackle to the purchase blocks (J) which are at the heads of the tackles leading down to the deck. The smaller drawings shows the complete rig with sail set and furled. It will be seen that the sail is provided with a reef band in the close reef position, this enables the reef to be tied off in the usual way should it be desirable to reinforce the roller reef during heavy weather. This precaution applies to the Cunningham rig also.

Howe's Patent Close Reefing Topsail.

This rig in a slightly modified form, not only survived into the era of the modern windjammer, but became the standard practice for all square rigged craft both large and small; with the exception perhaps of the fishing schooners of Brittany, which carry a small single topsail rigged with roller-reefing gear.

In its original form Captain Howe's rig consisted of a single topsail with an extra yard at the level of the lower-mastcap, Plate 30. The sail was in fact made in halves for ease in bending, but as the foot of the upper half was tightly laced to the same jack-stay as the head of the lower, it may be regarded as a single sail.

The idea behind the patent is very simple. If the halliards are let go, the upper half of the sail will hang in a bight on the fore—lee—side of the lower, where it will be completely blanketed and lie quiet; and so by the simple process of letting go the halliard the sail is automatically close reefed. Another claim in the original patent is that should the topmast carry away at the cap—the point at which it is most likely to go—the ship would be left with a close-reefed topsail still standing, whereas with the normal single topsail, or any of the self-reefing topsails, both yard and sail would go with the mast.

However the great point in favour of this rig was the complete absence of complicated mechanical gear to go wrong or jamb aloft, an advantage which, as we have already seen, caused it to outlive all other forms of topsail and be accepted as a universally standard rig for all ships. The double topsail and double topgallant as used to-day are both fundamentally the same as Howe's rig, the only real difference being that the upper sail is no longer laced to the yard below.

Many examples of these rigs, particularly Howe's will be found among the early clippers, but most of them were later converted to the ordinary double-topsail rig.

K

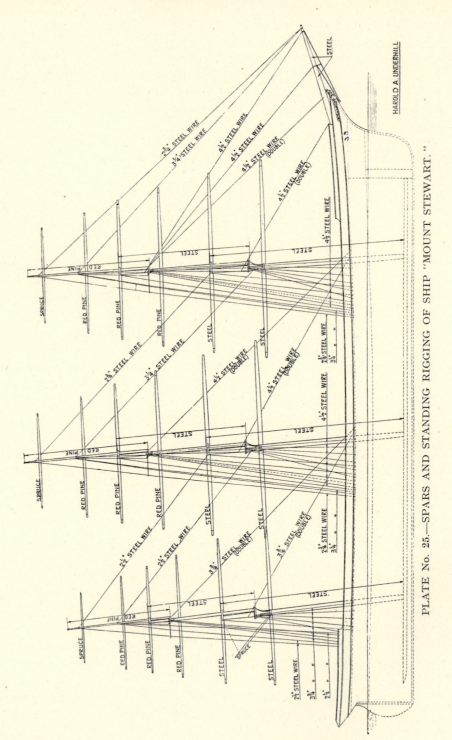

PLATE No. 25.—SPARS AND STANDING RIGGING OF SHIP "MOUNT STEWART."

HAROLD A. UNDERHILL

Perforated Sails.

The theory that wind held in the belly of the sail had a cushioning effect, and so reduced its efficiency, led to experiments in perforated sails. Holes about three feet in diameter were cut along the foot and up the leeches of sails for the purpose of allowing the wind to escape, as shown in the sketch Fig. 134, which is based upon a photograph of the barque *Invercauld*.

Fig. 134.

CHAPTER VI.

RUNNING RIGGING.

THE broad principle governing the lead and belaying of running rigging is, as with standing rigging, that the higher up the mast it goes the further aft will be its belaying point. Thus, taking any individual mast, the running gear of the course will be nearest the bow, then, moving aft, comes that of the lower-topsail, followed by the upper-topsail, topgallants, and royal in that order. This rule applies equally to main-rail and fife-rails alike.

The folding plate 51 shows the position and use of the belaying pins of the ship *Acamas*, and may be taken as typical of any modern square-rigger. Keys to this drawing will be found on pages 281 to 286, one being arranged numerically and the other under functional headings.

Plates 36, 37, and 38, are diagrammatic drawings indicating the number and position of holes in all fairleads on fore, main, and mizzen rigging respectively, and just what item of gear reeves through each. Further, I think they will give the reader a very clear mental picture of the grouping and sequence which governs the lead of all running-rigging. The first point to be noticed is that the gear of the course is grouped round No. 1 shroud; that of the lower-topsail round No. 2 shroud; upper-topsail round No. 3 and so on. Secondly it will be seen that on each three-hole fairlead the forward hole serves the most outboard point on the yard, i.e. leech-line, clew-line, or down-haul as the case may be; the centre hole serves the next line inboard, i.e. the outer-bunt-line, while the aftermost hole takes the line furthest inboard, namely the inner-bunt-line. In vessels rigged with three bunt-lines per side and no leech-line; the outer-bunt-line occupies the forward hole; the middle-bunt-line the second hole, and the inner-bunt-line the third.

Plate 39 shows the allocation of the holes in the plank fairlead in the decking of the top.

Another point is that certain gear, such as halliards, etc., does not reeve through fairleads on the stays, but goes straight to the pin. This type of gear is usually under heavy load and therefore taut, whereas at sea the bunt-lines, leech-lines etc., are kept as slack as possible to obviate cutting into, or undue chafe on, the sails, and require fairleads at frequent intervals if they are to be prevented from flaying about and becoming all jumbled up.

136

In many cases one pin holds several lines, but it will be seen that all lines on any one pin serve a common purpose, and would require to be cast off or belayed at the same time. For example. Pin No. 10 carries the leech-lines and bunt-lines of the fore course, all of which would be used when clewing up the sail. When describing the running gear I will always start at the sail or standing end, and follow it right back to the belaying pin, quoting the latter by number, which will of course refer to the number shown on Plate 51. I need hardly mention that the numbers are only used for easy reference in this book, and do not form any part of the ship's normal vocabulary.

I have included several plates of perspective diagrams showing the lead of running gear and the general location of the pins to which it belays. The position of these pins as shown in the diagrams must be regarded as only approximate, for while they are on the correct side of the ship, and in the neighbourhood of their true positions, they have in most cases been more widely spaced, or moved in some way with a view to separating the rigging as far as possible without destroying the general idea of the lead. The actual position and lead of all gear must be taken from the text and plate 51, which *does* show the true position of the pins in relation to the standing rigging.

There are many points which have to be watched in reeving off running-rigging, although they are mostly a matter of common sense; and if the function and movement of each item is considered before reeving, absurdities some-times seen in model work will be avoided. As an example of what I have in mind, examine the bunt-lines of the course shown in Plates 34 and 35. In the first plate which has the sails set, it will be seen that the blocks of the whips—purchases—on the bunt-lines are close up below the lead blocks under the top, while in Plate 35 with the sails clewed up, these same blocks have come down to just above the fairleads on the shrouds. Obviously they have to come down just as much as the foot of the sail goes up, yet I remember examining a very well built large scale model on which the rigger had come to grief over this very point. The sails were set, but the whip blocks on the bunt-lines and clew-garnets were only just above the fairleads, and would have been chock-a-block before the sail was one-third of the way up. This applies to all moving blocks, no matter what their particular purpose may be. Therefore the motto is, always visualize your gear in operation, and be certain that your moving blocks can reach both ends of their travel without fouling fixed objects or coming hard against their opposite numbers. You just *can't* haul a purchase block through a bull's-eye fairlead!

Another point, where wire pendants are used in conjunction with whips or rope purchases, as in the case of jib and staysail sheets; braces; halliards and the like, keep the rope purchase as short as possible, subject of course to its being able to fulfil its duty without the blocks coming together. This is a matter of economy. The wire pendant will probably last the life of the sail, but owing to friction on fairleads, belaying pins etc., the rope purchase or whip will require fairly frequent replacement.

Fairleads or lead blocks on heavy duty gear should never be placed too near to their belaying pins, but always leave room for the requisite number of men to get on the rope between fairlead and pin, so allowing the gear to be belayed while the whole party are still hanging on. Fairleads are used very generously on the running-rigging, not only for providing, as their name implies, a "fair lead" to the pin, but also to prevent the gear swaying about aloft and getting twisted up, or blocks banging against the masts. They vary considerably in type and construction, some forming an integral part of the spars, as in the case of the tops; or original ships furnishings as with those on the lower-shrouds. Others are added as and where they become necessary. Some of the former type have already been mentioned in a previous chapter, but a few of the latter will be given here.

The jib-downhauls usually pass through some form of fairlead outboard of the fo'castle head, the most common arrangement being timber battens seized to each leg of the fore-topmast stay. Holes are bored in the battens and through these the gear is led on its way inboard, (Fig. 135).

Another method is to fix these battens vertically to two of the fo'castle hand-rail stanchions, or alternatively stretch a rope, with bull's-eyes spliced in at intervals, between the knight-heads. However the arrangement shown in the sketch is the most usual.

A batten type of fairlead is also frequently used on the after side of the topmast cross-trees, or on the inside of the spreaders. Another use is at the head of the lower shrouds, where it is fixed on the underside and just below

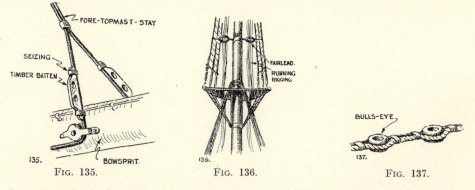

FIG. 135.   FIG. 136.   FIG. 137.

the point where the futtock-shrouds pass through. This fairlead lines up with the one built into the decking of the top, and the gear passes through both these before leading down the inside of the shrouds to the fairleads near the deck.

To steady the running gear in way of the topmast, it was common practice to use a large grommet, well parcelled with chafing gear and hung horizontally between the topmast shrouds and the lower-cap, (Fig. 136). The gear to the fife-rails was sometimes brought through bull's-eye fairleads seized between two lines which stretched from shroud to shroud across the ship, (Fig. 137). Finally we have the bulwark fairlead as used for the fore and main sheets.

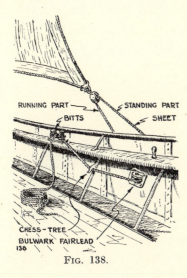

RUNNING PART —
BITTS
STANDING PART
SHEET
CHESS-TREE
BULWARK FAIRLEAD
138

Fig. 138.

This consists of a sheave built into the bulwarks at a suitable angle to lead the sheet square on to the chess-tree and so up to the bitts on the main rail, (Fig. 138).

Now for my oft repeated warning. The function and route taken by all the gear to be described in this chapter may be said to be common to all square-riggers, but the actual method of rigging may vary considerably. For example, the lower-bunt-lines on one ship may have whips to give extra purchase, while on another the same gear may run from sail to pin as a single line the whole way; obviously it is all a matter of the work to be done. The later day big steel carrier rigs whips on almost every conceivable line, and what is more, she needs them. The sails and gear are both large and heavy, but crews are small in number and largely composed of boys, so full use is made of the whip as being a comparatively inexpensive form of mechanical advantage. In the absence of definite information the model builder will have to use his common sense on this matter of detail, taking into consideration the period he is portraying; whether large or small crews would be available, and the relative size and weight of gear to be handled. Whips and purchases are not fitted unless they are necessary, as naturally they add to the cost of upkeep and make additional weight aloft.

This increase in weight of gear and decrease in size of crews at the end of the sailing ship era, represented her last struggle against the competition of steam, and resulted in the introduction of further mechanical aids, in the form of additional capstans in handy positions about the decks, and the use of brace and halliard winches, both of which will be described along with their respective gear.

It will be neccessary to refer to different types of tackle and purchases, and a list of those in general use are described and illustrated in Appendix II. to which the reader should refer if in any doubt. The most used is the common whip, which as we have already seen, may be found in almost any part of a ship's running gear. When used on gear which belays to the main-rail the standing end of the whip may either be made fast to an eye-bolt in the rail or other convenient fixture, or alternatively, seized to the standing rigging

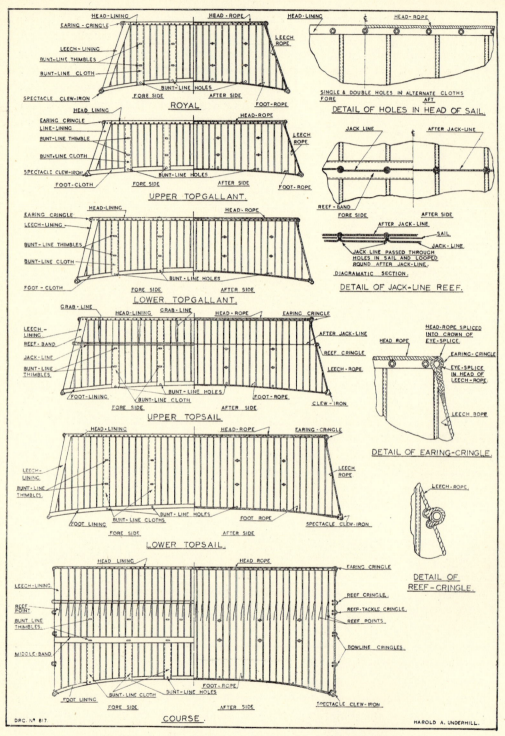

PLATE No. 26.—RANGE OF MODERN SQUARE SAILS.

immediately above the lowest fairlead as shown in Plates 34 and 35. The lower blocks of heavy purchases should always be shackled to eye-bolts in the deck or other convenient position.

We can now turn our attention to Plate 31 which illustrates the running rigging on the fore and aft canvas of a full-rigged ship. In modern vessels the staysail halliards are wire with a rope whip or purchase at the deck end, and in the plate referred to I have shown them direct to the head of the sail. On large staysails additional purchase is often obtained by shackling a single block to the head of the sail and seizing the halliard to the head of the stay.

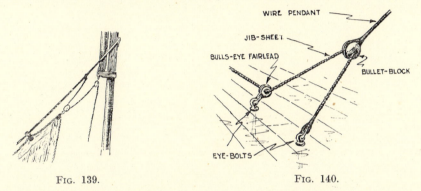

FIG. 139.   FIG. 140.

The lead is then from the head of the stay; through the single block on the sail; back up to a lead block on the mast and down to the deck where the usual whip is rigged, (Fig. 139).

The sheets of the head sails are double, one leading to port and the other starboard. The lee side is set up taut and the weather side left slack across the stay next abaft, ready to haul the sail over and set up taut when going about. Bullet-blocks are spliced into the ends of the jib-sheet pendants; this type of block has no corners or sharp edges to catch on the stay or chafe the sails, (Fig. 140). In the examples given in this chapter the jib-sheets are shown belayed to the main-rail, which is the usual arrangement, but some ships with long fo'castles had short fife-rails on that deck for belaying the jib-sheets.

Plate 51 shows the position of the eye-bolts and fairleads for the jib-sheets of the ship *Acamas*, but this will differ in different ships and the proper locations must be made to suit the cut of the headsails as shown on the sail and rigging plan. The lead of jib-sheets must always be arranged so that they exert equal tension on both leech and foot of the sail, and eye-bolts and fairleads will have to be placed accordingly. Fig. 141 illustrates this point, showing the right and wrong way to lead the sheets.

The remaining staysail sheets are usually single and passed over the stay when going about, although a lazy-sheet was sometimes rigged as shown on the mizzen topmast-staysail in Plate 31. The lazy-sheet is simply a single rope shackled to the clew of the sail and used to steady and assist it over the stay when going about. On these sails the standing part of the whip is bent to any convenient fixture; a ring-bolt or the standing rigging for example, and is of course moved from side to side as required.

The tacks of staysails are held down in the most convenient way. On headsails they may be seized to the foot of the stay; bent to the bowsprit jack-stay, or in the case of small diameter spars, take the form of a wire strop as shown in Fig. 131. Other staysail tacks will be seized to the foot of the stay or bent to a fixture on the mast.

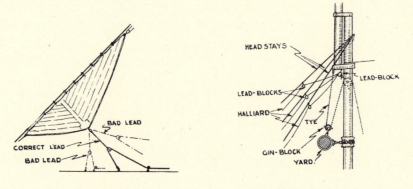

FIG. 141.   FIG. 142.

In the perspective diagram I have shown all the downhauls on the port side for the sake of convenience, they will of course be rigged on the same side of the sail as their lead blocks or fairleads. The downhaul lead blocks will be seized to the foot of the stay or any other suitable fixture, on the spike boom this would be the bowsprit jack-stays as shown in the drawing of the rigged boom on Plate 19. The lizards, which may be one or more in number according to the size of the sail, are seized to the hanks along the luff.

Additional lead blocks are sometimes rigged at the head of the stays, with the object of keeping the halliards from sagging on to the yards and becoming badly chafed. (Fig. 142).

Running-Rigging—Fore and Aft Sails.
Flying-Jib.

Halliard.—Shackled or bent to the head of the sail; taken up over a single lead block on the port side of the mast at the topgallant hounds; down inside No. 1 port topgallant backstay, passing through the fairlead at the cross-trees and terminating in a whip, the running part of which is reeved through the circular fairlead on the stay and belayed to pin No. 24 on the main rail port side.

Downhaul.—Shackled to the head of the sail; leads down the luff through one or more lizards; through lead block on port side of bowsprit; inboard through upper hole in port fairlead on fore topmast stay and belays to pin No. 1 on the fo'castle fife-rail.

Sheets.—Port and Starboard.—The wire pendants are shackled on to the clew-iron and have bullet-blocks spliced in their outer ends. Rope whips are bent to eye-bolts in the fo'castle deck and the running parts passed through the bullet blocks in the pendants; back through bull's eye fairleads on deck; over the break of the fo'castle and belayed to pin No. 6 port and starboard.

Tack.—Made fast to foot of stay or as found most convenient.

Outer-Jib.

Halliard.—Shackled to head of sail; led up over one sheave of a double block on the starboard side of the mast and immediately below the cross-trees; down inside the starboard topmast-backstay; set up with a whip, the fall of which reeves through the fairlead on No. 2 topmast-backstay to pin No. 22 on the starboard main-rail.

Downhaul.—Shackled to the head of the sail; leads down through the lizards on the luff and the lead block on the port side of the bowsprit; inboard through the second hole in the port fairlead and belays to pin No. 2 on the fo'castle fife-rail.

Sheets.—Port and starboard.—Rigged as for flying-jib and belayed to pin No. 7 on main rail port and starboard.

Tack.—As for flying-jib.

Jib.

Halliard.—Shackled to the head of the sail; leads up through single sheaved lead block below the cross-trees on the port side of the mast; down inside No. 1 port topmast-backstay; fall of whip leads through fairlead and belays to pin No. 21 on port main-rail.

Downhaul.—Shackled to head of sail; led down luff through lizards and lead block on starboard side of bowsprit; inboard through fairlead on starboard leg of fore-topmast-stay and belayed to pin No. 3 on fo'castle fife-rail.

Sheets.—Port and Starboard.—Rigged as for flying-jib and belayed to pin No. 8 on main-rail port and starboard.

Tack.—As for flying-jib.

Fore-Topmast-Staysail.

Halliard.—Shackled to head of sail; taken up over second sheave in double block on starboard side of mast below the cross-trees; down inside No. 1 starboard topmast-backstay; ends in a whip belayed to pin No. 20 on starboard main-rail.

Downhaul.—Shackled to head of sail; taken down through lizards on luff and lead block on starboard side; inboard to pin No. 4. on fo'castle fife-rail.

Sheets.—Port and starboard.—Rigged as for flying-jib. Standing part of whip bent to eye-bolt in the deck; fall leads up through bullet block in pendant; back through bull's-eye fairlead on deck and belays to bitts No. 9

Tack.—As for flying-jib.

Main-Royal-Staysail.

Halliard.—Shackled to head of sail; up over lead block on port side of mast at royal hounds; down inside port royal backstay and through fair-lead at the spreaders; terminating in a whip, the fall of which leads through the fairlead on the stay and belays to pin No. 63 on port main-rail.

Downhaul.—Shackled to head of sail; leads down luff through lizards; through lead block on after side of the foremast cap; through lubbers-hole in top; down to pin No. 31 on port side of fore fife-rail.

Sheet.—Single.—A wire pendant is shackled to the clew-iron and has a bullet-block spliced in outer end; a whip is rigged and belayed to pin No. 45 on main-rail port or starboard as required.

Tack.—Seized to stay just above fairlead on the fore-cap.

Main-Topgallant-Staysail.

Halliard.—Shackled to head of sail; leads up through lead block on starboard side of topgallant hounds; down inside the starboard topgallant-backstay; through fairlead at spreaders; and set up with a whip leading through fairlead on No. 1 starboard topgallant-backstay; belays on pin No. 60 on starboard main-rail.

Downhaul.—Shackled to head of sail; leads down through lizards, on luff of sail; through lead blocks at futtock-band, and belays on pin No. 35 on starboard side of fore fife-rail.

Sheet.—Rigged as main-royal-staysail and belays to pin No. 44 on main-rail, port or starboard as required.

Tack.—As for main-royal-staysail.

Main-Topmast-Staysail.

Halliard.—Shackled to head of sail; leads up through lead block on port side of topmast just below cross-trees; down inside first port topmast-backstay and set up with whip in the usual way to pin No. 56 on port main-rail.

Downhaul.—Shackled to head of sail; led down luff and through lizards; through lead block at foot of stay and down to pin No. 32 on port side of fore fife-rail.

Sheet.—Rigged as for main-royal-staysail and belays to pin No. 40 on main rail, port or starboard as required.

Tack.—As for main-royal-staysail.

Mizzen-Royal-Staysail.

When carried would be rigged as on main.

Mizzen-Topgallant-Staysail.

Halliard.—Shackled to head of sail; led up to lead block on port side of mast at topgallant hounds; down inside forward port topgallant-backstay; through fairlead on spreader; set up whip through fairlead on stay and belayed to pin No. 100 on port poop-rail.

Downhaul.—Shackled to head of sail. Leads down luff and through lizards; through lead block at foot of stay; belays on pin No. 65 on port side main fife-rail.

Sheet.—Rigged as main-royal-staysails; belays to pin No. 81 on main-rail, port or starboard as required.

Tack.—As for main-topgallant-staysail.

Mizzen-Topmast-Staysail.

Halliard.—Shackled to head of sail and led up to lead block immediately below the cross-trees on the starboard side of the topmast; down inside the forward starboard backstay, and set up with a whip in the usual way. Belays to pin No. 96 on the starboard poop-rail.

Downhaul.—Shackled to head of sail; leads down through lizards on luff; through lead block at foot of stay, and belays to pin No. 66 on starboard side of main fife-rail.

Sheet.—Rigged as for main-topmast-staysail and belayed to pin No. 77 on main-rail, port or starboard as required. Note. In the perspective diagram I have shown an alternative rig for the sheet, using a gun-tackle purchase in place of the common whip. This would be used on topmast-staysails of all large vessels, and eye-bolts would be provided in the deck on either side for hooking the lower block.

Tack.—As for main-topmast-staysail.

Spanker.

Head-Outhaul.—This may be either wire or chain and is shackled to the peak cringle of the sail; reeves through the sheave-hole in the peak of the gaff; inboard through a block at the lower cap. This block will be single if the peak halliard is a span shackled to the lower cap, or double if the halliard

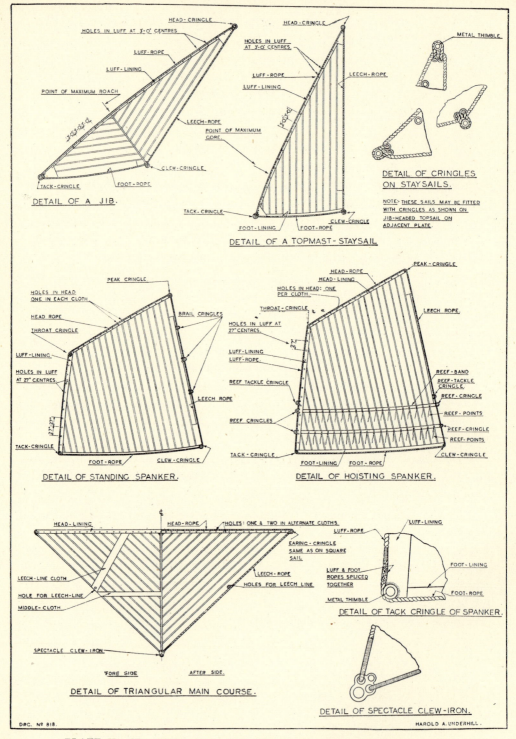

PLATE No. 27.---FORE AND AFT SAILS AND TRIANGULAR COURSE.

passes through the block and is set up in the top with rigging screw or lanyard; in this case the starboard sheave of the double block will take the halliard and the port sheave the spanker-head-outhaul. From the lead block the outhaul passes down to the upper block of a guntackle-purchase; the lower purchase block is shackled to an eye-bolt in the deck; the fall of the tackle is reeved through another lead block on deck and up to pin No. 95 on the port poop rail.

Head-Downhaul or *Head-Inhaul.*—Wire. Shackled to the peak-cringle of the sail; taken along below the gaff on the port side of the sail; through a single lead block, at the gaff goose-neck and down to the upper block of a gun-tackle purchase which is rigged as for the outhaul; through a lead block on deck and up to pin No. 94 on the port poop-rail.

Foot-Outhaul.—Wire. Shackled to the clew-cringle of the sail; reeved down over the sheave in the outer end of the boom; back along the underside of the boom, to reeve over one sheave of a double block on the mast at the boom goose-neck; down to belay to pin No. 133 on the after side of the mizzen spider-band.

Foot-Inhaul.—Shackled to the clew-cringle; leads in board to the second sheave of the block at the mast and down to pin No. 133 with the outhaul.

Brails.—Three in number. Middled at the brail-cringles on the leech of the sail; lead forward along port and starboard sides; down through their respective lead blocks on either side of the mast; down to the spider-band where they belay on pins No. 134 on port and starboard sides of the mast, three brails to a pin.

Sheet.—Two double blocks are shackled on to the "U" of the outer boom band, and two more double blocks are shackled to eye-bolts, one on either side of the deck. The sheet is double—or in two parts, one leading to port and one to starboard, each being reeved by splicing the fall into an eye on the lower block; up over one sheave of the upper block; down through the lower block and so on until all are taken up; finishing with the second sheave in the lower block and so up to pin No. 106 on the rail, port and starboard.

Boom-Guys.—Port and starboard.—These are used to steady the boom and are each made up of a wire pendant shackled to the side of the boom band, the outer end of the pendant is shackled to the upper block of a gun-tackle purchase, or in the case of small vessels, a whip. The standing part of the purchase or whip is made fast to an eye-bolt in the deck, and the fall belays to pin No. 105 on the rail port and straboard.

Vangs.—Port and starboard.—These are made up of wire pendants with gun-tackle purchases on the lower ends, the lower block of the purchase shackles into an eye-bolt in the deck, and the fall belays to pin No. 103 on the poop rail port and starboard.

Signal-Halliards.—These are reeved through a small jewel-block on the extreme end of the gaff, or alternately on a monkey-gaff at the cross-trees. The lower end is belayed on deck as most convenient at the time of use.

Running Rigging on Square-Sails.

We have already seen that halliards are necessary on topsails, togallants, royals and skysails, and that with double topsail and double topgallants the halliard is on the upper yard in each case. They have a very heavy duty to perform, not only in lifting and carrying the weight of yard and sail, but also partly transmitting the pull to the hull by acting as additional backstays; for this reason stout gear is used and usually set up well aft. Before the introduction of mechanical aid the heavy yards had to be hoisted by hand, a job which required the full crew in spite of the purchase obtained from two three-fold blocks. This was particularly so in the earlier days of the clipper period when single halliards were used, (Fig. 143A). With this rig the single wire halliard shackles directly to the chain tye at one end, and the upper purchase block at the other. The lower purchase block is shackled to an eye-bolt in the waterways, and the fall led up to the rail, either direct from the lower block, or from the upper and through a lead block on deck.

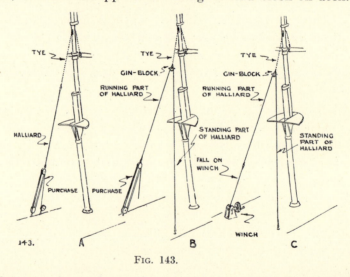

FIG. 143.

The first step forward was the introduction of the double halliard, (Fig. 143B). Here an iron block, termed a gin-block, is shackled to the after end of the chain tye, and the wire halliard reeves through this, one end being shackled to an eye-bolt in the deck and the other to the upper purchase block on the other side. This rig has two advantages; firstly, it does away with the unequal pull to one side of the mast, and secondly it gives the additional mechanical advantage of a whip.

The use of deck capstans as mentioned earlier in this chapter also went far to reduce the labour in hoisting yards, but the final stage was the introduction of the halliard winch in place of the rope purchase, (Fig. 143c). These winches are very simple, and although the supporting frame may vary in different makes, the mechanical design is the same. The principal feature is the drum, which not only does the hauling but also stores the wire taken in,

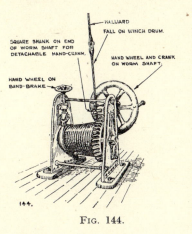

so there is no need to feed it off the winch and coil it as would be the case with a capstan. A large hand operated flywheel at one end drives the drum through a worm and pinion gear, while at the other end of the drum is a band brake. This winch is illustrated in the sketch Fig. 144.

FIG. 144.

The usual rig for a chain tye is to shackle it to the centre of the yard, from which point it goes up the mast and through a sheave-hole in the mast-head; down the after side to be shackled to the gin-block or wire halliard according to whether double or single halliards are rigged. An alternative arrangement is to arrange the tye as a whip on the fore side of the mast. In this case a gin-block is shackled to the centre of the yard, and the tye is made fast to the mast by being shackled to the under side of the cross-trees, or a masthead-strop in the case of topgallants. From the mast head the tye leads down the mast: through the gin-block on the yard; up through the sheave-hole in the mast head—reeving from the fore side; and down to the head of the halliard, (Fig. 142).

Reverting to halliards rigged with rope purchases, these latter should be kept as short as possible, subject of course to the blocks remaining a reasonable distance apart when the yard is fully hoisted. Purchases eat up a lot of rope, and in the case of the topsail-halliards, every extra foot of tackle requires seven additional feet of rope in the fall, so that if the upper purchase block in each square sail halliard of the ship on Plate 32 were to be only four feet higher than necessary, the additional rope required would be 210 feet. I make this point for the benefit of the model builder, because if he will get into the habit of always viewing his work from the combined angle of master and owner of a full size ship; first as to what is needed to do the work required, and secondly how can the results be obtained without waste of material, his model will really *look* right.

The best way to decide the position of the upper block is to work from the "hoisted" position, when the two blocks should be anything from six to nine feet apart. The travel of the upper block on single halliards will be

L

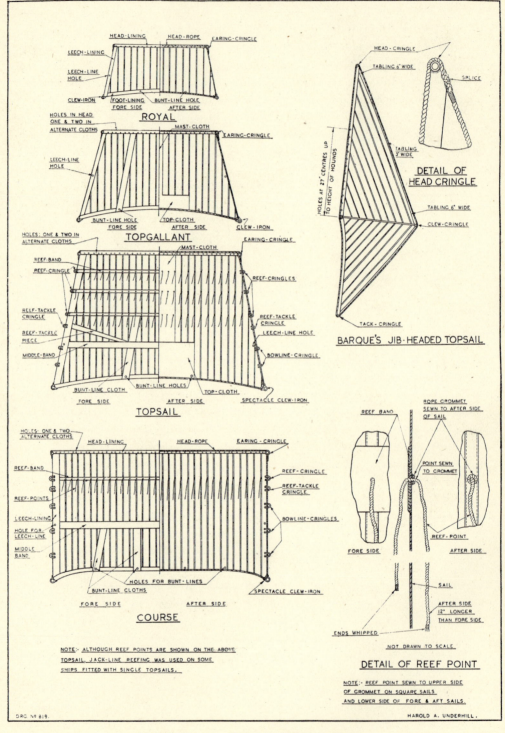

PLATE No. 28.—SINGLE SQUARE SAILS.

equal to the hoist of the yard, and on double halliards, twice this distance. Complications arise if the tye is rigged as a whip on the fore side of the mast, for then the after end of the tye will travel a distance equal to twice the hoist of the yard, and the upper purchase block of a single halliard will of course do the same; but should this type of tye be rigged with double halliards, the upper purchase block will travel a distance equal to four times the hoist of the yard. It will be appreciated that these points have to be closely watched in deciding the rig of the halliards, otherwise it is easy to arrange a rig which cannot be worked in practice.

I have mentioned the travel of the purchase block on a combination of the whip rigged tye and the double halliard, this however is more in the nature of a warning, as it is extremely unlikely that the two would, or for that matter could, be used together. If the after end of the tye descends twice the length of the hoist, as it does when the fore side is rigged as a whip, it obviously must come down below the level of the fore and aft stay which is set up to the lower mast-cap, and therefore double halliards would jamb taut across the stay before the yard could reach its hoisted position. So the combination could only be used in cases where the fore and aft stays were rigged sufficiently low down to allow the gin-block full travel. Not a very usual arrangement.

The whip rigged tye used in conjunction with the single halliard, provides the same mechanical advantage as the double halliard with the single tye, it is simply a matter of putting the whip on the tye instead of the halliard. Quite a number of iron and steel vessels rig their tyes as whips, using single halliards on the topsail yards; the upper yards can rig either single or double halliards, as there are no stays to foul. Both rope purchases and halliard winches are in general use with modern vessels, and either may be rigged with double or single halliards. Some of the later craft having single halliards and halliard winches, carried the latter nearer the centre line of the ship, so reducing the angular pull on the mast. One example which comes to mind is the steel four-mast barque *Viking*, she has all her halliard winches grouped round the fife-rails.

One rule is invariably followed in the rigging of square sail halliards; the fore-topsail halliard always belays or leads to a winch on the *port* side of the vessel, and all other halliards, both above it on the same mast, and abaft it on all other masts, are placed on alternate sides. This can best be explained in tabulated form as under:—

	Topsail Halliard	Topgallant Halliard	Royal Halliard	Skysail Halliard
Fore	Port	Starboard	Port	Starboard
Main	Starboard	Port	Starboard	Port
Mizzen	Port	Starboard	Port	Starboard
Jigger	Starboard	Port	Starboard	Port

An example of double halliards with single tyes is shown in the perspective diagram on Plate 32 which will be used to describe the lead. If single halliards are carried it simply means that the standing part, together with the gin-block on the after end of the tye, will be omitted, and the running side of the halliards shackled directly to the tye. The purchase and belaying pins will still be in the places described. In the same way, if halliard winches are used they will just take the place of the tackle and belaying pins. In modern craft single halliards may, as we have already seen, be rigged to winches near the centre line, but even so they will always have to be slightly to one side or the other to enable the halliard to clear the fore and aft stays, and that side will be as shown in the table given on previous page.

Fore Topsail Halliard.

Tye (A. on Plate 32).—Single chain. The tye shackles to the centre band or span on the yard and taken up the fore side of the mast; reeved over a sheave in topmast head immediately below cross-trees, and is completed by having an iron gin-block shackled on to the lower end. On topsail yards it is essential to make the length of the tye such that when the yard is in its lowest position, the gin-block will be only a foot or so below the sheave-hole in the mast. If the tye is made too long it will foul the royal-stay before the yard is at full hoist. On topgallant and royal yards this is not so important, as in modern ships there is no stay set up on the after side of the cross-trees, so there is plenty of room for the gin-block to descend as the yard goes up.

Halliard.—This consists of a long wire strop with a metal thimble spliced into each end. One end is shackled to an eye-bolt in the deck near the rail, or alternately to a chain-plate bolted to the ship's side and brought up through the main rail. Whichever type of anchorage is used it should be placed adjacent to the lower-cap-stay or the foremost topmast-backstay on the starboard side. This end of the wire forms the standing part of the halliard (A.2) and passes up and through the gin-block, on the other side of which it becomes the running-part (A.1) which shackles to the upper block of the rope purchase.

Purchase.—This is made up of two treble blocks, the lower one being shackled to an eye-bolt or chain-plate similar to that used on the standing part, and placed directly opposite on the port side. A third block—single— is shackled to an eye-bolt in the deck close to the lower purchase block and serves as lead block for the fall. The fall splices round a thimble on the underside of the upper block; leads down to the first sheave in the lower block; up to the first sheave in the upper block, and so on until all are taken up; finally leading off the last sheave in the top block, down through the single lead block on deck and up to pin No. 16 in the main-rail, port side.

If a halliard winch is fitted in place of the purchase, the free end of the wire fall on the winch drum will be eye-spliced or shackled into the thimble on the running end of the halliard, in place of the upper purchase block. This is shown in the sketch of the halliard winch (Fig. 144).

Fore-Topgallant-Halliard.

Tye (B).—Single chain. Rigged as on fore-topsail, and reeved through the sheave-hole in the topgallant-mast immediately below the topgallant-hounds.

Halliard.—Wire. Rigged as on the topsail; standing part (B.2) shackled to eye-bolt or chain-plate on port side in way of foremost topgallant-backstay reeved over sheave of gin-block on tye, and down (B.1) to upper purchase block.

Purchase.—Made up of two treble blocks and a lead block rigged as for topsail, but with lower block and lead block on starboard side in way of topgallant-backstay; fall belays to pin No. 23 on starboard main-rail.

Fore-Royal-Halliard.

Tye (C).—Single chain. Rigged as on topsail and reeved through sheave-hole in mast immediately below royal hounds.

Halliard.—Wire. Rigged as on topsail. Standing part (C. 2) shackled to eye-bolt or chain-plate on starboard side in way of royal-backstay; reeved through gin-block of tye; down port side (C. 1) to the upper purchase block. The purchase is made up of a three-sheave upper block, double-sheave lower block, and a single lead block. The lower block and lead block are shackled to eye-bolts or chain-plates on the port side. The fall is spliced round the thimble on the underside of the upper block; reeves down through the lower and so on until all sheaves are taken up, and finishes with the third one in the upper block; down to the lead block and up to pin No. 26 in the port main-rail.

Main-Topsail-Halliard.

Tye (D).—Single chain. Rigged and reeved as fore-topsail.

Halliard.—Wire. Standing part (D. 2) shackled to eye-bolt or chain-plate in way of lower-cap-stay or forward topmast-backstay on port side; reeved over sheave of gin-block and down (D. 1) to upper purchase block.

Purchase.—Rigged as on fore-topsail and belays to pin No. 55 on main-rail, starboard side.

Main-Topgallant-Halliard.

Tye (E).—Single chain. Rigged as on fore-topsail and reeved through sheave-hole immediately below the topgallant-hounds.

Halliard.—Wire. Standing part (E. 2) shackled to eye-bolt or chain-plate in way of topgallant-backstays starboard side; reeves through gin-block on tye and down (E. 1) to top purchase block.

Purchase.—Rigged as on fore-topsail and belayed to pin No. 61 on port main-rail.

Main-Royal-Halliard.

Tye (F).—Single chain. Rigged as on fore-topsail and reeved through sheave-hole immediately below royal-hounds.

Halliard.—Wire.   Standing part (F. 2) shackled to eye-bolt or chain-plate on port side in way of royal-backstay.   Reeved through gin-block on tye: down on starboard side (E. 1) to top purchase block.

Purchase.—Made up and reeved as on fore-royal; fall belayed to pin No. 62 on main-rail, starboard side.

Mizzen-Topsail-Halliard.

Tye (G).—Single chain. Rigged and reeved as on fore-topsail.

Halliard.—Wire. Standing part (G. 2) shackled to eye-bolt in the deck on starboard side of poop; reeved over sheave of gin-block on tye and down on port side (G. 1) to upper purchase block.

Purchase.—Rigged as on fore-topsail, with lower blocks shackled to eye-bolts in poop deck and fall taken up to pin No. 88 in poop-rail, port side.

Mizzen-Topgallant-Halliard.

Tye (H).—Single chain. Rigged as on fore-topsail and reeved through sheave-hole in mast immediately below the topgallant hounds.

Halliard.—Wire. Standing part (H. 1) shackled to eye-bolt in the deck on port side of poop, in way of the topgallant backstays; reeves through gin-block on the tye and down on the starboard side (H. 1) where it shackles to the upper purchase-block.

Purchase.—Rigged as on fore-topsail but with lower blocks shackled to eye-bolts in the poop deck in way of the starboard topgallant-backstays. Fall leads up to pin No. 101 on poop-rails, starboard side.

Mizzen Royal Halliard.

Tye (I)—Single chain. Rigged as on fore-topsail and reeved through sheave-hole in mast immediately below the royal hounds.

Halliard.—Wire. Standing part (I. 2) shackled to eye-bolt in the deck in way of the starboard royal-backstays; reeves through gin-block on tye and down on the port side (I. 1) to the top purchase block.

Purchase.—Rigged as on the fore-royal, with the lower blocks shackled to eye-bolts in the poop deck on the port side. The fall leads off the single block and up to pin No. 102 on the poop-rail, port side.

Methods of Clewing Square Sails.

Square sails may be divided into two general groups based upon the manner in which the clew-lines are rigged. The first group is made up of sails which clew up to the slings or quarters; and the second, sails clewing up to the yard-arms. On plate 34 I have given composite drawing illustrating both these arrangements, the half on the right showing sails clewed to slings and quarters; and the left having all sails, including the courses, clewed to the yard-arms. I have also taken advantage of this drawing to show on one side a single-topgallant above double topsails, and on the other double-top-gallants and double-topsails. Plate 35 shows the same spars with all the sails furled.

At one time all sails clewed up to slings or quarters, and it was only on the introduction of the double topsail that the practice of clewing up to the yard-arms became common. Even then the rig was for some time limited to those sails, and only gradually spread upwards to the topgallants and royals; and finally down to the courses. Generally speaking one may say that where single topsails are carried, all square sails will clew up to quarters or slings, while with double-topsails either method may be used on the yards above, although the earlier the ship the more likely it will be that the older way will be used, and it is only in the big ships of the carrier type that the courses will clew to the yard-arms.

The advantages of clewing up to the yard-arms are fairly obvious. The sail when furled is evenly distributed along the yard instead of being bunched up at the bunt, and thanks to the additional bunt-lines usually carried, it is under better control during the process of being clewed up. In spite of all this it took quite a long time for the rig to become popular with masters of the old school, their great objection being, that in harbour it was supposed to make the spars look heavy and clumsy, whereas sails furled to the bunt tended to accentuate the taper of the yards and left the arms clear. Incidentally double-topsails were also unpopular for much the same reason, they were considered to spoil the appearance aloft when the canvas was stowed, and in harbour, many clippers made a practice of hoisting the upper-topsail yards halfway up the topmasts after making a harbour stow of the sails. However, as the rig became more commonplace and generally accepted, the practice died out and yards were left down on the caps in what is today the general rule.

As the rig of each square sail will be the same on all masts in the ship, there is no need to take the masts separately in detail, but it will be sufficient

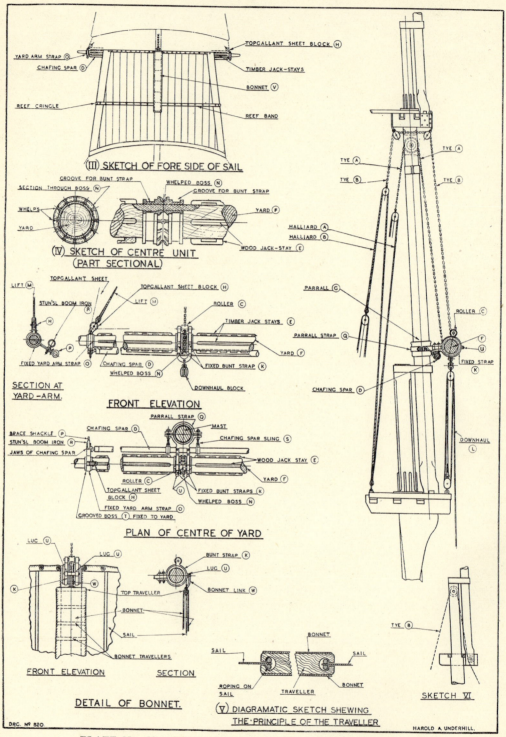

(III) SKETCH OF FORE SIDE OF SAIL

YARD ARM STRAP (O)
CHAFING SPAR (D)
REEF CRINGLE
TOPGALLANT SHEET BLOCK (H)
TIMBER JACK-STAYS
BONNET (V)
REEF BAND

(IV) SKETCH OF CENTRE UNIT (PART SECTIONAL)

GROOVE FOR BUNT STRAP
SECTION THROUGH BOSS (N)
WHELPS
YARD
WHELPED BOSS (N)
GROOVE FOR BUNT STRAP
YARD (F)
WOOD JACK-STAY (E)

SECTION AT YARD-ARM.

LIFT (M)
TOPGALLANT SHEET
STUN'SL BOOM IRON (R)
(H)
(P)
FIXED YARD ARM STRAP (O)
TOPGALLANT SHEET BLOCK (H)
LIFT (M)
ROLLER (C)
TIMBER JACK STAYS (E)
YARD (F)
CHAFING SPAR (D)
WHELPED BOSS (N)
FIXED BUNT STRAP (K)
DOWNHAUL BLOCK

FRONT ELEVATION

PLAN OF CENTRE OF YARD

BRACE SHACKLE (P)
STUN'SL BOOM IRON (R)
JAWS OF CHAFING SPAR
CHAFING SPAR (D)
PARRALL STRAP (Q)
MAST
CHAFING SPAR SLING (S)
WOOD JACK STAY (E)
YARD (F)
ROLLER (C)
TOPGALLANT SHEET BLOCK (H)
FIXED YARD ARM STRAP (O)
GROOVED BOSS (T) FIXED TO YARD
FIXED BUNT STRAPS (K)
WHELPED BOSS (N)

DETAIL OF BONNET.

LUG (U)
LUG (U)
(K)
TOP TRAVELLER
BONNET
SAIL
BONNET TRAVELLERS
BUNT STRAP (K)
LUG (U)
BONNET LINK (W)

FRONT ELEVATION   SECTION

(V) DIAGRAMATIC SKETCH SHEWING THE PRINCIPLE OF THE TRAVELLER

SAIL
BONNET
SAIL
BONNET
ROPING ON SAIL
TRAVELLER
BONNET

TYE (A)
TYE (A)
TYE (B)
TYE (A)
TYE (B)
HALLIARD (A)
HALLIARD (B)
PARRALL (C)
PARRALL STRAP (Q)
CHAFING SPAR (D)
ROLLER (C)
(F)
(U)
FIXED STRAP (K)
DOWNHAUL (L)

SKETCH VI

TYE (B)

DRG. Nº 820.

HAROLD A. UNDERHILL.

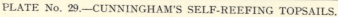

PLATE No. 29.—CUNNINGHAM'S SELF-REEFING TOPSAILS.

to treat Plate 34 as representing the fore-mast and follow all gear as such. For the main and mizzen it will be enough to quote the location and pin number of the belaying point, unless of course there should be some difference in the lead, in which case it will be described. In the same way, the jigger-mast of a four-mast ship or a five-mast barque will simply be a repeat of the other square rigged masts in the same ship.

Fore-Sail or Fore-Course.

Lifts.—The lifts of lower-yards are always rigged as running rigging. The outer end or standing-part has an eye-splice formed in the end—it will of course be understood that thimbles are used in all eye-splices even though not specifically mentioned here—which is then shackled to the lug on top of the yard-arm-band. The lift then leads up over the sheave of a single block on the side of the lower-mast cap; down through the lubbers-hole in the top, and shackled to the upper block of the purchase. The lower purchase block is shackled to an eye-bolt in the deck between the fife-rails, or to one of the lugs on the spider-band at the foot of the mast. The purchase is made up of two double-blocks, with the fall spliced into the thimble on the underside of the upper one; it is then led down through the lower block; up to the top one, and so on until all sheaves are taken up. From the last sheave in the upper block the fall may either lead straight to the pin, or be reeved through a bull's-eye fairlead at the deck and so back up to the rail. The port lift belays to pin No. 33 and the starboard lift to pin No. 37 on the port and starboard sides of the fife-rail respectively.

Clew-Garnets.—The rig of the clew-garnets will depend upon whether the sail clews up to the yard-arms or the bunt. The left hand detail on Plate 34 shows them as rigged in the big steel vessels which saw the close of the sailing ship era. The eye-splice of the outer end is shackled to the clew-iron on the sail, and the garnet leads up through a single block on the underside of the yard-arm-band; along below the yard and through a block on the quarter-band; down to the main-rail where it belays to pin No. 11 on the main-rail port and starboard. The drawing shows a whip rigged on the running end, this, as we have already seen, is optional, but is almost certain to be found in the big steel ship. An alternative is to rig the whip on the sail. The standing end of the clew-garnet is shackled to the underside of the yard-arm; leads down and through a block at the clew of the sail; up and through a block below the yard-arm-band; along below the yard and through a block at the quarter-band, and down to the deck as already described.

If the sail clews up to the bunt, as in the right hand detail on the plate, a block will be stropped to the thimble of the inner eye on the clew-iron, and the standing end of the clew-garnet shackled to the underside of the yard at the quarter-band, or to the lead block at this point. The garnet reeves down through the block at the clew; up through the block below the quarter-band, and down to pin No. 11 port and starboard.

Bunt-Lines.—The number of bunt-lines will vary according to the size of the sail and the period to which the ship belongs. Small craft, particularly in the days of the single topsail, frequently had only two bunt-lines and two leech-lines on the full width of the sail, while the modern steel barque may have as many as six or seven bunt-lines, or bunt-lines and leech-lines, across her courses. The rig of the bunt-lines may also differ in different ships. The modern practice is to run them vertically up the sail, but they may be inclined, or the centre ones vertical and the outer ones at an incline. However all these points will be made quite clear from the sail and rigging plan, or the model builder's knowledge of the ship in hand.

As our example I have taken the modern rig with the bunt-lines running vertically up the sail, should the reader be interested in a vessel where they are inclined, it is only a matter of moving the position of the lead blocks on the yard, otherwise the run of the gear will be exactly the same. The bunt-line blocks on the yard are seized to the jack-stay and rest on top of the sail as shown in the sketch Fig. 145. The lead blocks under the top are shackled to the eye-bolts below the rim in the positions show in the perspective sketch Fig. 44.

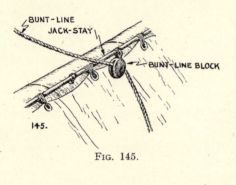

FIG. 145.

Bunt-lines are bent to the foot of the sail by means of bunt-lines-hitches or running hitches. The bunt-line-hitch is made by passing the end of the line through the cringle, or bunt-line-hole, in the foot of the sail and tying it round its own part with a clove-hitch (Fig. 146A), the complete hitch is then pulled up tight round the bolt-rope or rope cringle. The running hitch is made in the same way, except that instead of the clove-hitch the end makes one complete turn round its own part; the two parts of the round turn are seized together, forming a running noose (Fig. 146B), which is jammed tightly round the bolt-rope or cringle. The end of the bunt-line will of course be whipped before forming the hitches, this applies to all running rigging; the ends of *all* cordage must be whipped. A third alternative is to splice a toggle into the end of the bunt-line and pass it through the cringle, this method will only be used on sails having rope cringles on the foot. (Fig. 146c.)

From the foot of the sail the bunt-lines lead up through the thimble fairleads on the fore side; through their respective bunt-line blocks which are seized to the jack-stay of the yard; through their lead blocks below the

top and down forward of the foremost shroud, i.e. outside all rigging; through
the fairlead on No. 1 shroud, and all belay to pin No. 10 in the main-rail
port and starboard. The innermost bunt-line will of course go through the
block nearest the mast below the top. As already pointed out, whips may
be rigged on the bunt-lines if considered necessary.

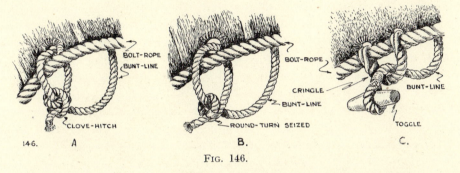

FIG. 146.

Leech-Lines.—These are not generally rigged on courses which clew up
to the yard-arms, but in this, like everything else, there are exceptions and
it is a point which must be settled from the sail plan or knowledge of the
actual vessel. Leech-lines are bent to the leech of the sail in the same way
as bunt-lines, using either bunt-line-hitch, running-hitch or toggle. From the
leech the line leads up the fore side of the sail; through thimble fairleads
if provided; through the leech-line block bent to the jack-stay of the yard;
through the outermost block below the rim of the top, and down to the deck
following the same route as the bunt-lines; belaying on the same pin, No. 10
port and starboard.

Slab-Lines.—These are not in general use and I have not included them
in Plate 34, but they can be seen in the sketch Fig. 16. They are bent to
the foot of the sail in the same manner as the bunt-lines; lead up the after
side; through lead blocks under the yard, and straight from these blocks
to pins provided on the fife-rail.

Reef-Tackle.—The modern steel ship does not as a rule have the reef-
tackles rigged, and therefore I have not shown it in the left hand detail on
Plate 34. It is however shown in the other half of the drawing. The standing
end of the reef-tackle is seized round the yard-arms, or any other convenient
fitting such as the neck of the outer-boom-iron in ships carrying stuns'l booms,
or to a thimble on the upper block shackled to the underside of the yard-arm-
band. The lower block is bent to the reef-tackle cringle on the leech of the
sail. From the yard-arm the reef-tackle reeves down through the block on
the sail; up through the block on the yard-arm; along below the yard and
through the quarter-block,—when reef-tackles are rigged a double block will
be used at the quarters, one sheave taking the clew-garnet and the other the
reef-tackle. From the quarter-block the fall leads down alongside the clew-

garnet, and may either belay to the same pin—No. 11 main-rail port and starboard—or to a spare pin if one is available adjacent to No. 11.

Sheet.—Chain or wire, rigged single or double. The single sheet shackles to the clew-iron on the sail; reeves in through the sheaved fairlead—No. 113 —in the bulwarks; under the chess-tree on the bulwark stanchion and belays to the bitts No. 38 on the main-rail port and starboard. In rigging the double sheet the standing end shackles to a chain-plate or eye-bolt—No. 112—on the outside of the bulwarks; reeves through a block shackled to the clew-iron on the sail; in through the sheaved fairlead—No. 113—in the bulwarks; up under the chess-tree and belays to the bitts No. 38. See sketch Fig. 138.

Tack.—Single wire. Has an eye-splice in one end, which shackles to the clew-iron on the sail. The tack is then taken forward, outboard of all gear; led in through a block or fairlead—No. 109A—on the fo'castle head port and starboard—or alternately this fairlead may be out on the cat-head— and belay to bitts—No. 109 port and starboard. As already described in chapter I., the weather tack and the lee sheet are set up taut, and the lee tack and weather sheet are slack when the ship is on a wind. (Fig. 18.)

Lazy-Tack and *Lazy-Sheet*.—Single wire or hemp, shackled to the clew-iron and coiled down on deck when not in use (Fig. 18). In use the lazy-tack belays to pin No. 5 port and starboard, and the lazy-sheet to pin No. 39 port and starboard, both on the main rail. These pins are of course alternative positions, for the one line may be used as either sheet or tack according to whether it is leading fore or aft.

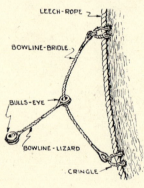

FIG. 147.

Bowline-Bridle and Lizard.—The bowline-bridle is a short wire span with an eye-splice at each end. The lizard is also a wire span but has a bull's-eye spliced in each end. The bridle is reeved through one of the bull's-eyes of the lizard, and then seized to the upper and lower bowline-cringles on the leech of the sail. The lizard should be sufficiently long to allow the bowline to be reeved through the outer bull's-eye by a man standing on the ship's rail. The bridle and lizard are shown in (Fig. 147).

Bowline.—Bowlines are used to keep taut the weather leech of the sail when close-hauled, and may be rigged either double or single. When rigged double, the standing end is bent to a convenient point on the bowsprit near the cap; leads inboard and through the outer bull's-eye of the lizard; back forward again and through a block seized to the bowsprit-cap; inboard to the fo'castle head where it belays at the most suitable point, such as the jib-downhaul pins, (Fig. 148). When rigged single it is bent directly on to the lizard.

Spilling-Lines.—These are an alternative to the bunt-lines, in fact they are bunt-lines which continue up the afterside of the sail instead of terminating at the foot. They are not commonly used in merchant craft and are only mentioned here as a matter of interest. The standing end is bent to the jack-stay of the yard and the running end passes down between the yard and the sail; the line continues down the afterside of the sail and through the bunt-

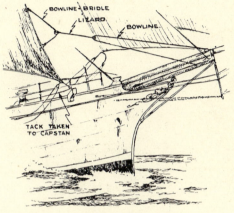

FIG. 148.

line-cringles at the foot; up on the fore side and through the bunt-line blocks on the yard; through the lead blocks below the rim of the top, and down to the pins usually occupied by the bunt-lines.

Fore-Lower-Topsail.

Clew-Lines.—In the modern rig clewing up to the yard-arms, the clew-line shackles to the clew-iron on the sail; leads up through a block on the underside of the yard-arm-band; along below the yard and through the quarter block; down through the fairlead in the decking of the top—see Plate 35—and is set up with a whip, the running part of which leads down through the

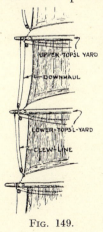

fairlead on No. 2 shroud and belays to pin No. 12 on the main-rail, port and starboard. The standing part of the whip is seized to No. 2 shroud immediately above the fairlead. When the sail is clewed up the block of the whip should be just above the fairlead on the shroud, otherwise it will foul the head of the shrouds at the mast when the sail is sheeted home.

An alternative method of rigging this clew-line is to make the standing end fast to the yard-arm; lead down and through a block shackled to the clew of the sail; up through the lead block on the yard-arm—(Fig. 149)—and so down to the deck as already described, except that no whip will be rigged, the line going direct to the pin via the usual fairleads.

FIG. 149.

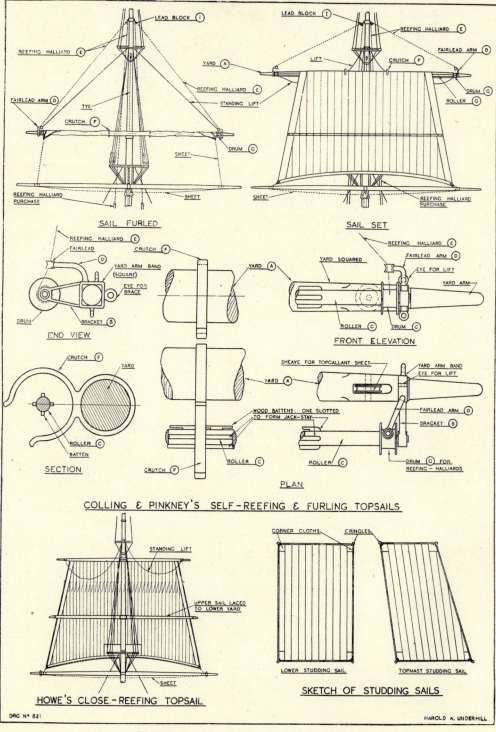

SAIL FURLED

SAIL SET

END VIEW

FRONT ELEVATION

SECTION

PLAN

COLLING & PINKNEY'S SELF-REEFING & FURLING TOPSAILS

HOWE'S CLOSE-REEFING TOPSAIL

SKETCH OF STUDDING SAILS

DRG Nº 821

HAROLD A. UNDERHILL

PLATE No. 30.—SELF REEFING TOPSAILS.

For clewing up to the quarters, one block is fitted on the underside of a band about one-third out from the mast, and another at the quarter-band. The clew-line is bent to the yard, or a thimble on the outer block as shown in the drawing; leads down through a block at the clew of the sail; back up and through the outer block; along below the yard to the quarter-block; down through the fairlead in the top; through the fairlead on No. 2 shroud and belays to pin No. 12 in the main-rail, port and starboard. No whip is rigged with this lead. The position of the outer clew-line block will vary slightly in different ships, but that shewn is perhaps the most common.

Bunt-Lines.—The rig of bunt-lines on topsails varies considerably in different ships, although the lead down to the deck may be said to be common to them all. The most usual arrangement is that shown on the left hand side of Plate 34. Here a double sheave block is seized to the forward topmast shroud, some little way above the level of the lower-topsail yard. In some of the early ships this block was right up at the cross-trees as in the case of the single topsail. The bunt-lines are bent at the foot of the sail as already described for the course; led up through the thimble fairleads on the fore side of the sail; through the bunt-line blocks seized to the jack-stay of the yard; up through the double block—one sheave for each buntline—on the topmast shroud, down through the fairlead-plank in the top; through the remaining two holes in the fairlead on shroud No. 2 and belayed on the same pin as the clew-line—No. 12 in the main-rail, port and starboard.

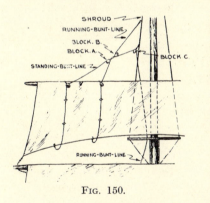

FIG. 150.

A variation of this rig is to bend the bunt-line to the outer bunt-line cringle on the foot of the sail; up through the fairleads on the fore side of the sail; through the outer bunt-line block on the yard; then reeve it through a single block—"A". (Fig. 150); pass it down through the inner bunt-line block on the yard; down the fore side of the sail and bend it to the inner bunt-line cringle. The total length of this standing bunt-line will be equal to about three times the depth of the sail. To the strop of the single block "A" shackle another single block "B" and seize a third single block "C" to the topmast shroud in place of the double lead block, and rather higher up. The running part of the bunt-line is seized to the shroud above block "C"; taken down and reeved through the top block "B" of the pair on the standing bunt-line; back up and through block "C" on the shroud, and down to the deck as already described. This sounds very complicated, but I think the sketch will make everything clear.

Another arrangement is shown in the right hand drawing on the plate referred to.   In this case the foot and the leech of the sail are joined by a span forming a combined standing bunt-line and leech-line, on which is reeved a free bull's-eye.   The running bunt-line is spliced round the score of the bull's-eye and taken up over the sheave of a single block on the topmast shroud: down to the deck as already described and belayed to pin No. 12.   It will be noted that in both this and the previous rig, only one line comes down to the deck instead of the usual two.   One point to watch in both these rigs is that the block on the topmast shroud is kept sufficiently high to allow the foot of the sail to reach the yard before the standing bunt-line comes chock-a-block with the lead block.

Sheet.—Chain.   Shackled to the clew of the sail; reeves through the cheek-block or sheave at the lower yard-arm; through the iron fairleads on the underside of the lower yard; through the iron clover-leaf block below the centre of the yard; and down the mast to the upper block of a three-fold purchase.   The lower block shackles to an eye-bolt in the deck or the large eyes on the spider-band at the foot of the mast.   The fall is spliced to a thimble on the lower block, and reeves through the upper block; down to the lower and so on until all sheaves are taken up, finishing with the third sheave in the *lower* block, from which it goes up to pin No. 28 on the spider-band round the mast.   Port and starboard.

Some ships rigged the lower-topsail sheets without a purchase.   In this case the chain continues down the mast, through a bull's eye fairlead or iron lead block on deck and up to pin No. 28.   To get the sheets well home a purchase would be clapped on the sheets as high as possible above the deck, with the lower block hooked to an eye on the lower spider-band.   This tackle will of course be removed when not in use.

Fore-Upper-Topsail.

Downhauls.—The standing end of the downhaul has an eye-splice by means of which it is shackled to the upper side of the lower-topsail yard-arm, using the lug on the yard-arm-band.   It is then taken up and through the block below the upper-topsail yard-arm; along below the yard and through the quarter-block; down between the rigging and the mast, and through the plank fairlead in the top, terminating in the block of a whip.   The standing part of the whip is seized to No. 3 shroud immediately above the three-hole fairlead; up through the block of the whip; down through the first hole in the fairlead on the shroud; and belayed to pin No. 13 in the main-rail, port and starboard.   The remarks regarding the position of the whip block on the lower-topsail clew-line will of course apply in this case.

Alternatively, the whip may be rigged on the yard-arm instead of the running end, (Fig. 149).   The standing end of the downhaul is seized to the upper-topsail yard-arm; led down and through a block on the upper side of the lower-topsail yard-arm-band; back up through the block below the upper-topsail yard-arm; along below the yard to the quarter block; straight down through the fairleads in the top and on the shroud and belayed on pin No. 13.

Bunt-Lines.—These are bent to the foot of the sail; led up through the fairlead thimbles on the fore side; through the bunt-line blocks seized to the jack-stay of the yard; up to a double lead block—one sheave for each bunt-line—shackled to the underside of the cross-trees; down and through the plank fairlead in the top; through holes No. 2 and 3 in the three-hole fairlead on No. 3 shroud, and belayed with the downhaul on pin No. 13 in the main-rail, port and starboard.

Sheets.—Chain. As the upper-topsail is taken in by lowering the yard instead of clewing up the sail, the sheets can be left standing except for occasionally taking up any slack due to stretch etc. They are therefore set up aloft instead of leading down to the deck. The chain is shackled to the clew-iron of the sail; reeved through the cheek-block or sheave in the lower-topsail yard-arm; through the iron fairleads below the yard; over one sheave of the iron clover-leaf block below the centre of the yard; terminating at the upper block of a rope purchase, the lower block of which is shackled to an eye-bolt on the rim of the top, forward of the topmast. The fall is attached to the upper block and reeved until the sheaves are taken up. After setting up taut, the fall is half-hitched round its own parts between the two blocks and finished off in round turns until all is expended and the end is then seized in place.

Another method is to reeve the sheet as described above, and after leaving the clover-leaf block it is taken back along its own part in the series of half-hitches; finally the end is whipped to the standing part. This is indicated diagrammatically on the upper-topgallant sheet in Plate 34.

Many smaller vessels do not rig sheets on upper-topsails, but shackle the clew of the sail directly to a large shackle on the lower-topsail yard-arm. This fitting is shown in the detail of wooden yards on Plate 18.

Fore-Lower-Topgallants.

Clew-Lines.—Shackled to the clew-iron on the sail; taken up through the block below the yard-arm; along below the yard and through the quarter-block; down through the fairlead at the cross-trees; through the plank fairlead in the top; down through the first hole in the three-hole fairlead on No. 4 shroud and belayed to pin No. 15 in the main-rail, port and starboard. Whips may be rigged on the end of the clew-lines if considered necessary, or arranged on the yard-arms as shown in Fig. 149 for the lower-topsail yard.

Bunt-Lines.—Bent to the foot of the sail; led up the fore side and through the thimble fairleads on the sail; through the bunt-line blocks seized to the

M

jack-stay; up through a double block—one sheave for each bunt-line—seized to the forward shroud of the topgallant rigging; down through a fairlead at the cross-trees; through the fairlead plank in the top; down through the second and third holes in the fairlead on No. 4 shroud, and belayed on pin No. 15, main-rail, port and starboard—with the clew-lines. The alternative methods already described may be used to rig the bunt-lines of any sail to which they could be applied.

Sheet.—The upper sheets are usually composed of a combination of chain, wire and rope purchase. The chain is used in way of blocks and sheaves when the sheet is under load, this may be taken to mean that the sheet will be chain from the clew of the sail to just past the clover-leaf block when sail is set. The object of this is, that under load the sheet will be continually running backward and forward a few inches each way, due to the working of the spars, etc., and in so doing the portion round the sheaves will be bending and straightening over and over again, which would soon fatigue wire just as you can break a piece of wire by bending it backwards and forwards. With chain it is different, each link is a separate unit and the chain can run round the sheave without bending the actual metal. There is no need to carry chain past what is the last sheave when sail is set, for although the wire will be hauled round some of the sheaves when sail is furled, it is not then under load and continually working, but only travels over the sheaves once each way, i.e., going up and coming down. One other point is that the sheets of the upper sails have to pass a number of fairleads, for which wire has the advantage of being smaller and running more freely.

Now to return to the lower-topgallant sheets. The chain is shackled to the clew-iron of the sail; led through the cheek-block or sheave in the upper-topsail yard-arm; along through the iron fairleads below the yard; through the clover-leaf sheet block below the centre of the yard and so down. The wire will be spliced into the chain just below the clover-leaf block, the splice being neatly made to enable it to run through the blocks; it then passes down through the fairlead in the cross-trees; through the plank fairlead in the top, and shackles to the block of the whip. The standing part of the whip is made fast to shroud No. 4 immediately above the fairlead; leads up through the block of the whip; and belays on pin No. 14 in the main-rail, port and starboard.

Fore-Upper-Topgallant.

Downhaul.—The eye-splice in the standing end is shackled to the lower-topgallant yard-arm; leads up through the block below the upper-topgallant yard-arm; along below the yard and through the quarter-block; down and through the fairlead in the cross-trees; down through the plank fairlead in the top, and ending in the single block of the whip. The standing part of the whip is seized to No. 5 shroud immediately above the three-hole fairlead; reeved through block of the whip, back down through the first hole in the fairlead on the stay and belays to pin No. 17 in the main-rail port and starboard. Alternatively the downhaul may be rigged with the whip at the yard-arm as shown in Fig. 149, instead of between the top and the deck.

Bunt-Lines.—These are bent to the foot of the sail; led up through the thimble fairleads on the fore side; through bunt-line blocks seized to the jack-stay on the yard; through a double sheave block—one sheave for each bunt-line—at the topgallant-hounds; down the mast and through the fairlead at the cross-trees; through the plank fairlead in the top; through the second and third holes in the three hole fairlead on No. 5 shroud and belayed on pin No. 17 in the main-rail, port and starboard—with the downhaul.

Sheet.—Chain. Shackled to the clew-iron of the sail; led down through the cheek-block or sheave in the lower-topgallant yard-arm; along through the iron fairleads below the yard; through the clover-leaf block below the centre of the yard, and either set up at the cross-trees with a rope purchase, or hitched along its own part and seized, all as described for the upper topsail sheet.

Single Fore-Topgallant.
(Clewing up to Slings.)

Although I have taken as my example a single topgallant which clews up to the slings, this of course only illustrates one of the many combinations possible, and single topgallants may also clew up to the quarters or the yard-arms, in fact the latter may be said to be the most common rig with ships of the iron and steel period.

The lead of the bunt-lines and leech-lines is also subject to many variations, only a few of which can be mentioned here. So again the model builder must be guided by his sail and rigging plan, or such information as can be obtained by research and from photographs. However I will have more to say about plans and photographs later in this chapter.

We will start with the rig as shown on the right hand side of Plate 34.

Clew-Lines.—A single block is shackled to the band at the slings, and another bent to the thimble in the clew-iron on the after side of the sail—(Fig. 121). The standing-end of the clew-line is bent to the yard, outside the band just mentioned, or may be shackled to a thimble on the upper block. From the yard it is taken down the after side of the sail; through the block at the clew; up and through the block at the slings; down through the fairlead in the cross-trees; through the plank fairlead in the top; through the fairlead on No. 4 shroud, and is belayed on pin No. 15 in the main-rail, port and starboard.

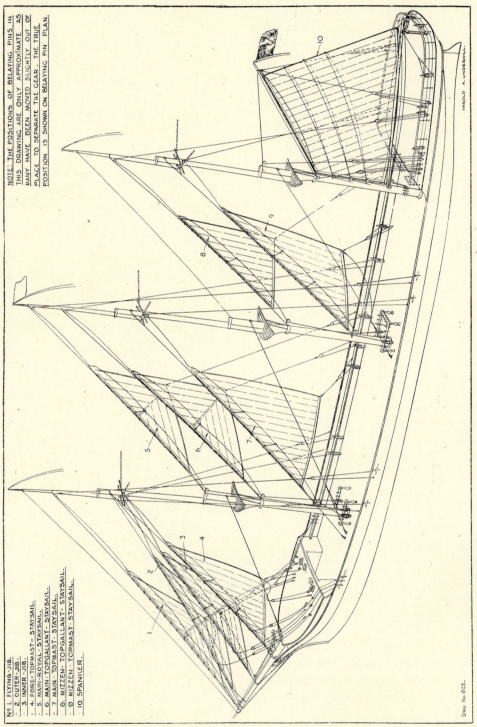

NOTE: THE POSITIONS OF BELAYING PINS IN THIS DRAWING ARE ONLY APPROXIMATE AS MANY HAVE BEEN MOVED SLIGHTLY OUT OF PLACE TO SEPARATE THE GEAR. THE TRUE POSITION IS SHOWN ON BELAYING PIN PLAN.

No 1. FLYING-JIB.
" 2. OUTER-JIB.
" 3. INNER-JIB.
" 4. FORE-TOPMAST-STAYSAIL.
" 5. MAIN-ROYAL-STAYSAIL.
" 6. MAIN-TOPGALLANT-STAYSAIL.
" 7. MAIN-TOPMAST-STAYSAIL.
" 8. MIZZEN-TOPGALLANT-STAYSAIL.
" 9. MIZZEN-TOPMAST-STAYSAIL.
" 10. SPANKER.

DRG No 622.

HAROLD A. UNDERHILL.

PLATE No. 31.—RUNNING RIGGING ON FORE AND AFT SAILS.

Bunt-Lines.—In this example there is only one per side. It is bent to the foot of the sail in the usual way; taken diagonally up through the fairlead thimbles on the fore side of the sail; through the bunt-line block seized to the jack-stay of the yard; through one sheave of the double block at the topgallant-hounds—the other sheave being for the leech-line—down the mast and through the fairleads in the cross-trees and decking of the top; through the fairlead on No. 4 shroud and belayed on Pin No. 15 in the main-rail port and starboard.

One alternative is shown in Fig. 151A. Here two bunt-lines are rigged per side, one serving as combined bunt-line and leech-line. The inner one leads as described above, but the standing-end of the outer is bent to the leech-line cringle on the leech of the sail; taken down the fore side, and reeved through a bull's-eye attached by a short strop to the outer bunt-line cringle on the foot of the sail; up through the thimble fairlead(s) on the sail; through the outer bunt-line block seized to the jack-stay of the yard; through the second sheave of the double block at the hounds; down through fairleads in the cross-trees, top, and on No. 4 shroud, and belays with the bunt-line on pin No. 15 port and starboard. This lead may be reversed by bending the line to the bunt-line-cringle at the foot of the sail, and the bull's-eye to the leech-line-cringle. However this is not so common.

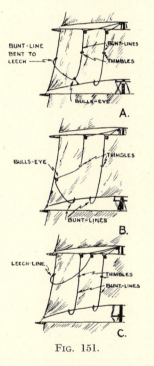

FIG. 151.

The four-mast barque *Star of Lapland*, owned by the Alaska Packers Association, is one example of outer bunt-lines "snaked" up the face of the sail, and there are other variations of this lead. The *Star of Lapland* bent her outer bunt-lines to the usual cringle at the foot of the sail; then across and through a bull's-eye on the leech; back into the original line by reeving through the normal thimble fairlead on the sail; up and through the outer buntline block on the yard, and so down the mast to the deck, (Fig. 151B). She was, by the way, rigged with double topsails and topgallants.

Leech-Lines.—Bent to the leech-line-cringle on the leech of the sail; across the fore side and up through the leech-line-block seized to the jack-stay of theyard; up over the second sheave of the double block at the hounds; down through the fairleads in the cross-trees, top, and on No. 4 shroud, and belayed with the bunt-lines on pin No. 15 in the main-rail, port and starboard.

When more than one bunt-line is carried per side, the leech-line may either be rigged outside the outer bunt-line as shown on the course in Plate 34, or the leech-line block on the yard may be placed inside the outer bunt-line block, as in (Fig. 151c) in which case the leech-line crosses the outer bunt-line on the fore side of the sail. This lead may apply to any sail, including the courses.

Sheets.—The chain is shackled to the clew of the sail; reeved down through the cheek-block or sheave in the topsail yard-arm; along through fairleads below the yard; through the clover-leaf block below the centre of the yard and extends a few feet down the mast. At this point the wire is bent on, and continues through the plank fairlead in the top; is spliced round or shackled to the block of the whip. The standing end of the whip is seized to a convenient eye-bolt or on No. 4 shroud, and is reeved through the block; down through the fairlead on the shroud, and belayed on pin No. 14 in the main-rail, port and starboard.

Fore-Royal.

Clew-Lines.—Shackled to the clew of the sail; led up and through the block below the yard-arm; along below the yard and through the quarter-block; down the mast and through fairleads in the cross-trees, and top; through No. 1 hole in the three-hole fairlead on No. 6 shroud; belayed to pin No. 19 in the main-rail, port and starboard.

When the sail clews up to the slings or the quarters, the clew line is bent to the thimble on the inside of the clew-iron; leads up through a block below the sling of the yard, and so down to the deck as described above.

Bunt-Lines.—Bent to the foot of the sail; led up through the fairlead thimbles on the fore side; through the bunt-line block seized to the jack-stay of the yard; through a double block at the royal-hounds—one sheave for each bunt-line; down the mast and through fairleads in cross-trees, and top; through Nos. 2 and 3 holes in the fairlead on No. 6 shroud, and belays with the clew-line on pin No. 19 in the main-rail, port and starboard.

When the sail clews up to the slings the lead of the bunt-lines will be the same, although they will be reduced one per side as shown in the plate.

Leech-Lines. (When rigged)—Bent to the leech of the sail; led across the fore side and through the leech-line-block on the yard; over one sheave of the bunt-line lead block at the royal hounds; down through fairleads in the cross-trees and top; through No. 2 hole in the fairlead on No. 6 shroud —in this example No. 3 hole would be occupied by the bunt-line; and belayed with the bunt-line on pin No. 19 in the main-rail, port and starboard.

Sheets.—The chain is shackled to the clew of the sail; reeved down through the cheek-block or sheave in the topgallant yard-arm; along below the yard and through the clover-leaf block below the centre; bent on to the wire, which continues down the mast and through fairleads in cross-trees and top; and belays on pin No. 18 in the main-rail, port and starboard.

Before going any further I had better point out that in producing the three fairlead diagrams, Plates 36, 37 and 38, and in quoting the shrouds down which the various items of gear are led, I have based my description on a vessel rigged with six shrouds per side and carrying royals above double-topgallants and double-topsails. In the case of a vessel carrying the same number of sails aloft, but having only five shrouds, the fairlead and all the gear for the royal would be carried on the lower-cap-stay. On the other hand should she carry six shrouds but have single topgallants aloft, then the gear of the royals would move forward to the fifth shroud. If in setting out your belaying pins, you always start with the courses on No. 1 shroud and work aft, you can't go far wrong. The pins serving such gear as staysail halliards etc., will of course be placed adjacent to their respective stays, no matter whether the square-sail gear finishes on the fifth or sixth shroud, or on the cap-stay.

Main-Sail or Main-Course.

Lifts.—Rigged as on fore-sail; belayed on pin No. 64 in main-rail, port and starboard.

Clew-Garnets.—As on fore-sail; belayed on pin No. 47 in main-rail, port and starboard.

Bunt-Lines.—As on fore-sail; belayed on pin No. 46 in main-rail, port and starboard.

Leech-Lines.—As on fore-sail; belayed with bunt-lines on pin No. 46 port and starboard.

Slab-Lines.—(If carried). As on fore-sail.

Reef-Tackles.—(If carried). As on fore-sail.

Sheets.—Made up as on fore-sail. Single sheet leads from clew of sail; through sheaved fairlead No. 117 in bulwarks; under chess-tree on the rail stanchion, and belays on the bitts No. 74 on the main-rail, port and starboard.

Double sheets are shackled to the eye-bolt or chain-plate No. 116 on the outside of the bulwarks; leads through a single block on the clew of the sail; in through the sheaved fairlead No. 117; under the chess-tree and belays on bitts No. 74 port and starboard.

Tack.—Made up as on fore-sail; led forward and is belayed on the fore-sheet bitts No. 38 on the weather side of the main-rail.

Lazy-Tack and Lazy-Sheet.—Made up as on fore-sail; when in use as lazy-tack it belays on pin No. 39 port or starboard as required.

Bowline-Bridle and Lizard.—Rigged as on fore-sail.

Bowline.—Standing-end is hitched to the main-topmast-stay just above the fore fife-rail; the running-end is then reeved through the outer bull's eye in the lizard; taken forward to the fore fife-rail and belayed on either pin No. 30 on the port side, or pin No. 34 on the starboard.

Main-Lower-Topsail.

Clew-Lines.—As on fore-lower-topsail; belayed on pin No. 48 in main-rail, port and starboard.

Bunt-Lines.—As on fore-lower-topsail; belayed on pin No. 48 port and starboard—with the bunt-lines.

Sheets.—As on fore-lower-topsail; belayed on pin No. 70 port and starboard on spider-band round mast.

Main-Upper-Topsail.

Downhaul.—As on fore-upper-topsail; belayed on pin No. 49 in main-rail, port and starboard.

Bunt-Lines.—As on fore-upper-topsail; belayed with downhaul on pin No. 49 main-rail, port and starboard.

Sheets.—Rigged and set up aloft as on fore-upper-topsail.

Main-Lower-Topgallant.

Clew-Lines.—As on fore-lower-topgallants; belayed on pin No. 51 in main-rail, port and starboard.

Bunt-Lines.—As on fore-lower-topgallant; belayed on pin No. 51 main-rail, port and starboard—with the clew-lines.

Sheets.—As on fore-lower-topgallant; belayed on pin No. 50 in main-rail port and starboard.

Main-Upper-Topgallant.

Downhaul.—As on fore-upper-topgallant; belayed on pin No. 52 in main-rail, port and starboard.

Bunt-Lines.—As on fore-upper-topgallant; belayed with downhaul on pin No. 52 in main-rail, port and starboard.

Sheet.—As on fore-upper-topgallant; rigged and set up aloft.

Single Main Topgallant.

Clew-Lines.—As on fore-topgallant; belayed on pin No. 52 in main-rail, port and starboard.

Bunt-Lines.—As on fore-topgallant; belayed on pin No. 51 in main-rail, port and starboard.

Leech-Lines.—As on fore-topgallant; belayed with the bunt-lines on pin No. 51 port and starboard.

Sheets.—As on fore-topgallant; belayed on pin No. 50 in main-rail, port and starboard.

Main-Royal.

Clew-Lines.—As on fore-royal; belayed on pin No. 54 in main-rail, port and starboard.

Bunt-Lines.—As on fore-royal; belayed with bunt-lines on in No. 54 port and starboard.

Leech-Lines.—(When rigged.) As on fore-royal; belayed with bunt-line on pin No. 54 in main-rail, port and starboard.

Sheets.—As on fore-royal; belayed on pin No. 53 in main-rail, port and starboard.

Cro'jack or Mizzen-Course.
This sail is not carried in all ships.

Lifts.—As on fore-sail; belayed on pin No. 135 on the mizzen spider-band.

Clew-Garnets.—As on fore-sail; belayed on pin No. 83 in main-rail, port and starboard.

Bunt-Lines.—As on fore-sail; belayed on pin No. 82 in main-rail, port and starboard.

Leech-Lines.—As on fore-sail; belayed on pin No. 82 with the bunt-lines.

Reef-Tackle.—(When carried). As on fore-sail.

Sheet.—Rigged as on fore-sail; led inboard through the normal mooring fairlead on the after end of the poop, and belayed on bitts No. 104 on port and starboard sides of the poop. If rigged double; standing-end shackles to chain-plate outside hull and adjacent to the fairlead; running-part is reeved through a single block on the clew of the sail; in through the fairlead and belayed on the bitts—No. 104.

Tack.—Rigged as on fore-sail; taken forward and belayed to main-sheet bitts No. 74 on the weather side.

Lazy-Tack and Lazy-Sheet.—Rigged as on fore-sail; when in use as lazy-tack will be belayed on pin No. 75 port, or 76 starboard, whichever is required.

Bowline-Bridle and Lizard.—As on fore-sail.

Bowline.—Standing-end bent to the mizzen topmast-stay above the main

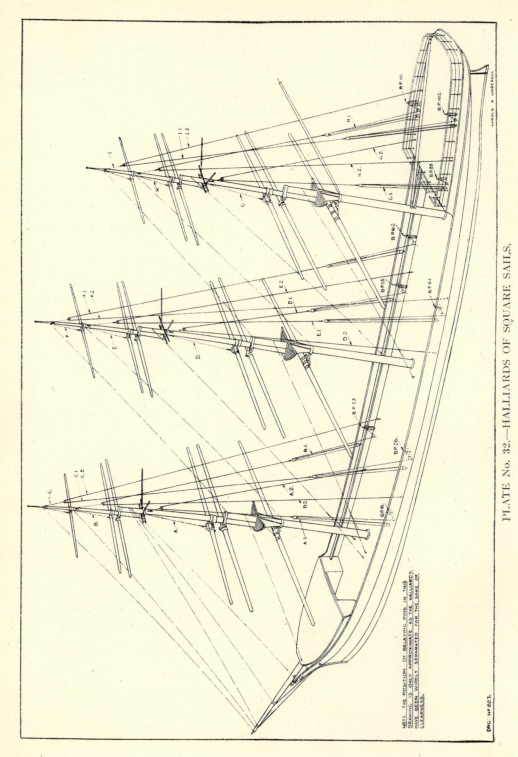

NOTE. THE POSITION OF BELAYING PINS IN THIS DRAWING IS ONLY APPROXIMATE AS THE HALLIARDS HAVE BEEN WIDELY SEPARATED FOR THE SAKE OF CLEARNESS.

DRG. No 823.

HAROLD A. UNDERHILL

PLATE No. 32.—HALLIARDS OF SQUARE SAILS.

fife-rail. Running-part reeved through outer bull's-eye on the lizard and and belayed to any convenient pin in main fife-rail.

Spilling-Lines.—As on fore-sail.

Mizzen-Lower-Topsail.

Clew-Lines.—As on fore-lower-topsail; belayed on pin No. 84 in poop rail, port and starboard.

Bunt-Lines.—As on fore-lower-topsail; belayed with clew-line on pin No. 84 in poop rail, port and starboard.

Sheet.—As on fore-lower-topsail; belayed on pin No. 108 on mizzen spider-band, port and starboard.

Mizzen-Upper-Topsail.

Downhauls.—As on fore-upper-topsail; belayed on pin No. 85 in poop rail, port and starboard.

Bunt-Lines.—As on fore-upper-topsail; belayed with down-hauls on pin No. 85 poop rail, port and starboard.

Sheets.—As on fore-upper-topsail: rigged and set up aloft, or shackled to yard-arms.

Mizzen-Lower-Topgallant.

Clew-Lines.—As on fore-lower-topgallant; belayed on pin No. 87 on poop rail, port and starboard.

Bunt-Lines.—As on fore-lower-topgallant; belayed with clew-lines on pin No. 87, port and starboard.

Sheet.—As on fore-lower-topgallant; belayed on pin No. 86 poop rail, port and starboard.

Mizzen-Upper-Topgallant.

Downhauls.—As on fore-upper-topgallant; belayed on pin No. 90 poop rail, port and starboard.

Bunt-Lines.—As on fore-upper-topgallant; belayed with downhaul on pin No. 90 port and starboard.

Sheets.—Rigged and set up aloft as on fore-upper-topgallant.

Single-Mizzen-Topgallant.

Clew-Lines.—As on fore-topgallant; belayed on pin No. 87 in poop rail, port and starboard.

Bunt-Lines.—As on fore-topgallant; belayed with the clew-lines on pin No. 87 port and starboard.

Leech-Lines.—As on fore-topgallant; belayed on pin No. 87 with clew-lines and bunt-lines, port and starboard.

Sheet.—As on fore-topgallant; belayed on pin No. 86 poop rail, port and starboard.

Mizzen-Royal.

Clew-Lines.—As on fore-royal; belayed on pin No. 92 on poop rail, port and starboard.

Bunt-lines.—As on fore-royal; belayed on pin No. 92 on poop rail, port and starboard.

Leech-Lines.—As on fore-royal; belayed with bunt-lines on pin No. 92 in poop rail, port and starboard.

Sheets.—As on fore royal; belayed on pin No. 91 in poop rail, port and starboard.

Single Topsails.

So far I have said little about the gear on single topsails, but I think that by now, the reader will have sufficiently grasped the general principles to be able to rig the single sail without further detailed description. Fig. 152

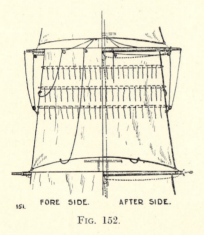

FORE SIDE.   AFTER SIDE.

151.

Fig. 152.

shows the fore and aft sides of a typical single sail, and clearly indicates the gear carried. The lead down to the rail will be as already described, and its belaying points will be grouped round No. 2 shroud. The number and arrangement of bunt-lines and leech-lines will vary in different ships, but this will not affect the run of the gear down the mast. Single topgallants will of course be rigged over single topsails.

What happens to the running gear when the sails are unbent and the ship left under bare poles? This will be of interest to many model builders, as the great majority of models show ships with sails unbent. Personally I think this rather a pity. On a model of decent size, sails properly furled look very well and show the model rigged as for sea without the sails hiding most of the work. I never did like the look of a ship "High and dry" on a stand with all canvas set, I feel that if the sails are to be sheeted home it should be on a water line model. However this is just a personal angle, and no doubt there is much one can say against it.

Incidentally, in building a model with sails furled, it is very necessary to see that they do not look clumsy or heavy, and the sails should be made specially for the purpose of furling. It is rarely possible to obtain material of scale *thickness*, and the depth of the sail should be reduced out of scale, until it is found by experiment just what is required to produce a furl of true proportions. When this has been found the sails should be properly made—except for depth—and bent to the yards. The result at this stage will look extremely silly, for such sails as double-topsails or topgallants may prove to be only half their proper depth, but this will not matter on a show-case model as sails once furled are not likely to be set again, it would be several months spare time work to cast off all gear and re-belay!

The same thing applies to staysails, the length along the foot will be to scale, but the luff and leech will require to be shortened. With standing spankers the luff will be to scale and the foot and head reduced, while with spankers set on hoisting gaffs the opposite will apply.

When the sails of a ship are unbent, and stowed away in the sail room, and she is likely to lay up for some length of time; much of the running gear, such as bunt-lines, etc., will be unreeved and stowed away too; sheets, clew-lines and downhauls will be left rigged at all times as they tend to stiffen the yards. If the turn round is likely to be rapid, then the lighter gear may remain aloft, and the modeller may make his own choice as to whether he rigs it or not.

The drawing on the edge of Plate 39 shows the appearance of the yard-arms when sails are unbent. It will be seen that in each case, the clew-line and sheet have been unshackled from the clew of the sail and shackled together to form a continuous line. They are then set up taut and so keep the yards well supported. Without this the lower-topsail and lower-topgallant yards, which have no lifts, would be hanging solely from their trusses and would tend to sag at the yard-arms. The upper-topsail and upper-topgallant sheets may either be seized to their own parts as shown, or alternatively the downhaul can be unshackled from the yard-arm and shackled to the end of the sheet.

Staysail halliards and downhauls are usually shackled together near the foot of the stay, all ready to go back on to the sail when it is bent. Bunt-line, leech-lines, etc., when left aloft, will be hitched to their own parts at the bunt-line or leech-line block on the yard, or hitched to the jack-stay near the block.

Braces.

In designing the lead of braces it is necessary to see that they do not impede the lowering of the yards. If, for example, the lead block on the adjacent mast is placed level with the yard in its hoisted position, the brace will have to be slacked away before the yard can come down. This can best be explained on the diagram Fig. 153, where "A" is the yard at full hoist; "B" the yard down; "C", "D" and "E" alternative positions for the lead block

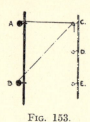

FIG. 153.

on the adjacent mast. It will be clear that if the lead block is on the same level as the hoisted yard—position "C", the distance "A"-"C" is much shorter than "B"-"C", and should the yard be let go in a hurry without first slacking away the braces, it will probably jamb half way down, or something will carry away. Obviously the best position for the lead block would be "D" which is half way down the travel of the yard, for in this case the braces would slacken off and tighten up again as the yard came down, finishing just as taut as when at full hoist.

There may be many reasons why it is not possible to obtain this ideal position; the braces must pass between the head of one sail and the foot of another on the mast next abaft, and even if that mast is fore-and-aft rigged, the lead block must be attached to the nearest convenient fixture on the mast. The location of the lead block must therefore always be something of a compromise, and when the ideal position "D" cannot be obtained, it is advisable to take the next best below, rather than above.

Another point which requires watching is the lead of the cro'jack braces on a full-rigged ship. If the mizzen mast is stepped rather close abaft the main relative to length of the yards, as was often the case in the older ships, the cro'jack braces may foul the main backstays when the yards are braced up. This should be worked on paper, and if necessary special bands fitted some distance in from the yard-arms; the brace pendants will then be shackled to these bands instead of to the yard-arms, so bringing the braces nearer the centre of the yard and making them run clear of the main rigging when braced up.

Plate 33 shows the brace layout of a full-rigged ship, this of course is not the only arrangement, but may be taken as typical. One ship which differed was the *Joseph Conrad*, ex-*George Stage*, but she was a very small vessel for ship rig, so small in fact that her life-boats completely filled the space between the fore and main rigging. In her case the lower braces led back to the tops instead of down to the rail. In the case of a barque rigged craft the lead would be as shown, except that all braces would lead aft as the fore and main. This plate must be regarded as a diagram and not a working drawing, for I have moved several belaying pins slightly out of position and omitted the braces from the starboard side, all for the purpose of separating the rigging and making the drawing easy to read. The true lead of the gear and the position of pins will be perfectly clear from the text and the fairlead and belaying pin drawings.

Fore-Mast.

Fore-Brace.—The wire pendant has an eye-splice round a thimble at either end, one being shackled to the lug on the after side of the yard-arm-band and the other to the eye of a single block. Sometimes the pendant is spliced round the actual block instead of being attached by shackle.

The fall is spliced into an eye on the underside of the block on the pendant; reeved through a single block shackled to the bulwarks—for the sake of clearness I have shown this block low down in the drawing, in actual practice it would be on top of the bulwarks. From this last block it passes through the block on the pendant; down and through the forward sister-block on the main-rail; forward along the rail and belays on pin No. 41 port and starboard.

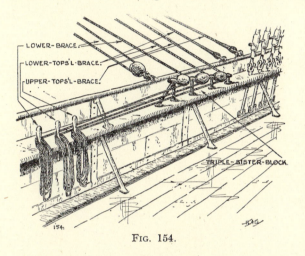

LOWER-BRACE.

LOWER-TOPS'L-BRACE.

UPPER-TOPS'L-BRACE.

TRIPLE-SISTER-BLOCK.

FIG. 154.

Fig. 154 shows the nest of three sister-blocks on the main-rail. The blocks are arranged in line and inclined down towards the stern. They are supported on four iron stanchions of varying length bolted on top of the rail, and connected to the blocks in such a way that the latter are free to rotate on their common centre line, so adjusting themselves to the angle of their individual braces.

Fore-Lower-Topsail-Brace.—The pendant is shackled to the after side of the yard-arm-band, and has a single block either shackled or spliced on the outer end.

The running-part of the brace is seized to the fork of the main-stay just forward of the top, or may be shackled to an eye-bolt on some part of the top if this arrangement will clear the foot of the main-topsail. It then reeves through the block on the pendant and is spliced into the eye of a single block. At this point I will remind the reader of my previous warning. The lengths of the pendants and running-parts of all braces, must be carefully worked out to ensure that the yard can swing in either direction without the block on the running-part fouling either pendant block or bulwarks.

The fall has an eye-splice in the standing-end, by means of which it is shackled to the chain-plate or eye-bolt on top of the bulwarks. The running-end is reeved through the single block on the running-part of the brace; back over the sheave of the centre sister-block; forward along the main-rail to pin No. 42 port and starboard.

Fore-Upper-Topsail-Brace.—The pendant is shackled to the after side of the yard-arm-band and has a single block on the outer end.

The running-part is seized to the head of the main-topmast-stay, or may be shackled to an eye-bolt at the cross-trees if such lead will clear the foot of the main topgallant sail. It then leads forward through the block on the pendant and is eye-spliced into the eye of a single block.

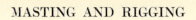

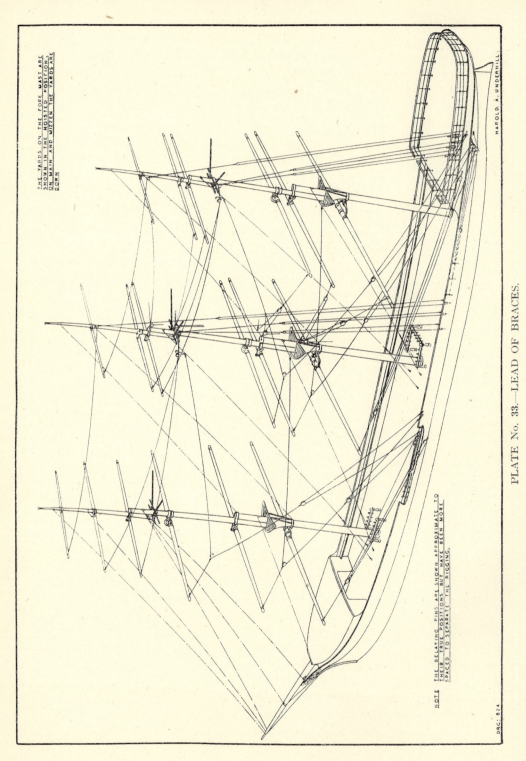

THE YARDS ON THE FORE MAST ARE SHOWN IN THE HOISTED POSITION, ON MAIN AND MIZZEN THE YARDS ARE DOWN

NOTE THE BELAYING PINS ARE SHOWN APPROXIMATELY TO THEIR TRUE POSITIONS, BUT HAVE BEEN MORE SPACED TO SEPARATE THE RIGGING.

DRG. 824   HAROLD A. UNDERHILL.

PLATE No. 33.—LEAD OF BRACES.

The fall is shackled to a chain-plate or eye-bolt on top of the bulwarks; taken forward and through the single block on the running-part; back and through the aftermost sister-block; forward along the main-rail and belayed on pin No. 43 port and starboard.

Fore-Lower-Topgallant-Brace.—This is a single wire and is shackled to the lug on the after side of the yard-arm-band; led aft and over one sheave of a pair of double lead blocks on short strops seized to the head of the main-topmast-stay. The object of these blocks is to keep both upper and lower topgallant braces down below the foot of the main topgallant sail. From the lead-block on the stay the brace is taken up and over one sheave of a double block on the side of the mast below the cross-trees; down abaft the mast and inside the main-topmast backstays, and spliced into the eye of a single block. This block should be about midway between the cross-trees and the deck when the yards are square to ensure free travel without fouling. On the drawing these blocks have been placed where they can best be seen, and not necessarily at their correct levels. The lower part of the brace is in the form of a whip, the standing-end of which is seized to No. 1 main-topmast-backstay near the rail. The running-part of the whip is reeved through the block on the brace; brought down inside No. 2 Main-topmast-backstay and reeved through the forward hole in the fairlead on this stay—see Plate 37, and belayed to pin No. 57 on the main-rail, port and starboard.

Fore-Upper-Topgallant-Brace.—Single wire, shackled to the after side of the yard-arm-band; reeved over the second sheave of the double block on the main-topmast-stay; over the second sheave of the double block on the side of the mast below the cross-trees; and spliced into the eye of a single block for the whip. The standing-end of the whip is seized to the foot of No. 3 main-topmast-backstay; reeved through the single block on the end of the brace; down through the after hole of the fairlead on No. 2 main-topmast-backstay and belayed on pin No. 58 in the main-rail, port and starboard.

Fore-Royal-Brace.—Single wire, shackled to the after side of the yard-arm-band; reeved through a single block on the side of the mast at the main-topgallant-hounds—note, if necessary lead blocks may be rigged on the main-topgallant-stay to keep the brace below the foot of the main-royal sail. If used these lead blocks would be rigged as shown on the main-topmast-stay for the topgallant braces, although of course only single blocks would be required. From the lead block at the hounds the brace goes down inside the backstay and is spliced into the eye of a single block for the whip. The standing end of the whip is seized to the main-topmast-capstay or other convenient point; taken up and through the block; down through the single bull's-eye fairlead on No. 3 main-topmast back-stay and belayed on pin No. 59 in the main-rail, port and starboard.

N

It should be noted that while whips are described on all braces in this example, this does not always apply, and many small vessels carry the upper braces down to the pin direct without using any form of purchase.

Main-Mast.

Bumkin.—The lead blocks of the three lower braces on the main mast are carried outside the vessel on a bumkin—Fig. 155. This consists of a

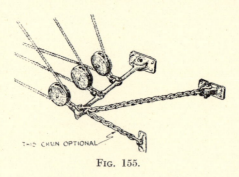

THIS CHAIN OPTIONAL

FIG. 155.

metal bar—wood in some of the older ships—attached to the side of the ship by means of a hinged bracket, which allows it to be swung forward out of the way when in port. The bumkin is held out, and the pull of the braces taken by, a chain which is shackled to a plate on the side of the hull. On the fore side of the bumkin are three metal eyes to which the brace blocks are shackled.

Main-Brace.—The wire pendant shackles to the after side of the yard-arm-band, and has a single block on the outer end.

The fall is spliced into an eye on the underside of the pendant block leads down through a single block on the side of the hull. This block will be up at deck level not low down as shown in the drawing which has been drawn so for the sake of clarity. From the ship's side the fall goes up and over the sheave of the single block on the pendant; back through the outer block on the bumkin; forward and through a fairlead in the bulwarks just on the fore side of the break of the poop; along the top of the main-rail and belays on pin No. 78 in the rail, port and starboard.

Main-Lower-Topsail-Brace.—The wire pendant shackles to the after side of the yard-arm-band and to a single block at the outer end.

The running-part is seized to the mizzen-stay, or shackled to the mizzen top if this will allow the brace to clear the foot of the mizzen-topsail. It is taken forward and through the block on the pendant; the end being spliced into the eye of a single block.

The fall shackles to a chain-plate on the side of the hull at the deck level and above the bumkin; is led forward and through the single block on the running-part; back through the centre lead block on the bumkin; forward through the fairlead in the bulwarks and belays on pin No. 79 in the main-rail port and starboard.

Main-Upper-Topsail-Brace.—The wire pendant shackles to the after side of the yard-arm-band and has a single block on the outer end.

The running-part is seized at the head of the mizzen-topmast-stay, or if it will clear the foot of the mizzen-topgallant, to any convenient point at the cross-trees. It is then taken forward and through the block on the pendant, and spliced into the eye of a single block.

The fall is shackled to a chain-plate on the ship's side above the bumkin; reeved through the block on the running-part of the brace; back through the inner block on the bumkin; forward through the fairlead in the bulwarks; along the top of the main rail and belayed on pin No. 80 port and starboard.

Main-Lower-Topgallant-Brace.—Single wire, shackled to the after side of the yard-arm-band; led aft and over one sheave of a pair of double blocks on short strops seized to the head of the mizzen-topmast-stay; up over one sheave of a double block on the side of the mast below the mizzen cross-trees; down inside the mizzen-topmast-backstays and spliced into the eye of the single block of the whip.

The standing-end of the whip is seized to No. 1 mizzen-topmast-back-stay; taken up and through the block on the brace; down through the forward hole of the fairlead on No. 2 topmast-backstay and belayed on pin No. 97 in poop rail, port and starboard. Plate 39.

Main-Upper-Topgallant-Brace.—Single wire, shackled to the after side of the yard-arm-band; led over the second sheave of the double block on the mizzen-topmast-stay; over the second sheave of the double block below the cross-trees; down inside the mizzen-topmast-backstays and spliced into the eye of a single block for the whip.

The standing end of the whip is seized to No. 3 mizzen-topmast-backstay; reeved through the block on the brace; down through the after hole in the fairlead on No. 2 mizzen-topmast-backstay and belayed on pin No. 98 in the poop rail, port and starboard.

Main-Royal-Brace.—Single wire, shackled to the after side of the yard-arm-band; taken aft and through a single block on the side of the mast at the mizzen topgallant-hounds—if necessary additional lead blocks may be fitted on the mizzen-topgallant-stay to keep the brace below the mizzen royal sail, if used these should be on short wire strops as described for the fore-topgallant-braces. From the block at the hounds the brace comes down inside the backstay and is spliced into the eye of a single block for the whip.

The standing-part of the whip is seized to the mizzen-topmast-capstay just above the rail; led up and through the single block on the brace; down through the single bull's-eye fairlead on No. 3 mizzen-topmast-backstay and belayed on pin No. 99 in the poop rail, port and starboard.

Mizzen-Mast.

Cro'jack-Brace.—The wire pendant shackles to the fore side of the yard-arm-band; or if rigged to a special band inside the yard-arm to a lug on *top*

of the band and so clear of the jack-stay and sail.   A single block is spliced
on to the end of the pendant.

The running-part is shackled to the afterside of the main top; taken
aft and over the sheave of the single block on the pendant; forward and over
one sheave of a double block shackled to the after side of the cheeks of the
main top; down abaft the mast and belayed on pin No. 67 in the main fife-
rail, port and starboard.   No whip is rigged on this brace, as the height from
belaying pin to lead block at main top is less than the distance travelled by
the yard-arm, and therefore the block of a whip would foul at either end before
the yard could complete its swing in either direction.   This applies to the
mizzen-topsail-brace also.

Mizzen-Lower-Topsail-Brace.—The wire pendant is shackled to the fore
side of the yard-arm-band, and spliced into the eye of a single block at the
other end.

The running-part shackles with the cro'jack-brace on the after side of
the main top; it is then led aft and through the single block on the pendant;
forward and over the second sheave of the double block below the top—the
first sheave being taken up by the cro'jack-brace; down abaft the mast and
belayed on pin No. 68 in the main fife-rail, port and starboard.

Mizzen-Upper-Topsail-Brace.—The wire pendant is shackled to the fore
side of the yard-arm-band, and the outer end spliced into the eye of a single
block.

The running-part is seized to the foot of the mizzen-royal-stay immediately above the main lower-mast cap; taken aft and over the sheave of the
single block on the pendant; forward and over one sheave of a double block
on the after side of the main-cap—the second sheave is used for the corresponding brace on the opposite side; down abaft the mast and the after rim
of the top; belays on pin No. 69 in the main fife-rail, port and starboard.

Mizzen-Lower-Topgallant-Brace.—Single wire, shackled to the fore side
of the yard-arm-band; led forward and over one sheave of a pair of double
blocks shackled abaft the main cross-trees; down abaft the mast and belayed
on pin No. 71 in the main fife-rail, port and starboard.   Note, whips are
optional on the upper braces of the mizzen-mast.

Mizzen-Upper-Topgallant-Brace.—Single wire, shackled to the fore side
of the yard-arm-band; led forward over the second sheave of the double
block abaft the main cross-trees; down abaft the mast and belayed on pin
No. 72 in the main fife-rail, port and starboard.

Mizzen-Royal-Brace.—Single wire, shackled to the fore side of the yard-
arm-band; led forward and over one sheave of a double block on the after
side of the main topmast-cap—the second sheave is for the corresponding
brace on the opposite side. From the lead block the brace is taken down abaft
the mast and belayed on pin No. 73 in the main fife-rail, port and starboard.

Brace Winches.

The Jarvis brace winch, Fig. 156, operates the three lower braces, i.e. upper-topsail; lower-topsail, and lower-yard respectively, and may be described briefly as six tapered drums arranged in pairs and keyed on to three parallel shafts, each pair controlling the port and starboard braces of the same yard. Above the centre pair of drums is a fourth shaft having handles or cranks

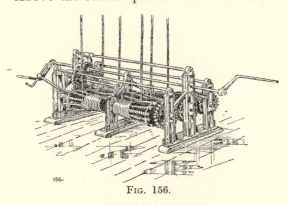

156.

FIG. 156.

on either end, and geared to all three drum shafts. Rotation of the hand crank causes all drums to turn together, and as the port and starboard braces wind on their respective drums from opposite fore and aft sides, one will pay out as the other winds in.

At first sight one would expect to haul in on one side exactly the same amount of brace as is paid out on the other, this *is* the case while the yard is in the neighbourhood of right angles to the centre line of the ship, but as it swings round, the *brace* from the yard-arm which is abaft the mast travels faster than that of the arm which is forward of it. When the yard is at an angle of about 45° to the centre line, the brace from the arm abaft the mast travels about 23 inches for every 17 inches of the brace on the other side, and this difference increases or decreases as the yard goes further round or returns to the square position. All this may perhaps sound rather complicated or even fantastic, but the reader need not accept my word for it as it can easily be checked, either on the drawing board or by calculation, and the fact remains that the winch is so designed to take care of this difference in travel. It is in fact very simple, and all a matter of the changing relation between the angles of the braces on opposite sides of the ship. By the way when trying it out on the drawing board, remember that the yard does not pivot on its own centre, but on the end of an arm—the truss or parral—extending back at right angles to it.

This difference in the travel of opposite braces on the same yard, is taken care of by means of the tapering drums of the winch. In reeving the braces on the drums they are always attached to the small end, and, assuming the yards to be square across the ship, wound on until the centre of the drum is reached, from this point they go to their respective yard-arms via lead blocks which will be described later.

As the centres of all the drums are of the same diameter, it is obvious that at this point the speed of paying out and hauling in on opposite drums will be identical, as is required while the yards are square across.   But as the drums rotate the brace is wound on to an ever increasing diameter on one drum, while its opposite number is unwinding off the steadily decreasing diameter of the other.   The same applies as the yard is swung back, the difference between the two sides decreasing until just at the moment when the yard is square across, the two sides of the brace are respectively running off and on the drums at a point where they are equal in diameter, and therefore hauling in and paying out at the same speed. As the yard continues to swing the braces continue winding on and off their respective drums, and as the centre line of the drum is passed, the brace which was the faster becomes the slower and vice versa.   In this way the winch automatically compensates for the difference in travel, and reduces it to one common speed at the winch shaft.

The drums are built up of iron bars having scores in them to ensure the brace winding fair and not over-riding, and are "nested" as shown in the diagram on Plate 40 to make the winch as compact as possible.   Locking pawls and brakes are provided to give adequate control over the winch, and allow it to be locked when the yards are round in the required position.   The final trim of the yards can be obtained by means of hand tackle as will be described later.

Lead of Braces to the Brace Winch.

As a general description, one may say that when brace winches are fitted the braces are rigged as usual, except that what is normally the standing-end, instead of being shackled or seized to a fixed point is extended back to the winch, so that in actual fact both ends are running-ends.   However we will follow the lead of the braces and make everything clear. All braces above the upper-topsail are reeved in the usual way and belay on their normal pins.

Plate 40 shows a typical arrangement.   A large size single block is provided on either side of the cross-trees above the brace winch.   These blocks are shackled to the lower eyes of two short pendants which are put over the mast with the topmast-backstays.

Two wire pendants are also provided on either side of the lower-mast below the top.   These are formed by making a long wire strop with a metal thimble eye-spliced into each end, the strop is then passed round the mast at the standing-rigging and the two parts seized together to form a long and short leg hanging down through the lubbers-hole.   The part round the mast will be well parcelled and served, and when the pendant is finished the long leg should extend about one-third down the lower-mast.   The pair on the opposite side is made in the same way.

A large size single block is shackled into each of the four pendant eyes, and to steady the pendants and prevent the blocks banging against the mast, short wire spans having an eye-splice in each end are seized between the pendants. Additional spans are seized between the pendants and the shrouds, making a continuous stay from shroud to shroud as shown in the detail on Plate 40. The object of the lead blocks below the top is merely to carry the brace over the deck.

A large diameter double sheave block is shackled to the bulwarks in way of No. 1 shroud; the braces are then reeved as follows.

Lower-Brace.—The usual wire pendant and single block are shackled to the yard-arm. The brace reeves on the forward drum of the brace winch as already described—port brace on one drum, starboard on the other. From the drum it passes up and through the lower lead block below the top; down and through the outer sheave of the lead-block on the bulwarks; forward and through the pendant block; back and through the forward sister-block of the nest on the rail; along on top of the rail and belayed on the forward pin of the group of three, port and starboard. I am not quoting the pins by number, as the rig now being described will of course apply to all the square-rigged masts in the ship, the pins are however the same as those used for the braces without winches.

Lower-Topsail Brace.—Has the usual wire pendant and single block. The brace is reeved on the centre drum, port and starboard; taken up and through the upper lead-block below the top; down and through the inner sheave of the double block on the bulwarks; up and through the pendant block on the yard; down and through the centre sister-block; forward along the mainrail and belayed on the centre belaying pin, port and starboard.

Upper-Topsail-Brace.—Pendant and single block on the yard-arm as usual. The brace is reeved on the after drum of the winch—port and starboard; taken up abaft the mast; through the lead-block below the cross-trees; through the block on the pendant from the yard-arm; and spliced into the eye of a single block. The whip is made fast to an eye-bolt on the bulwarks; led up and through the single block on the brace; back through the after sister-block on the rail; forward along the rail and belayed on the aftermost of the three pins, port and starboard.

There are two minor alternatives to the above, one is to reeve the lower-topsail-brace the same as the upper. To do this two pairs of lead-blocks are fitted below the cross-trees and only one—for the lower-brace—below the top. Another version is to rig whips—as shown on the upper-topsail in the plate—on all three braces, keeping the rest of the lead just as described. However these are very small details and must be settled from the reader's own knowledge of his particular vessel.

The object of the braces belaying on pins as well as reeving on the winch, is to provide a means of taking up any slack due to stretch, or unequal travel

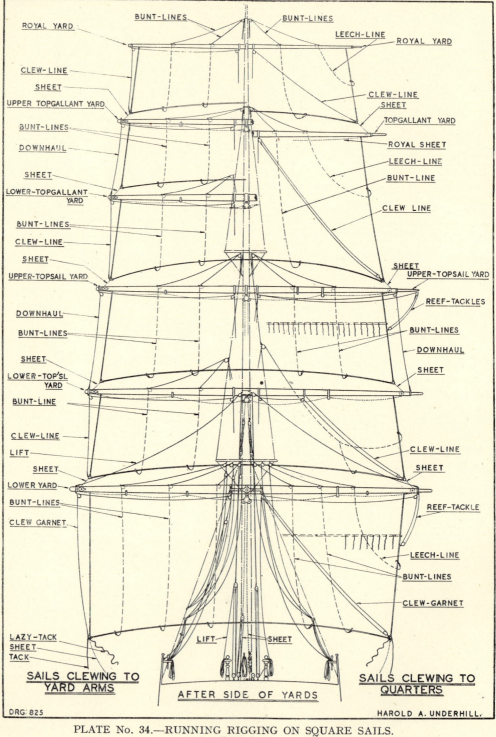

ROYAL YARD

BUNT-LINES   BUNT-LINES

LEECH-LINE   ROYAL YARD

CLEW-LINE

SHEET

UPPER TOPGALLANT YARD

CLEW-LINE
SHEET

TOPGALLANT YARD

BUNT-LINES

DOWNHAUL

ROYAL SHEET

LEECH-LINE

BUNT-LINE

SHEET

LOWER-TOPGALLANT
YARD

CLEW LINE

BUNT-LINES

CLEW-LINE

SHEET

UPPER-TOPSAIL YARD

SHEET
UPPER-TOPSAIL YARD

REEF-TACKLES

DOWNHAUL

BUNT-LINES

BUNT-LINES

DOWNHAUL

SHEET

SHEET

LOWER-TOP'SL
YARD

BUNT-LINE

CLEW-LINE

LIFT

SHEET

LOWER YARD

BUNT-LINES

CLEW GARNET

CLEW-LINE

SHEET

REEF-TACKLE

LEECH-LINE

BUNT-LINES

CLEW-GARNET

LAZY-TACK

SHEET

TACK

LIFT   SHEET

**SAILS CLEWING TO
YARD ARMS**

AFTER SIDE OF YARDS

**SAILS CLEWING TO
QUARTERS**

DRG. 825   HAROLD A. UNDERHILL.

PLATE No. 34.—RUNNING RIGGING ON SQUARE SAILS.
(Sails Set.)

beyond the capacity of the winch to compensate, and for final trimming of the yards. In fact it provides a simple and speedy adjustment for the length of the braces.

Braces of a Brig or Snow.

Most of the square sail gear is the same whether the vessel be rigged as a ship or barque; brig or brigantine; snow or barquentine. The exception is the lead of the braces on a brig or snow rigged vessel, and there are several arrangements peculiar to these rigs, three of which are shown on Plate 41. The upper sketch shows what was perhaps the final development of the brig rig—the term brig is of course intended to include that of the snow also. The lead of the braces on the fore-mast is as already described for the ship rig, namely, the upper braces leading back to the main-mast, and the running-parts of the lower braces going down to the rail. On the main the upper braces are led forward to the fore-mast, and the lower braces down to the rail at the stern.

In the second sketch the fore-mast is rigged as just described, but on the main all braces, including the lower ones, lead forward to the fore-mast. This rig is in fact exactly like the main and mizzen masts of a ship rigged vessel.

The third example is the oldest rig of all. In this case none of the braces lead down to the ship's side, all those on the fore mast leading to the main, and the braces on the main going to the after side of the fore-mast.

Incidentally I have taken advantage of these sketches to illustrate the differences between the brig and the snow. The two upper ones are brigs and the lower a snow. This has nothing to do with the lead of the gear, the only difference being that the spanker of the brig is hooped on the lower-mast itself, while that of the snow is hooped to a small trysail-mast abaft the lower main-mast.

In this chapter I have based most of my details on a full-rigged ship because it is the most complicated rig, and if that is mastered the reader will have no difficulty in rigging a barque. After all, if you strip the yards off the mizzen—as was in fact done with many ship-rigged vessels during the last days of sail—you have the complete barque rig, the only difference in the case of a vessel built as a barque being that the mizzen lower-mast and spanker will be rather larger in proportion, and she would have a topmast but no topgallant. If you want a four-mast barque, it is only a matter of adding another square-rigged mast and you have it.

The brigantine and barquentine rigs are simply a square-rigged mast as already described with one or more fore and aft rigged masts abaft it. The fore and aft sails will most likely have hoisting gaffs instead of the standing gaff of the full-rigged ship, but as the gear on these will be much the same as that of the coasting schooner, there is no need to repeat it here.

Studding-Sails.

Studding-sails, or stun'sls as they are more commonly called, belong to the clipper era, and disappeared with the passing of the thorough bred. The call for speed was replaced by the demand for carrying capacity and economy in running, and the later day ship had neither need for, nor the men to handle these flying kites.

There is a tendency to regard the rig of stun'sl gear as something mysterious and beyond all understanding; something in the nature of a secret passed down, only to be lost in the end; but there really is nothing extraordinary about it. It is true that the lead of the gear is rarely seen in any sail and rigging plan, but as will be seen later, that may be said to apply to running gear in general. It is also true that stun'sl gear varied considerably in different ships, but that is understandable when one remembers that most of it was sent aloft and reeved off only when required, and did not form part of the permanent gear of the ship. It is to be expected that ship masters would form their own pet ideas and theories as to the best place for this or that block and have these ideas carried out in their own ships.

Two types of spar were used in setting stun'sls; a yard which was laced to the head, and a boom to extend the foot. The upper stun'sls-booms were carried on the square yards immediately below the sails they served, and were supported by the inner and outer boom-irons as detailed in chapter III.

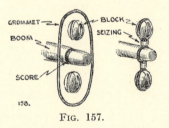

GROMMET   BLOCK

BOOM   SEIZING

SCORE

158.

Fig. 157.

The booms themselves were of constant diameter for the length which doubles on the yard, and tapered from the outer boom-iron to the end. The diameter at the end of the taper should be two-thirds the diameter at the heel. The inner end—or heel—has a hole bored through it, or in some cases thumb-cleats fitted, for the heel-lashing; while the outer end has a score round its circumference a few inches in, this is to take the strop of the jewel-block, or blocks. (Fig. 157).

Small single sheaved blocks called jewel-blocks, are attached to the spar by means of a large grommet which passes round both blocks and spar, with a seizing between them, so forming a combined block strop and spar band as in the sketch referred to. The topmast-stuns'l-boom has a jewel-block above and below the boom, while the rest have blocks on top only.

The lower-stun'sl-boom or swinging-boom, is attached to the ship's side by means of a goose-neck bolted to the bulwark plating, or in the case of ship's having their standing-rigging set up to outside channels, the goose-neck is on the outer edge of the fore-channels in way of No. 1 shroud. Lower-stun'sls are not carried on the main, so no boom is required. When not in use the boom is swung aft along the hull and the after end clamped in a bracket projecting from the ship's side. This bracket has sufficient projection to line up with the channels, or to allow for the curvature of the hull in the case of ships having the standing-rigging set up inside the bulwarks. At sea in areas where stuns'ls were not likely to be rigged, the boom would be unshipped and carried on deck with the spare spars. In harbour the spar was often used as a boat-boom to which boats in the water were made fast to keep them clear of the ship's side.

The boom may either be fitted with rigging bands as shown in Plate 42 or thumb cleats forming stops may be used. Also in older vessels a large hook in the end of the boom and an eye-bolt in the channels, took the place of the goose-neck.

Upper stun'sl-booms were rigged out and in on their respective yards by means of a light tackle known as a jigger. When rigged out, the inner jigger-block was hooked into a wire strop reeved through the hole in the heel of the boom, and the outer block hooked to a grommet on the neck of the outer-boom-iron; the fall led along the yard, see sketch on Plate 42. For rigging in the boom, the outer-block was transferred to some fixed point inboard, such as the truss of the yard or a strop round the mast, and the boom hauled in along the yard. When once the boom was rigged out it was held in position by a heel-lashing round the boom; through the hole in the heel; and round the neck of the inner-boom-iron.

The proportions of stun'sl-booms will be given in chapter IX, but the size and shape of the sails will require to be taken from the sail and rigging plan. If this is not available it is possible to form some idea of the size of the sails from certain known factors. Firstly the length of stun'sl-booms, these are usually half the total length of the yard on which they are carried. Secondly, the stun'sl-boom doubles on the yard one-third its own length, plus of course the length taken up by the heel-lashing; and from this the outboard projection of the boom can be obtained, which fixes the width of the sail at the foot.

Stun'sl-yards have a slight taper from the centre towards the outer ends, which are provided with thumb-cleats for lashing out the head-earings, and allowance must be made for the earings when estimating the length of the yards. The head of the sail is laced to the yard by passing the line round the yard and through the eyelets in the sail, this may be done as a simple spiral lacing, or half-hitched at every turn. The halliard may either be bent to the centre of the yard with thumb-cleats on either side to prevent slipping, or the thumb-cleats may be fitted one-quarter in from either end with a span between them to which the halliard is bent.

Plate 42 is a perspective drawing illustrating a suite of stun'sls and their gear, and in the following description the numbers quoted will refer to those shown on the plate.

Rigging the Lower-Studding-Sail-Boom or Swinging-Boom.

Martingale (1)—The object of the martingale is to prevent the boom rising under the pull of the sail. The outer end is shackled to the lug below the centre-band, or in the case of older ships, would be spliced round the boom against centre stops. By the way, although this band is referred to as the centre-band, it is really fitted at a point one-third in from the outer end. From the boom the martingale goes down and through a block shackled to an eye-bolt on the ship's side; up the side and over the rail; and belayed to the most convenient pin in the main-rail. The martingale was not rigged in all ships.

Boom-Guys. (2)—A single block is shackled to either side of the centre-band, one forward and the other aft. The forward guy is made fast on the fo'castle; taken back and reeved through the block on the forward side of the boom; led forward again and belayed to a convenient point near the standing-end. The after guy is made fast to the main rigging; led forward and through the block on the boom, and back to a point near No. 1 main shroud.

Topping-Lift. (3)—This shackles to the top of the inner-band, or is spliced round the boom in the case of older ships; reeves through a single block seized to the yard-arm-band of the lower-yard; up and through a single block on a short strop round the mast above the lower-cap; down through the lubbers-hole and belayed to the spider-band or fife-rail.

Lower-Studding-Sail.

Yard.—The lower-stun'sl-yard does not extend the full width of the sail but is laced along the outboard side of the head. The length should be twice the projection of the sail beyond the topmast-stun'sl-boom, plus an allowance for the earings.

Outer-Halliard. (4)—The lower-stun'sl has two halliards, the outer one is bent to the centre of the stun'sl-yard; reeved up through a jewel-block on the underside of the topmast-stunsl'-boom; up and through a single block on the end of a pendant put over the topmast at the cross-trees (5); down and through a lead-block on deck at the foot of the mast; up to the spider-band and belayed.

There are several alternative leads for this halliard beyond the jewel-block on the topmast-stun'sl-boom. One is to hook the second lead-block to a short strop at the lower-cap instead of the cross-trees; another, to seize this lead-block to the standing-rigging below the top. However, the method shown in the plate has the obvious advantage of taking the pull well up the mast and so putting less load on the topmast-stun'sl-boom. The lower you place the lead-block, the more weight the boom will have to carry.

Inner-Halliard. (6)—The second halliard supports the inner half of the sail. A single block is bent to the inner earing-cringle at the head of the sail and another block seized to the rim of the top, or to the topmast-rigging at the top. The fall is reeved through these blocks and the running-end taken down to the deck where it is belayed.

Alternatively the inner-block may be hooked to a strop put round the topmast immediately above the lower-cap. This of course will give a more upward pull to the head of the sail. Another alternative is to seize the inner block to the quarter-band of the lower-yard, and so to the deck.

Clew-Line or Tripping-Line. (7)—The clew-line is bent to the outer clew of the sail; taken up and through a jewel-block seized to the inner end of the lower stun'sl-yard; led along below the lower-yard and through a single block seized to the quarter-band; down to the deck and belayed on the fife-rail.

Instead of putting the last named block on the yard, it may be seized to the lower rigging, or any other convenient point that will provide a good lead down to the deck.

Tack. (8)—The tack is bent or toggled to the outer clew of the sail; reeved through a small block on top of the outer end of the swinging-boom; taken aft and through a single block on the main shrouds at bulwark level; down to the pin-rail and belayed on any convenient pin.

If the vessel has the standing-rigging set up to outside channels, the lead block will be shackled to an eye-bolt on the fore edge of the main-channels, and the tack taken inboard through the nearest port.

Sheets. (9)—The sheets are double. A single line long enough to form both sheets, is middled and the bight put through the inner clew-cringle; the

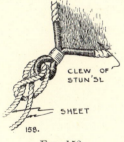

two ends are then reeved through the bight and pulled taut, (Fig. 158). There are two ways of reeving the sheets, one as shown in Plate 42 where the sheet is reeved through a single block at the goose-neck of the swinging-boom; brought over the rail and belayed on deck. The other sheet is brought over the rail and is available for use as a lazy-sheet. The second method dispenses with the block on the boom, and the two sheets are led fore and aft respectively and belayed on the main-rail to convenient belaying pins.

CLEW OF STUN'SL

SHEET

158.

FIG. 158.

Topmast-Studding-Sail.

Yard.—This extends the full width of the head of the sail and is laced as already described.

Halliard. (10)—All upper stun'sls have single halliards bent to the centre of the yard. From the yard the halliard reeves through a jewel-block seized to the neck of the outer boom-iron on the topsail-yard—upper-topsail in the case of vessels rigged with double yards; up and through a single block hooked into a short strop at the topmast-cap; down to the deck and belayed.

Alternatively it may be rigged along the underside of the topsail-yard, with the lead block made fast at the quarters instead of the topmast-cap; and so down to the deck. This rig however has many very obvious disadvantages, the greatest being lack of strength. In the rig shown in the drawing the weight is taken on the mast direct, and the halliard acts as an additional lift tending to support the yard-arm, while in the alternative rig the whole weight of the stun'sl gear is a dead load on the yard-arm, and the downward pull of the halliard to the deck must be taken by the topsail-tye in addition to its normal load.

Tack. (11)—The tack is bent or toggled to the outer clew of the sail; reeved through a small block on the top of the topmast-stun'sl-boom; taken aft to the standing-rigging of the mast next abaft; through a lead-block on the rigging and down to the pin-rail where it belays.

Brace. (Not shown in the drawing)—A brace was sometimes rigged from the topmast-stun'sl-boom. The forward end was spliced round the end of the boom; the brace then led aft; through a lead-block adjacent to that of the tack and so down to the deck.

Sheets. (12)—These are double and bent to the sail as in the case of the lower-stun'sl, but one side is left longer than the other. The short leg is reeved through a single block seized to the neck of the inner-boom-iron on the lower-yard; through a block seized to the rim of the top, or to the foot of the topmast-rigging; down to the deck and belayed. The long-sheet or deck-sheet is taken down well forward of the sails it serves and belayed on deck.

An older rig was to middle the line forming the sheets, making them of equal length, one part was then taken forward and the other aft. In the case of the fore-topmast-stun'sl the fore part of the sheet went to the fo'castle, and the after part came down just aft of the fore-rigging. On the main-mast the fore part came down at the fore-rigging, and the after part just abaft the main

Downhaul. (13)—The downhaul is bent to the outer end of the topmast-stun'sl-yard; led down through a bull's-eye or thimble on the outer leech of the sail, midway between the head and the foot; through a small block or bull's-eye at the outer clew-cringle; down on the fore side of the lower-stun'sl and course and belayed on deck.

Topgallant-Studding-Sail.

Yard.—As on the topmast-stun'sl.

Halliard. (14)—Bent to centre of yard; reeved through a jewel-block on the extreme end of the topgallant yard-arm—the neck of the outer-boom-iron if royal stun'sls are carried; up through a single block hooked into a strop put round the mast immediately above the topgallant-hounds; and down to the top where it is made fast to any convenient fixture.

If the topmast-stuns'l is rigged below the yard as described as an alternative, then the topgallant-stun'sl will be rigged in the same way, but the disadvantages already mentioned will apply here too.

Tack. (15)—Bent or toggled to the outer-clew-cringle of the sail; reeved through a single block or bull's-eye on top of the topgallant-stuns'l-boom. From this point it may either lead aft to the rail as already described for the tack of the topmast-stun'sl, or down to its own top and made fast to the foot of the topmast-rigging, or it may be taken through a block in the top and so down to the deck.

Sheet. (16)—The sheet is rigged with a long and short leg as already mentioned for the topmast-stuns'l. The short leg is made fast round the topsail-yard at the inner-boom-band. The long leg goes down to the top where it is made fast to one of the topmast shrouds.

Downhaul. (17)—The downhaul is made fast to the outer end of the topgallant-stun'sl-yard; led down the leech of the sail; through a jewel-block or bull's-eye at the outer clew; down to the top where it is made fast to one of the topmast shrouds.

An alternative is to bend the downhaul to the inner end of the stuns'l-yard, and take it direct to the top without any block or bull's-eye on the sail.

Royal-Studding-Sail.

When royal-stuns'ls are carried they are rigged as shown for the topgallant.

Burtons.

Additional tackles called top-burtons were often rigged between the mast-caps and the yards, with the object of giving extra support to the yard-arms while the stun'sls were being carried. They were only a temporary rig and were sent down again when the stuns'ls were taken in.

I think I have now covered all the gear found in a normal square-rigger and I hope, put all readers in a position to read and understand even the most complicated sail and rigging plan, but before going any further I would like to add a few words on the use of plans.

Shipbuilders' arrangement drawings usually require a certain amount of editing if they are to represent the vessel as finally launched, also there are the changes made to the ship during her sea career. These have to be considered if the model builder wishes to represent some particular period. The difference between the original design and the final product will be readily understood by anyone accustomed to shipbuilding practice, or for that matter engineering or architecture, for I expect there are very few buildings which are completed exactly in accordance with the original small scale design!

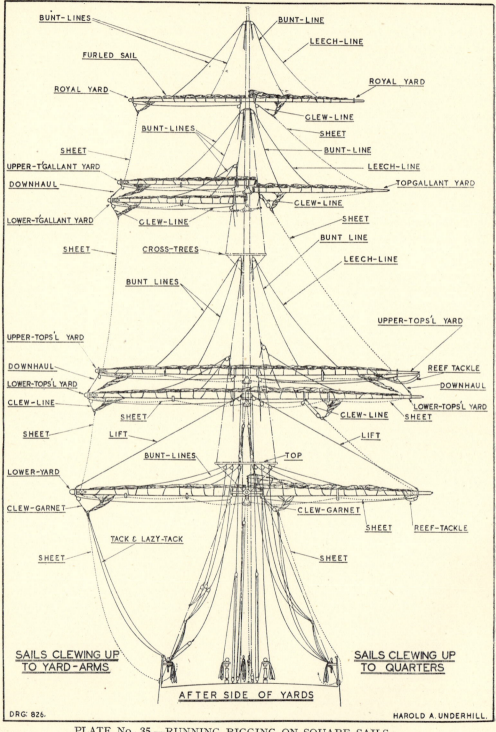

PLATE No. 35.—RUNNING RIGGING ON SQUARE SAILS.
(Sails Furled.)

When the builder knows the general requirements of the vessel he has to build and has decided on the principal features; the lines, arrangement drawing, and sail plan are produced to a relatively small scale, and these, after approval, form the basis on which the ship is built. These arrangement drawings, which have to illustrate the ship as a whole, are necessarily too small to be used for constructional work, and large scale detail drawings of each section and component have to be made. It is during this process of detailing that snags and difficulties not apparent in the small scale drawings, come to light and are rectified, or improvements proposed and incorporated in the ship.

The building of the vessel is not held back until all the detail drawings are completed, but the drawing work is usually just in advance of the constructional progress, and these alterations and modifications develop from time to time throughout the whole building period. To embody them all in the original arrangment drawings would mean continual erasing and alteration, therefore it is usually considered sufficient to annotate the actual yard copies "see revised detail number so and so". It is true that in building such as a modern liner, builders usually provide the owners with a set of arrangement drawings revised right up to the time the vessel leaves the yard, but that does not apply to the period in which we are now interested.

I hope I have shown why builders' arrangments drawings may differ slightly from the actual ship, and also that the construction of the vessel may spread over anything up to a hundred or so drawings—it may run into four figures in the case of the modern liner. All this may have little to do with the subject of masting and rigging, but I have made the point because so many model builders seem to think that three or four relatively small scale drawings, should be able to furnish detailed information regarding every conceivable fitting in the ship.

The foregoing notes apply to the latter end of the sailing ship era, and the further back one goes the less information will be found on paper. Many old master builders were men who could use an adze and dress a spar or frame by eye alone, but when it came to drawing could hardly draw a straight line. In such yards the hull would be designed by carving a half-model from the solid and cutting it up to get the run of the frames, the rest of the construction would be worked out on the spot by the shipwright.

As a matter of interest I have included Plate 43 which is reproduced from the actual builders' spar plan of the barque *Gloamin* built at Nova Scotia in 1870. The builder has merely provided the dimensions of the spars, leaving the shipwright, sailmaker and rigger to do the rest in their respective departments, and a very good job they would make of it too, for such men were real craftsmen and took great pride in their work. This particular drawing is perhaps an extreme example, but only in that the draughtsmanship is very

o

crude; very few drawings of this period contained more information, except perhaps to show the outline of the sails.

Even in the days of the composite and iron ship, sail and rigging plans rarely include more than the masts and spars, standing-rigging, sails and perhaps the braces. It is only in the plans of the sail training ships built in the present century that one will find sails and running-rigging shown in detail, and the reason seems fairly obvious. By the time these ships were built, few yards could hope to produce riggers with sufficient experience to rig one of these big sailing ships without the aid of fully detailed drawings. And so it comes about that only after the sailing ship had ceased to be built as a commercial proposition, do we find builders' plans showing full rigging details.

The point I have tried to make is that the prospective model builder, who for instance, aims at a really good model of one of the clippers, may devote a lot of time and money to searching for and obtaining the original sail plan of the ship he wants, only to find that he is still a long way from having all the information he needs. Therefore, while chasing the original plans, don't neglect all other sources of information, such as photographs and old prints, for you will probably need them all before you can arrive at a true picture of just how the vessel was rigged.

During the last twenty odd years I have had occasion to re-draw a considerable number of plans, amending and completing arrangement drawings, and producing complete sail and rigging plans, in an endeavour to record the ships as they really went to sea rather than as originally conceived by their designers. It takes a lot of research work, even though in some cases I have been fortunate enough to have the freedom of the builder's records and plan store, and so able to borrow the large scale yard details and specifications which supplied full information on everything except the lead of the running gear. That of course was invariably left to the riggers, and possibly the future master of the vessel, holding a watching brief on behalf of the owners. Other ships I knew or they had been commanded by friends, who were always only too pleased to assist in compiling a lasting record of their old loves.

With earlier ships it is necessary to go further afield, and before making any start on the drawing board a few months should be devoted to buying, begging or borrowing every possible photograph or print you can lay your hands on. Advertise for them, also for anyone who sailed in her or knew her well, and in this direction the Colonial papers are usually very helpful. Keep at it until it is obvious that you have pumped all sources dry, and only then should you think of starting work. By the way do not despise the loan of photographic groups taken aboard the ship. At first sight they may appear useless, being 98 per cent group with only a very poor 2 per cent of ship in the background, but that 2 per cent may include say a few feet of the topsail-yard-arm, showing a single block perched on top with two lengths of line doing the Indian rope trick above it, but that block has informed you that her upper-topsail-downhauls were rigged with a whip on the yard-arms; or the mate may be leaning nonchalantly against a bit of iron work which you *should* recognise as the corner of a Jarvis winch, and so you have learned that at some time or another she had brace winches added. All very simple if you know what you are looking at when you see it, and I hope that having read so far, you will.

Having collected all the data you can get, don't just jump all over the place, but work systematically taking each item of gear in turn. Go carefully through all your collection searching for light on that particular item, do not neglect any scrap of evidence, for you will often find a lead in the most unlikely places. It is quite possible that one photograph or print will contradict another, that frequently happens, for shipmasters had a very free hand in the rigging of their ships, and one man's meat was often another man's poison. This is particularly true with regard to the lead of running-rigging.

This reference to the idiosyncrasies of shipmasters reminds me of an old skipper friend of mine, who by the way spent much of his early sea time in Craig's "Counties". He had a rooted objection to spreaders at the cross-trees. It appears that at some time or another he had served in a ship fresh from the builder's yard, and on which the thumb-cleats of the spreaders had been fitted too far aft and were not sufficiently strong. During the first heavy blow the thumb-cleats sheared, and having been wrongly placed, left the backstays very slack, with the result that all the top-hamper above the cross-trees went over the side before they could set up the stays. In spite of the fact that this was one case of failure against thousands which never gave any trouble, he never again trusted spreaders, and declared that on gaining his first command he took the backstays out of the cleats and set them up taut, just seizing them to the spreaders so that the latter took no active part in supporting the masts. He passed on many years ago, but his hatred remained with him to the end, and any mention of spreaders was like waving a red flag in front of a bull. After a few years in steam he retired from the sea and took up model building as a hobby, he turned out three very fine little ships, a "County" and two "Cutty Sarks", but flatly refused to put spreaders on any of them, although he well knew that both ships carried them. It was useless to point out that his models lost their value as true pictures of the orginals, all protests were met with "I won't rig those damn things in any ship of mine, full size or model" and there the matter always ended.

To return to the use of plans. Do not trust too blindly to the diameters of masts and spars as measured directly off a print, but before finishing them off check them with the standard tables of relative diameters to length, just to make sure that they are not over size. It is always better to err a little on the thin side rather than make them too heavy. In full size practice one would never measure from a print, but always work from quoted dimensions. In model work, owing to the small scale, it is not possible to show dimensions on the drawing, so it is always advisable to check such things as spar diameters.

A certain amount of inaccuracy in reproduction is unavoidable. The original pencil drawing will be dead to scale in all details, but this drawing is not suitable for the production of prints, and an ink-on-cloth copy must be made. This copy, or tracing, forms the negative from which the prints are made, and to get good results the lines must be dense and black. The ink line if it is to print well, can never be made as fine as the pencil original, and the extra thickness of two lines can make several inches difference to the diameter of a spar drawn to a small scale. There is also the risk of slight shrinkage in exposing, developing, and washing the sensitized paper comprising the print. I mention this to explain why there may at times be an infinitesimal difference between two prints of the same ship.

I hope I have not created the impression that all ship modelling necessarily involves months of tedious labour in the way of general preparation, to do so would be entirely wrong. In the first place my remarks apply only to models of specific vessels, and secondly, research work is never tedious, no matter how long it may take. I will go as far as to say that it can well be the most interesting and fascinating part of the whole job, providing infinitely more pleasure than even the actual construction of the model.

What I do want to drive home is that if you build, what for the want of a better term I will call a "named" ship, then do be certain of your details before putting them in model form. A well built model is a lasting record and one which may ultimately find its way into some collection, where, in view of its having been built during the last years of sail, it may take on the authoritative cloak of a "contemporary model".

I maintain that one should never name a model after a specific vessel, unless quite certain that such detail as is shown is really true to that ship. If there is any doubt of this, then simply call the model "A clipper—or whatever it is—of such and such period", or if you must name it, use a fictitious one which is not in the registers of the period; or one so common that it could not be attributed to any one vessel. I think model makers owe this much to future generations, and this is particularly true of well built models, for the better the craftsmanship the greater will be the faith placed on its accuracy. I know that all students of early naval architecture will endorse this view, for endless hours have been spent in trying to reconcile apparently authentic contemporary models with equally authoritative documentary evidence, only to find in the end that one has been sent off on a false trail by inaccuracy or artistic licence on the part of the model builder. So please do not name a good model unless it really *is* a true model of that ship. One other small point.

It adds greatly to the historical value of a model if it is signed and dated by the builder, and a good place for this is the bottom of the hull where it can be seen through the hatch.   I have seen old models signed on the housing of the mainmast, but this is not likely to be found until the model reaches the stage of needing complete restoration.

By this time the reader will have decided that I regard most model makers in poor esteem, but this is far from being the case.   I am a keen model builder myself, and I know from experience that the majority of sailing ship modellers are enthusiastic students of their subject.   I have—and will continue to the end of the book—been using the spur to goad on the few who are prepared to let small, but none the less important, details slide.   I also admit that I take a poor view of the man who hacks out a solid chunk of wood; gives it three masts—its only possible resemblance to the original—and inflicts it on the world as a "Cutty Sark" or "Thermopylae", for there is no more justification for this, than for a painter to religiously paint his lay figure and leave it to posterity as a portrait of a famous man.

CHAPTER VII.

COASTERS AND SMALL CRAFT.

THERE is a deep rooted fallacy that the sailing coaster must necessarily be tubby and slow, and one must admit that there were examples of the floating box type, also that to-day many are dowdy and ill kept. But all this applies equally well to the big sailing ship, she went through exactly the same phase, and it seems unfair to remember only the "hard-up" days of the coaster while singing the praises of the clipper in her prime.

There are many reasons for this outlook, but one is very obvious. The sailing coaster outlived her larger sister, and was still plentiful and to be seen in most ports and harbours at a time when the deep-water sailer had already become a museum piece, and so the somewhat down at the heel coaster of living memory is accepted as representative of the type, while the big ship is remembered as the clipper in her hey'day. One may hope that with the passage of time, the poverty stricken coaster will recede into her proper perspective and the true sailing coaster, the prim little ship of fifty years ago, will receive her well deserved place in the annals of sail.

The introduction of the auxiliary engine did not improve the sailer, and usually resulted in spars and rigging being cut down, or if left aloft, neglected and allowed to become very bedraggled in appearance. However, in spite of all the tattered rigging, patched sails and fished spars of the final struggle for existence, many sweet lined hulls were to be found by those with eyes to see them. The squalor was, after all, only skin deep and could not hide the beauty that was the real ship.

Another very wrong idea, no doubt the outcome of this age of floating cities, is that these small ships are only suitable for coastal waters. There were certain trades in which speed and rapid turn round were of the greatest importance. Trades such as fresh fruit, where it was essential to get the goods from tree to consumer in the shortest possible time; where small quantities and speedy transit meant delivery in good condition, while large vessels, with the longer time taken to get the goods alongside and loaded, would result in deterioration before the ship was even full and ready for sea. The Mediterranean fruit; Newfoundland fish, and the West Indian trades all produced fleets of small craft, including brigs, brigantines, and perhaps most-popular of all, topsail schooners. These vessels were in most cases thoroughbreds, having perfect lines and carrying stuns'ls and every possible flying kite. It must not, however, be thought that these offshore traders had the monopoly of fine craft, for when the coastal trade was at its height there were many firms owning quite large fleets of very smart little coasters.

The small sailer put up a gallant fight against power competition, and right up to the middle of the twenties an odd schooner or so managed to pick up Newfoundland and Mediterranean charters, although that represented just about the last kick. When they were squeezed off their original routes, many of these clipper schooners gravitated to the British coastal trade, and some survived to see the end of that too, for they were staunch little ships and well built. At one time a large percentage of the country's commerce was carried coastwise in sail, either from port to port for consumption within the country, or taken to some of the larger ports for loading into the big deep-watermen, bot sail and steam. There were also one or two special coastal trades for which a particular type of craft was largely used, the most widely known being the collier brigs of the East Coast, which we have already mentioned in connection with the bentinck fore-sail.

Steam gradually crowded the sailing coaster out of port after port, just as it had crowded so many of them off the deep-sea routes, until she was left with only the small tidal creeks and harbours into which the steamer could not or would not go. For a time it seemed that she might continue to pick up a few, if rather poor, charters acting as feeder for the larger craft, but then the small handy Dutch motor vessel appeared on the coast, and as she was both cheap to run and also willing to go anywhere where there was a few inches of water, her arrival just about put "paid" to the sailer. In the end about the only thing left to the schooner was china clay, and in this trade the survivors struggled on, just about meeting expenses and nothing more. Even that could only be done by the strictest economy, and I have often watched crews discharging by means of the hand dolly winch, while a modern crane stood idle alongside because the freight would not stand the cost of its hire. In any case why hurry? In all probability a quick turn round would only result in lying up on the mud somewhere waiting for another cargo, which may be long enough in offering, or may never turn up at all, in which case she would just stay on the mud until she rotted to pieces. Small wonder that the sailing coaster became very shabby during her last few years. She had no money to spend on upkeep, and if she had what was the use when any voyage might well be the last.

At the outbreak of the present war—1939—there were still a few sailing coasters scraping a living together, and also a fleet of French schooners which made regular visits to the Welsh ports. These latter vessels by the way rigged single topsails, with roller-reefing gear. The war 1914-18 took a very heavy toll of sailing craft, including coasters, and no doubt the same will apply this

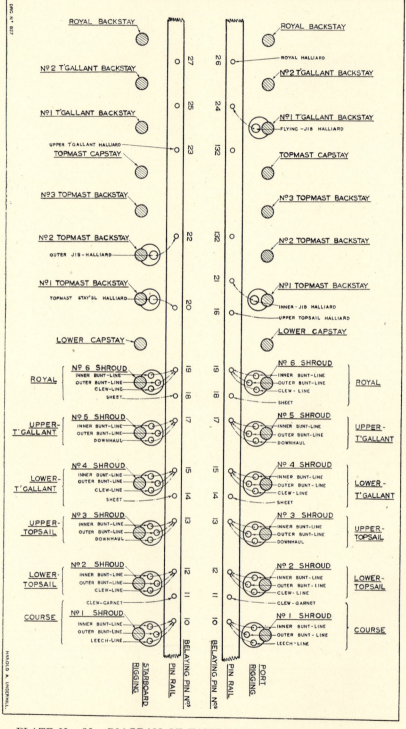

PLATE No. 36.—DIAGRAM OF FAIRLEADS IN FORE RIGGING.

time, at least as far as sailing craft are available, so it seems quite probable that coastwise sail will have completely disappeared by the time peace is declared. Even the Thames barge, which by the way made quite long coastal trips, is almost a thing of the past.

The barquentine, or brig-schooner as she is sometimes referred to in old books, does not appear to have had much of a place in the old off-shore fleets, although many brigs, of which the *Waterwitch* was a good example, were cut down and re-rigged as three-mast barquentines during their coasting days. Incidentally the brig was considered one of the handiest and most powerful rigs, and, as I pointed out in *Sailing Ship Rigs and Rigging*, forms a very large percentage of the craft on Lloyd's Register of Shipping at the end of the last century. But the cost of upkeep was high in relation to the size of the vessel, and of course the rig needed a much larger crew than a schooner rigged craft of the same size, so on the grounds of economy the brig was one of the first rigs to die out, followed by that of the brigantine.

The three-mast topsail schooner proved to be a good all round rig for coastal work, and a large number of exceedingly fine vessels were turned out. Like her two-masted sister she generally crossed four yards on the fore-mast, a lower-yard to which no sail was bent, although a square running sail might be set flying below it; above this yard were either single topsail, topgallant and royal, or alternatively double topsails and topgallant, Plate 47. In time the upper yard—either royal or topgallant—disappeared, and two square sails, upper and lower topsails, became the accepted rig, while in some cases only a small single topsail was carried. This single sail bore little resemblance in cut to the accepted idea of a single top'sl, for its spread usually exceeded its hoist to such an extent that it was little larger than a normal lower-topsail.

The older schooners all carried bowsprits and jib-booms as already described for larger craft, but the single spar standing bowsprit was introduced and gradually superseded the older rig, until in the end the majority of coasters carried the timber "spike" boom. The coasting trade produced a number of very pretty ketches, with clipper stems and long tapering bowsprits. This rig is quite distinct from the ketch rig as used by fishermen. With the latter the bowsprit is a running spar which can be brought inboard along the deck, while a single jib is set flying, whereas the trading ketch carries a standing bowsprit, or even bowsprit and jib-boom, and has four or more head-sails hanked to stays.

The small ships like their bigger sisters, also had various rigs made up of unorthodox combinations of standard components, such as three-mast-schooners with topmasts on the fore and main, and a pole mizzen; the main-topsail schooner; the schooner-ketch, and many others which will be dealt with in the next chapter. Should the reader wish to build one of these rigs, he can get all the information he requires by taking the various components now to be described and assembling them as required. The fore and aft schooner was quite common on the coast, particularly with the auxiliaries, but as a true sailer it was never so popular in this country as the topsail-schooner. Anyone working on a model of a British fore and after will be able to take the details from the top-sail-schooners illustrated here, simply omitting the yards from the fore mast, and remembering of course that as there will be no lower-topsail yard, the fore-cap will not require the boss for the crane.

There is no need to treat the rigging of the coaster in great detail, as it follows very closely that of the larger vessel. The difference is mainly a matter of proportion and arrangement rather than one of general principle. In the first place the spars are lighter for a given length, but as will be seen from the tables at the end of the book this applies to all spars of the fore and aft rig. The diameters of a barque's fore and aft mast for example, may be reduced by one-fifth on the same given length. In the same way the hoist of a modern coaster's square sails is very small in proportion to width, so that for a given length of yard she usually carries a smaller superficial area and therefore the yard may have a smaller relative diameter.

For the purpose of description I propose to take the coaster as she was in the final period, by which time the gear had been reduced to the most simple form, but I hope to be able to indicate what one might expect to find in one of these ships during the clipper period of some sixty years ago. In any case the clipper schooner offers little difficulty, the fore and aft canvas has remained more or less unchanged, and except for the number carried, the only difference on the square sails is that the early clippers rigged their bunt-lines, etc., rather like the larger vessels. As for the standing-rigging, the change here lies in the fact that when the topgallant mast vanished the number of backstays could be reduced. To sum up; the out and out clipper carried a bigger sail plan, with stuns'l booms on the yards, and for that reason needed more standing-rigging to support the mast. Also the running-gear on the square sails was a little more elaborate, and the masts may have a little more rake, but all these points will be available on whatever drawing the model builder is using. For the rest it is safe to say that the details will remain much the same.

As a spar the spike boom requires little in the way of description. The heel has the usual square tenon checked into the fore side of the pawl-bitt of the windlass. Forward of the heel the housing may be either square or octagonal as far as the bed, which of course is square and bolted down to the head timbers of the hull. Outboard the spar is round and fitted with three bands in the positions shown on Plate 45. The spike boom is not pierced with sheave-holes for the head-stays as in the case of a jib-boom.

Except in the matter of proportion, a slightly smaller diameter—length ratio, a schooner's masts differ very little from the timber spars of a ship or barque, the actual constructional details may be said to be the same. The principal difference is that they consist of lower-mast and topmast only, and that decked tops are not fitted. The construction of a schooner's fore cross-trees—Plate 46—follows that of a normal top except that the rim and decking are omitted. Checks, trestle-trees, and cross-trees are built, as already described for the larger vessel, but the arms of the cross-trees are either bored or notched for the topmast-rigging, and spreaders, usually wood, although sometimes of iron, extend aft to brace the topmast-backstays. The forward cross-tree is slightly shorter than the after one, so making the topmast-rigging taper forward, to allow the yards their maximum swing.

A schooner's main, and in the case of three-masters, mizzen also, cross-trees are exactly the same as the fore except that the forward cross-tree, which passes between the lower-mast and topmast, is extended out to the full beam of the vessel in way of that particular mast, while the after one on each mast extends only a few inches beyond the outer faces of the trestle-trees on either side.

The mast-caps are usually iron and quite normal in design. That on the fore mast of a topsail schooner will of course have the boss to carry the crane of the lower-topsail yard, unless she carries a single topsail. If she is fore and aft rigged the boss will be omitted and the fore-cap made to the same design as the main and mizzen. The caps are provided with eyes for the various blocks to be described with the running-rigging, these may of course differ in different ships, and previous remarks regarding designing the cap to suit the vessel will also apply here.

The gaffs have timber jaws as shown in the detail on Plate 46. Timber jaws are also provided on the booms of earlier vessels, but most of the later ships have iron goose-necks. When timber jaws are fitted on the booms, a collar is built round the mast to carry the weight, and supported by four wooden brackets spiked in position below it. The lower end of the bearing block of the gaff is cut square to sit on the collar and so keep the actual jaws up above it, this will be clearly seen in the detail mentioned. The yards are normal in every way except, as already stated, their relative diameter to length may be smaller.

Plate 44 is the sail and rigging plan of a two-mast topsail schooner during the closing years of coastwise sail, and shows the rig as it is perhaps best remembered. By this time few vessels carried more than two square-sails—upper and lower topsails—and the running bob-stay rig had become the generally adopted arrangement throughout the trade. Plate 47 shows the sail and rigging plan of a three-mast topsail schooner crossing double-topsails and topgallant. This drawing is based on the well known schooner *Jane Banks*, and is a reconstruction showing her as I imagine she appeared

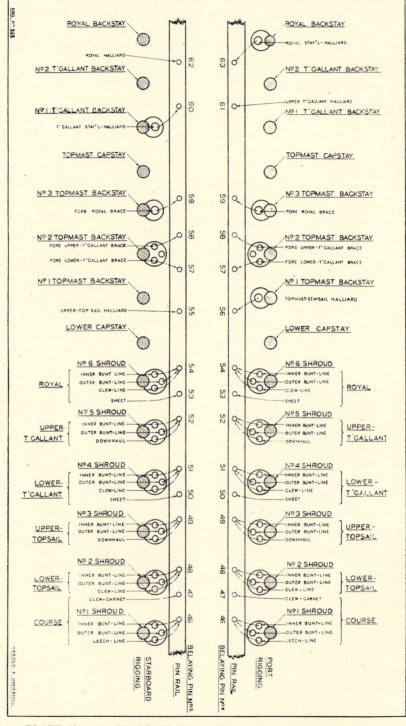

PLATE No. 37.—DIAGRAM OF FAIRLEADS IN MAIN RIGGING.

in her prime. However it is *not* authoritative, having been produced solely from a few notes and details taken aboard her some eight or ten years ago, by which time of course she only crossed the upper and lower topsails. She still had the original fore-topmast with topgallant pole, and her head-stays were set up as drawn, so it would only require the replacement of the topgallant yard to restore her to the rig shown. It is possible that my records may contain data which would either confirm or contradict this reconstruction, but as mentioned in the preface, this is being written during the war period at a time when practically all my material has been stored for safety; and in any case I am not free to devote the time to research, which is not really necessary in view of the fact that the drawing is offered *not* as a plan of the *Jane Banks*, but merely an illustration of a three-mast schooner of the period, and as such it will serve perfectly.

We will start with the standing-rigging, taking first the modern—to use the word in a relative sense—spike-boom as shown in Plates 44 and 45. The most noticeable feature, and one that is peculiar to the coaster, is the arrangement of the double bob-stay. A chain-plate of the type illustrated in Fig. 76c is fitted in the stem near the water line, and to this the lower ends of both-bobstays are shackled. The bob-stays are of chain and the upper end of the inner one is shackled to a thimble or heart; a similar thimble or heart is shackled to the underside of the inner-band and the bob-stay and set up with a lanyard. The topsail schooner *Two Sisters* had a different arrangement for the inner-bob-stay. In her case the upper end shackled to the inner-band; then passed down and through an iron block shackled to the stem at the water line; came up alongside the stem-on the starboard side; over the rail and belayed inside the bulwarks. This however is the only instance I know of this particular lead being used, although of course there may be plenty of others.

To return to our example. The upper end of the outer-bob-stay is shackled to a small iron block. The running-part, which is also of chain is shackled to the underside of the outerband; reeved through the iron block on the standing-part; up and through an iron block on the underside of the centre-band; back along the spar; through a fairlead in the starboard bow and belayed inside the bulwarks.

A single bowsprit-guy is rigged on either side, these are wire with a thimble spliced in the outer end and a heart in the inner end. The outer thimble shackles to the outer band on the bowsprit, and the inner end sets up with a lanyard to a heart on the cat-head, or other convenient point on either bow. One foot-rope is rigged on each side, the outer ends being provided with either thimbles spliced in and seized to the shackles of the bowsprit-guys, or alternatively the two foot-ropes are joined in a cut-splice, forming an eye to fit snugly round the end of the boom. The eye is wormed, parcelled and served before being put over the end of the spar. Turks-heads or knots are formed on the foot-rope at intervals to provide a foot grip for men on the boom; the inner ends of the foot-ropes are spliced round lanyard-thimbles and set up to eye-bolts on the bulwarks on either side of the spar. They are supported at intervals by stirrups consisting of short lengths of wire with an eye-splice in each end. The upper ends are seized to the bowsprit-guys, and the lower to the foot-rope, Plate 45.

Plate 47 shows another arrangement of the spike-boom, and no doubt indicates the transition stage between the older bowsprit and jib-boom and the rig just described. A single chain bob-stay is carried, the lower end being shackled to the chain-plate near the water line and the upper set up to the after edge of the inner-band with hearts and lanyard. An iron martingale is bolted to a lug on the fore side of the inner-band, as detailed in an earlier chapter. This martingale is a simple iron bar with jaws forged on the upper end and an eye on the fore and after faces of the lower end; no thumb-cleats are provided, as in this rig the head-stays do not pass through the boom and along over the martingale, the latter being merely a stiffener to the spar itself. Two chain martingale-stays are carried; their lower ends being united by a single shackle which connects them to the forward eye on the bottom of the martingale. The outer-martingale-stay shackles to a lug below the outer-band, and the inner-stay to the centre-band.

The martingale-back-ropes are also chain and lead one to either bow. The forward ends of both back-ropes go on a single shackle on the after eye of the martingale, while the after ends set up on either bow with hearts and lanyards. Either one or two bowsprit-guys may be fitted on each side, the outer ones are rigged between the outer-band and the bow as described for Plate 45. The inner guys—when carried—are shackled to the inner-band, or to an additional band immediately abaft it, and are set up at the cat-heads for bow with hearts and lanyards. The foot-ropes and stirrups are rigged a or the other arrangement.

The head-stays coming down to the outer and centre bands respectively are reeved through bull's eyes and set up to the band next abaft with hearts and lanyards, or turned on thimbles and seized back to their own parts. By the way, all bands except the outer one have a shackle facing forward as well as the one to which the bull's eye is attached. The jib-stay, which comes down to the inner-band, may either be set up as above, or alternatively iron blocks may be shackled to the lugs on either side of the band—it is when this is done that the additional band for the inner-bowsprit-guys may be necessary, although it can be avoided if the lugs for the guys are kept well down on the lower quarters of the band, and the lugs for the blocks placed slightly above the centre line. These two iron blocks serve the same purpose as the cheek-blocks on the steel spike-boom. The stay has a short leg spliced into the lower

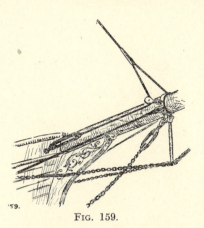

FIG. 159.

end, and one part is reeved through each iron block; taken aft and set up at the bows with hearts and lanyards on either side close in to the sides of the spar. Alternatively the ends may be turned on thimbles and seized back to their own standing-parts at the bows. The arrangement of these two blocks is shown in the sketch. (Fig. 159).

The lead of the head-stays on a schooner differs from that of a fully square-rigged mast, further, there are several ways of rigging the stays, as will be seen from the diagrammatic sketches in Fig 159. The first point to note is that there are two stays set up to the head of the lower-mast instead of the usual one. The inner one, or fore-stay, is quite normal and is set up inside the hull. The next stay, which on a fully square-rigged mast would be the fore-topmast-stay, but is here termed the jib-stay; extends between the inner-band—or bowsprit-cap if bowsprit and jib-boom are carried—and the lower-mast head. The next stay, the outer-jib-stay, has several alternative positions for its upper end; it may be taken to the topmast immediately above the lower-topsail-yard, (Fig. 160A); or it may go to a shoulder on the topmast above the sheave-hole for the upper-topsail-tye, leaving a short topgallant pole above, (Fig. 160B). This rig will of course always be used when a topgallant-yard is crossed, and several of the ships so rigged today are vessels which at one time carried topgallant-yards. Another alternative is to carry the stay right up to the mast-head and bed it on the same stops as the flying-jib-stay, (Fig. 160C). Lastly there is the arrangement shown in Fig. 160D. Here the fore-stay,

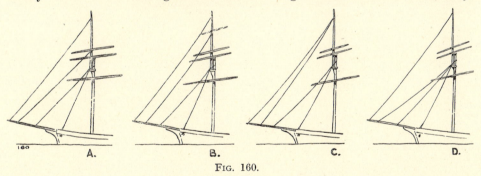

A.   B.   C.   D.

FIG. 160.

jib-stay, and outer-jib-stay all lead in to the cross-trees of the lower-mast, leaving only the flying-jib-stay to go to the head of the topmast, this however is not a very common rig. When the rig shown in sketch "A" is used, the stay is supported on the topmast by thumb-cleats as shown in Plates 44 and 48. These cleats must be so placed as to keep the stay sufficiently high to allow the lower-topsail-yard to swing freely, and yet low enough to clear the foot of the upper-topsail. A pair of thumb-cleats are also fitted on the mast immediately above the stay to act as stops for the upper-topsails yard; if these were not fitted the parral would jamb on the stay when the yard was down. There would also be a lot of unnecessary wear on the eye of the stay.

Now for the standing-rigging. The order of placing the rigging over the masts is exactly the same as laid down for the square-rigger, although for the sake of convenience I may not describe it in that order. On the fore-mast there are usually four shrouds per side, made up in pairs and put over the masthead with the forward pair on the starboard side first, and the rest in rotation. The lower ends are turned on dead-eyes and set up with lanyards to chain-plates at the vessel's side.

Next comes the fore-stay. This will be single wire, not double as with the bigger ship. A large eye is formed in the head and wormed, parcelled, served and leathered in the usual way, or over-parcelling and painting may take the place of the leather. This eye is placed over the lower-mast head, and may either be carried on thumb-cleats on the doubling, or bedded down on top of the lower-rigging. The "V" of the eye should be well forward of the topmast to allow the latter to be struck when required. The lower end of the stay has a short leg spliced into it, forming an inverted "Y". These legs are passed down on either side of the bowsprit; reeved through bull's-eyes shackled to eye-bolts in the deck; set up taut and seized back to their own standing-parts. Another method was to pass them round the bowsprit housing from opposite sides, and after setting up taut, seize each leg to its opposite number in the manner indicated in Fig. 98. except that in the schooner the stay is inboard of the stem head. Thumb-cleats must of course be provided on the spar to prevent the stay from sliding. Some modern coasters have a much simpler arrangement. The lower end of the stay is spliced round a metal thimble at a point about four feet above the level of the bowsprit; a short length of chain is then put in a noose round the bowsprit-housing and the end brought up to meet the stay.

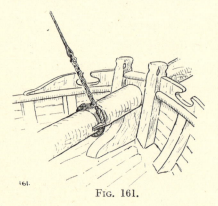

The stay is then set up taut with a tackle, and while held taut, the chain and stay are shackled together with the result as shown in Fig. 161. If the first method is used the two legs will have to be wormed, parcelled and served before setting up, while in the latter arrangement the chain noose requires well parcelling where it is in contact with the spar, the spar may also be metal sheathed in way of the chain.

Fig. 161.

The jib-stay goes over the mast-head in the same way, and the lower end may either reeve through a bull's-eye on top of the inner-band and set up aft, or have a short leg spliced in; be led aft through iron blocks on either side of the band, and set up to the bows with hearts and lanyards. Whichever method is used the stay will be wormed, parcelled and served from just above the level of the bowsprit.

The topmast-shrouds, two per side, are made up in pairs, the starboard pair going first over the mast-head. The heads of the shrouds are bedded down at the topmast-hounds, and only go right to the mast-head when no topgallant-mast, or pole, is carried, as in the case of Plate 44. The lower ends are turned on lanyard-thimbles after passing through the holes or notches in the arms of the cross-trees, and the rigging is set up with lanyards to the futtock-band as shown in Fig. 97D. Rope ratlines are rigged on the topmast-rigging, although either rope, or wood or iron battens are quite common for the lower-shrouds.

The outer-jib-stay has an eye-splice formed in the head, which after being wormed, parcelled and served, must be a snug fit on the mast at whichever point it is rigged. The lower end reeves through the bull's-eye on the inner-band; is taken aft, and set up to the shackle on the band next abaft. The flying-jib-stay is rigged in the same manner, with the lower end reeving through a bull's-eye on the outer-band.

The later day coaster with her two square topsails was usually content with a single backstay, this was put over the mast head immediately below the pole; came down through a notch in the end of the spreader and set up with dead-eyes to the chain-plates on the hull. Older ships and vessels carrying topgallants or topgallants and royals naturally rigged more backstays, and in the drawing on Plate 47 I have shown two topmast-backstays coming down from the topmast-hounds and set up with dead-eyes and lanyards, and a single topgallant-backstay set up on deck with hearts and lanyards. This latter arrangement is optional, dead-eyes and chain-plates on the hull can be used for this stay if desired. All these backstays will of course have to be provided with cleats on the spreaders, although the outer one may rest in notches in the extreme end as described for the first example.

The yards follow the larger practice in all details. The lower-yard has the usual iron truss, a little lighter in construction of course, but otherwise the same. The yard-arms are perfectly normal, with sheave-holes for the sheets as detailed in the chapter on timber spars, but no jack-stays are fitted on the lower-yard as this does not carry a standing square sail. This yard has foot-ropes rigged but no stirrups, as not having any sail to furl, there is not the same need for men along the yard.

The lower-topsail-yard usually has an iron crane as shown in the drawings, although some vessels attached this yard to the topmast by means of a timber

P

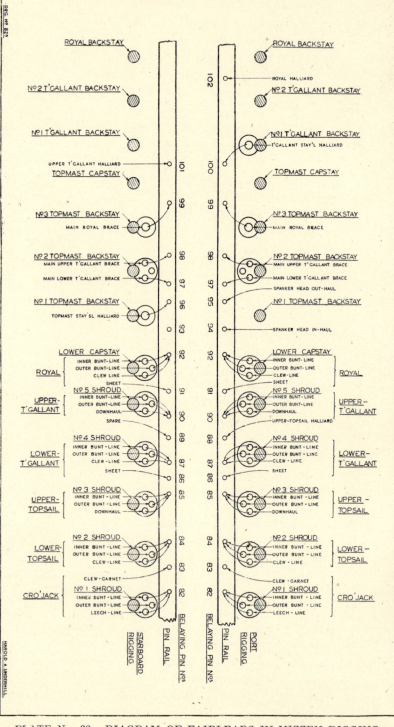

PLATE No. 38.—DIAGRAM OF FAIRLEADS IN MIZZEN RIGGING.

parral resting on top of the cap. However this was generally the result of a vessel having been converted from single to double topsails, in which case the old mast-cap would not have the bracket for the crane, and by using the wood parral the expense of fitting a new cap was avoided. It is most likely that the original topsail-yard would simply be let down on to the cap and a new upper yard provided, or possibly the original rig included a topgallant, which could be moved down and used as an upper-topsail, in which case the change could be made without any new or even altered spars, quite a consideration in the later days of coastwise sail.

The upper yards are typical timber spars, with wooden parrals as detailed on Plate 18. In most cases the upper yards were too small to require stirrups on the foot-ropes and so these were rarely seen, but should they be needed they are rigged in the usual way.

The main and mizzen masts have three shrouds per side, set up with dead-eyes and lanyards to the chain-plates on the hull. The main and mizzen topmasts have a single shroud per side, this leads down through notches or holes in the ends of the long cross-tree, and is set up on deck between Nos. 1 and 2 shrouds with hearts, or lanyard-thimbles, and lanyards.

The remaining fore and aft stays are extremely simple. Between the fore and main masts is a triatic stay of single wire; the fore end is spliced round a metal thimble and shackled to a lug on the afterside of the fore-cap. The after end, which finishes several feet short of the main-mast, is spliced round a lanyard-thimble, and the stay set up with a lanyard to a corresponding thimble on the fore side of the main-cap.

The eye of the main-topmast-stay is put over the main-topmast-hounds; the fore end reeves through a bull's-eye on the after side of the fore-cap, and is set up abaft the mast at the fore-cross-trees with thimbles and lanyards. On three-mast schooners two stays lead aft from the main-topmast-hounds. One reeves through a bull's-eye on the fore side of the mizzen-cap, and is set up at the mizzen cross-trees with lanyards and thimbles. The other stay reeves through a bull's-eye or jewel-block at the mizzen topmast-hounds; down the fore side of the topmast and set up, either at the cross-trees or on deck, with thimbles and lanyards. That completes the standing-rigging of a typical coasting schooner, and I think I have given it in sufficient detail, that together with Chapter IV, it should enable the reader to rig one of these vessels without much difficulty.

The next job will be the running-rigging. That on the head-sails is just as described for the larger vessel, consisting of halliard, downhaul and double sheets, so there is no need for repetition here. It will be noticed that the fore-staysail has a row of reef-points, this of course is different from the ship or barque rigged craft, but very few fully square-rigged fore-masts have fore-staysails, as such sails would be of little use behind the square fore-sail. Some coasters rig a boom, on the foot of the fore-staysail, and when this is done the fore end is attached to the foot of the stay, with the sheet block shackled to a band at the inner end.   A single sheet is of course used, as there is no need for it to be led aft to give proper set to the sail.   A single block is also carried on top of the band, this is for the topping-lift, (Fig. 162) which usually takes the form of a single wire pendant with a short gun-tackle-purchase at the lower end.   The upper end of the pendant may either be seized to the "V"

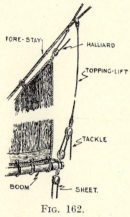

FIG. 162.

of the fore-stay or take the form of a large eye round the mast at the cross-trees and coming down the fore side of the lower-yard.   However a small eye in the head of the pendant and seized to the "V" of the stay is the most usual method.   This topping lift by the way, is also used as a fish-tackle on such rare occasions as it is desired to get the anchors over the bows and on deck.   When no boom is rigged, the fore-staysail halliards are pressed into service for the same duty.

As already mentioned, a square fore-sail is not carried, but at times a square sail is set flying below the lower-yard when running, and some schooners keep the halliards of this sail permanently rigged. Plate 49 is a detailed drawing of the square sails of a modern coaster, and on this these halliards are shown in chain-dot line. It will be seen that a single block is shackled to the underside of each yard-arm-band.   The halliards, or outhauls, are each spliced round a thimble on the underside of their respective blocks; reeved down and through another single block; up and through the block on the yard-arm to which they have been spliced, and the fall taken down to the rail.   When not in use the two lower blocks are seized together with the end of a spare line, leaving an end long enough to reach down to the deck when the two blocks are up at the yard.   Both halliards are then hauled in until the lower blocks—lashed together—are hanging centrally below the yard, with the length of line hanging down to act as downhaul when they are wanted on deck for bending the sail.   A few fore and aft schooners had this sail hooped to the yard, rather like a curtain on a pole, and when not in use it was furled up and down on the fore side of the mast—we will deal more fully with this later—in which case the lower, or inner, as they are then, blocks are always bent to the sail.   The plate shows the lower blocks hauled up below the yard as when not in use.

The lifts of the lower-yard are shackled to eyes on the upper side of the yard-arm-bands; reeved through single blocks at the mast-cap; and so down to the deck where they have a short rope tackle of single blocks.   The foot-ropes have their outer ends seized to the brace-pendant shackle, and the inner ends to the opposite side of the iron truss. Thimbles are spliced into either end of the footropes to take the lashings.

The square sails are of course bent to iron jack-stays in the usual way, and there is nothing out of the way in the lead of their gear, so just the briefest description is all that is necessary. Almost all lower-topsails clew up to the quarters as shown on the plate and detailed on the sail plans, although one does meet an odd schooner with all her square topsails clewing up to the yard-arms, but she is rather to be regarded as the exception which proves the rule. The clew-lines are bent to the clew-iron; reeved through a block on the quarter-band; through another block at the slings and so down to the deck.

The lower-topsail-sheets are of chain and shackled to the clew-irons; reeved through the sheave-holes in the lower-yard-arms; along below the yard and through the iron clover-leaf block at the slings; down to a point above the deck, where they terminate in gun-tackles, the falls of which are belayed to the spider-band. The upper blocks of these tackles should be so placed that when the sail is sheeted home they are a few feet above the spider-band. The rules regarding economy in cordage apply as much to the coaster as the big ship.

163.

FIG. 163.

Bunt-lines are rarely rigged on the modern coaster, but such ships as do carry them have a very simple rig as shown in Fig. 163. It consists of a span bent to the bunt-line-cringle on one side; reeved through a bull's-eye on the end of a single bunt-line; and bent to the cringle on the other side of the sail. The bunt-line proper reeves through a block at the mast and so down to the deck. Alternatively the single bunt-line may be bent to a cringle in the centre of the foot of the sail and the span omitted. Buntlines on the older ships, paricularly the clipper-schooners, were of course more fully rigged and closely resembled the big ship practice of the day.

The upper-topsail has a chain tye reeved through the sheave-hole immediately below the topmast-hounds, and down abaft the mast. From this point it may be rigged with either single or double halliards, with the usual purchase of the running-part on the port side. Standing-lifts are rigged from the topmast hounds and shackled to the yard-arms. Sheets are not used on the upper-topsail, but the clews are set up taut with lanyards reeved through the clew-irons and large shackles through the lower-topsail-yard as shown in the detailed drawing of timber yards in Plate 18. The downhauls shackle to the lower-topsail yard-arms; reeve through blocks on their own yard-arms; along below the yard and through blocks at the slings and so down to the deck.

When a topgallant-yard is crossed the halliard is rigged as for the upper-topsail, but of course with the hauling part on the starboard side of the ship. The sheets are chain for such length as will reeve through the various blocks.

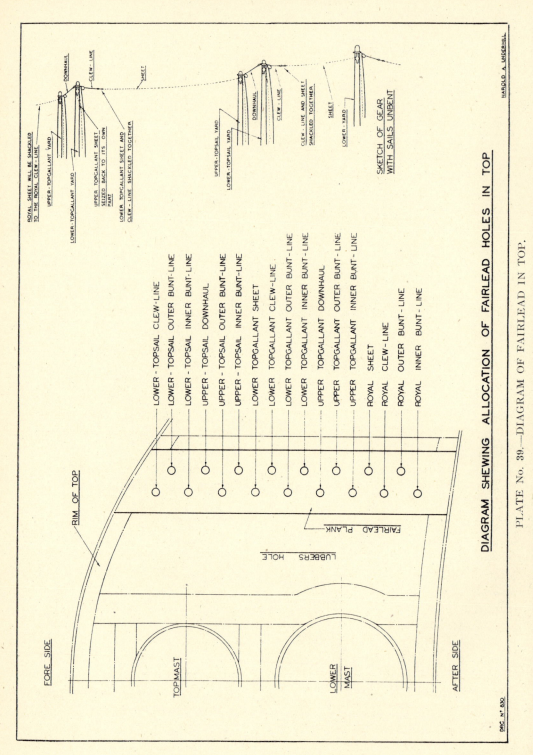

DIAGRAM SHEWING ALLOCATION OF FAIRLEAD HOLES IN TOP

PLATE No. 39.—DIAGRAM OF FAIRLEAD IN TOP.

the remainder being single wire. The lead can be followed from the sail plan of the three-mast schooner, or from the description already given in previous chapters. Standing-lifts are rigged from the topgallant-hounds to the yard-arms. The clew-lines lead from the clew-irons; up to blocks at the quarters; through blocks at the slings, and so down to the deck.

The lower yard-arms have short wire brace pendants with a single block at the outer end, and all made up as described for the big ship. The standing-end of the brace has an eye spliced in it and is seized to No. 1 shroud on the main-mast, at a point about one-quarter of the way down from the cross-trees; it then reeves through the block on the pendant; back and through a single block seized to the shroud about twenty feet above the rail, and so down to a belaying pin inside the main shrouds.

Similar brace pendants are also rigged on the upper yards. The lower-topsail-brace is seized on to the triatic-stay just forward of the main-cap; or to a grommet round the main-topmast immediately above the cap; leads forward and through the block on the pendant; back and over one sheave of a double block on the side of the main-cap—the second sheave is for the upper-topsail-brace—and so down to the deck. The upper-topsail-brace follows exactly the same lead; the standing end of the brace is seized to the same point as the brace below; leads forward and through the block on the pendant; back and through the second sheave in the double block at the mast-cap, and so down to the deck. When a topgallant is carried the standing-end of the brace is seized to the head of the main-topmast-stay, otherwise the lead is as for the topsail-yards.

This brings us to the running-rigging on the gaff-sails and gaff-topsails. Plate 48 is a large scale detail of a schooner's gaff-fore-sail, and it will be seen that two reef-bands are carried. The foot of the sail is bent to a timber jack-stay fitted along the upper side of the boom, while the head is laced to the gaff with a running lacing. The peak is made fast with an earing which makes several round turns round the spar, and additional turns out round a thumb-cleat on top of the spar; these latter serve to haul taut the head of the sail. The throat is bent to an eye or plate below the gaff-jaws; the clew is bent to the end of the boom with an earing similar to that at the peak, while the tack may either be seized to an eye on the boom or made fast to pins on the mast as shown in Fig. 164.

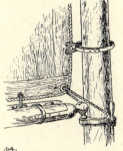

FIG. 164.

The throat-halliard is reeved through two double blocks, one on the mast and the other on the gaff. The upper block is shackled to an iron crane bolted through the mast just below the cross-trees, and the lower block to an eye-plate above the gaff-jaws. The halliard is spliced round a thimble on the underside of the upper block, and reeved through both blocks until all sheaves are expended, finishing at the upper block, and so down to the deck.

The peak-halliard blocks on the gaff may either be stropped or shackled direct to the spar, or more usually, attached to the gaff by means of wire spans, an arrangement which has the advantage of distributing the load more

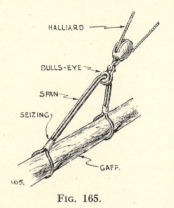

FIG. 165.

evenly along the spar. This rig is clearly shown in Fig. 165. Each span is made up of a length of wire with its ends spliced together to form an endless becket, which when completed is reeved through a hard wood bull's-eye, and the bights so formed pushed along the gaff to the required positions against the thumb-cleats already provided. When in position the two parts of the becket are seized together close to the spar, so forming an eye at either end of the span and resting against the thumb-cleats which keep the eyes from moving out of place. The bull's-eyes on the spans have metal strops to which single blocks are shackled, and when these are in position the gaff is ready for the halliard. The standing-part of the halliard is shackled to the lower eye-bolt on the afterside of the mast head; reeves through alternate blocks on the gaff and mast, finishing at the upper block abaft the mast-head and so down to the rail on the starboard side. The blocks abaft the mast are shackled to eye-bolts which are either bolted or riveted right through the timber spar.

The rig described above and illustrated in the plates is certainly that most commonly used, but there are variations of course. One is to belay both ends of the peak-halliard on deck. In this case an additional single block is shackled to the mast, using the lower eye-bolt to which the standing end of the halliard is normally made fast. The halliard then starts from a belaying pin in the main-rail on the port side; leads up and through the lower block abaft the mast-head; reeves through alternate blocks on gaff and mast, finishing at the top block on the mast, from which point it is taken down to the deck and belayed to a pin in the main-rail starboard side. Another alternative which is very commonly used on the mizzen of three-masters when the mizzen is smaller than the main, is for the standing-end of the halliard to be seized round the gaff at a point about one-third in from the peak, taking the place of the usual inner span. It then leads up to a single block at the middle eye-bolt abaft the mast—the lower one is not fitted with this rig—through a block on a span at the peak; back to the upper block on the mast, and down to the belaying pin in the main-rail starboard side.

The topping-lift of the fore-sail serves the dual purpose of supporting the boom when sail is taken in or reefed, and preventing the gaff sagging to leeward when sail is set. It is in fact a combined topping-lift and vang. A short wire pendant having a bull's-eye or metal thimble spliced in the outer end, is attached to the peak of the gaff. The topping-lift is single wire with an eye spliced in either end; the lower eye is shackled to the upper side of the outer-band on the boom; the upper eye reeved through the thimble or bull's-eye on the pendant, and shackled to the lower block of a gun-tackle-purchase. The upper block of the purchase shackles to an eye on the fore side of the main-cap, and the fall leads down to the spider-band.

The sheet block is double and may be attached to the spar by any of the methods already described. I should perhaps mention that the luff of the sail is bent to timber hoops on the lower-mast.

With the exception of the topping-lift and the alternative rig for the mizzen peak-halliard, the lead of the gear on both main and mizzen sails is the same as on the fore. The main-topping-lift of the three-master is formed by rigging a short wire pendant from the mizzen cross-trees, and to this pendant is shackled the upper block of a gun-tackle-purchase. The lower block of the purchase is shackled to the outer-band on the boom, and the fall belayed on the mizzen spider-band. To prevent the peak of the main-gaff sagging to leeward a separate tackle is rigged. A short wire strop having a thimble or bull's-eye in one end and an eye-splice the other, is shackled to the fore side of the mizzen-cap. A wire pendant is then seized to the peak of the main-gaff; reeved through the bull's-eye on the short pendant; and the lower end shackled to the upper block of a gun-tackle-purchase set up on deck. All this will be found on the sail plan on Plate 47.

The topping-lift on the main-mast of a two-master or the mizzen of a three, is rigged in the usual way. The lift is shackled to the upper side of the outer-band on the boom; reeved through a block on the side of the mizzen-cap; and is set up on deck with a three-fold purchase. A few of the larger coasters rigged double lifts, that is to say one on each side of the sail, but this is very unusual. The topping-lift should be well provided with chafing gear at close intervals between the boom and the mast.

The rig of the jib-headed topsails on main and mizzen is very simple. The halliard shackles to the head of the sail, reeves through a block at the topmast-hounds, and so down to the deck. The downhaul is also shackled to the head-cringle and leads down to the deck in the same way. The sheet, or outhaul, is bent to the clew of the sail; reeves through a jewel-block—or in some cases a cheek-block on the starboard-side—at the peak of the gaff; through a single block below the gaff-jaws and so down to the deck. The inhaul is also bent to the clew; reeves through a block below the gaff-jaws on the side opposite to the sheet, and down to the deck. The tack is bent to the tack of the sail and belayed to the spider-band round the foot of the mast. The luff of the sail may be bent to hoops on the topmast between the lower-cap and the hounds; hanked to a wire stay leading from the topmast-hounds and setting up on deck with a tackle, or the sail may be set flying.

Before leaving the schooner I had better mention two sails frequently found in the fore and afters. These are the running-square sail and the raffee-topsail. It is quite usual for fore and aft schooners to carry a standing yard on the lower fore-mast. This yard is supported by a truss like that of the normal yard, and has the same lifts and braces. There are various ways of rigging the running square-sail, it may either be set flying, hooped along the yard itself, or hanked to a wire stay set up taut immediately below the yard, rather like an inverted jack-stay, but without stanchions of course. In both the latter cases the bunt of the sail is bent to the centre of the yard, and when being set the head is hauled out to each yard-arm by means of the outhauls already described, and illustrated on Plate 49. When taken in the sail hangs vertically in front of the mast, and is furled by winding a gasket round and round the bunched canvas. The raffee-topsail is triangular and sets between the yard and the mast-head. As a rule this sail is furled along the top of the yard, and is hoisted by a halliard to the mast-head.

That I think brings us to the end of the gear of the every-day coaster, and together with the details already given for the big ship should enable the modeller to make a reasonably good job of rigging a ship of this type. On this last point it always seems to me to be a pity that so little interest should be taken by the model builder in these grand little ships, which to my mind are worthy of the best that can be put into them. There is everything to be said for them from the model builder's point of view, for not only is the rig relatively simple, but the prototype being a small ship, allows the model to be on a fairly large scale without becoming cumbersome in size, and the hull is an ideal type for good plank on frame construction.

Before going on to the barquentine rig I would like to say just a few words about the various other types of small craft which were at one time common in both deep-sea and coastal trades. The brig and snow require little mention from the constructional point of view, for their masts are normal square-rigged masts such as will be found in any ship or barque rigged vessel, although smaller vessels of the coasting trade were often rather more lightly rigged, having no yards above the topgallants. In the case of the snow there is also the addition of the trysail-mast abaft the main, but this has been illustrated in the details of timber spars. The brigantine has the normal square-rig forward with a schooner's main abaft it. By the way I am using the term brigantine in its modern sense, for what we now call a brigantine is really an herma-phrodite-brig. The true brigantine has a fully square-rigged fore-mast with a topsail-schooner's *fore-mast* as a main, in other words, she carried square-sails on the topmast of her fore and aft rigged main. However the true brigantine vanished long ago, and the hermaphrodite-brig is now always accepted as being a brigantine.

The small barquentine may be divided into two distinct classes, each with very marked, if somewhat small, differences in rigging, and major differences in hull design. The first class ranges from say 150 to 250 tons register, and has the typical three-mast schooner hull. She is flush-decked throughout, or at the most has a quarterdeck raised only a few inches above the main-deck, with hatches and all fittings arranged as in the schooner. The second type averages about 500 tons and is usually a very handsome craft, with good sheer and sweeping bows. The deck arrangement follows more closely that of the big ship. A small anchor deck at the level of the main-rail in the bows; a relatively large deckhouse with boats on top; a quarterdeck raised to the level of the topgallant-rail and surrounded by a teak rail on turned wood pillars, with the coach roof of the after accommodation forming a small monkey poop up through it. Yes, the majority of these little ships were a delight to the eye, even if they did not have all the majestic rigging of the ship or barque. In fact I think a well balanced barquentine rig can be every bit as good to look at as any other rig. Of course the big steel barquentine is another matter, with all their spars of the same size on each mast, many of them had the "made by the mile and sold by the yard" look, and as for some of the conversions, ex ships and barques, well the less said the better!

However, I am wandering from the point. The small type of barquentine usually has a fore-mast with a very short topgallant, and crossing only four yards, lower, double topsail, and single topgallant. Her standing and running-rigging is also kept as simple as possible, four shrouds on the fore, and three on the main and mizzen are generally considered ample for a ship of this class. The main and mizzen masts are rigged as for the schooner, with the wide single cross-tree and one stay on each side supporting the topmast. Her main and mizzen also carry the schooner's jib-headed topsails above the gaff-sails.

The larger class is a different vessel altogether. Her fore-mast is usually well proportioned and crosses a royal over double-topsails and a single-topgallant. Both standing and running rigging follow big ship practice; five shrouds per side on the fore-mast, with two or three topmast and topgallant backstays, and a royal backstay. Bunt-lines, clew-lines, etc., are all rigged as on her larger sister. On the fore and aft masts four shrouds are rigged per side, while instead of the single wide cross-tree she carries a miniature top, or in a few cases a pair of short cross-trees like those on the fore-mast of a topsail-schooner. The topmast has stops or hounds about one-third down from the head, dividing it into topmast and topgallant-pole; and instead of being supported by a single wire on either side, two topmast shrouds are rigged. These are set up like those on a schooner's fore-mast; from the topmast-hounds down through the rim of the top and set up to the futtock-band with lanyards. Topmast and topgallant backstays extend between the topmast and topgallant hounds respectively and the ship's rail, where they are all set up with dead-eyes to chain-plates in the normal way.

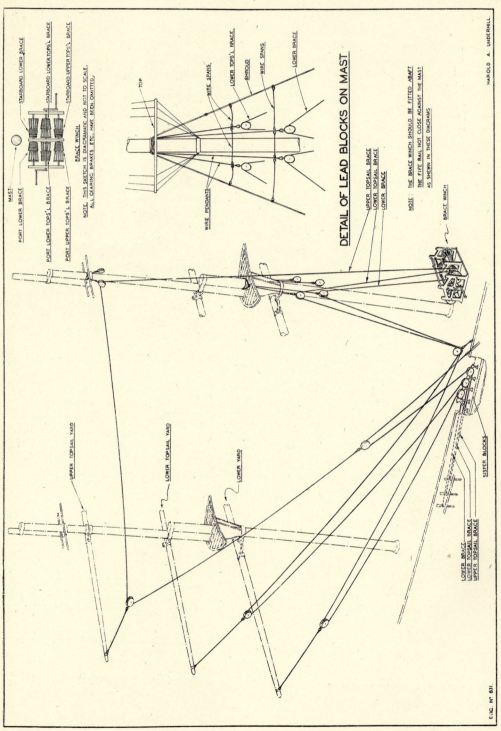

DETAIL OF LEAD BLOCKS ON MAST

STARBOARD LOWER BRACE
STARBOARD LOWER TOPS'L BRACE
STARBOARD UPPER TOPS'L BRACE
BRACE WINCH
MAST
PORT LOWER BRACE
PORT LOWER TOPS'L BRACE
PORT UPPER TOPS'L BRACE

NOTE. THIS SKETCH IS DIAGRAMATIC AND NOT TO SCALE. ALL GEARING BRAKES ETC. HAVE BEEN OMITTED.

TOP
WIRE SPANS
LOWER TOPS'L BRACE
SHROUD
WIRE SPANS
LOWER BRACE
WIRE PENDANTS

UPPER TOPSAIL BRACE
LOWER TOPSAIL BRACE
LOWER BRACE
BRACE WINCH

NOTE: THE BRACE WINCH SHOULD BE FITTED ABAFT THE FIFE RAIL NOT CLOSE AGAINST THE MAST AS SHEWN IN THESE DIAGRAMS

UPPER TOPSAIL YARD
LOWER TOPSAIL YARD
LOWER YARD

SISTER BLOCKS
LOWER BRACE
LOWER TOPSAIL BRACE
UPPER TOPSAIL BRACE

ENG. N° 831.

HAROLD A. UNDERHILL.

PLATE No. 40.—LEAD OF BRACES TO BRACE WINCH.

A jib-headed topsail is carried on the mizzen, but not on the main. A triatic-stay is rigged from the after side of the main-cap to the fore side of the mizzen, and a mizzen-topmast-stay and topgallant-stay extend down from their respective hounds to the after side of the main-cap. A mizzen-topmast-staysail, hanked to the stay takes the place of the jib-headed main-topsail of the smaller type of craft. The mizzen mast is generally slightly smaller than the main in every respect, which gives the whole rig perfect balance to the eye. Hoisting gaffs are most commonly used on both masts, but there are one or two examples where the mizzen has a standing gaff and the sail brailed in to the mast. Having once built a model of one of these little vessels, I can assure the reader that they are excellent ships for the purpose.

There used to be quite a large number of small barques of 500 to 700 tons, which were very pretty little craft and well worth study, but from the rigging point of view need no special mention for their spar plans were simply the larger ship scaled down. I have also mentioned the trading ketch, but here again the details already given in this chapter will be sufficient to cover that rig should it be required.

CHAPTER VIII.

UNUSUAL RIGS.

THERE can be no doubt as to where to begin a chapter on unusual rigs, the obvious point is with the Vinnen Schooners. These ships are—or should it be, were, for I am not certain whether any are still afloat in this sixth year of the war—certainly unique in rig, and carry a sail plan which has never been used in any other vessel. There have been many strange rigs from time to time during the long era of sail, but with the exception of the five-mast barquentine *Transit* of 1800, none of them stood quite alone, all having some vessel more or less akin in some way or another. There is a wide difference in the grounds on which the *Transit* and the Vinnen ships can claim to be unusual, for whereas the rig of the former was really that of a barquentine, every single component forming it was completely unorthodox, while with the Vinnen fleet the components were normal, but their assembly produced an entirely new rig.

Perhaps the nearest approach to the Vinnen rig was the famous six-master *Great Eastern*, and one may be permitted to wonder to what extent, if any, the designer of the Vinnen schooners drew inspiration from Brunel's masterpiece. However the *Great Eastern* was a steam ship with auxiliary sail, whereas the Vinnen ships are sailers with an auxiliary engine. As it seems just possible that there may be some link between the two designs, and as an interesting comparison, I will just refresh the readers' memory regarding the *Great Eastern*; although as a true steamer she has no real place here. She had six masts, but how they were named I do not know, and for the sake of convenience I propose to number them from the bow. No. 1 was a short pole mast with a fore-staysail set up to the stem head, and a gaff fore-sail. Nos. 2 and 3 both carried topmasts and crossed a lower-yard, topsail-yard and topgallant-yard, they also had a standing gaff. Nos. 4 and 5 also carried topmasts, but they were only fore and aft rigged, while No. 6 reverted to a short pole-mast like No. 1 and carried only a gaff-sail. Speaking generally I should think the complete arrangement was just about as ugly as any rig could be, and from this angle there certainly is no connection between the *Great Eastern* and the schooners, for the latter were very fine looking ships even though out of the ordinary.

There were five of these schooners, all sisters built from the same design between the years 1921 and 1922. Their names were *Adolph Vinnen, Carl Vinnen, Christle Vinnen, Sussane Vinnen* and *Werner Vinnen*, of which perhaps the Carl was the best known. They were quite large ships of 1827 tons register, and their rig, as will be seen from the sail and rigging plan on Plate 50 consisted of five masts all of the same dimensions. The fore and mizzen crossed four yards each and set upper and lower topsails with a single topgallant above, while a running square-sail was permanently bent to a mast-track below the lower-yards. This sail was furled vertically up and down the fore side of the masts, and hauled out to the yard-arms by means of outhauls as already described for the topsail coasting schooner. All square-sails clewed up to the yard-arms as is usual with modern vessels, and carried the normal number of bunt-lines, etc. The gaffs had iron jaws which completely encircled the masts instead of the usual open type, but the luffs of the sails followed normal practice in having hoops on the lower-masts. The main, jigger and after-mast carried no yards, but were typical fore and afters. The rig is very pleasing and the ships well proportioned, although from the point of view of appearance I think they would be improved by the omission of the yards from the mizzen, leaving the rig that of a five-mast topsail schooner, that however is merely a personal opinion. In *Sailing Ships Rigs and Rigging* I referred to the many and various names suggested from time to time for this rig, but I still hold that "Two-topsail schooner" is about as near as one can get. This name is derived from the old "Two-topsail" or "Main-topsail" schooners of the last century, and in view of the fact that the second range of topsails are carried on the mizzen and not the main, the former title is the obvious one to use.

The two-topsail schooner is not a freak but an accepted rig, although it was never very common, and in its original form the alternative name of "Main-topsail" schooner is the most suitable. It consisted of a two-masted schooner having square topsails and topgallants on the main as well as the fore topmast. This is distinct from a brig in that, (a) both masts carry gaff-sails, (b) both carried lower-mast and topmast only, and were therefore not fully square-rigged, and (c) neither mast carried a course. I do not know just when this rig went out of use, but it must be a long time ago.

Next comes the jackass-barque, the variations of which are almost legion, and round about which many wordy battles have raged. Incidentally the term "jackass-rig"—as distinct from jackass-barque—is often used to describe any unusual combination of masts and spars. For the jackass-barque the only factors really necessary to qualify for entry into the ranks seem to be that there must be at least one fully square rigged mast, and that the arrangement of the masts must not be in accordance with any known rig; beyond that there are no limits. All the components of a jackass rig may be perfectly normal or otherwise in themselves, but their combination and assembly must not comprise any accepted rig. There were jackass-barques consisting of a fully square-rigged fore-mast, followed by a fore and aft main with square topsails on the topmast and a normal fore and aft mizzen bringing up in the rear.

Then there was the famous *Olympic* with her two fully square rigged masts followed by two normal fore and aft rigged masts, a kind of three-mast barque with an extra mast thrown in for luck. In both these examples each mast taken alone was a normal spar, it was only the combination which was out of the ordinary. Incidentally the *Olympic* was later cut down to a four-mast barquentine by taking out the square-rigged main-mast and replacing it by a fore and after, but even then she was far from being a good looking ship, for although the hull was very shapely the mast spacing was unbalanced. No doubt it looked alright in her old rig, for with the two square-rigged masts forward and the two fore and afters aft, they automatically divided themselves into two groups, and so long as each pair looked right, the space joining them did not seem to matter. But as a barquentine the spacing looked all wrong, there was a long gap between the fore and main; then a very short one between the main and mizzen; a greater space between mizzen and jigger, and an even longer one from that mast to the stern; it all had a very patched up look.

In the little ships we have several examples of unorthodox rig, and one which, although never really common, could be seen in fair numbers, was a

FIG. 166.

form of staysail schooner sometimes called a schooner-brigantine, (Fig. 166). It will be seen that she has the normal spars of a topsail schooner; the fore-mast consisting of a lower-mast and topmast on which are crossed double-topsails and a single topgallant, without any square-sail—or fore-sail—below the lower-yard. Her main-mast is also perfectly normal in both construction and rig, but between the masts, instead of the usual gaff fore-sail she has a range of staysails. Is she a schooner or a brigantine? Well your guess is as good as mine, for to the best of my knowledge the rig has never been defined and really has no name. But as her principal spars are those of a schooner, and, for other reasons which I will mention later, there is more of the schooner in her than anything else, I personally think she should be so called. The same rig appeared as a three-master and of course raised the question of schooner or barquentine, but again I feel satisfied that one must accept her as the former. After all the essential factor in defining the brigantine and barquentine is that both rigs must have a *fully* square-rigged fore-mast, which to my mind definitely rules out the rig shewn in **Fig. 166**, and her three-masted counterpart, as neither have the sails or spars of full square rig. Perhaps the best description would be "square-rigged staysail-schooner", anyway the reader can take his choice.

The above is not the only variation of this rig, for it appears in many "shades", and some incline more towards the brigantine. There is the case where the fore-mast carries a standing fore-course bent to the yard in the usual way. In fact as far as sails are concerned she has the full complement to make her square-rigged forward, but the actual spars of the fore-mast are still those of the schooner, namely a lower-mast and topmast, although in this case the lower-mast is relatively shorter and carries a top but no top-mast cross-trees. What is she? I think one must let her into the brigantine class, even though she is still not a true brigantine as her fore-mast does not carry a fidded topgallant. I know that this is rather a case of splitting hairs, but at one end of the scale you have the schooner, and at the other the brigantine, and there must be a line of demarcation somewhere, the question is just where is it? If for any reason you particularly wish to identify these rigs I suggest that the titles of square-rigged staysail schooner or schooner-brigantine are as near as you will get to it, or in the case of the three-master call her a schooner-barquentine, but I repeat, these are only my own suggestions and must not be regarded as authoritative.

FIG. 167.

In much the same category is the schooner-ketch, (Fig. 167), although she could not possibly be mistaken for other than she is, except perhaps when seen from dead end on when she will look like a normal topsail-schooner.

Q

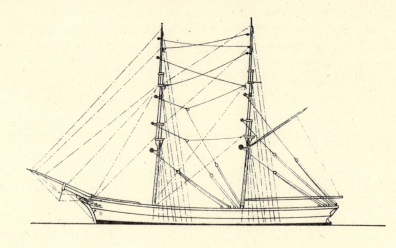

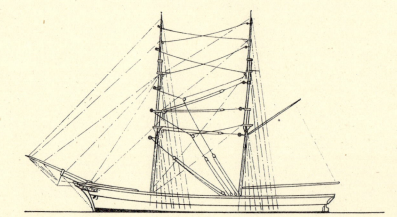

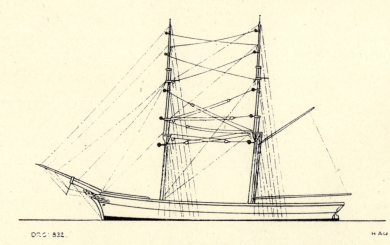

PLATE No. 41.—BRACES OF A BRIG OR SNOW.

Another name, and I think a more appropriate one, is topsail-ketch. Her main-mast is a true topsail-schooner's fore-mast and crosses double-topsail yards. The gaff and boom are proportionately longer than would be the case with the schooner because the mizzen mast is stepped much further aft. This of course applies to any coasting ketch, topsail or otherwise, and if the yards are removed from the topsail-ketch the rig is perfectly normal. The topsail ketch was at one time quite common on the East Coast as the rig of the Billy-Boy, although the latter's hull was of course of a particular type.

With the three-mast schooners one often finds vessels with topmasts on the fore and main and only a pole mast for the mizzen, this applies particularly to the fore and afters and auxiliary craft. I am of course not referring to ships which lost their mizzen-topmast during the last few years of sail, and did not think it worth while replacing, particularly if they had an auxiliary engine. I remember the schooner *Ryelands* trudged up and down the coast for several years with what looked like, and probably was, a broom handle nailed to the mizzen above the cross-trees in lieu of a topmast. Incidentally she also had one of her booms fished with old planks and a length of chain, although just how long it remained so I cannot say. I rather suspect that the broom handle "topmast" was not merely a sign of hard times, but also a touch of "auxiliaryitus", and that like many others she thought more of her engine than her spars, however perhaps I am being unfair to the old girl.

Some years ago I saw a three-mast fore and aft schooner which was something in the nature of a double-yoked ketch, at least she looked like a ketch with an off-shoot growing aft. She had three pole masts, of which the fore-mast was the largest, then followed the main and mizzen, each successively smaller than the one before. I can't say that the general effect was one to be admired, and I have often wondered whether she was built that way, or whether her original rig had carried a larger main. It is just possible that her main may have been lost or damaged, and replaced by a spar which happened to be available at the time, and unfortunately was just between the fore and mizzen in length. I have often wondered, but I don't suppose I will ever know.

Another rig which is very uncommon among the merchant craft of this country, although it has come more to the fore in the yachts of the last few years, is the fore and aft staysail schooner. This as its name suggests, is a schooner rig in which all sails except the aftermost one are carried on stays between the masts or out to the bowsprit. There are several variations in the lead of the stays, but the principle is the same in them all. The only commercial craft of this rig that I can call to mind as being built in this country is the *John Williams*, whose sail and rigging plan I produced in *Sailing Ship Rigs and Rigging*.

I have limited this book to the various rigs which could at one time or

another be seen round the coasts of this country, but if one were going further
afield, then the number of small craft with rigs which to us are unusual, would
require not a chapter but a book. I would not care to have to name all the
queer combinations which, up to a year or so ago, could be found in the Mediterranean alone. Fore and afters of all sorts and sizes; brigs, brigantines of
strange rig; mixtures of square, fore and aft and lateen rig all in one craft
and so on. Perhaps I may be allowed to wander sufficiently far from the
straight and narrow path, to mention two Italian rigs which I always find
interesting. The first is the two-mast fore and aft schooner, with masts stepped
well-forward—both pole masts by the way—so that the fore is right in the
eyes of the ship, an enormous bowsprit and jib-boom almost as long as the
ship herself and a main-boom to match. These vessels usually have rather
pretty hulls, with a shapely stem and plenty of sheer. The other rig is the
polacre brigantine. The polacre rig consists of a pole mast crossing three or
more square yards, but having no cross-trees or topmast-rigging other than
backstays. When taking in sail all the upper yards come down in a bunch,
so that the topsail, topgallant and royal are all together at a point where
the lower-mast-cap would normally be.

Now we come to what was the most interesting "unusual" rig ever turned
out, that of the *Transit*. Unlike the Vinnen sisters this was not merely an
unusual combination of ordinary spars, but every detail was unlike anything
that had ever been used before, or for that matter, since, and from keel to
truck she was designed as a complete breakaway from all the shipping world
of her time understood. Her hull design and construction certainly has no
real place here, and all I will say in that direction is that she had very small
beam in relation to length, and that all her sections flaired outward the whole
way from keel to rail, so that for her entire length she was "V" section, or
wider on deck than at the water line. That alone must have been a shock
to the shipping fraternity of her age, for those were the days of excessive
tumble-home on the topsides, and for that matter, except perhaps for certain
naval types, a certain amount of tumble-home is to be found in all ships
right up to the present day. But if the hull proved a shock there was
more to come, for the sail and rigging design must have been positively
staggering!

The ship was designed—or should one say invented, for she was covered
by a fourteen years patent—by Captain R. H. Gower, a practical seaman who
had seen service with the Hon. East India Company; and she was the outcome
of his observations and experiments carried out while in command of normal
ships. Captain Gower raised the money from various sources and personally
supervised the building of the vessel and it is reported that thanks to his
simplified system of framing and the absence of curves in the topsides, he
was able to use ordinary house carpenters for most of the construction, only

calling in shipwrights when she was ready for planking. However the hull construction is another story, and we cannot go any further into it here.

The rigging of the ship as covered by the patent specification has no parallel either before or since, but there seems some doubt as to just how far the details of the original specification were carried out in the actual building of the ship, for a contemporary painting shows many of the details as being of more or less normal construction. This however is not conclusive proof that Gower did not build exactly to his specification, although for reasons which I will give later, I think it probably correct. It is of course possible that the artist may be at fault; he may have based his picture on sketches made some distance from the vessel, and having got the main outline and features correctly drawn, filled in the smaller details from his knowledge of the accepted practice of the time. If this is the case no one could blame him, for mast construction had remained more or less unchanged since the days of the old circular fighting top of "egg-cup" design, and for that matter, except for the introduction of iron and steel, has remained much the same up to the present day.

She was designed and built as a five-master, square-rigged on the foremast and fore and aft rigged on the remainder; she was in fact a five-mast barquentine, although none of the contemporary reporters seem to have known just what to call her, for they simply played safe and referred to her as the five-masted sailing vessel *Transit*. She was later reduced to four masts, but just when it is difficult to say, although it seems to have been during the somewhat lengthy period between completion and proceeding on her first voyage; a period spent by her designer in unsuccessful efforts to interest the Admiralty and larger shipping companies in his idea.

Fig. 168 is a reconstruction based upon the details given in the original patent specification, but I want to make it quite clear that this is my own

FIG. 168.

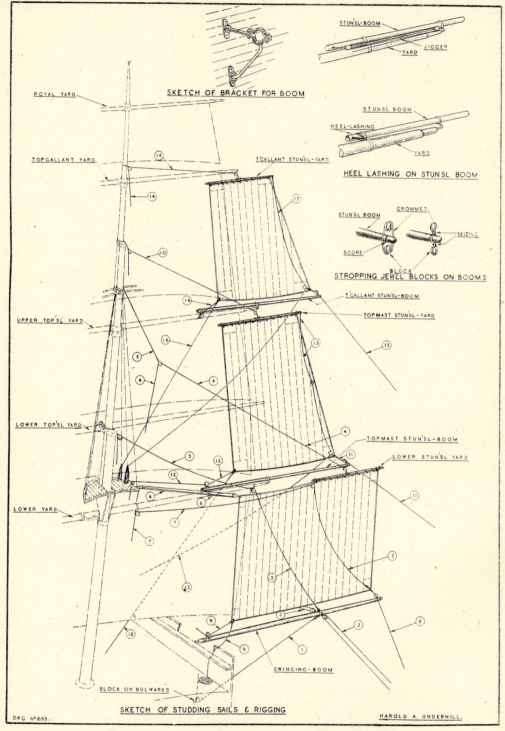

SKETCH OF BRACKET FOR BOOM

HEEL LASHING ON STUN'SL BOOM

STROPPING JEWEL BLOCKS ON BOOMS

SKETCH OF STUDDING SAILS & RIGGING

DRG Nº 833.

HAROLD A. UNDERHILL.

PLATE NO. 42.—STUN'SLS AND STUN'SL RIGGING.

drawing and is not authenticated beyond the fact that the *details* agree with those of the specification. I have no complete sail and rigging plan, and have simply assembled the individual masts shown in the specification in the proportions *I think* may have been used. Fig. 169 is a copy of the vessel as shown

FIG. 169.

in the contemporary painting, and comparison of the two will reveal the several differences to which I have already referred.

To start with the rig as specified. Generally; each mast was to be self supporting and have no standing-rigging connecting it to its neighbours. To gain that end the masts were rigged flag-pole fashion, that is to say each was stayed to four points, one point on each side forward of the mast, and one on each side abaft it. No fore and aft stays were rigged on the centre line of the vessel, and the topmasts of the fore and afters were to be rigged with the doublings on one side instead of forward of the lower-masts, this was supposed to enable them to be struck without fouling the sails.

On the lower fore-mast the top—or in the case of small vessels, single cross-trees—was to be placed on top of the mast-cap, and above instead of below the doublings, an arrangement of which I must admit I fail to see the advantage. This position of the top is our first point of difference between the picture and the specification, for the former clearly shows the top in the normal place. It is possible, and I think quite likely, that the ship was so built, but on the other hand when the artist came to work up his original sketches and saw where he had put the top, he may have thought he had been suffering from a touch of the sun, and decided to put things right before anyone noticed it. One could certainly sympathize with him, for to arrive back in the studio and find that you had perched the top daintily on the mast-head like a sun bonnet, would be enough to shake any self respecting marine artist. One only expects that kind of thing in modern commercial art, and our painter of the year 1800 could hardly know that.

The next amazing feature was that the lower-yard was to be above the fore-stay, and the fore-course have a triangular hole cut in it to allow the stay to pass through. The foot of the sail was to lace to a boom, our old friend the bentinck-boom in fact, although with the addition of the lacing. The reef-points were to be along the foot of the sail, and tied round the boom instead of the yard. I do not know how the crew were to get at these points when tying down a reef, but no doubt the inventor had made some provision for this. It will be seen that the fore-course is another point of difference between the original design and the painting, the artist has omitted the sail and boom and placed the yard in its normal position below the stay.

The topsail is more or less ordinary except that crow's-feet were attached to the foot on either side of the mast, and from these, lines extended down to the spider-band on the mast. The object of this was to stretch the sail flat, although the same end could have been gained by lacing the foot of the sail to the yard below. There is nothing to be said about the topgallant, that seems quite ordinary.

The fore and aft masts were even more unorthodox than the fore, and must have been a real shock to the sailors of that day. Each fore and aft mast carried three sails, which the designer calls, course, topsail and topgallant respectively. The courses and topsails are truly rectangular in shape, the former extending from the lower-mast cap to a point just above the deck, and the topsail from the cap to the topmast-hounds. The luffs of both these sails were laced to their respective masts. The course was extended by two spars or sprits, having jaws on their inner ends to fit the mast. These spars ran diagonally across the sail; the upper one extending upwards to the peak, and the lower down to the clew, and they were held against the sail by means of canvas straps sewn across them at intervals; these were intended to keep the sail flat when the sprits were on the windward side. A throat halliard extended from the jaws of the upper sprit to the cap on the lower-mast head, and another tackle was rigged between the jaws of the lower sprit and the deck. Hauling on both these tackles tended to pull the sprits nearer to the horizontal position, so forcing the peak and clew diagonally outwards and stretching the sail flat and taut. The canvas straps were made longer as they neared the jaws, which allowed for the necessary movement of the sprit during the process of tensioning down the tackles.

The topsail has a single sprit rigged in the same way and furnished with a tackle between the jaws and the topmast-hounds. This sail was provided with brails, and when taken in was simply brailed back to the mast with the sprit running up and down abaft it. The topgallant also had a single sprit, and one brail which followed the leech of the sail; reeved through a sheave in the mast-head and so down to the deck. The topsail sheet reeved through a block on the upper sprit of the course; in and through a block at the lower-cap, and so down to the deck. The course had a sheet which belayed to the spider-band of the mast next abaft, while a second sheet or vang led from the peak of the sail to the lower-cap of the mast next abaft. A vang was also rigged between the peak of the topsail sprit and the topmast-hounds of the mast next abaft.

If one compares the fore and aft masts as laid down in the specification with those shown in the painting, it will be noted that the unusual construction and rig of the masts themselves has been faithfully reproduced; the four point staying; doublings on the side, and diagonal cross-trees to suit the placing of the stays, are all correctly shown, which to my mind is a very strong point in the artist's favour. It seems hardly likely that he would accurately record the rigging details on fore and aft masts, and yet fail to notice some extremely odd arrangements on the fore. This however brings us to another point of difference, it will be seen that while the painting shows the courses and topsails rectangular in shape, the topgallants have become normal jib-headed sails; also the sprits have been omitted and gaffs and booms used instead, although of course, owing to the shape of the sails the gaffs are horizontal. Here again we have little to go on in deciding which is correct for the ship as built, but contemporary reports seem to suggest that the sprits gave a lot of trouble during her trials, and it is quite possible that they were abandoned and replaced by gaffs and booms as shown in the painting.

There is a possible explanation which would cover all the points of difference, and one which I think most likely correct, although it is purely supposition on my part without any concrete evidence to support it, and under the present circumstances I have no opportunity for further research to test it. The employment of house carpenters instead of shipwrights, and the use of old wire re-layed for the standing-rigging; or for that matter, the fact of Captain Gower building the craft himself instead of entrusting her to a ship-builder, all seem to point to a need for economy. Therefore it seems reasonable to suggest that he may have had the offer of a square-rigged mast out of a salvaged vessel, and decided to use it as a fore-mast, so saving the expense of a new one. This is rather borne out by the height of the fore-mast as shown in the painting, where it is much higher than the fore and afters, while the text and sketches of the patent both suggest that all masts were intended to be equal. Here again it seems most unlikely that the painter would make such a glaring mistake if it were not true to the actual ship. At this stage, the construction of the first ship, Captain Gower would no doubt anticipate his rig creating sufficient interest to be repeated in another, giving him an opportunity to incorporate the rest of his ideas in this next vessel, which, the rig having passed the experimental stage, he could reasonably expect

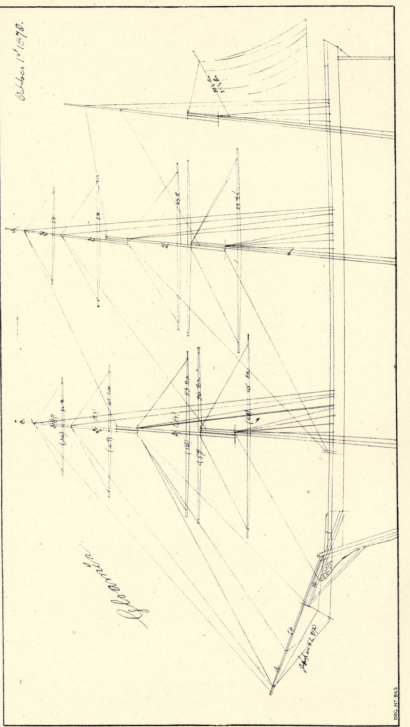

PLATE No. 43.—MAST AND RIGGING PLAN FOR BARQUE "GLOAMIN."

(Reproduced from the original drawing.)

to build without the need for improvisation on the grounds of economy. After all, the modifications intended for the fore-mast represented a very small part of the design as a whole, and he may have been quite willing to forgo them if by so doing he could save the cost of a new fore-mast. There is no evidence to suggest that the fore and aft masts were not built to the specification, in fact both the painting and such other evidence as there is all point the other way, and suggest that they were. The sprits appear to have proved extremely temperamental, and on these grounds I think it quite possible that they were abandoned in favour of gaffs and booms. All this is pure conjecture, but it would explain why a picture, painted at a time when artists did as a rule understand the ships they painted, should differ to such an extent from the ship as designed.

Captain Gower appears to have tried very hard to interest both the Admiralty and the Hon. East India Company in his rig, and even got so far as to be allowed to test the ship against one of the crack Naval sloops of the day. During these trials *Transit* seems to have actually sailed rings round the naval vessel, beating her on every point of sailing in spite of the fact that a large part of *Transit's* crew had been shipped for the test, and had no previous experience with the rig. Reading between the lines of such meagre information as is available, it would seem that the sloop got very peeved about the whole business and just packed up and sailed off home. Even then *Transit* added insult to injury and further disturbed the ruffled feathers by beating her soundly on the way, arriving at the anchorage some fourteen hours ahead of her rival. What foolish tactics! they proved altogether too much for my Lords of the Admiralty, who decided, like the man seeing his first elephant, that there was no such animal, and apparently turned both the blind eye and the deaf ear to all appeals for recognition of the trials. The East India Company were also nibbling at the idea, but they too cooled off, perhaps as a matter of policy, and in the end Captain Gower had to take her to sea to earn her keep.

She sailed in convoy, and immediately proceeded to demonstrate her superiority over both convoy and escort by sailing round them all, proving over and over again that she was not only fast, but handled beautifully under all conditions. If Captain Gower had any ideas that such tactics might cause My Lords to reconsider their attitude, he ought to have known better. During the war with France she was often chased by privateers and war vessels, but none seem to have been able to make up on her, except on one occasion when she was reported to have indulged in a cat and mouse game, but in this instance the mouse was doing the playing. From all reports it appears that she consistently outsailed and outweathered all ships of her time, but her design was too revolutionary and nothing ever came of it. It must have been a great disappointment to her designer that in spite of all she had done, no one would admit any interest in her, and although an undoubted success she should be regarded as a white elephant. She was certainly not a pretty ship judged by accepted standards, but that may be said of many vessels of more orthodox rig, and it is a great pity that she failed to gain the recognition she deserved, for had she done so we to-day might have been better informed as to her build.

In describing *Transit* I have said that she was barquentine rigged, but that the reporters of the day did not know what to call her. This of course is quite understandable, for the term barquentine was not coined until about half a century later, in fact I think it was about 1869 or 1870 before it was at all commonly used. Prior to that it was quite usual to refer to the rig as a three-masted brig, although its relation to the brig seems to be rather obscure. However the nomenclature of rigs has undergone so many changes that it is difficult to trace the origin of many, and one has to be very circumspect in trying to visualize rigs as described before the middle of the last century, for the same term may represent entirely different rigs at different periods. Even so, the use of the term three-masted brig for the rig we now call the barquentine, has to me always been difficult to understand, I would have said that the normal ship rig was about the only one to which the term could reasonably apply, however that is all beside the point. The development of the barquentine and brigantine rigs is a subject which offers scope for interesting research, and I hope that when I get back to civilian life I may devote a little time to it.

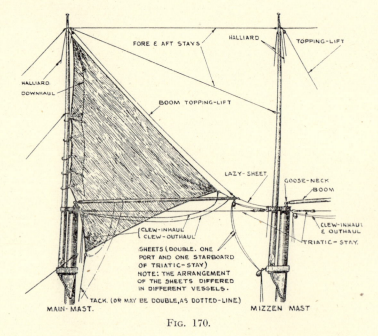

Fig. 170.

Apart from the vessels which were completely unorthodox in rig, there are several well known examples of additional spars being carried on what were otherwise normal sail plans. For instance there was the four-mast barquentine *Oberon* with booms on her mizzen and jigger topmast-staysails.   These booms were carried in goose-necks on the main and mizzen mast heads respectively —Fig. 170—and the sheets were taken aft to the cap of the mast next abaft. This arrangement gave the vessel a rather untidy look aloft when all canvas was furled, but it was a labour saving rig devised by her master, and obviated the need for passing the sheets over the triatic-stay every time the ship went about.

The four-mast barquentine *Renfield* crossed a single yard on the mizzen lower-mast, and on this a running square-sail and, I believe, raffee-topsail were set, while, if my memory is not at fault, several other barquentines of the same fleet carried these square yards on all the fore and aft masts.

Another interesting little ship was that beautiful barquentine *Tacora*. She was rather out of the ordinary in the arrangement of the square yards on the fore-mast, there was however a good reason for this.   *Tacora* was built as a four-mast fore and aft schooner, but on the advice of her master was converted to a four-mast barquentine, a change which turned out to be well worth while as it improved her performance all round.   This conversion was made without removing the original fore-mast, by the simple process of building a top between the cross-trees and the deck, and of course re-rigging the mast accordingly thus converting the original fore and aft mast into a square-rigged lower-mast and pole topmast, while by fitting additional hounds for the topgallant rigging,

Fig. 171.

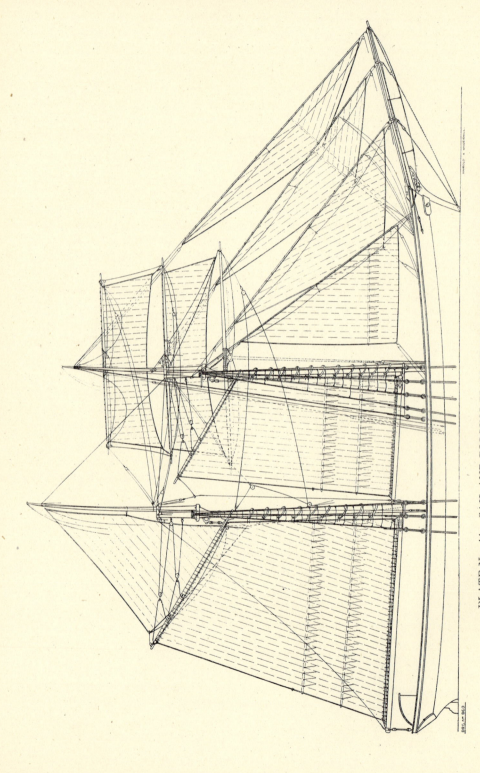

PLATE No. 44.—SAIL AND RIGGING PLAN OF TWO-MAST TOPSAIL SCHOONER.

the original topmast became the topgallant and royal. This will be seen in the sketch Fig. 171.

This new rig gave her a fore-topmast which was rather short to accommodate double topsails, so a single topsail yard was crossed, even then this sail was very little deeper than a normal upper-topsail. The original schooner rig had rather long doublings, which of course remained so on the converted fore-mast, so that the topgallant yard was rather high even when down on the cap. This under normal circumstances would have left a large gap between the topgallant and topsail yards when the canvas was taken in, but *Tacora* always kept her topsail yard well up the topmast—as shown in the sketch— when sail was furled, resulting in a range of evenly spaced single yards, which gave the ship a very smart and almost dainty appearance aloft. This, together with her yacht like hull, earned her the reputation of being the most beautiful barquentine ever turned out, and personally, I think she deserved it.

The four-mast topsail schooner rig is certainly not unorthodox, but it was never very commonly used. There were however one or two well known Baltic schooners so rigged, and of course we have one modern example in the Spanish training ship *Juan Sebastian de Elcano*, a steel auxiliary vessel of 3220 tons, launched in 1900. Her sail and rigging plan is reproduced in *Sailing Ship Rigs and Rigging*.

CHAPTER IX.

USE OF TABLES AND FORMULAE.

I HAVE several times stressed the point regarding care in making spars and rigging in correct proportions. I am not suggesting that badly proportioned models are in the majority, far from it, but in my opinion, of those models which are below par, more are spoiled in this way than any other, and I think it safe to say that in nine cases out of ten it is due to spars and gear being too thick and heavy. The odd one we will put down as the model where the masts are too long for the hull, for I do not think I have ever seen a single one where the builder has erred on the light side. Why should this be I wonder?

With the sailor made model built at sea there is good reason, for he had neither photographs nor drawings to show him the ship as a whole, and as pointed out in a previous chapter, he was naturally impressed by the diameter and thickness of everything. These were dimensions he could actually see, whereas lengths were usually so great that from his viewpoint they simply stretched away in the distance, providing little idea of proportion. The net result was that he generally exaggerated everything and produced an over sparred and over rigged model. Yes, over emphasis is both understandable and excusable in the model built at sea. One must also remember that the sailor had few tools and even less material suitable for fine work.

Models by the model maker ashore are a different matter. They are usually built under better conditions where both tools and materials are available, and what is more to the point, photographs or drawings to work from. Under such circumstances thick and clumsy spars and rigging are neither understandable nor excusable. It is not a question of scale or measurement, although that after all is simple enough, but just one of direct comparison between photograph or drawing and the model, and it seems unbelievable that anyone should be unable to make direct visual comparison.

One possible explanation is that in the makers anxiety to see quick results they may perhaps have proceeded to rig and fit each individual spar as soon as it is made, instead of completing all the spars before doing any rigging at all. I know this ought not to make any difference, each spar *should* be properly proportioned in itself, but none the less it is certainly easier to judge the spars as a whole rather than individually.

My advice is to make all your spars, and finish them except for the final slight polish. Then step the masts and cross the yards, binding them in place by means of thread. Now compare the model with the photograph; try to look at it from the same angle, and then from all other viewpoints. If possible leave it temporarily rigged for a day or so, going back to look at it from time to time. It is surprising how you can spot faults in a thing you thought perfect when first finished, if only you leave it for a time and go back to it with an open mind. If you are not too good at judging proportions you may try the following, which may help to bring the model and the photograph nearer to par. Take a piece of cardboard and cut out the centre as if to frame the photograph, then, holding cardboard and photograph side by side at arms length and looking through the hole in the card, walk backwards away from the model until it occupies the same place in the opening as the ship does in the photograph. It is of course an advantage to place the model against a suitable background, as this will throw the spars in good sharp outline. This method will give a good idea of comparison between photograph and model.

If you feel that the spars are the slightest bit on the heavy side, then for goodness sake thin them down, for if they look heavy at this stage they will be even worse when you have added jack-stays, foot-ropes, etc., and it is always better to err on the thin side. Remember also that in all probability your photograph will be of the vessel with sails bent, so the thickness you see when comparing it with your model, will include the furled sail on top of the yard, for which of course you must make suitable allowance.

When working from scale drawings there is less risk of badly proportioned spars, but even here it will be as well not to trust too explicitly to the diameters measured from the plan, for as already explained the lines always thicken up in the process of reproduction, and the safest way is to check your diameters with the appropriate spar table in this chapter.

The diameters of all spars bear a definite relation to their length, and in this chapter I have included a number of tables showing the diameters of spars of all kinds and covering a wide range of given lengths, together with the basic formulae from which the various tables have been calculated, so that even though the actual size required is not given, the model maker can work it out for himself.

Table No. 1 has been compiled from Lloyd's standard specifications and tables of scantlings for iron and steel lower-masts, and shows the relative diameters at heel, partners, hounds and head, for masts ranging from 48 feet

R

to 99 feet in overall length.   This length is measured from the top of the keelson to the upper side of the lower-mast cap, the dimensions of the topmast should also be worked out before finally deciding on those of the lower-mast, for should the length of the topmast be such as to require a given diameter which is greater than that of the lower-mast at the cap, the lower-mast would need to be increased in diameter—not length of course—until the two masts are at least equal at that point. To take an example. Assume the length of the lower-mast to be 81 ft., and that of the topmast 54 ft. From table No. 1 we find that the head of the lower-mast requires to be 18 ins. diameter, while from table No. 2 we get the heel of the topmast as 19 ins. diameter. The distance between the topmast heel and the lower-mast cap is relatively short, and the taper on the topmast over this length can be ignored for all practical purposes. Obviously it would look bad to have the topmast of greater diameter than the lower, so the latter would be increased to 19 inches at the cap, and the remaining diameters increased in proportion.

TABLE No. 1.

PROPORTIONS OF IRON OR STEEL LOWER-MASTS.

| Extreme Length | Partners (Given Dia.) | Diameters | | | Extreme Length | Partners (Given Dia.) | Diameters | | |
		Heel	Hounds	Head			Heel	Hounds	Head
Ft.	Ins.	Ins.	Ins.	Ins.	Ft.	Ins.	Ins.	Ins.	Ins.
48	16	13	13½	11	75	25	19½	21	16½
51	17	13½	14	11½	78	26	20	21½	17½
54	18	14	15	12	81	27	21	22½	18
57	19	15	15½	12½	84	28	22	23	18½
60	20	16	16½	13½	87	29	22½	24	19½
63	21	16½	17½	14	90	30	23	25	20
66	22	17	18½	14½	93	31	24	26	20½
69	23	18	19	15½	96	32	25	26½	21
72	24	19	20	16	99	33	26	27	21½

This checking of one spar against another must be carried out right through the spar plan before finally fixing their dimensions, and before any time is expended on making them. To take another example, although an extremely unlikely one; some vessels had relatively short bowsprits carrying very long jib-booms, and this could be carried to a point where the given diameter of the jib-boom would exceed that of the bowsprit at the cap, in which case the bowsprit would of course have to be increased in diameter to suit the jib-boom.

Table No. 2 shows the relative diameters of iron or steel topmasts at various points along their length, and like table No. 1 has been compiled from Lloyd's specification and tables. This particular table requires no special mention, except perhaps with regard to pole-masts—that is to say lower-mast and topmast in one as shown in Fig. 1c. For the purpose of calculating the respective diameters, a pole-mast is treated as two spars. From keelson to the upper side of the lower-cap-band—the band fitted where the lower-cap would be on a fidded mast—is treated as the lower-mast, and above this point regarded as the topmast, and the dimensions taken from tables Nos. 1 and 2 respectively. If, as may well be the case, the heel of the topmast and the head of the lower-mast do not work out at the same diameter, whichever is the smaller will be increased to the diameter of the larger, so forming a continuous spar.

The fore and aft rigged mast of a barque may have all its diameters one-fifth less than those of a square-rigged mast of the same length. This rule will of course also apply to the fore and aft rigged masts of iron or steel barquentines and schooners.

In composite built vessels it is probable that the topmasts will be timber spars, the dimensions of which will be obtained from table No. 6. The lower-masts will be normal iron spars with dimensions as in table No. 1 and of course the rule regarding increasing the lower-mast when necessary to bring its diameter up to that of the topmast still applies.

TABLE No. 2.

PROPORTIONS OF IRON OR STEEL TOPMASTS.

Measured Length	Diameters			Measured Length	Diameters		
	Heel	Hounds	Head		Heel	Hounds	Head
Ft.	Ins.	Ins.	Ins.	Ft.	Ins.	Ins.	Ins.
32	12	$10\frac{1}{2}$	9	50	18	16	$13\frac{1}{2}$
34	$12\frac{1}{2}$	11	$9\frac{1}{2}$	52	$18\frac{1}{2}$	$16\frac{1}{2}$	14
36	13	$11\frac{1}{2}$	10	54	19	17	$14\frac{1}{2}$
38	14	$12\frac{1}{2}$	$10\frac{1}{2}$	56	20	18	15
40	$14\frac{1}{2}$	13	11	58	$20\frac{1}{2}$	$18\frac{1}{2}$	$15\frac{1}{2}$
42	15	$13\frac{1}{2}$	$11\frac{1}{2}$	60	21	19	16
44	16	14	12	62	22	20	$16\frac{1}{2}$
46	$16\frac{1}{2}$	$14\frac{1}{2}$	$12\frac{1}{2}$	64	23	21	17
48	17	15	13	66	24	22	$17\frac{1}{2}$

Even if iron or steel topmasts are carried, the topgallants and royals will usually be timber spars, but in the case of the few big ships which are rigged with metal spars throughout, the proportions of these upper masts will be based on table No. 2.

Table No. 3, which is also compiled from Lloyd's, gives the relative proportions of iron or steel bowsprits, and it will be noted that the given length is stated as being "outboard" of the hull and does not include the housing. This is in fact measured from the forward end of the bed, which may or may not be the point where the spar leaves the hull. In most cases the bed will extend along outside the forward bulkhead to a point just abaft the figure-head, and it will be from this that the spar will be measured. The measured length is really the unsupported length to the outer face of the bowsprit-cap. The diameters given in the table, which by the way is intended for bowsprits carrying jib-booms, are taken at the heel, bed and bowsprit cap. For the proportions of the jib-boom, which will of course be timber, see table No. 9.

Iron and steel spike-booms are not specifically provided for in Lloyd's tables, but the proportions of these spars can be arrived at by measuring from bed to the outer edge of the cap-band the band equal to the bowsprit-cap on a spar carrying a jib-boom—and fixing the dimensions to this point as for a bowsprit with a timber jib-boom. Beyond this point the spar is continued in a taper until the extreme length is reached, at which point the diameter will be about 10 ins. or 12 ins. In full size practice the design of such spar would be submitted to Lloyd's for approval before the work was started.

TABLE No 3.

PROPORTIONS OF IRON OR STEEL BOWSPRITS.

Length	Diameters			Length	Diameters		
	Bed	Heel	Cap		Bed	Heel	Cap
Ft.	Ins.	Ins.	Ins.	Ft.	Ins.	Ins.	Ins.
14	16½	14	12	21	25½	21	17½
15	17½	15	12½	22	26½	22	18½
16	19	16	13	23	28	23	19
17	20	17	14	24	29	24	20
18	21½	18	15	25	30	25	21
19	23	19	16	26	31½	26	21½
20	24½	20	16½	27	33	27	22

Table No. 4 is from Lloyd's standard specification for the construction of iron or steel yards, and gives the diameters at slings, quarters, and yard-arms. The measured length of a yard is taken over the actual metal, excluding the timber yard-arm plugs, or in other words it is measured from outside to outside of yard-arm-bands. The use of the table requires no explanation, but it may be as well to point out that in the majority of cases the lighter yards will be constructed of timber, even in iron and steel vessels. This is illustrated in Plate 25 which is the spar plan for the ships *Mount Stewart* and *Cromdale* from which it will be seen that all yards above the lower-topsail are of timber. It was only with the few last big carriers that all masts and spars were of steel throughout.

TABLE No. 4.

PROPORTIONS OF IRON OR STEEL YARDS.

Measured Length	Slings (Given Dia.)	Quarters			At Yard-Arm Band	Measured Length	Slings (Given Dia.)	Quarters			At Yard-Arm Band
		1st	2nd	3rd				1st	2nd	3rd	
Ft.	Ins.	Ins.	Ins.	Ins.	Ins.	Ft.	Ins.	Ins.	Ins.	Ins.	Ins.
32	8	$7\frac{7}{8}$	$7\frac{1}{4}$	6	4	68	17	$16\frac{1}{2}$	$15\frac{1}{4}$	$12\frac{3}{4}$	$8\frac{1}{2}$
36	9	$8\frac{3}{4}$	$8\frac{1}{8}$	$6\frac{3}{4}$	$4\frac{1}{2}$	72	18	$17\frac{1}{2}$	$16\frac{1}{4}$	$13\frac{1}{2}$	9
40	10	$9\frac{3}{4}$	9	$7\frac{1}{2}$	5	76	19	$18\frac{1}{2}$	$17\frac{1}{8}$	$14\frac{1}{4}$	$9\frac{1}{2}$
44	11	$10\frac{3}{4}$	10	$8\frac{1}{4}$	$5\frac{1}{2}$	80	20	$19\frac{1}{2}$	18	15	10
48	12	$11\frac{3}{4}$	$10\frac{3}{4}$	9	6	84	21	$20\frac{1}{2}$	19	$15\frac{3}{4}$	$10\frac{1}{2}$
52	13	$12\frac{5}{8}$	$11\frac{3}{4}$	$9\frac{3}{4}$	$6\frac{1}{2}$	88	22	$21\frac{1}{2}$	$19\frac{3}{4}$	$16\frac{1}{2}$	11
56	14	$13\frac{5}{8}$	$12\frac{5}{8}$	$10\frac{1}{2}$	7	92	23	$22\frac{1}{2}$	$20\frac{3}{4}$	$17\frac{1}{4}$	$11\frac{1}{2}$
60	15	$14\frac{5}{8}$	$13\frac{1}{2}$	$11\frac{1}{4}$	$7\frac{1}{2}$	96	24	$23\frac{3}{4}$	$21\frac{5}{8}$	18	12
64	16	$15\frac{5}{8}$	$14\frac{3}{8}$	12	8	100	25	$24\frac{3}{4}$	$22\frac{5}{8}$	$18\frac{3}{4}$	$12\frac{1}{2}$

Table No. 5 gives the relative dimensions of timber lower-masts ranging from 50 ft. to 99 ft. in length, and has been compiled from the following formulae.

$$\frac{\text{Measured length in feet}}{3} = \text{Given diameter in inches.}$$

The measured length is over all, taken from the underside of the heel tenon to the top of the cap tenon. The remaining diameters are calculated as under, and given to the nearest $\frac{1}{16}$ in.

$$1Q. = \frac{GD \times 60}{61} : 2Q. = \frac{GD \times 14}{15} : 3Q. = \frac{GD \times 6}{7} :$$

$$Hs. = \frac{GD \times 3}{4} : Hd. = \frac{GD \times 5}{8} : Hl. = \frac{GD \times 6}{7} :$$

1Q., 2Q. and 3Q. represent 1st, 2nd and 3rd quarters respectively, and Hs., Hd. and Hl., the hounds, head and heel, respectively.

This represents the standard practice for arriving at the proportions of timber lower-masts, but of course the rule that the lower-mast at the head must never be less than the given diameter of the topmast, applies here just as with the metal spars, and the diameters of the lower-mast may have to be increased to agree with this.

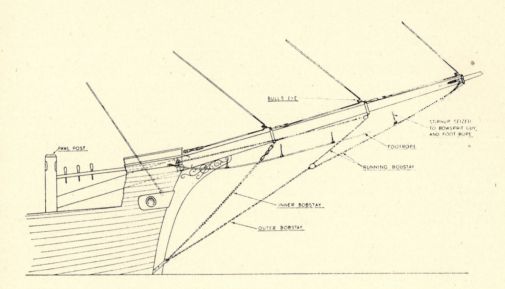

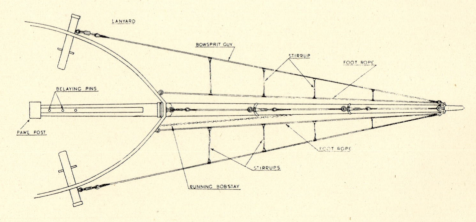

PLATE No. 45.—BOWSPRIT OF COASTING SCHOONER.

TABLE No. 5.

PROPORTIONS OF TIMBER LOWER-MASTS.

Measured Length	Given Diameter	Quarters 1st	Quarters 2nd	Quarters 3rd	Hounds	Head	Heel	Measured Length	Given Diameter	Quarters 1st	Quarters 2nd	Quarters 3rd	Hounds	Head	Heel
Ft.	Ins.	Ins.	Ins.	Ins.	Ins.	Ins.	Ins.	Ft.	Ins.	Ins.	Ins.	Ins.	Ins.	Ins.	Ins.
50	16 1/2	16 3/16	15 3/8	14 3/16	12 3/8	10 5/16	14 1/8	75	25	24 9/16	23 5/16	21 7/16	18 3/4	15 5/8	21 3/8
51	17	16 3/4	15 7/8	14 9/16	12 3/4	10 11/16	14 9/16	76	25 1/2	25 1/16	23 13/16	21 7/8	19 1/8	15 15/16	21 7/8
52	17 1/2	17 1/4	16 3/8	15	13 1/8	10 15/16	15	77	25 3/4	25 5/16	24 1/16	22 1/16	19 5/16	16 1/8	22 1/8
53	17 3/4	17 1/2	16 9/16	15 1/4	13 5/16	11 3/16	15 1/4	78	26	25 9/16	24 1/4	22 5/16	19 1/2	16 1/4	22 1/4
54	18	17 11/16	16 13/16	15 1/2	13 1/2	11 9/16	15 7/16	79	26 1/2	26 1/16	24 3/4	22 3/4	19 7/8	16 5/8	22 3/4
55	18 1/2	18 1/8	17 1/4	15 7/8	13 7/8	11 5/8	15 13/16	80	26 3/4	26 5/16	25	22 7/8	20 1/16	16 3/4	22 7/8
56	18 3/4	18 7/16	17 1/2	16 1/16	14 1/16	11 3/4	16 1/8	81	27	26 9/16	25 3/16	23 3/16	20 1/4	16 15/16	23 1/8
57	19	18 11/16	17 3/4	16 5/16	14 1/4	11 7/8	16 1/4	82	27 1/2	27 1/16	25 11/16	23 9/16	20 5/8	17 3/16	23 9/16
58	19 1/2	19 3/16	18 3/16	16 3/4	14 5/8	12 3/16	16 3/4	83	27 3/4	27 5/16	25 15/16	23 3/4	20 13/16	17 3/8	23 3/4
59	19 3/4	19 7/16	18 7/16	16 15/16	14 13/16	12 7/16	17	84	28	27 9/16	26 1/8	24	21	17 1/2	24
60	20	19 11/16	18 11/16	17 3/16	15	12 9/16	17 3/16	85	28 1/2	28 1/16	26 9/16	24 7/16	21 3/8	17 13/16	24 3/8
61	20 1/2	20 3/16	19 1/8	17 9/16	15 3/8	12 13/16	17 5/8	86	28 3/4	28 5/16	26 13/16	24 5/8	21 9/16	18	24 5/8
62	20 3/4	20 7/16	19 3/8	17 13/16	15 9/16	13	17 7/8	87	29	28 1/2	27	24 7/8	21 3/4	18 3/16	24 7/8
63	21	20 11/16	19 5/8	18	15 3/4	13 3/16	18	88	29 1/2	29	27 1/2	25 5/16	22 1/8	18 7/16	25 1/4
64	21 1/2	21 1/8	20 1/16	18 7/16	16 1/8	13 1/2	18 3/8	89	29 3/4	29 1/4	27 3/4	25 1/2	22 5/16	18 5/8	25 1/2
65	21 3/4	21 3/8	20 1/4	18 5/8	16 5/16	13 5/8	18 5/8	90	30	29 1/2	28	25 3/4	22 1/2	18 13/16	25 3/4
66	22	21 5/8	20 1/2	18 7/8	16 1/2	13 13/16	18 7/8	91	30 1/2	30	28 1/2	26 1/16	22 7/8	19 1/8	26
67	22 1/2	22 1/8	21	19 5/16	16 7/8	14 1/8	19 1/4	92	30 3/4	30 1/4	28 11/16	26 3/8	23 1/16	19 5/16	26 3/8
68	22 3/4	22 3/8	21 1/4	19 1/2	17 1/16	14 1/4	19 1/2	93	31	30 1/2	28 15/16	26 5/8	23 1/4	19 7/16	26 5/8
69	23	22 5/8	21 1/2	19 3/4	17 1/4	14 7/16	19 3/4	94	31 1/2	31	29 3/8	27	23 5/8	19 11/16	27
70	23 1/2	23 1/8	21 15/16	20 3/16	17 5/8	14 3/4	20 3/16	95	31 3/4	31 1/4	29 5/8	27 1/4	23 13/16	19 13/16	27 3/8
71	23 3/4	23 3/8	22 3/16	20 3/8	17 13/16	14 7/8	20 5/16	96	32	31 1/2	29 7/8	27 7/16	24	20	27 9/16
72	24	23 5/8	22 7/16	20 9/16	18	15 1/16	20 9/16	97	32 1/2	32	30 3/8	27 7/8	24 3/8	20 5/16	27 7/8
73	24 1/2	24 1/8	22 7/8	21	18 3/8	15 3/8	21	98	32 3/4	32 1/4	30 1/2	28 1/16	24 9/16	20 1/2	28 1/8
74	24 3/4	24 3/8	23 1/16	21 1/4	18 9/16	15 1/2	21 1/4	99	33	32 1/2	30 13/16	28 1/4	24 3/4	20 5/8	28 3/8

Table No. 6 covers the dimensions of topmasts ranging from 14 ft. to 60 ft. and has been compiled from the following:—

$$\frac{\text{Measured length in feet}}{3} = \text{Given diameter in inches.}$$

$$1Q. = \frac{GD \times 60}{61} : 2Q. = \frac{GD \times 14}{15} : 3Q. = \frac{GD \times 6}{7} :$$

$$Hs. = \frac{GD \times 9}{13} : Hd. = \frac{GD \times 6}{11} .$$

The measured length is of course taken from the heel to the top of the topmast-cap, and the given diameter is at the point where the topmast passes through the lower-cap. The heel will be formed square and made up to fill the space between the trestle-trees and cross-trees of the lower-mast. If the mast is either square or octagonal between the lower-cap and the heel, such formation will be left on the spar outside the given diameter and not shaved down from it. Under certain circumstances, to be described later, this table may also be used for sizing topgallant and royal masts, but in that case, and when the topgallant and royal are formed as one spar, the diameter given for the head will be omitted and that for the hounds taken as the end of the spar.

TABLE No. 6

PROPORTIONS OF TIMBER TOPMASTS.

Total Length	Dia. at Cap and Sq. of Heel	Quarters			Hounds	Head	Total Length	Dia. at Cap and Sq. of Heel	Quarters			Hounds	Head
		1st	2nd	3rd					1st	2nd	3rd		
Ft.	Ins.	Ins.	Ins.	Ins.	Ins.	Ins.	Ft.	Ins.	Ins.	Ins.	Ins.	Ins.	Ins.
35	$11\frac{5}{8}$	$11\frac{1}{2}$	$10\frac{7}{8}$	10	$8\frac{1}{16}$	$6\frac{3}{8}$	48	16	$15\frac{3}{4}$	$14\frac{15}{16}$	$13\frac{3}{4}$	$11\frac{1}{4}$	$8\frac{3}{4}$
36	12	$11\frac{13}{16}$	$11\frac{1}{4}$	$10\frac{5}{16}$	$8\frac{5}{16}$	$6\frac{9}{16}$	49	$16\frac{3}{8}$	$16\frac{1}{4}$	$15\frac{5}{16}$	$14\frac{1}{16}$	$11\frac{3}{8}$	$8\frac{15}{16}$
37	$12\frac{3}{8}$	$12\frac{3}{8}$	$11\frac{9}{16}$	$10\frac{5}{8}$	$8\frac{5}{8}$	$6\frac{3}{4}$	50	$16\frac{5}{8}$	$16\frac{3}{8}$	$15\frac{9}{16}$	$14\frac{1}{4}$	$11\frac{9}{16}$	$9\frac{1}{8}$
38	$12\frac{5}{8}$	$12\frac{7}{16}$	$11\frac{13}{16}$	$10\frac{7}{8}$	$8\frac{13}{16}$	$6\frac{13}{16}$	51	17	$16\frac{3}{8}$	$15\frac{5}{8}$	$14\frac{9}{16}$	$11\frac{13}{16}$	$9\frac{5}{16}$
39	13	$12\frac{13}{16}$	$12\frac{3}{16}$	$11\frac{3}{16}$	9	$7\frac{1}{8}$	52	$17\frac{3}{8}$	$17\frac{1}{8}$	$16\frac{1}{4}$	$14\frac{7}{8}$	$12\frac{1}{16}$	$9\frac{1}{4}$
40	$13\frac{3}{8}$	$13\frac{3}{16}$	$12\frac{7}{16}$	$11\frac{7}{16}$	$9\frac{5}{16}$	$7\frac{5}{16}$	53	$17\frac{5}{8}$	$17\frac{3}{8}$	$16\frac{7}{16}$	$15\frac{5}{8}$	$12\frac{1}{4}$	$9\frac{1}{4}$
41	$13\frac{5}{8}$	$13\frac{7}{16}$	$12\frac{3}{4}$	$11\frac{3}{4}$	$9\frac{7}{16}$	$7\frac{7}{16}$	54	18	$17\frac{3}{8}$	$16\frac{13}{16}$	$15\frac{7}{16}$	$12\frac{1}{2}$	$9\frac{5}{16}$
42	$14\frac{5}{8}$	$13\frac{13}{16}$	$13\frac{1}{16}$	12	$9\frac{3}{4}$	$7\frac{5}{8}$	55	$18\frac{3}{8}$	$18\frac{1}{4}$	$17\frac{3}{16}$	$15\frac{1}{4}$	$12\frac{3}{4}$	$10\frac{1}{16}$
43	$14\frac{3}{8}$	$14\frac{3}{16}$	$13\frac{7}{16}$	$12\frac{3}{8}$	$9\frac{15}{16}$	$7\frac{3}{4}$	56	$18\frac{5}{8}$	$18\frac{3}{8}$	$17\frac{7}{16}$	16	$12\frac{15}{16}$	$10\frac{3}{16}$
44	$14\frac{5}{8}$	$14\frac{7}{16}$	$13\frac{5}{8}$	$12\frac{9}{16}$	$10\frac{1}{8}$	$7\frac{15}{16}$	57	19	$18\frac{3}{4}$	$17\frac{1}{4}$	$16\frac{5}{16}$	$13\frac{3}{16}$	$10\frac{7}{16}$
45	15	$14\frac{13}{16}$	14	$12\frac{7}{8}$	$10\frac{7}{16}$	$8\frac{1}{8}$	58	$19\frac{3}{8}$	$19\frac{1}{4}$	$18\frac{1}{8}$	$16\frac{5}{8}$	$13\frac{7}{16}$	$10\frac{9}{16}$
46	$15\frac{3}{8}$	$15\frac{1}{4}$	$14\frac{3}{4}$	$13\frac{3}{16}$	$10\frac{5}{8}$	$8\frac{3}{8}$	59	$19\frac{5}{8}$	$19\frac{3}{8}$	$18\frac{7}{16}$	$16\frac{15}{16}$	$13\frac{5}{8}$	$10\frac{3}{4}$
47	$15\frac{5}{8}$	$15\frac{3}{4}$	$14\frac{5}{8}$	$13\frac{7}{16}$	$10\frac{7}{8}$	$8\frac{1}{2}$	60	20	$19\frac{3}{4}$	$18\frac{3}{4}$	$17\frac{3}{16}$	$13\frac{7}{8}$	$10\frac{15}{16}$

NOTE:—The Heel to be square with sides not less than the Diameter at the Cap.

The separately fidded royal mast had gone out of use by the period in which we are interested, and the topgallant and royal had become one spar. However, like the combined lower-mast and topmast, they are measured separately for the purpose of calculating their respective diameters. The topgallant is measured from heel to topgallant-stops, and the royal from the topgallant-stops, which of course forms the heel of the royal-mast, to the royal-stops. Above this is the short pole whose diameter is made to suit the depth of the royal-stops.

There are three methods of arriving at the proportions of the combined mast. The first is to calculate the given diameter of each mast, and using table No. 6., or the formulae from which it is compiled, fix the diameters at the various quarters of each spar, omitting the head of course, because the highest point on each mast will be the stops or hounds. If the difference between the diameters of the hounds of the topgallant and the heel of the royal is not sufficient to form an adequate stop for the topgallant-rigging, then the diameters of the topgallant will have to be increased accordingly.

The second method is to base all diameters on the given diameter of the topgallant-mast. This method takes no account of the length of the royal-mast, but assumes that this will bear the normal relation to the length of the topgallant, and for that reason this method is of no use when the royal is above normal length.

The third way is to calculate all diameters for the topgallant and make the royal two-thirds of these dimensions.

In application the first method requires no explanation. The given diameter of each mast is obtained by the usual formula:—

$$\frac{\text{Measured length in feet}}{3} = \text{Given diameter in inches.}$$

and having arrived at the given diameters of the two masts, the remaining diameters are obtained from table No. 6, making any adjustment necessary to provide sufficient depth for the topgallant-stops.

To use the second method it is only necessary to obtain the measured length and given diameter of the topgallant-mast, then the remaining proportions of the combined spar can be obtained as follows:—

$$\frac{\text{GDT} \times 10}{13} = \text{TS} \quad \text{and} \quad \frac{\text{GDT} \times 3}{5} = \text{RS.}$$ Where GDT = Given diameter of topgallant; TS. = Outside diameter of topgallant-stops, and RS. = Outside diameter of royal-stops. Obviously the heel of the royal-mast will be TS. less the depth of the stop and the diameter of the pole will equal RS, less the depth of the royal-stop.

For the third method the topgallant is worked out in detail, and then all equivalent positions on the royal are made one-third smaller in diameter.

TABLE No. 7.

PROPORTIONS OF TOPGALLANT AND ROYAL MASTS.

Measured Length of Topgallant Mast	Given Diameter of Topgallant Mast	Dia. at Topgallant Stops	Dia. at Royal Stops	Measured Length of Topgallant Mast	Given Diameter of Topgallant Mast	Dia. at Topgallant Stops	Dia. at Royal Stops
Ft.	Ins.	Ins.	Ins.	Ft.	Ins.	Ins.	Ins.
14	$4\frac{3}{4}$	$3\frac{11}{16}$	$2\frac{5}{16}$	30	10	$7\frac{3}{4}$	6
15	5	$3\frac{7}{8}$	$3\frac{1}{16}$	31	$10\frac{3}{8}$	8	$6\frac{1}{4}$
16	$5\frac{3}{8}$	$4\frac{1}{8}$	$3\frac{1}{4}$	32	$10\frac{3}{4}$	$8\frac{1}{4}$	$6\frac{1}{2}$
17	$5\frac{3}{4}$	$4\frac{7}{16}$	$3\frac{1}{2}$	33	11	$8\frac{1}{2}$	$6\frac{5}{8}$
18	6	$4\frac{5}{16}$	$3\frac{5}{8}$	34	$11\frac{3}{8}$	$8\frac{3}{4}$	$6\frac{7}{8}$
19	$6\frac{3}{8}$	$4\frac{7}{8}$	$3\frac{7}{8}$	35	$11\frac{3}{4}$	9	$7\frac{1}{16}$
20	$6\frac{3}{4}$	$5\frac{1}{4}$	$4\frac{3}{16}$	36	12	$9\frac{1}{4}$	$7\frac{5}{16}$
21	7	$5\frac{3}{8}$	$4\frac{1}{4}$	37	$12\frac{3}{8}$	$9\frac{1}{2}$	$7\frac{7}{16}$
22	$7\frac{3}{8}$	$5\frac{11}{16}$	$4\frac{1}{2}$	38	$12\frac{3}{4}$	$9\frac{13}{16}$	$6\frac{3}{4}$
23	$7\frac{3}{4}$	6	$4\frac{3}{4}$	39	13	10	$7\frac{13}{16}$
24	8	$6\frac{3}{16}$	$4\frac{7}{8}$	40	$13\frac{3}{8}$	$10\frac{5}{16}$	$8\frac{1}{16}$
25	$8\frac{3}{8}$	$6\frac{7}{16}$	$5\frac{1}{16}$	41	$13\frac{3}{4}$	$10\frac{9}{16}$	$8\frac{1}{4}$
26	$8\frac{3}{4}$	$6\frac{3}{4}$	$5\frac{1}{4}$	42	14	$10\frac{7}{8}$	$8\frac{7}{16}$
27	9	$6\frac{15}{16}$	$5\frac{7}{16}$	43	$14\frac{3}{8}$	$11\frac{3}{16}$	$8\frac{5}{8}$
28	$9\frac{3}{8}$	$7\frac{1}{8}$	$5\frac{5}{8}$	44	$14\frac{3}{4}$	$11\frac{1}{2}$	$8\frac{7}{8}$
29	$9\frac{3}{4}$	$7\frac{1}{2}$	$5\frac{7}{8}$	45	15	$11\frac{5}{8}$	9

It will now be appreciated how necessary it is to complete all mast dimensions before deciding on the spar plan as a whole. What is more, a lot of extra work may be saved if a start is made at the royal and continued down all the other masts in rotation, for it could possibly happen that all spars up to the royal worked out exactly right in relation one to the other, but if the royal proved larger than expected it might be necessary to increase each mast below.

Table No. 7 shows the proportions of combined topgallant and royal masts worked out by the second method. The measured lengths quoted are of course for the topgallant alone, and cover masts ranging from 14 ft. to 45 ft. By the way the given diameter of the topgallant is taken at the topmast-cap. The heel will be squared out to fill the space in the topmast cross-trees

TABLE No. 8.

PROPORTIONS OF TIMBER BOWSPRITS.

Dia. at Bed	Quarters			Outer End	Heel	Dia. at Bed	Quarters			Outer End	Heel
	1st	2nd	3rd				1st	2nd	3rd		
Ins.	Ins.	Ins.	Ins.	Ins.	Ins.	Ins.	Ins.	Ins.	Ins.	Ins.	Ins.
$12\frac{1}{2}$	$12\frac{1}{4}$	$11\frac{7}{16}$	10	$8\frac{3}{8}$	$10\frac{11}{16}$	$21\frac{1}{2}$	$21\frac{3}{16}$	$19\frac{3}{4}$	$17\frac{1}{4}$	$14\frac{5}{16}$	$18\frac{7}{16}$
13	$12\frac{3}{4}$	$11\frac{15}{16}$	$10\frac{7}{16}$	$8\frac{5}{8}$	$11\frac{3}{16}$	22	$21\frac{5}{8}$	$20\frac{3}{16}$	$17\frac{5}{8}$	$14\frac{11}{16}$	$18\frac{13}{16}$
$13\frac{1}{2}$	$13\frac{1}{4}$	$12\frac{7}{16}$	$10\frac{13}{16}$	9	$11\frac{5}{8}$	$22\frac{1}{2}$	$22\frac{1}{16}$	$20\frac{5}{8}$	18	15	$19\frac{5}{16}$
14	$13\frac{3}{4}$	$12\frac{7}{8}$	$11\frac{1}{4}$	$9\frac{3}{8}$	12	23	$22\frac{5}{8}$	$21\frac{1}{8}$	$18\frac{7}{16}$	$15\frac{5}{16}$	$19\frac{3}{4}$
$14\frac{1}{2}$	$14\frac{1}{4}$	$13\frac{5}{16}$	$11\frac{5}{8}$	$9\frac{11}{16}$	$12\frac{7}{16}$	$23\frac{1}{2}$	$21\frac{1}{8}$	$21\frac{9}{16}$	$18\frac{13}{16}$	$15\frac{5}{8}$	$20\frac{3}{16}$
15	$14\frac{3}{4}$	$13\frac{15}{16}$	12	10	$12\frac{7}{8}$	24	$23\frac{9}{16}$	22	$19\frac{1}{4}$	16	$20\frac{5}{8}$
$15\frac{1}{2}$	$15\frac{1}{4}$	$14\frac{3}{16}$	$12\frac{7}{16}$	$10\frac{3}{8}$	$13\frac{5}{16}$	$24\frac{1}{2}$	$24\frac{1}{16}$	$22\frac{7}{16}$	$19\frac{5}{8}$	$16\frac{5}{16}$	21
16	$15\frac{3}{4}$	$14\frac{11}{16}$	$12\frac{13}{16}$	$10\frac{11}{16}$	$13\frac{3}{4}$	25	$24\frac{9}{16}$	$22\frac{7}{8}$	20	$16\frac{11}{16}$	$21\frac{7}{16}$
$16\frac{1}{2}$	$16\frac{3}{16}$	$15\frac{1}{8}$	$13\frac{3}{16}$	11	$14\frac{3}{16}$	$25\frac{1}{2}$	$25\frac{1}{16}$	$23\frac{3}{8}$	$20\frac{7}{16}$	17	$21\frac{7}{8}$
17	$16\frac{11}{16}$	$15\frac{5}{8}$	$13\frac{5}{8}$	$11\frac{3}{8}$	$14\frac{5}{8}$	26	$25\frac{9}{16}$	$23\frac{7}{8}$	$20\frac{13}{16}$	$17\frac{5}{16}$	$22\frac{5}{16}$
$17\frac{1}{2}$	$17\frac{3}{16}$	16	14	$11\frac{11}{16}$	15	$26\frac{1}{2}$	$26\frac{1}{16}$	$24\frac{3}{8}$	$21\frac{1}{4}$	$17\frac{11}{16}$	$22\frac{3}{4}$
18	$17\frac{11}{16}$	$16\frac{9}{16}$	$14\frac{7}{16}$	12	$15\frac{7}{16}$	27	$26\frac{9}{16}$	$24\frac{3}{4}$	$21\frac{5}{8}$	18	$23\frac{3}{16}$
$18\frac{1}{2}$	$18\frac{3}{16}$	$16\frac{15}{16}$	$14\frac{13}{16}$	$12\frac{5}{16}$	$15\frac{7}{8}$	$27\frac{1}{2}$	27	$25\frac{1}{4}$	22	$18\frac{5}{16}$	$23\frac{9}{16}$
19	$18\frac{11}{16}$	$17\frac{7}{16}$	$15\frac{1}{4}$	$12\frac{11}{16}$	$16\frac{5}{16}$	28	$27\frac{1}{2}$	$25\frac{11}{16}$	$22\frac{7}{16}$	$18\frac{11}{16}$	24
$19\frac{1}{2}$	$19\frac{3}{16}$	$17\frac{15}{16}$	$15\frac{5}{8}$	13	$16\frac{3}{4}$	$28\frac{1}{2}$	28	$26\frac{1}{16}$	$22\frac{13}{16}$	19	$24\frac{7}{16}$
20	$19\frac{11}{16}$	$18\frac{3}{8}$	16	$13\frac{3}{8}$	$17\frac{3}{16}$	29	$28\frac{1}{2}$	$26\frac{5}{8}$	$23\frac{3}{8}$	$19\frac{5}{16}$	$24\frac{7}{8}$
$20\frac{1}{2}$	$20\frac{3}{16}$	$18\frac{7}{8}$	$16\frac{7}{16}$	$13\frac{5}{8}$	$17\frac{5}{8}$	$29\frac{1}{2}$	29	$27\frac{1}{16}$	$23\frac{5}{8}$	$19\frac{11}{16}$	$25\frac{5}{16}$
21	$20\frac{5}{8}$	$19\frac{3}{16}$	$16\frac{13}{16}$	14	18	30	$29\frac{1}{2}$	$27\frac{1}{2}$	24	20	$25\frac{3}{4}$

Table No. 8 shows the proportions of timber bowsprits, which, unlike metal ones, are measured over all from the after side of the heel tenon to the fore side of the cap tenon, but the measured length is rarely used, for it is common practice to make the given diameter of the bowsprit the same as that of the main-mast. The given diameter is measured at the bed and the remaining measurements taken at the heel, 1st, 2nd and 3rd, quarters and at the cap. These various proportions are arrived at as follows:—

$$\text{Hl.} = \frac{\text{GD} \times 6}{7} : \text{1Q.} = \frac{\text{GD} \times 60}{61} : \text{2Q.} = \frac{\text{GD} \times 11}{12} :$$

$$\text{3Q.} = \frac{\text{GD} \times 4 :}{5} \ \text{Hd.} = \frac{\text{GD} \times 2}{3}$$

It is on these figures that table No. 8 has been based.

It is usual practice to make the bed of the spar either square or octagonal, such formation is of course outside the given diameter.

Table No. 9 shows the proportions of jib-booms, and, when carried, flying-jib-booms. The measured length of a jib-boom is over all, and the given diameter taken at the bowsprit cap. It is more usual in modern practice to make the spar of equal diameter from the bowsprit-cap to the heel, having a taper on the outer portion only, but should the spar taper inboard as well, that portion will be made to suit the heel-chock and not to any standard rule.

TABLE No. 9.
PROPORTIONS OF JIB BOOMS.

Measured Length	Given Dia. to nearest ¼"	Quarters			End	Measured Length	Given Dia. to nearest ¼"	Quarters			End
		1st	2nd	3rd				1st	2nd	3rd	
Ft.	Ins.	Ins.	Ins.	Ins.	Ins.	Ft.	Ins.	Ins.	Ins.	Ins.	Ins.
30	$8\frac{3}{4}$	$8\frac{9}{16}$	$8\frac{1}{16}$	$7\frac{5}{16}$	$5\frac{7}{8}$	47	$13\frac{3}{4}$	$13\frac{1}{2}$	$12\frac{5}{8}$	$11\frac{1}{2}$	$9\frac{3}{16}$
31	9	$8\frac{13}{16}$	$8\frac{1}{4}$	$7\frac{1}{2}$	6	48	14	$13\frac{11}{16}$	$12\frac{7}{8}$	$11\frac{11}{16}$	$9\frac{3}{8}$
32	$9\frac{1}{4}$	$9\frac{1}{16}$	$8\frac{1}{2}$	$7\frac{3}{4}$	$6\frac{3}{16}$	49	$14\frac{1}{4}$	$13\frac{15}{16}$	$13\frac{1}{16}$	$11\frac{7}{8}$	$9\frac{1}{2}$
33	$9\frac{3}{4}$	$9\frac{1}{2}$	9	$8\frac{1}{8}$	$6\frac{1}{2}$	50	$14\frac{1}{2}$	$14\frac{3}{16}$	$13\frac{5}{16}$	$12\frac{1}{8}$	$9\frac{11}{16}$
34	10	$9\frac{3}{4}$	$9\frac{3}{16}$	$8\frac{3}{8}$	$6\frac{11}{16}$	51	$14\frac{3}{4}$	$14\frac{7}{16}$	$13\frac{9}{16}$	$12\frac{5}{16}$	$9\frac{7}{8}$
35	$10\frac{1}{4}$	10	$9\frac{7}{16}$	$8\frac{9}{16}$	$6\frac{7}{8}$	52	15	$14\frac{5}{8}$	$13\frac{3}{4}$	$12\frac{1}{2}$	10
36	$10\frac{1}{2}$	$10\frac{1}{4}$	$9\frac{5}{8}$	$8\frac{3}{4}$	7	53	$15\frac{1}{2}$	$15\frac{1}{8}$	$14\frac{1}{4}$	$12\frac{15}{16}$	$10\frac{3}{8}$
37	$10\frac{3}{4}$	$10\frac{1}{2}$	$9\frac{7}{8}$	9	$7\frac{3}{16}$	54	$15\frac{3}{4}$	$15\frac{3}{8}$	$14\frac{1}{2}$	$13\frac{1}{8}$	$10\frac{1}{2}$
38	11	$10\frac{3}{4}$	$10\frac{1}{8}$	$9\frac{3}{16}$	$7\frac{3}{8}$	55	16	$15\frac{5}{8}$	$14\frac{11}{16}$	$13\frac{3}{8}$	$10\frac{11}{16}$
39	$11\frac{1}{2}$	$11\frac{1}{4}$	$10\frac{9}{16}$	$9\frac{5}{8}$	$7\frac{11}{16}$	56	$16\frac{1}{4}$	$15\frac{7}{8}$	$14\frac{15}{16}$	$13\frac{9}{16}$	$10\frac{7}{8}$
40	$11\frac{3}{4}$	$11\frac{1}{2}$	$10\frac{13}{16}$	$9\frac{13}{16}$	$7\frac{7}{8}$	57	$16\frac{1}{2}$	$16\frac{1}{8}$	$15\frac{3}{16}$	$13\frac{3}{4}$	11
41	12	$11\frac{3}{4}$	11	10	8	58	17	$16\frac{5}{8}$	$15\frac{5}{8}$	$14\frac{3}{16}$	$11\frac{3}{8}$
42	$12\frac{1}{4}$	12	$11\frac{1}{4}$	$10\frac{1}{4}$	$8\frac{3}{16}$	59	$17\frac{1}{4}$	$16\frac{13}{16}$	$15\frac{13}{16}$	$14\frac{3}{8}$	$11\frac{1}{2}$
43	$12\frac{1}{2}$	$12\frac{3}{16}$	$11\frac{1}{2}$	$10\frac{7}{16}$	$8\frac{3}{8}$	60	$17\frac{1}{2}$	$17\frac{1}{16}$	$16\frac{1}{16}$	$14\frac{5}{8}$	$11\frac{11}{16}$
44	13	$12\frac{11}{16}$	$11\frac{15}{16}$	$10\frac{7}{8}$	$8\frac{11}{16}$	61	$17\frac{3}{4}$	$17\frac{5}{16}$	$16\frac{5}{16}$	$14\frac{13}{16}$	$11\frac{7}{8}$
45	$13\frac{1}{4}$	$12\frac{15}{16}$	$12\frac{3}{16}$	$11\frac{1}{16}$	$8\frac{7}{8}$	62	18	$17\frac{9}{16}$	$16\frac{1}{2}$	15	12
46	$13\frac{1}{2}$	$13\frac{3}{16}$	$12\frac{3}{8}$	$11\frac{1}{4}$	9	63	$18\frac{1}{4}$	$17\frac{13}{16}$	$16\frac{3}{4}$	$15\frac{1}{4}$	$12\frac{3}{16}$

The formations of the jib-boom requires a little care, for the dimensions given by the formulae represent the minimum diameters of the spar, and such stops as may be required will have to be allowed for on top of this. The best way to set out this spar is to draw it—either on paper or on the timber ready squared for making it—as worked out from the tables, then set up the stops in their respective positions and revise the tapers to join up with the other diameters of the stops. By this means the diameter at the bottom of each stop will be the required diameter of the spar at that point.

The basic taper of the spar is obtained from the followg, and it is from these figures that the table has been calculated:—

$$\frac{\text{Measured length in feet}}{24} = \text{Given diameter in inches.}$$

and the various other diameters are obtained from:—

$$1Q. = \frac{GD \times 40}{41} : 2Q. = \frac{GD \times 11}{12} : 3Q. = \frac{GD \times 5}{6}$$

$$\text{and the end} = \frac{GD \times 2}{3}$$

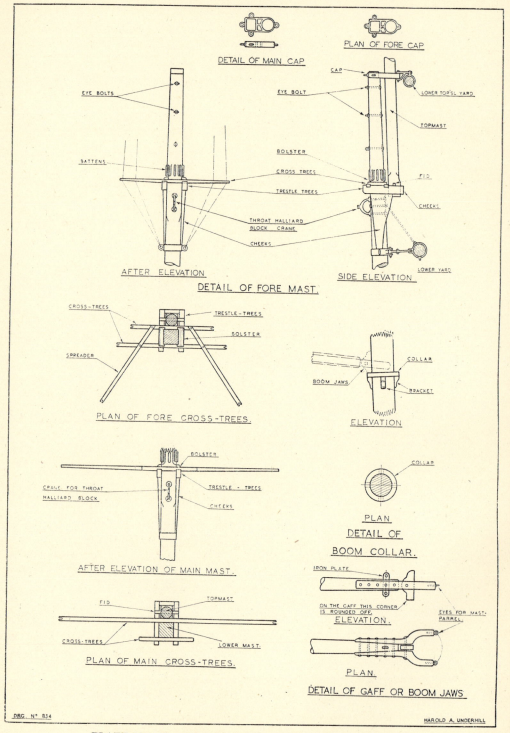

DETAIL OF MAIN CAP

PLAN OF FORE CAP

EYE BOLTS

CAP

EYE BOLT

LOWER TOP'SL YARD

TOPMAST

BATTENS

BOLSTER

CROSS TREES

TRESTLE TREES

FID

THROAT HALLIARD
BLOCK CRANE

CHEEKS

CHEEKS

AFTER ELEVATION

SIDE ELEVATION

LOWER YARD

DETAIL OF FORE MAST.

CROSS-TREES

TRESTLE-TREES

BOLSTER

SPREADER

PLAN OF FORE CROSS-TREES.

COLLAR

BOOM JAWS

BRACKET

ELEVATION

BOLSTER

CRANE FOR THROAT
HALLIARD BLOCK

TRESTLE - TREES

CHEEKS

COLLAR

PLAN

DETAIL OF
BOOM COLLAR.

AFTER ELEVATION OF MAIN MAST.

IRON PLATE

FID

TOPMAST

ON THE GAFF THIS CORNER
IS ROUNDED OFF.

ELEVATION.

CROSS-TREES

LOWER MAST.

EYES FOR MAST-
PARREL.

PLAN OF MAIN CROSS-TREES.

PLAN.

DETAIL OF GAFF OR BOOM JAWS

DRG. Nº 834

HAROLD A. UNDERHILL

PLATE No. 46.—COASTING SCHOONER'S MAST DETAILS.

All iron and steel yards are constructed on a constant diameter-length ratio, but with timber yards it is different, the relation of diameter to length varies with the position of the yard. Thus a metal yard 48 ft. long would be 12 ins. diameter at the slings, which is of course the given diameter, no matter whether it was used as a lower-yard, topsail-yard, or for that matter royal-yard. But a timber yard 48 ft. long would be $12\frac{1}{2}$ ins. diameter for a lower-yard; 12 ins. diameter for a topsail, and $9\frac{7}{8}$ ins. for a topgallant. The royal may either be made on the same length-diameter ratio as the topgallant, or alternatively its diameter may be made one-half that of the topsail-yard on the same mast, irrespective of the length of the royal. Table No. 10 shows the respective given diameters for lower; topsail; and topgallant yards having measured lengths ranging from 30 ft. to 92 ft. Where double topsail yards are carried, both upper and lower yards will have the same length-diameter ratio.

TABLE No. 10.
DIAMETER AT SLINGS FOR WOODEN LOWER, TOPSAIL, TOPGALLANT AND ROYAL YARDS.

Length of Yard	Dia. at Slings			Length of Yard	Dia. at Slings			Length of Yard	Dia. at Slings		
	Lower	Topsail	Topgallant & Royal		Lower	Topsail	Topgallant & Royal		Lower	Topsail	Topgallant & Royal
Ft.	Ins.	Ins.	Ins.	Ft.	Ins.	Ins.	Ins.	Ft.	Ins.	Ins.	Ins.
30	$7\frac{3}{4}$	$7\frac{1}{2}$	$6\frac{1}{4}$	51	$13\frac{1}{4}$	$12\frac{3}{4}$	$10\frac{3}{8}$	72	$18\frac{3}{4}$	18	$14\frac{3}{4}$
31	8	$7\frac{1}{4}$	$6\frac{3}{8}$	52	$13\frac{1}{2}$	13	$10\frac{5}{8}$	73	19	$18\frac{1}{4}$	15
32	$8\frac{1}{4}$	8	$6\frac{5}{8}$	53	$13\frac{3}{4}$	$13\frac{1}{4}$	$10\frac{7}{8}$	74	$19\frac{1}{4}$	$18\frac{1}{2}$	$15\frac{1}{4}$
33	$8\frac{5}{8}$	$8\frac{1}{4}$	$6\frac{3}{4}$	54	14	$13\frac{1}{2}$	$11\frac{1}{8}$	75	$19\frac{1}{2}$	$18\frac{3}{4}$	$15\frac{3}{8}$
34	$8\frac{7}{8}$	$8\frac{1}{2}$	7	55	$14\frac{1}{4}$	$13\frac{3}{4}$	$11\frac{1}{4}$	76	$19\frac{3}{4}$	19	$15\frac{1}{2}$
35	$9\frac{1}{8}$	$8\frac{3}{4}$	$7\frac{1}{4}$	56	$14\frac{1}{2}$	14	$11\frac{1}{2}$	77	20	$19\frac{1}{4}$	$15\frac{3}{4}$
36	$9\frac{3}{8}$	9	$7\frac{1}{2}$	57	$14\frac{3}{4}$	$14\frac{1}{4}$	$11\frac{5}{8}$	78	$20\frac{1}{4}$	$19\frac{1}{2}$	16
37	$9\frac{5}{8}$	$9\frac{1}{4}$	$7\frac{3}{4}$	58	15	$14\frac{1}{2}$	$11\frac{7}{8}$	79	$20\frac{1}{2}$	$19\frac{3}{4}$	$16\frac{1}{4}$
38	$9\frac{7}{8}$	$9\frac{1}{2}$	$7\frac{7}{8}$	59	$15\frac{3}{8}$	$14\frac{3}{4}$	12	80	$20\frac{3}{4}$	20	$16\frac{3}{8}$
39	$10\frac{1}{8}$	$9\frac{3}{4}$	$8\frac{1}{8}$	60	$15\frac{5}{8}$	15	$12\frac{1}{4}$	81	21	$20\frac{1}{4}$	$16\frac{5}{8}$
40	$10\frac{3}{8}$	10	$8\frac{1}{4}$	61	$15\frac{7}{8}$	$15\frac{1}{4}$	$12\frac{1}{2}$	82	$21\frac{1}{4}$	$20\frac{1}{2}$	$16\frac{7}{8}$
41	$10\frac{5}{8}$	$10\frac{1}{4}$	$8\frac{3}{8}$	62	$16\frac{1}{4}$	$15\frac{1}{2}$	$12\frac{5}{8}$	83	$21\frac{1}{2}$	$20\frac{3}{4}$	17
42	$10\frac{7}{8}$	$10\frac{1}{2}$	$8\frac{5}{8}$	63	$16\frac{3}{8}$	$15\frac{3}{4}$	$12\frac{7}{8}$	84	$21\frac{3}{4}$	21	$17\frac{1}{4}$
43	$11\frac{1}{8}$	$10\frac{3}{4}$	$8\frac{7}{8}$	64	$16\frac{5}{8}$	16	$13\frac{1}{8}$	85	22	$21\frac{1}{4}$	$17\frac{3}{8}$
44	$11\frac{3}{8}$	11	9	65	$16\frac{7}{8}$	$16\frac{1}{4}$	$13\frac{1}{4}$	86	$22\frac{3}{8}$	$21\frac{1}{2}$	$17\frac{5}{8}$
45	$11\frac{5}{8}$	$11\frac{1}{4}$	$9\frac{1}{4}$	66	$17\frac{1}{4}$	$16\frac{1}{2}$	$13\frac{1}{2}$	87	$22\frac{5}{8}$	$21\frac{3}{4}$	$17\frac{3}{4}$
46	12	$11\frac{1}{2}$	$9\frac{1}{2}$	67	$17\frac{3}{8}$	$16\frac{3}{4}$	$13\frac{3}{4}$	88	$22\frac{7}{8}$	22	18
47	$12\frac{1}{4}$	$11\frac{3}{4}$	$9\frac{5}{8}$	68	$17\frac{5}{8}$	17	$13\frac{7}{8}$	89	$23\frac{1}{8}$	$22\frac{1}{4}$	$18\frac{1}{4}$
48	$12\frac{1}{2}$	12	$9\frac{7}{8}$	69	$17\frac{7}{8}$	$17\frac{1}{4}$	$14\frac{1}{8}$	90	$23\frac{3}{8}$	$22\frac{1}{2}$	$18\frac{3}{8}$
49	$12\frac{3}{4}$	$12\frac{1}{4}$	10	70	$18\frac{1}{8}$	$17\frac{1}{2}$	$14\frac{3}{8}$	91	$23\frac{5}{8}$	$22\frac{3}{4}$	$18\frac{5}{8}$
50	13	$12\frac{1}{2}$	$10\frac{1}{4}$	71	$18\frac{3}{8}$	$17\frac{3}{4}$	$14\frac{1}{2}$	92	$23\frac{7}{8}$	23	$18\frac{7}{8}$

Table No. 10 has been compiled from the following formulae:—

$$\frac{\text{Measured length in feet} \times 7}{27} = \text{GD of lower-yard in inches.}$$

$$\frac{\text{Measured length in feet} \times 3}{12} = \text{GD of topsail yard in inches.}$$

$$\frac{\text{Measured length in feet} \times 11}{54} = \text{GD of topgallant yard in inches.}$$

The royal may either be calculated as for the topgallant or made one-half its own topsail yard. The measured length is taken over the yard-arm-bands.

Having arrived at the given diameter for each type of yard, the remaining proportions will be found from table No. 11 which covers a range of yards from 6 ins to 23½ ins given diameter, rising by ½ ins. By the way in all these tables the given diameters have been calculated to the nearest ¼ ins, which explains why at times sizes make irregular jumps although the measured length increases by even feet.

Table No. 11 has been calculated from:—

$$1Q. = \frac{GD \times 30}{31} : 2Q. = \frac{GD \times 7}{8} : 3Q. = \frac{GD \times 7}{10}$$

$$\text{and yard-arm} = \frac{GD \times 3}{7}$$

TABLE No. 11.

PROPORTIONS OF TIMBER YARDS.

Dia. at Slings	Diameter at Quarters			Yard Arm	Dia. at Slings	Diameter at Quarters			Yard Arm	Dia. at Slings	Diameter at Quarters			Yard Arm
	1st	2nd	3rd			1st	2nd	3rd			1st	2nd	3rd	
Ins.	Ins.	Ins.	Ins.	Ins.	Ins.	Ins.	Ins.	Ins.	Ins.	Ins.	Ins.	Ins.	Ins.	Ins.
6	5 13/16	5 1/4	4 1/4	2 9/16	12	11 5/8	10 1/2	8 7/16	5 3/16	18	17 3/8	15 3/4	12 5/8	7 1/4
6½	6 1/4	5 11/16	4 9/16	2 13/16	12½	12 1/8	10 15/16	8 3/4	5 3/8	18½	17 15/16	16 3/16	13	7 7/16
7	6 3/4	6 1/8	4 15/16	3	13	12 9/16	11 3/8	9 1/4	5 9/16	19	18 7/16	16 5/8	13 5/16	8 3/16
7½	7 1/4	6 9/16	5 1/4	3 1/4	13½	13 1/16	11 13/16	9 1/2	5 13/16	19½	18 7/8	17 1/16	13 11/16	8 3/8
8	7 3/4	7	5 5/8	3 7/16	14	13 9/16	12 1/4	9 13/16	6	20	19 3/8	17 1/2	14	8 9/16
8½	8 1/4	7 7/16	6	3 11/16	14½	14 1/16	12 11/16	10 3/16	6 1/4	20½	19 7/8	17 15/16	14 3/8	8 3/4
9	8 3/4	7 7/8	6 5/16	3 7/8	15	14 1/2	13 1/8	10 1/2	6 7/16	21	20 3/8	18 3/8	14 3/4	9
9½	9 3/8	8 5/16	6 11/16	4 1/16	15½	15	13 9/16	10 7/8	6 11/16	21½	20 13/16	18 13/16	15 1/16	9 1/4
10	9 11/16	8 3/4	7	4 5/16	16	15 1/2	14	11 1/4	6 7/8	22	21 5/16	19 1/4	15 7/16	9 7/16
10½	10 1/8	9 3/16	7 3/8	4 1/2	16½	16	14 7/16	11 9/16	7 1/16	22½	21 13/16	19 11/16	15 3/4	9 11/16
11	10 5/8	9 5/8	7 3/4	4 3/4	17	16 1/2	14 7/8	11 15/16	7 5/16	23	22 5/16	20 1/8	16 1/8	9 7/8
11½	11 1/8	10 1/16	8 1/16	4 15/16	17½	17	15 5/16	12 1/4	7 1/2	23½	22 3/4	20 9/16	16 7/16	10 1/16

Opinions differ very considerably on the form of booms, and they are quoted variously as having the maximum diameter in the centre; one-third of the way out from the mast, and lastly making the greatest diameter in way of the sheet block. The reader can take his choice, but examination of a number of known examples suggests that the most common practice was to make the comparatively short booms on the spankers of square-rigged craft with the major diameter in the centre, but the booms of large fore and aft sails, such as the big barquentines, with the greatest diameter one-third out from the mast. These two types of boom differ in another way, the smaller which for easy reference I will call a spanker-boom, was usually the same diameter at both ends, while the larger—which I will call a fore and aft boom

—had the end at the mast larger than the outer end. I have given both types in tables Nos. 12 and 13 which detail spanker and fore and aft booms respectively.

The measured length is of course over all, and the given diameter the maximum diameter, no matter where it be placed. The length-diameter ratio seems to have been got over by the simple process of making the spanker-boom the same diameter as the lower fore-topsail yard. I have checked a number of known examples and find they differ very considerably, but by averaging them I have arrived at the following, which may at least be a guide to the modeller wishing to fix the boom diameter:—

$$\frac{\text{Measured length in feet} \times 11}{48} = \text{Given diameter in inches.}$$

This applies to both types of boom. However as the model maker may like to fix his own length-diameter ratio, I have not quoted any measured lengths in either table.

The various diameters for spanker-booms as shown in table No. 12 have been calculated from the following:—

$$1Q. = \frac{GD \times 40}{41} : 2Q. = \frac{GD \times 11}{12} : 3Q. = \frac{GD \times 5}{6}$$

$$\text{and the ends} = \frac{GD \times 2}{3}$$

TABLE No. 12.

PROPORTIONS OF SPANKER BOOMS.

Given Diameter	Quarters			Ends	Given Diameter	Quarters			Ends
	1st	2nd	3rd			1st	2nd	3rd	
Ins.	Ins.	Ins.	Ins.	Ins.	Ins.	Ins.	Ins.	Ins.	Ins.
$5\frac{1}{2}$	$5\frac{3}{8}$	$5\frac{1}{16}$	$4\frac{5}{8}$	$3\frac{11}{16}$	$11\frac{1}{2}$	$11\frac{3}{16}$	$10\frac{9}{16}$	$9\frac{3}{8}$	$7\frac{11}{16}$
6	$5\frac{7}{8}$	$5\frac{1}{2}$	5	4	12	$11\frac{3}{4}$	11	10	8
$6\frac{1}{2}$	$6\frac{3}{8}$	$5\frac{15}{16}$	$5\frac{7}{16}$	$4\frac{3}{8}$	$12\frac{1}{2}$	$12\frac{1}{4}$	$11\frac{7}{16}$	$10\frac{7}{16}$	$8\frac{3}{8}$
7	$6\frac{7}{8}$	$6\frac{7}{16}$	$5\frac{7}{8}$	$4\frac{11}{16}$	13	$12\frac{3}{4}$	$11\frac{15}{16}$	$10\frac{7}{8}$	$8\frac{3}{4}$
$7\frac{1}{2}$	$7\frac{3}{8}$	$6\frac{7}{8}$	$6\frac{5}{16}$	5	$13\frac{1}{2}$	$12\frac{1}{4}$	$12\frac{1}{16}$	$11\frac{3}{16}$	9
8	$7\frac{13}{16}$	$7\frac{3}{8}$	$6\frac{3}{4}$	$5\frac{3}{8}$	14	$13\frac{5}{8}$	$12\frac{13}{16}$	$11\frac{11}{16}$	$9\frac{3}{8}$
$8\frac{1}{2}$	$8\frac{5}{16}$	$7\frac{13}{16}$	$7\frac{1}{8}$	$5\frac{11}{16}$	$14\frac{1}{2}$	$14\frac{3}{16}$	$13\frac{1}{4}$	12	$9\frac{11}{16}$
9	$8\frac{13}{16}$	$8\frac{1}{4}$	$7\frac{1}{2}$	6	15	$14\frac{5}{8}$	$13\frac{3}{4}$	$12\frac{1}{2}$	10
$9\frac{1}{2}$	$9\frac{5}{16}$	$8\frac{3}{4}$	$7\frac{15}{16}$	$6\frac{3}{8}$	$15\frac{1}{2}$	$15\frac{3}{16}$	$14\frac{3}{16}$	$12\frac{15}{16}$	$10\frac{3}{8}$
10	$9\frac{13}{16}$	$9\frac{1}{4}$	$8\frac{3}{8}$	$6\frac{11}{16}$	16	$15\frac{5}{8}$	$14\frac{5}{8}$	$13\frac{3}{8}$	$10\frac{11}{16}$
$10\frac{1}{2}$	$10\frac{3}{16}$	$9\frac{5}{8}$	$8\frac{3}{4}$	7	$16\frac{1}{2}$	$16\frac{1}{8}$	$15\frac{1}{8}$	$13\frac{13}{16}$	11
11	$10\frac{13}{16}$	$10\frac{1}{8}$	$9\frac{3}{16}$	$7\frac{3}{8}$	17	$16\frac{13}{16}$	$15\frac{13}{16}$	$14\frac{1}{4}$	$11\frac{3}{8}$

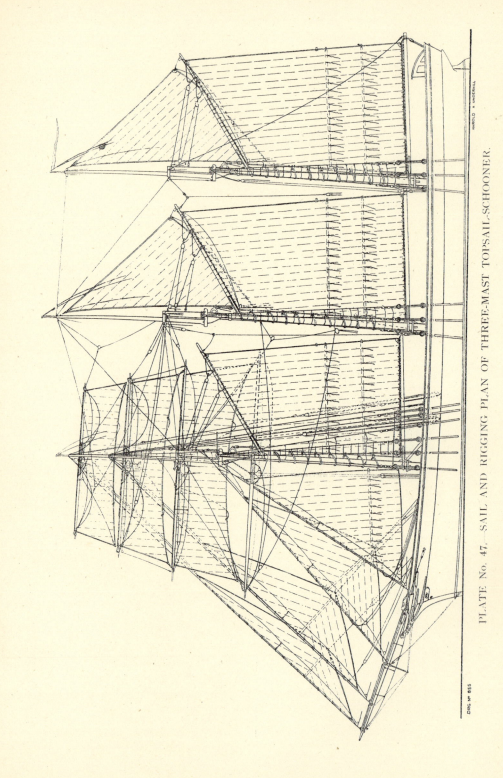

DRG No 855

PLATE No. 47. SAIL AND RIGGING PLAN OF THREE-MAST TOPSAIL-SCHOONER.

HAROLD A. UNDERHILL.

In table No. 13 the proportions of booms used on larger fore and aft sails have been calculated from the following :—

$$1Q. = \frac{GD \times 40}{41} : 2Q. = \frac{GD \times 12}{13} : 3Q. = \frac{GD \times 7}{8}$$

$$\text{fore end} = \frac{GD \times 2}{3} \text{ and after end} = \frac{GD \times 3}{4}$$

TABLE No. 13.
PROPORTIONS OF FORE AND AFT BOOMS.

Given Diameter	Quarters			Outer End	Mast End	Given Diameter	Quarters			Outer End	Mast End
	1st	2nd	3rd				1st	2nd	3rd		
Ins.	Ins.	Ins.	Ins.	Ins.	Ins.	Ins.	Ins.	Ins.	Ins.	Ins.	Ins.
6	5 7/8	5 9/16	5 1/4	4	4 1/2	12	11 3/4	11 1/16	10 1/2	8	9
6 1/2	6 3/8	6	5 11/16	4 3/8	4 7/8	12 1/2	12 1/4	11 1/2	10 15/16	8 3/8	9 3/8
7	6 7/8	6 1/2	6 1/8	4 11/16	5 1/4	13	12 11/16	12	11 7/16	8 11/16	9 3/4
7 1/2	7 5/16	6 15/16	6 9/16	5	5 11/16	13 1/2	13 3/16	12 1/2	11 13/16	9	10 1/8
8	7 13/16	7 3/8	7	5 3/8	6	14	13 11/16	12 7/8	12 1/4	9 3/8	10 1/2
8 1/2	8 5/16	7 7/8	7 7/16	5 11/16	6 7/16	14 1/2	14 1/8	13 7/16	12 11/16	9 11/16	10 7/8
9	8 13/16	8 5/16	7 7/8	6	6 3/4	15	14 5/8	13 7/8	13 3/16	10	11 1/4
9 1/2	9 5/16	8 13/16	8 5/16	6 3/8	7 1/8	15 1/2	15 1/8	14 5/16	13 9/16	10 3/8	11 5/8
10	9 13/16	9 1/4	8 3/4	6 11/16	7 1/2	16	15 5/8	14 3/4	14	10 11/16	12
10 1/2	10 3/16	9 3/4	9 1/8	7	7 7/8	16 1/2	16 1/8	15 1/4	14 7/16	11	12 3/8
11	10 3/4	10 3/16	9 5/8	7 3/8	8 1/4	17	16 5/8	15 3/4	14 7/8	11 3/8	12 3/4
11 1/2	11 3/16	10 5/8	10 1/16	7 11/16	8 5/8	17 1/2	17 1/8	16 3/16	15 5/16	11 11/16	13 3/16

The measured length of a gaff is the length of the actual spar, i.e. taken from the inside of the jaws to the outer end, and the given diameter, or maximum diameter is usually placed from 4 ft., to 6 ft. out from the face of the mast.

The given diameter of a gaff is often stated as being the same as that of its own boom, but this does not seem to be carried out to any great extent in actual practice, perhaps because the gaff is usually supported at close intervals by the spans of the peak halliards. I have checked twenty-seven vessels of which I have the spar dimensions, and in one case only does the gaff have the same given diameter as the boom. The majority of the remaining twenty-six work out exactly to the formula given below, and such as differ are obviously only the result of the diameter being taken to the nearest half-inch, so I don't think the modeller will go far wrong from the following:—

$$\frac{\text{Measured length in feet}}{4} = \text{Given diameter in inches.}$$

The remaining diameters have been calculated from the following, which have been used in compiling table No. 14.

$$1Q. = \frac{GD \times 40}{41} : 2Q. = \frac{GD \times 11}{12} : 3Q. = \frac{GD \times 4}{5}$$

$$\text{and the end} = \frac{GD \times 5}{9}$$

S

TABLE No. 14.

PROPORTIONS OF GAFFS.

Measured Length	Given Diameter	Quarters 1st	Quarters 2nd	Quarters 3rd	End	Measured Length	Given Diameter	Quarters 1st	Quarters 2nd	Quarters 3rd	End
Ft.	Ins.	Ins.	Ins.	Ins.	Ins.	Ft.	Ins.	Ins.	Ins.	Ins.	Ins.
21	5 1/4	5 1/8	4 13/16	4 1/4	2 15/16	41	10 1/4	10	9 3/8	8 1/4	5 11/16
22	5 1/2	5 3/8	5 1/16	4 7/16	3 1/16	42	10 1/2	10 1/4	9 5/8	8 7/16	5 7/8
23	5 3/4	5 5/8	5 5/16	4 5/8	3 3/16	43	10 3/4	10 1/2	9 7/8	8 5/8	6
24	6	5 7/8	5 1/2	4 13/16	3 3/8	44	11	10 3/4	10 1/8	8 13/16	6 1/8
25	6 1/4	6 1/8	5 3/4	5	3 1/2	45	11 1/4	11	10 3/8	9	6 1/4
26	6 1/2	6 3/8	6	5 1/4	3 5/8	46	11 1/2	11 1/4	10 9/16	9 1/4	6 7/16
27	6 3/4	6 5/8	6 1/4	5 7/16	3 3/4	47	11 3/4	11 1/2	10 3/4	9 7/16	6 9/16
28	7	6 7/8	6 7/16	5 5/8	3 7/8	48	12	11 3/4	11	9 5/8	6 11/16
29	7 1/4	7 1/8	6 11/16	5 13/16	4 1/16	49	12 1/4	12	11 1/4	9 13/16	6 7/8
30	7 1/2	7 3/8	6 13/16	6	4 3/16	50	12 1/2	12 1/4	11 1/2	10	7
31	7 3/4	7 9/16	7 1/8	6 3/16	4 5/16	51	12 3/4	12 7/16	11 3/4	10 3/16	7 1/8
32	8	7 13/16	7 3/8	6 3/8	4 7/16	52	13	12 11/16	11 15/16	10 7/16	7 1/4
33	8 1/4	8 1/16	7 9/16	6 5/8	4 9/16	53	13 1/4	12 15/16	12 3/16	10 5/8	7 7/16
34	8 1/2	8 5/16	7 13/16	6 13/16	4 3/4	54	13 1/2	13 3/16	12 7/16	10 13/16	7 1/2
35	8 3/4	8 9/16	8 1/16	7	4 7/8	55	13 3/4	13 7/16	12 5/8	11	7 11/16
36	9	8 13/16	8 1/4	7 1/4	5	56	14	13 11/16	12 7/8	11 1/4	7 13/16
37	9 1/4	9 1/16	8 1/2	7 7/16	5 1/8	57	14 1/4	13 7/8	13 1/8	11 7/16	7 15/16
38	9 1/2	9 5/16	8 5/8	7 5/8	5 5/16	58	14 1/2	14 1/4	13 5/16	11 5/8	8 1/16
39	9 3/4	9 9/16	8 15/16	7 13/16	5 7/16	59	14 3/4	14 7/16	13 9/16	11 13/16	8 1/4
40	10	9 3/4	9 3/16	8	5 9/16	60	15	14 11/16	13 3/4	12	8 3/8

As there is little call for studding-sail-yards and booms I will simply give the formula from which they are calculated, and the reader will then be able to work out the sizes for himself.

The given diameters of both yards and booms are obtained from:—

$$\frac{\text{Overall length in feet}}{5} = \text{Given diameter in inches.}$$

The booms are made of equal diameter for the first third of their length, from this they taper down to two-thirds the given diameter at the outer end Studding-sail-yards have the same proportions but they taper to both ends.

All rope, both wire and hemp, is measured by its circumference in inches, and is so quoted in the following tables. I have given the sizes of all gear in detail, although for the majority of models its main purpose will be to serve as an indication of general proportion rather than for exact reproduction, and I suggest that the small scale modeller fix the size of some principal item, say main-stay or main-shrouds, and judge the remainder from this. For large scale models, say 1/4 in. to the foot or over, it will of course be possible to get all the gear fairly accurately to size, and the easiest way will be to convert the circumferences to diameters, the sizes can then be measured directly on an ordinary scale rule as used by draughtsmen.

From the modeller's point of view the modern wire rigged vessel has the advantage of requiring relatively few sizes of standing-rigging as compared with the hemp rigged craft, even so, on small scale work the best he can do will be to fix the scale size of the main gear and graduate the rest down from it, using such material as it is possible to get. Here again I say review your gear as a whole before making any attempt at rigging. You will find it an advantage to lay out your entire stock of rigging material and carefully measure each size on the scale from which you are building your model, and having decided just what size each would represent, label each spool or hank with its scale size, i.e. 5 in. wire, 3 in. wire and so on. This will save a great deal of time and possible error during the process of rigging, for having arrived at the size of gear the actual ship would carry for the rigging in hand, you have only to look round your stock to find the nearest scale size you have. Time spent in general preparation before starting the actual model building or rigging is never time wasted, far from it, it is in fact time saved, but apart from that, it invariably results in better workmanship. To have to estimate the scale size of your material every time you change to some different item of rigging, soon makes the job tedious and often results in a tendency to accept sizes without knowing whether they are really right or not.

An evening spent in reducing all your stock material to scale dimensions and marking it, will repay you over and over again, and if you are really interested in model work the job will be neither dull nor tedious. During the actual rigging you simply go to your stock, much as you might go to the rigging loft in full size practice, and select the size, or nearest size to that wanted. I think it an advantage to carry this out right through the whole construction of the model, on the hull, for example, lay in a small stock of wood in a range of sections such as can be purchased from most model or handicraft shops, and having settled the scale of the model, note the scale sizes of the various timber sections. The result is that as the model proceeds you can select at once the size of material required for any particular job, But there, I am wandering from the subject!

Table No. 15 gives the sizes of steel wire rigging for vessels ranging from 3000 down to 300 tons register, and is based on Lloyd's standard specification. This table also indicates the number of stays or shrouds per side, and, in the case of fore and aft stays, whether they are to be single or double. A double stay is of course two wires of the size indicated, side by side and seized together as described in chapter IV. It will be seen that the table does not give any indication of the size of topmast and topgallant shrouds, but these can be obtained by means of table No. 16.

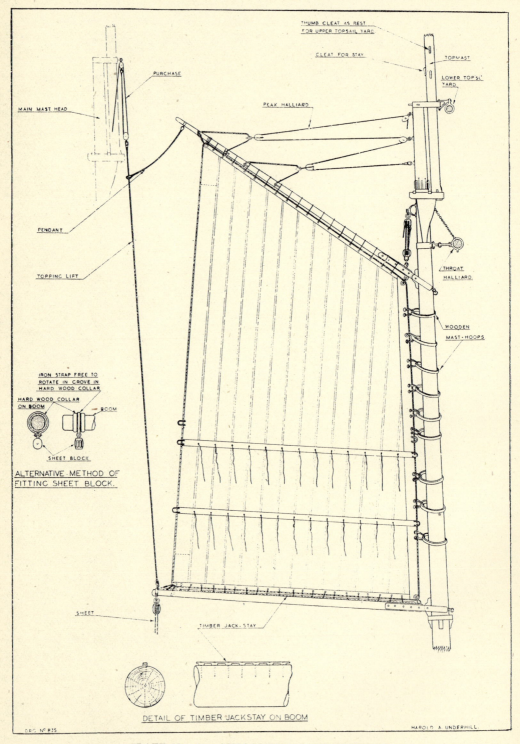

THUMB CLEAT AS REST
FOR UPPER TOPSAIL YARD

CLEAT FOR STAY

TOPMAST

LOWER TOP'S'L
YARD

PURCHASE

MAIN MAST HEAD

PEAK HALLIARD

PENDANT

TOPPING LIFT

THROAT
HALLIARD

WOODEN
MAST-HOOPS

IRON STRAP FREE TO
ROTATE IN GROVE IN
HARD WOOD COLLAR

HARD WOOD COLLAR
ON BOOM

BOOM

SHEET BLOCK

ALTERNATIVE METHOD OF
FITTING SHEET BLOCK.

SHEET

TIMBER JACK-STAY

DETAIL OF TIMBER JACKSTAY ON BOOM

DRG N° B 35

HAROLD A. UNDERHILL.

PLATE No. 48.—SCHOONER'S GAFF-FORESAIL.
(Note.—Arrow referring to throat halliard is pointing to lower yard in error.)

TABLE No. 15.

SIZE OF STEEL WIRE STANDING RIGGING.

COMPLIED FROM LLOYD'S STANDARD SPECIFICATION

Size of Vessel in Registered Tons	Fore & Main or Mizzen	Masts														Bowsprit					
		Lower Shrouds		Lower Capstays		Topmast Backstays		Topgallant Backstays		Lower Stays		Topmast Stays		Topgallant Stays		Inner Bobstay Iron Bar		Outer Bobstay Chain		Shrouds Chain	
		Number per side	Size	Number per side	Size	Number per side	Size	Number per side	Size	D. or S.	Size	D. or S.	Size	D. or S.	Size	D. or S.	Size	D. or S.	Size	Number per side	Size
3000/3500	F	6	5½	2	5½	3	5½	2	4¼	D	5½	D	5½	S	4¼	S	4⅛	S	2 1/16	2	1⅛
	M	5	4½	1	4½	3	4½	2	3¼	D	4½	D	4½	S	3¼						
2600/2999	F	6	5¼	2	5¼	3	5¼	2	4⅛	D	5¼	D	5¼	S	4⅛	S	4⅛	S	2 1/16	2	1⅛
	M	5	4⅜	1	4⅜	3	4⅜	2	3⅛	D	4⅜	D	4⅜	S	3⅛						
2300/2599	F	6	5	1	5	3	5	2	3⅞	D	5	D	5	S	3⅞	S	4	S	2	2	1 1/16
	M	5	4¼	1	4¼	3	4¼	2	3	D	4¼	D	4¼	S	3						
2000/2299	F	6	4⅞	1	4⅞	3	4⅞	2	3¾	D	4⅞	L	4⅞	S	3¾	S	3⅞	S	1 15/16	2	1 1/16
	M	5	4⅛	1	4⅛	3	4⅛	2	2⅞	D	4⅛	D	4⅛	S	2⅞						
1800/1999	F	6	4¾	1	4¾	3	4¾	2	3½	D	4¾	D	4¾	S	3½	S	3¾	S	1⅞	2	1
	M	5	4	1	4	3	4	2	2¾	D	4	D	4	S	2¾						
1600/1799	F	6	4½	1	4½	3	4½	2	3¼	D	4½	D	4½	S	3¼	S	3⅝	S	1 13/16	2	1
	M	5	3¾	1	3¾	3	3¾	2	2½	D	3¾	D	3¾	S	2½						
1400/1599	F	6	4¼	1	4¼	3	4¼	2	3	D	4¼	D	4¼	S	3	S	3½	S	1¾	2	⅞
	M	5	3½	1	3½	3	3½	2	2¼	D	3½	D	3½	S	2¼						
1200/1399	F	6	4⅛	1	4⅛	3	4⅛	2	2¾	D	4⅛	D	4⅛	S	2¾	S	3¼	S	1⅝	2	⅞
	M	5	3¼	1	3¼	3	3¼	2	2⅛	D	3¼	D	3¼	S	2⅛						
1000/1199	F	6	4	1	4	3	4	2	2⅝	D	4	D	4	S	2⅝	S	3	S	1½	2	13/16
	M	5	3	—	—	3	3	2	2	D	3	S	3	S	2						
800/999	F	5	3¾	1	3¾	2	3¾	2	2½	D	3¾	D	3¾	S	2½	S	2½	S	1⅜	2	¾
	M	5	2⅞	—	—	2	2⅞	1	1⅞	S	2⅞	S	2⅞	S	1⅞						
700/799	F	5	3½	1	3½	2	3½	1	2⅜	D	3½	D	3½	S	2⅜	S	2¼	S	1 5/16	1	¾
	M	5	2¾	—	—	2	2¾	1	1¾	S	2¾	S	2¾	S	1¾						
600/699	F	5	3¼	1	3¼	2	3¼	1	2¼	D	3¼	S	3¼	S	2¼	S	2	S	1¼	1	11/16
	M	4	2⅝	—	—	2	2⅝	1	1⅝	S	2⅝	S	2⅝	S	1⅝						
500/599	F	5	3	—	—	2	3	1	2⅛	D	3	S	3	S	2⅛	S	2	S	1¼	1	⅝
	M	4	2½	—	—	1	2½	1	1½	S	2½	S	2½	S	1½						
400/499	F	4	2¾	—	—	2	2¾	1	2	D	2¾	S	2¾	S	2	S	2	S	1¼	1	9/16
	M	3	2⅜	—	—	1	2⅜	1	1⅜	S	2⅜	S	2⅜	S	1⅜						
300/399	F	4	2½	—	—	2	2½	1	1¾	D	2½	S	2½	S	1¾	S	2	S	1 3/16	1	9/16
	M	3	2¼	—	—	1	2¼	1	1¼	S	2¼	S	2¼	S	1¼						

NOTE—F indicates Fore and Main Masts.
M indicates Mizzen Mast.
D indicates Double Stay.
S indicates Single Stay.
All sizes are given in Circumference in Inches.

For vessels of four or five Masts; or having Pole Masts; or Double Topgallants. See Notes in this Chapter.

The following table is a rough guide to the relative proportions of wire standing rigging, and is only intended to assist the model builder in deciding the sizes of such rigging as is not included in table No. 15. The use of the table is quite simple. The main-stay is taken as the basis of all other rigging and is represented by 1·0. The size of the remaining gear is obtained by multiplying the size of the main-stay by the figure shown in the appropriate column of the table. For example. Suppose the size of the main-stay—or main-shrouds for that matter for they are both the same size—has been fixed as 5 ins. then the main-topmast-shrouds would be 5ins × 0·9 = 4·5 ins, or $4\frac{1}{2}$ in. wire. Or the mizzen-topmast-shrouds would be got by 5 ins. × 0·778 = 3·89 ins., use 4 inches as the nearest standard wire.

TABLE No. 16.

RELATIVE SIZES OF WIRE STANDING RIGGING.

Description	Bowsprit	Fore Mast	Main Mast	Mizzen Mast
Inner Bobstay (Iron Bar)	0·805	—	—	—
Outer Bobstay (Iron Bar)	0·805	—	—	—
Bowsprit Shrouds	1·000	—	—	—
Lower Shrouds	—	1·000	1·000	0·834
Lower Stays (Double)	—	1·000	1·000	0·834
Lower Capstays	—	1·000	1·000	0·834
Topmast Shrouds	—	0·900	0·900	0·778
Topmast Backstays	—	1·000	1·000	0·834
Topmast Capstays	—	1·000	1·000	0·834
Topmast Stays (Double)..	—	1·000	1·000	0·834
Topgallant Shrouds	—	0·772	0·772	0·555
Topgallant Backstays	—	0·722	0·722	0·555
Topgallant Stay	—	0·722	0·722	0·555
Inner Jib-Stay	—	1·000	—	—
Outer Jib-Stay	—	1·000	—	—
Royal Stays	—	0·611	0·611	0·555
Royal Backstays	—	0.611	0·611	0·555

A great number of wood, composite, and iron ships were rigged with wire set up with dead-eyes and lanyards, and it is very important in model work that these may be made to scale. Next to the bowsprit gear, the setting up of the standing-rigging with dead-eyes and lanyards is perhaps the most conspicuous and if badly proportioned can mar the whole effect. The usual tendency is to make the dead-eyes too large, so that they rather resemble a row of shields hanging in the lower rigging, and if combined with lanyards which are too thin, can look very bad indeed. On the other hand dead-eyes must not be too small, for to bend a rope, either wire or hemp, round too small a radius is to kink and weaken it. There is a ratio, varying with the nature of the material, between the circumference of the rope and the minimum radius round which it may be bent without losing strength, and all sheaves, dead-eyes and thimbles are designed to keep just outside this danger line.

Another point I wish to make is that the lanyards must obviously be in keeping with the size of rigging they support, and it would not be much use using a 4½ in. wire shroud if it was to be set up with lanyards made from a clothes-line. As a matter of fact where wire rigging is used the hemp lanyard is often larger than the wire stay or shroud it supports. For example, a 4¾ in. wire shroud requires a 6 in. hemp lanyard through the dead-eyes, so it will be seen how wrong it is to use a very thin material for lanyards.

TABLE No. 17.
SIZE OF DEAD-EYES FOR WIRE RIGGED SHIPS.

Size of Vessel in Tons Register	Fore & Main or Mizzen	Lower Shrouds & Capstays		Topmast Shrouds		Topmast Backstays & Capstays		Topgallant Backstays		Royal Backstays	
		Dia. of Dead-Eye	Size of Lanyard	Dia. of Dead-Eye	Size of Lanyard	Dia. of Dead-Eye	Size of Lanyard	Dia. of Dead-Eye	Size of Lanyard	Dia. of Dead-Eye	Size of Lanyard
1800 - 2000	M & F	12	6	9	4½	12	6	9	4½	9	4½
	Miz.	10	5	8	3	10	5	7½	3¾	7½	3¾
1600 - 1799	M & F	11½	5¾	9	4½	11½	5¾	8½	4¼	8½	4¼
	Miz.	9½	4¾	8	4	9½	4¾	7	3½	7	3½
1400 - 1599	M & F	11	5½	8	4	11	5½	8	4	8	4
	Miz.	9	4½	7	3½	9	4½	6½	3¼	6½	3¼
1200 - 1399	M & F	10½	5¼	8	4	10½	5¼	7½	3½	7½	3½
	Miz.	8½	4¼	7	3½	8½	4¼	6½	3¼	6½	3¼
1000 - 1199	M & F	10	5	7½	3½	10	5	7½	3¾	7½	3¾
	Miz.	8	4	6½	3¼	8	4	6	3	6	3
800 - 999	M & F	9½	4¾	7½	3½	9½	4¾	7	3½	7	3½
	Miz	8	4	6½	3¼	8	4	6	3	6	3
700 - 799	M & F	9	4½	7	3½	9	4½	7	3½	7	3½
	Miz.	7½	3¾	6	3	7½	3¾	6	3	6	3
600 - 699	M & F	8½	4¼	6½	3¼	8½	4¼	6½	3¼	6½	3¼
	Miz.	7½	3¾	6	3	7½	3¾	6	3	6	3
500 - 599	M & F	8	4	6½	3¼	8	4	6½	3¼	6½	3¼
	Miz.	7	3½	6	3	7	3½	6	3	6	3
400 - 499	M & F	7½	3¾	6	3	7½	3¾	6	3	6	3
	Miz.	7	3½	6	3	7	3½	6	2½	6	2½
300 - 399	M & F	7	3½	6	2½	7	3½	6	2½	6	2½
	Miz.	6½	3¼	6	2½	6½	3¼	6	2½	6	2½

Dead-eye diameters in inches: lanyards circumference in inches.

Table No. 17 indicates the diameters of dead-eyes, and the size of lanyards to be used at various points on wire rigging, for vessels ranging from 2000 tons down to 300 tons register. The size of dead-eyes for hemp rigging will be covered in a later table.

As already explained there is a limit to which cordage may safely be bent, and therefore the *thickness* of a dead-eye is not governed by the size of groove required to receive the standing-rigging, but by the minimum radius round which the lanyard can be bent without loosing strength. Table No. 18 shows the usual relation between diameter and thickness of a range of dead-eyes suitable for wire standing-rigging, and may serve as a useful guide when making these fittings.

TABLE No. 18.

PROPORTIONS OF DEAD-EYES.

Diameter	16″	15″	14″	13″	12½″	12″	11½″	11″	10½″
Thickness	9″	8½″	8″	7½″	7″	7″	6½″	6½″	6″
Diameter	10″	9½″	9″	8½″	8″	7½″	7″	6½″	6″
Thickness	6″	5½″	5½″	5″	5″	4½″	4½″	4″	4″

Hemp rigging naturally requires to be much greater in circumference than steel wire for an equal load, so that the standing-rigging of the old hemp rigged craft has a much more bulky look than her modern wire rigged sister. Of course the majority of vessels of our period were wire rigged, but it is possible that the reader may be interested in one of the old stagers which survived into the era of steel, and I have therefore included table No. 19 which covers the standing-rigging of vessels ranging from 150 tons to 1200 tons register. Like the table on wire rigging it also includes the number of stays or shrouds per side. It will be noticed that no double stays are shown, but all such stays are as double on modern ships are simply made of a single large stay. This is in accordance with the usual practice when hemp is used throughout.

TABLE No. 19.

SIZE OF STANDING RIGGING ON HEMP RIGGED CRAFT.

Size of Vessel in Tons Register	Mast	Masts: Shrouds: Lower: Size	Masts: Shrouds: Lower: Number per side	Masts: Shrouds: Topmast: Size	Masts: Shrouds: Topmast: Number per side	Masts: Shrouds: T'gallant: Size	Masts: Shrouds: T'gallant: Number per side	Masts: Backstays: Topmast: Size	Masts: Backstays: Topmast: Number per side	Masts: Backstays: T'gallant: Size	Masts: Backstays: T'gallant: Number per side	Masts: Backstays: Royal: Size	Masts: Backstays: Royal: Number per side	Masts: Fore & Aft Stays: Lower	Masts: Fore & Aft Stays: Topmast	Masts: Fore & Aft Stays: Topgallant	Masts: Fore & Aft Stays: Royal	Bowsprit: Shrouds (Chain)	Bowsprit: Number per side	Bowsprit: Bobstays	Bowsprit: Number per side	Jibboom: Guys	Jibboom: Martingale-Stay	Jibboom: Martingale Back-Ropes	Jibboom: Flying-Jibboom Guys
		Ins.		Ins.		Ins.		Ins.		Ins.		Ins.		Ins.	Ins.	Ins.	Ins.	Ins.		Ins.		Ins.	Ins.	Ins.	Ins.
150-200 Barque Rig	F.&M.	6	4	4	3	2½	2	5	1	2½	2	1½	1	8	5	2½	1½	½	1	5/8	1	4	4½	2½	2½
	Miz.	5	3	4	1	—	—	3	2	2	2	1¼	1	5	3	2	1½								
201-300 Barque Rig	F.&M.	7	5	4	3	3	2	5½	2	3	2	2	2	10	5½	3	2	9/16	1	5/8	1	4	5	3	2½
	Miz.	5	4	3¼	2	—	—	3½	2	2	2	1¼	1	6	3½	2	1½								
301-450 Barque Rig	F.&M.	7½	5	4½	3	3	2	5½	2	3	2	2	2	12	5½	3¼	2	5/8	1	¾	1	4	5½	3½	2½
	Miz.	5½	4	3½	2	—	—	4	2	2	2	1¼	1	6	4	2½	1½								
451-600 Ship Rig	F.&M.	8	6	5	3	3½	2	6	3	3½	2	2¼	2	13	6	3½	2¼	5/8	1	¾	1	4½	6	4	2¾
	Miz.	6	4	4	3	2½	2	4½	2	2½	2	1¼	1	6½	4¼	2½	1½								
601-800 Ship Rig	F.&M.	9	7	5½	4	3½	2	6½	3	4	2	2¼	2	14	6½	3½	2¼	¾	2	7/8	1	4½	6½	4	3
	Miz.	6	5	4½	4	3	2	4½	2	3	2	1½	1	7	4½	3	1¾								
801-1200 Ship Rig	F.&M.	10	7	6	4	4	2	7	3	4½	2	2½	2	15	7	4	2½	¾	2	1	2	5	7	4½	3
	Miz.	6½	6	5	4	3	2	4½	2	3	2	2	1	7½	5	3	2								

NOTE:—F. & M. indicates Fore & Main Masts.
Miz. indicates Mizzen Mast.
Size of all cordage given in inches circumference.
This table is based on the use of single Fore and Aft stays in accordance with the practice of the period.

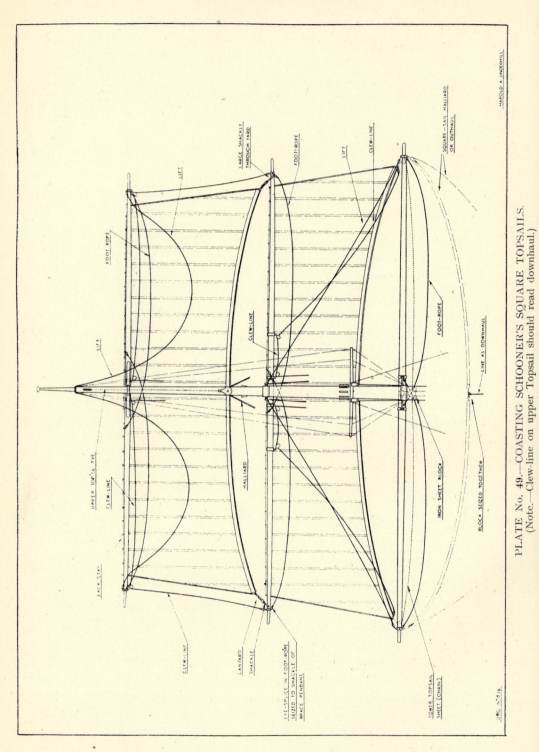

PLATE No. 49.—COASTING SCHOONER'S SQUARE TOPSAILS.
(Note.—Clew-line on upper Topsail should read downhaul.)

Table No. 20 shows the diameter of dead-eyes and circumference of lanyards for hemp rigged craft covering the same range as table No. 19. It will be noted that hearts are shown for the larger bowsprit gear, and it was usual to use lanyard thimbles instead of dead-eyes on some of the lighter rigging about the masts, such as the topgallant-shrouds. All this is indicated in the table.

TABLE No. 20.
SIZE OF DEAD-EYE AND LANYARDS ON HEMP RIGGED SHIPS.

Size of Vessel in Tons Register	Fore & Main or Mizzen	Lower Shrouds		Topmast Shrouds		Topmast Backstays		Topgallant Shrouds		Topgallant Backstays		Royal Backstays		Bobstays		Bowsprit Shrouds	
		Dia. of Dead-Eye	Size of Lanyard	Dia. of Dead-Eye	Size of Lanyard	Dia. of Dead-Eye	Size of Lanyard	Dia. of Dead-Eye	Size of Lanyard	Dia. of Dead-Eye	Size of Lanyard	Dia. of Dead-Eye	Size of Lanyard	Hearts or Thimbles	Size of Lanyard	Hearts or Thimbles	Size of Lanyard
150-200 (Brig)	F. & M.	8	3	6	2	8	3	T	1	T	1¼	T	½	T	2	T	2
	Miz.	—	—	—	—	—	—	—	—	—	—	—	—				
201-300	F. & M.	10	3½	6	2	8	3	T	1	T	1¼	T	½	H	2½	H	2
	Miz.	8	2½	6	1½	6	1¾	T	1	T	1	T	½				
301-450	F. & M.	11	4	6	2	8	3	T	1¼	T	1½	T	¾	H	3	H	2½
	Miz.	8	2½	6	2	6	1¾	T	1	T	1	T	½				
451-600	F. & M.	11	4	7	2½	8	3	T	1½	6	1½	T	¾	H	3½	H	2½
	Miz.	8	2½	7	2	7	2	T	1¼	T	1	T	¾				
601-800	F. & M.	14	4½	8	2½	9	3	T	1½	6	1½	T	1	H	4	H	2½
	Miz.	8	3	7	2	7	2	T	1¼	T	1¼	T	¾				
801-1100	F. & M.	16	5	9	3	10	3¼	T	2	6	2	T	1	H	4	H	2½
	Miz.	9	3	8	2½	8	2½	T	1½	T	1½	T	1				

NOTE:—F. & M. indicates Fore & Main Masts.
Miz. indicates Mizzen Mast.
H. indicates Heart.
T indicates Lanyard-Thimble.
Dead-eyes are given in inches diameter.
Lanyards are given in inches circumference.

The size of running rigging cannot be detailed to the same extent as standing rigging, for much will depend upon the size and shape of the sails it serves, which will of course govern the duty performed. On the other hand the modern tendency was to make everything as uniform as possible with a view to limiting the number of sizes to be carried as spares, so here again the period of the prototype may make a considerable difference in the sizes of running-rigging. As time went on wire was used more and more for running-rigging, until at the end of the era there was relatively little cordage except in the form of tackles and purchases. Chain also came more into the picture,

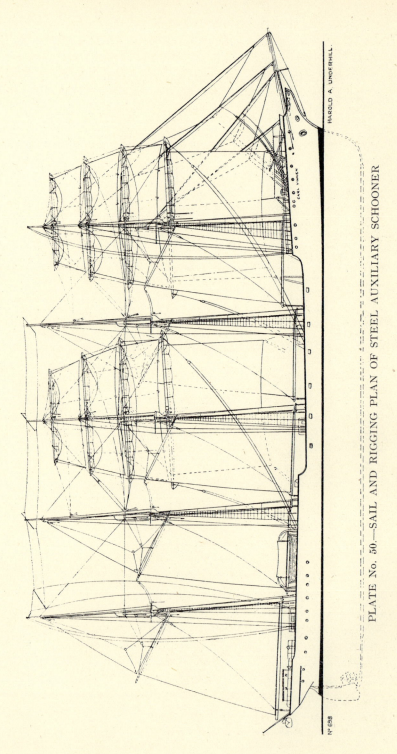

PLATE No. 50.—SAIL AND RIGGING PLAN OF STEEL AUXILIARY SCHOONER

for in the early hemp rigged ships, cordage was used for the sheets of square-sails, whereas with the later ships sheets were entirely of chain, or of wire with chain inserts in way of blocks and fittings.

The following tables have been included as a guide for the large scale model builder, and are based on sizes known to have been used in hemp

TABLE No. 21.

APPROXIMATE SIZES OF RUNNING RIGGING ON SQUARE SAILS.

Description of Gear	Barque 300 Tons				Ship 1,500 Tons			
	F. & M.		Mizzen		F. & M.		Mizzen	
	Hemp	Wire	Hemp	Wire	Hemp	Wire	Hemp	Wire
	Ins.	Ins.	Ins.	Ins.	Ins.	Ins.	Ins.	Ins.
Lower-Yard Lifts	4	1¾	—	—	4	1¾	2½	1
Lower-Braces	3	1½	—	—	4	1¾	2½	—
Lower-Sheets	4	1¾	—	—	5	2	—	—
Lower-Tacks	4	1¾	—	—	5	2	—	—
Lower-Clew-Garnets	2	¾	—	—	3½	1⅝	—	—
Lower-Leech-Lines	2	¾	—	—	2½	1	—	—
Lower-Bunt-lines	2½	1	—	—	3	1½	—	—
Lower-Slab-Lines	2	1	—	—	2	1	—	—
Lower-Bowline and Bridle	3	1½	—	—	4	1¾	—	—
Lower-Studding-Sail Halliards	2½	1	—	—	3	1½	—	—
Lower-Studding-Sail Inner Halliards	2½	1	—	—	3	1½	—	—
Lower-Studding-Sail Sheets	2½	1	—	—	3	1½	—	—
Lower-Studding-Sail Tack	2½	1	—	—	3	1½	—	—
Lower-Studding-Sail Tripping-Line	1½	⅝	—	—	2	¾	—	—
Lower-Studding-Sail Swinging-Boom-Guys	2½	1	—	—	3	1½	—	—
Topsail-Tye	C	C	—	—	C	C	C	C
Topsail-Halliard	2½	1	—	—	3	1½	2½	1
Topsail-Lifts	3	1½	—	—	3½	1⅝	3	1½
Topsail-Braces	2½	1	—	—	3	1½	2½	1
Topsail-Sheets	C	C	—	—	C	C	C	C
Topsail-Clew-lines	2¼	1	—	—	3½	1⅝	2	¾
Topsail-Bunt-Lines	2¼	1	—	—	3	1½	2	¾
Topsail-Reef-Tackles	2½	1	—	—	3	1½	2¼	1
Topsail-Bowline and Bridle	2½	1	—	—	3	1½	—	—
Topsail-Studding-Sail-Halliards	2½	1	—	—	3½	1⅝	—	—
Topsail-Studding-Sail-Sheets	2½	1	—	—	3¼	1⅝	—	—
Topsail-Studding-Sail-Tacks	2½	1	—	—	3½	1⅝	—	—
Topsail-Studding-Sail-Downhaul	1½	⅝	—	—	2½	1	—	—
Topgallant-Tye	C	C	—	—	C	C	C	C
Topgallant-Halliard	2½	1	—	—	3½	1⅝	2¼	1
Topgallant-Lifts	2¼	1	—	—	3	1½	2	¾
Topgallant-Braces	1½	⅝	—	—	2¼	1	1½	⅝
Topgallant-Sheets	2½	1	—	—	3¾	1¾	2	¾
Topgallant-Clew-lines	1½	⅝	—	—	2	¾	1½	⅝
Topgallant-Bunt-Lines	1½	⅝	—	—	2	¾	1½	⅝
Topgallant-Studding-Sail-Halliards	1½	⅝	—	—	2½	1	—	—
Topgallant-Sheets	2	¾	—	—	2	¾	—	—
Topgallant-Downhauls	—	—	—	—	1½	⅝	—	—
Royal-Tye	C	C	—	—	C	C	C	C
Royal-Halliard	2	¾	—	—	2½	1	2	¾
Royal-Lifts	1½	⅝	—	—	2	¾	1	½
Royal-Braces	1	½	—	—	2	¾	1	½
Royal-Sheets	1½	⅝	—	—	2¼	1	1	½

Note:—F. & M. indicates Fore & Main Masts
Mizzen indicates Mizzen-Mast.
C indicates Chain.

rigged ships. The vessels represented are one of 1500 tons and one of 300 tons register and may be said to be typical of large and small vessels respectively. Alongside the figures for hemp I have included another column which will give the model maker a rough idea of the equivalent size of wire to be used for the same duty. Table No. 21 gives the running-gear on square-sails, and table No. 22 does the same for fore and afters.

These tables do not cover the whole range of running-rigging, nor is it intended that they should be regarded as a standard specification to which all ships would be rigged, but they will at least give the reader some general idea of the proportion of one item to another.

TABLE No. 22.

APPROXIMATE SIZE OF RUNNING RIGGING ON FORE AND AFT SAILS.

Description of Gear	Barque 300 Tons				Ship 1500 Tons			
	F. & M.		Mizzen		F. & M.		Mizzen	
	Hemp	Wire	Hemp	Wire	Hemp	Wire	Hemp	Wire
	Ins.	Ins.	Ins.	Ins.	Ins.	Ins.	Ins.	Ins.
Flying-Jib-Halliard	2	$\frac{3}{4}$	—	—	$2\frac{1}{2}$	1	—	—
Flying-Jib-Downhaul	$1\frac{1}{2}$	$\frac{5}{8}$	—	—	2	$\frac{3}{4}$	—	—
Flying-Jib-Sheets	2	—	—	—	$2\frac{1}{2}$	—	—	—
Flying-Jib-Sheet-Pendants	$3\frac{1}{4}$	$1\frac{1}{2}$	—	—	4	$1\frac{3}{4}$	—	—
Jib-Halliards	$2\frac{1}{2}$	1	—	—	$3\frac{1}{4}$	$1\frac{1}{2}$	—	—
Jib-Downhauls	2	$\frac{3}{4}$	—	—	$2\frac{1}{2}$	1	—	—
Jib-Sheets	$2\frac{1}{4}$	—	—	—	3	—	—	—
Jib-Sheet-Pendants	$3\frac{1}{2}$	$1\frac{5}{8}$	—	—	$4\frac{1}{2}$	$1\frac{7}{8}$	—	—
Lower-Staysail-Halliards	$2\frac{1}{2}$	1	2	$\frac{3}{4}$	3	$1\frac{1}{2}$	$2\frac{1}{2}$	1
Lower-Staysail-Downhauls	2	$\frac{3}{4}$	$1\frac{1}{2}$	$\frac{5}{8}$	$2\frac{1}{2}$	1	2	$\frac{3}{4}$
Lower-Staysail-Sheets	$2\frac{1}{4}$	—	2	—	3	—	$2\frac{1}{2}$	—
Lower-Staysail-Sheet-Pendants	$3\frac{1}{2}$	$1\frac{5}{8}$	3	$1\frac{1}{2}$	$4\frac{1}{2}$	$1\frac{7}{8}$	4	$1\frac{3}{4}$
Topmast-Staysail-Halliards	$2\frac{1}{2}$	1	2	$\frac{3}{4}$	3	$1\frac{1}{2}$	$2\frac{1}{2}$	1
Topmast-Staysail-Downhauls	2	$\frac{3}{4}$	$1\frac{1}{2}$	$\frac{5}{8}$	$2\frac{1}{2}$	1	2	$\frac{3}{4}$
Topmast-Staysail-Sheets	$2\frac{1}{2}$	—	2	—	$3\frac{1}{2}$	—	3	—
Topmast-Staysail-Sheet-Pendants	$3\frac{1}{2}$	$1\frac{5}{8}$	3	$1\frac{1}{2}$	$4\frac{1}{2}$	$1\frac{7}{8}$	4	$1\frac{3}{4}$
Topgallant-Staysail-Halliard	2	$\frac{3}{4}$	$1\frac{1}{2}$	$\frac{5}{8}$	$2\frac{1}{2}$	1	2	$\frac{3}{4}$
Topgallant-Staysail-Downhaul	$1\frac{1}{2}$	$\frac{5}{8}$	$1\frac{1}{2}$	$\frac{5}{8}$	2	$\frac{3}{4}$	$1\frac{1}{2}$	$\frac{5}{8}$
Topgallant-Staysail-Sheets	2	—	$1\frac{1}{2}$	—	$2\frac{1}{2}$	—	2	—
Topgallant-Staysail-Sheet-Pendants ..	$3\frac{1}{4}$	$1\frac{5}{8}$	3	$1\frac{1}{2}$	4	$1\frac{3}{4}$	$3\frac{1}{2}$	$1\frac{5}{8}$
Spanker Peak-Halliards	—	—	$2\frac{1}{2}$	1	—	—	4	$1\frac{3}{4}$
Spanker-Throat-Halliard	—	—	$2\frac{1}{2}$	1	—	—	4	$1\frac{1}{4}$
Spanker-Sheets	—	—	$2\frac{1}{2}$	—	—	—	$3\frac{1}{2}$	—
Spanker-Topping-Lifts	—	—	3	$1\frac{1}{2}$	—	—	$4\frac{1}{2}$	$1\frac{7}{8}$
Spanker-Head & Foot Outhauls	—	—	2	1	—	—	$3\frac{1}{2}$	$1\frac{5}{8}$
Spanker-Brails, Head & Foot Inhauls ..	—	—	$1\frac{1}{2}$	$\frac{5}{8}$	—	—	2	$\frac{3}{4}$
Spanker-Vangs	—	—	2	$\frac{3}{4}$	—	—	2	$\frac{3}{4}$
Spanker-Vang-Pendants	—	—	$2\frac{1}{2}$	1	—	—	$3\frac{1}{2}$	$1\frac{5}{8}$
Spanker-Boom-Guy-Pendants	—	—	3	$1\frac{1}{2}$	—	—	$3\frac{1}{2}$	$1\frac{5}{8}$
Spanker-Boom-Guys	—	—	$2\frac{1}{2}$	—	—	—	$3\frac{1}{2}$	—

APPENDIX I.

PURCHASES AND TACKLES IN COMMON USE ON RUNNING RIGGING.

In the following sketches and description I have indicated the various standing and running parts as they are likely to be when forming part of a sailing ship's running-rigging. When these same tackles are used for other purposes their various components may function differently, and what is now shown as a running part become stationary and vice versa, although the composition and rig of the tackle remains the same. For example, the Simple Whip—Fig. 172—is shown as rigged to give extra purchase on a halliard, clew-line, etc., so the block is bent to the end of the moving line and one end of the fall becomes the standing part, but when used for lifting a weight, the block would be stationary and the object to be lifted attached to one end of the fall. In the same way, the Runner and Tackle is shown with the upper block attached to the moving object, while both the standing end of the runner and the lower block of the tackle are shackled to eye-bolts in the deck, whereas for raising a heavy weight, one or both of these would be attached to the object to be lifted and the upper single block remain stationary.

The point I wish to make is that while the components of the various tackles will remain unchanged, their actual rig and function may be varied according to requirements.

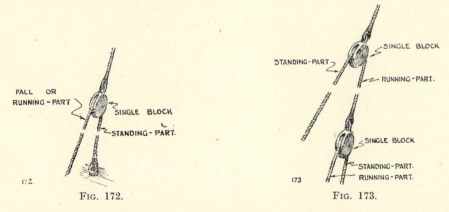

FIG. 172.   FIG. 173.

Simple-Whip.—This is the most simple form of purchase used. A single block is bent to the end of the line to which purchase is to be applied. The standing end of the fall is made fast to some convenient fixture such as an eye-bolt or part of the vessel's standing-rigging, the running end reeved through the block and taken down to its belaying point. This form of purchase is largely used on staysail-halliards and sheets, clew-lines, downhauls, etc. (Fig. 172).

Whip and Runner.—This might be described as one whip super-imposed on another, or a double whip. The first whip is rigged as for the simple-whip, but the running end terminates in a single block instead of continuing down to the belaying point. Through this block a second whip is reeved, the running part of which goes down to the belaying point. This tackle was much used on the halliards of single-topsails and topgallants in the smaller ships of the early clipper era.

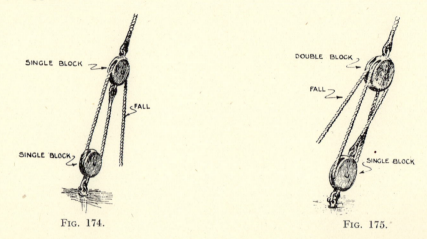

FIG. 174.　　　　　　　　　　　FIG. 175.

Gin-Tackle Purchase.—This is composed of two single blocks, the upper one bent to the end of the moving line and the lower shackled to a convenient eye-bolt. The fall is spliced round a thimble on the heel of the upper block; reeves down through the lower block; up and through the upper block and is belayed as required (Fig. 174).

Luff-Tackle Purchase.—This has a double and single block. The double block is made fast to the moving line and the single shackled to the deck; The fall is spliced round a thimble on the single block; reeves over one sheave of the double block; down through the single; back through the double and belays as convenient (Fig. 175).

Runner and Tackle.—This is really a simple whip with a luff-tackle purchase on the fall. A single block is bent to the moving line. The standing part of the runner—or whip—shackles to a convenient fixture, and the running part bent to the upper block of a luff-tackle. The double halliard rigged on square yards is really a runner and tackle, except that a three-fold purchase—Fig. 178—takes the place of the luff-tackle (Fig. 176).

Two-Fold Purchase.—This consists of two double blocks. The fall is spliced to the heel of one; reeved through each in turn until all sheaves are taken up, and so down to the belaying point (Fig. 177).

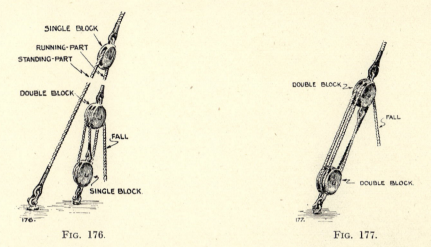

FIG. 176.   FIG. 177.

Three-Fold Purchase.—Made up of two treble blocks. The fall being spliced to the heel of one and reeved through each in turn until all sheaves are taken up (Fig. 178).

There are of course other forms of purchase such as the Top-burton, the Long-tackle, and so on, using fiddle-blocks, shoe-blocks, shoulder-blocks, sister-blocks, etc., but these all belong more to the days of hemp standing-rigging and are not in common use today, and therefore are of no interest to us.

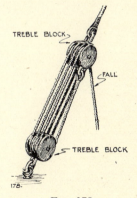

FIG. 178.

T

APPENDIX II.
SAILING SHIP DRAWINGS.

THE publishers can supply sets of sailing ship plans specially drawn by the Author to scales suitable for model construction and consisting of Lines Drawing; General Arrangement Drawing with Deck Plans; Sail & Rigging Plan including all running-rigging, and, in certain cases, additional sheets providing scale details of individual deck fittings, masts, spars, rigging, etc.

The aim of these drawings is to provide authentic data for those interested in the sailing ship period, or desiring to build models of named ships. They are based on original drawings and specifications, from which all essential information has been condensed into three or more sheets of convenient size averaging 30 ins. $\times$ 22 ins.

With a view to illustrating the ship as she actually went to sea, the original details have been edited as far as possible by personal survey of such vessels as were available from the author's own records and research work, or both, but the author will always be pleased to learn of any changes which, through the lack of information, may not have been embodied or noted on the drawings, so that such information can be added.

The undermentioned ships are at present available, together with a few sets for the construction of simple models not intended to represent any particular vessel.

Acamas.—Steel full-rigged ship. A large modern ship rigged vessel of 1860 tons

Albert Rickmers.—Steel three-mast barque. This is a good example of the modern three-mast barque, she is perhaps better remembered as *Penang.*

Archibald Russell.—Steel four-mast barque. A very well known unit of the grain fleet and a frequent visitor to this country in the last days of sail.

Carl Vinnen.—Steel auxiliary five-mast two-topsail schooner. This vessel has already been mentioned and illustrated in Chapter VIII.

Coriolanus.—Iron full-rigged ship. The *Coriolanus* was known as "Queen of the Jute Clippers" and is said to have been one of the most beautiful iron ships ever turned out.

Cromdale.—Steel full-rigged ship. A very fine example of one of the later day wool clippers.

Cutty Sark.—Composite full-rigged ship. This famous tea and wool clipper needs no further mention.

Discovery.—Wood auxiliary steam barque. This particular set is not claimed to be correct in detail for Captain Scott's famous ship, as at the time the drawings were compiled the actual vessel was not available.

Emma Ernest.—Wood three-mast topsail schooner. A typical coaster and a vessel well known to Londoners as the *Seven Seas*, moored off the Embankment.

Endeavour.—Bark (1768) this is Captain Cook's famous vessel and these drawings are very fully detailed as the result of careful research work, and really authentic and suitable for perfect scale models.

Fame.—Composite brig. This is one of the famous Bengal Pilot Brigs. (See Hoogly Pilot Brig).

Formby.—Steel full-rigged ship. Reputed to have been the first vessel to be constructed of steel.

France (II).—Steel auxiliary five-mast barque. This, the second five- mast barque of that name was the largest sailing craft ever built.

Halcyon.—Steel lee-board ketch. The *Halcyon* is a modern coasting ketch of the barge type.

Helen Barnet Gring.—A typical American four-mast fore and aft schooner.

Juan Sebastian De Elcano.—Steel four-mast topsail-schooner. This Spanish Train-in Shipg was designed in Great Britain and is an extremely fine looking craft and an excellent subject for a model.

Lady Daphne.—200-ton Thames sailing barge. This is a typical example of the large coasting barge so well known on the South coast.

Leon.—A pretty little wood brigantine of 302 tons, built at Laurvig, Norway, in 1880. The plans include a full construction drawing for a plank on frame model. Scale $\frac{1}{8}'' = 1'\ 0''$.

Loch Etive.—Iron full-rigged ship. One of the famous "Loch Line" clippers.

Loch Sunnart.—Iron full-rigged ship. Sister ship of *Loch Etive.*

Magdalene Vinnen (II).—Steel auxiliary four-mast barque. This is the second four-mast barque of that name and is a typical modern ship with mid-ship bridge deck.

Marie Sophie.—Wood brig. The *Marie Sophie* is a good example of the trading brig in her prime.

Mount Stewart.—Steel full-rigged ship. Sister ship of *Cromdale.*

Mozart.—Steel four-mast barquentine. A well-known and typical example of the modern steel barquentine.

Oamaru.—Iron full-rigged ship. This was one of the famous colonial clippers, and a good looking ship, with long poop and fine lines.

Penang.—Steel three-mast barque. (Ex-*Albert Rickmers*).

Pommern.—Steel four-mast barque. Another old friend and regular visitor with the grain ships.

Queen Margaret.—Steel four-mast barque, referred to by Lubbock as "one of the fastest and most beautiful carriers of the nineties."

Raven.—Wood brigantine. A good example of the trading brigantine once so common in both off shore and coasting trades.

Ross-Shire.—Steel four-mast barque. A well remembered member of Thomas Law's fleet of sailing ships.

Runnymede.—Wood snow. This is an interesting old stager with square stern and single topsails.

Statsraad Lehmkual.—Steel three-mast barque. A typical modern training ship.

Three Brothers.—Rye smack. Ketch rigged.

Timaru.—Iron full-rigged ship. Sister ship of the iron clipper *Oamaru.*

Torrens.—Composite ship. Well known as the favourite ship of Joseph Conrad.

Valerian.—Brixham trawler. This is a very comprehensive set with a view to providing all possible detail of these fine boats.

Waterwitch.—Wood three-mast barquentine. Another old favourite of the British coast, she was the last real square-rigger on the coast.

William Ashburner.—Three-mast topsail-schooner. This very fine schooner was one of the last sailing ships in our coastal trade, and will be remembered with pleasure by many lovers of these little craft.

COASTING SCHOONER.—This is a typical two-mast Topsail schooner. The sail plan of which is shown in plate 44.

40-GUN FRIGATE.—(Circa 1790). This is a very complete set of plans, with separate, drawings of each individual spar, deck fitting, etc., all to a scale of $\frac{1}{4}'' = 1'\ 0''$. Also full sail and rigging plans showing the lead of all standing and running gear.

12-GUN BRIG OF WAR.—This set has been produced for super detail $\frac{1}{4}$-in. scale models of one of the old 12-gun brigs, which many will remember as sail training ships in the Royal Navy.

HOOGHLY PILOT BRIG.—These brigs will be well remembered by all who served in the Calcutta trade in the days of sail, and the plans, which are to a scale of $\frac{1}{4}'' = 1'\ 0''$ have been compiled from the actual yard details. This particular vessel was one of the last sailers in the Hooghly Pilot Service.

SCOTTISH ZULU.—The Zulu is perhaps the finest of all Scottish fishing types and these drawings, to a scale of $\frac{1}{2}'' = 1'\ 0''$, were originally produced by the author for presentation to the Society for Nautical Research. They are full working drawings of the *Muirneag* and are the result of a most complete survey, which was made just before she was broken up. They include full constructional and fitting out details, as well as notes and sketches on the use of the gear. They are perhaps the most complete record of this type of vessel yet produced.

ELIZABETHAN GALLEON.—Suitable for a small decorative model, typical of the Elizabethan period.

COASTING KETCH.—These drawings are of a typical West Country trading ketch and make an excellent subject for a model.

RING NET BOAT.—One of the modern cruiser sterned fishermen of the Scottish coast.

SHIPS BOATS.—A range of details including Lines, Sections, Construction Plans and details of ships boats as carried by the sailing Man-of-War.

MUZZLE LOADING GUNS.—A range of old time muzzle loading guns as carried in the days of sail.

MASTING & RIGGING.—Large scale prints of most of the full page plates in this book are available, approximate size $30'' \times 22''$ and can be supplied as either white or blue prints.

The above list will of course be added to from time to time.

Particulars on application to Brown, Son & Ferguson, Ltd., 52-58 Darnley Street, Glasgow, S.1.

APPENDIX III.

TERMINOLOGICAL KEY TO BELAYING PIN LAYOUT.
See Folding Plate No. 51.

Name of Gear		Type	Side	Position	No
FORE MAST.					
HEAD SAILS.					
Flying-jib-halliard		BP.	P.	MR.	24
Flying-jib-downhaul		,,	P.	HFR.	1
Flying-jib-sheets		,,	P. & S.	MR.	6
Outer-jib-halliard		,,	S.	MR.	22
Outer-jib-downhaul		,,	P.	HFR.	2
Outer-jib-sheet		,,	P. & S.	MR.	7
Inner-jib-halliard		,,	P.	MR.	21
Inner-jib-down-haul		,,	S.	HFR.	3
Inner-jib-sheet		,,	P. & S.	MR.	8
Fore-topmast-staysail-halliard		,,	S.	MR.	20
Fore-topmast-staysail-downhaul		,,	S.	HFR.	4
Fore-topmast-staysail-sheets		Bitts	P. & S.	Deck	9
SQUARE—SAILS.					
Fore-sail.	Leech-lines and Bunt-lines	BP.	P. & S.	MR.	10
Fore-sail.	Clew-garnets	,,	P. & S.	MR.	11
Fore-sail.	Sheets	Bitts	P. & S.	MR.	38
Fore-sail.	Lazy-sheet	BP.	P. & S.	MR.	39
Fore-yard-lift.	(Port)	,,	P.	FFR.	33
Fore-yard-lift.	(Starboard)	,,	S.	FFR.	37
Fore-tack		Bitts	P. & S.	Deck	109
Fore-lazy-tack		BP.	P. & S.	MR.	5
Fore-brace		,,	P. & S.	MR.	41
Fore-lower-topsail.	Bunt-lines & Clew-lines	,,	P. & S.	MR.	12
Fore-lower-topsail.	Sheets	,,	P. & S.	S-B.	28
Fore-lower-topsail.	Brace	,,	P. & S.	MR.	42
Fore-upper-topsail.	Halliard	,,	P.	MR.	16
Fore-upper-topsail.	Downhaul & Bunts-lines	,,	P. & S.	MR.	13
Fore-upper-topsail.	Sheets (Set up aloft)	—	—	—	—
Fore-upper-topsail.	Brace	BP.	P. & S.	MR.	43
Fore-lower-topgallant.	Bunt-lines & Clew-lines	,,	P. & S.	MR.	15
Fore-lower-topgallant.	Sheets	,,	P. & S.	MR.	14
Fore-lower-topgallant.	Brace	,,	P. & S.	MR.	57
Fore-upper-topgallant.	Halliard	,,	S.	MR.	23
Fore-upper-topgallant.	Downhaul & Bunt-lines	,,	P. & S.	MR.	17
Fore-upper-topgallant.	Sheets (Set up aloft)	—	—	—	—
Fore-upper-topgallant.	Brace	BP.	P. & S.	MR.	58
Fore-royal.	Halliard	,,	P.	MR.	26
Fore-royal.	Bunt-lines & Clew-lines	,,	P. & S.	MR.	19
Fore-royal.	Sheets	,,	P. & S.	MR.	18
Fore-royal.	Brace	,,	P. & S.	MR.	59
MAIN-MAST.					
STAYSAILS.					
Main-topmast-staysail-halliard		BP.	P.	MR.	56
Main-topmast-staysail-downhaul		.,	P.	FFR.	32
Main-topmast-staysail-sheet		,,	P. & S.	MR.	40
Main-topgallant-staysail-halliard		,,	S.	MR.	60
Main-topgallant-staysail-downhaul		,,	S.	FFR.	35
Main-topgallant-staysail-sheet		,,	P. & S.	MR.	44
Main-royal-staysail-halliard		,,	P.	MR.	63
Main-royal-staysail-downhaul		,,	P.	FFR.	31
Main-royal-staysail-sheet		,,	P. & S.	MR.	45

TERMINOLOGICAL KEY TO BELAYING PIN LAYOUT—*Cont.*

Name of Gear	Type	Side	Position	No
SQUARE—SAILS.				
Main-sail. Leech-lines & Bunt-lines	BP.	P. & S.	MR.	46
Main-sail. Clew-garnets	,,	P. & S.	MR.	47
Main-sail. Sheets	Bitts	P. & S.	MR.	74
Main-sail. Tack. (On fore-sheet bitts)	Bitts	P. & S.	MR.	38
Main-sail. Lazy-tack	BP.	P. & S.	MR.	39
Main-yard-lifts	,,	P. & S.	MFR.	64
Main-brace	BR.	P. & S.	MR.	78
Main-bowline. (Starboard)	,,	S.	FFR.	34
Main-bowline. (Port)	,,	.P.	FFR.	30
Main-lower-topsail. Buntlines & Clew-lines	,,	P & S.	MR.	48
Main-lower-topsail. Sheets	,,	P. & S.	S-B	70
Main-lower-topsail. Brace	,,	P. & S.	MR.	79
Main-upper-topsail. Halliard	,,	S.	MR.	55
Main-upper-topsail. Downhaul & Bunt-lines	,,	P. & S.	MR.	49
Main-upper-topsail. Sheets. (Set up aloft)	—	—	—	—
Main-upper-topsail. Brace	BP.	P. & S.	MR.	80
Main-lower-topgallant. Bunt-lines & Clew-lines	,,	P. & S.	MR.	51
Main-lower-topgallant. Sheets	,,	P. & S.	MR.	50
Main-lower-topgallant. Brace	,,	P. & S.	PR.	97
Main-upper-topgallant. Halliard	,,	P.	MR.	61
Main-upper-topgallant. Downhaul & Bunt-lines	,,	P. & S.	MR.	52
Main-upper-topgallant. Sheets (Set up aloft)	—	—	—	—
Main-upper-topgallant. Brace	BP.	P. & S.	PR.	98
Main-royal. Halliards	,,	S.	MR.	62
Main-royal. Bunt-lines & Clew-lines	,,	P. & S.	MR.	54
Main-royal. Sheets	,,	P. & S.	MR.	53
Main-royal. Brace	,,	P. & S.	PR.	99
MIZZEN—MAST.				
STAYSAILS AND SPANKER				
Mizzen-topmast-staysail-halliard	BP.	S.	PR.	96
Mizzen-topmast-staysail-downhaul	,,	S.	MFR.	66
Mizzen-topmast-staysail-sheet	,,	P. & S.	MR.	77
Mizzen-topgallant-staysail-halliard	,,	P.	PR.	100
Mizzen-topgallant-staysail-downhaul	,,	P.	MFR.	65
Mizzen-topgallant-staysail-sheet	,,	P. & S.	MR.	81
Spanker-head-outhaul	,,	P.	PR.	94
Spanker-head-downhaul	,,	P.	PR.	94
Spanker-foot-outhaul, also Inhaul	,,	Mid.	S-B	133
Spanker-brails	,,	P. & S.	S-B.	134
Spanker-sheet	,,	P. & S.	PR.	106
Spanker-vangs	,,	P. & S.	PR.	103
Spanker-boom-guys	,,	P. & S.	PR.	105
SQUARE SAILS.				
Cro'jack. Leech-lines & Bunt-lines	BP.	P. & S.	MR.	82
Cro'jack. Clew-garnets	,,	P. & S.	MR.	83
Cro'jack. Sheets	Bitts	P. & S.	Deck	104
Cro'jack. Tack. (On main-sheet bitts)	,,	P. & S.	MR.	74
Cro'jack. Lazy-tack. (Port)	BP.	P.	MR.	75
Cro'jack. Lazy-tack. (Starboard)	,,	S.	MR.	76
Cro'jack-yard. Lifts	,,	P. & S.	S-B	135
Cro'jack-brace	,,	P. & S.	MFR.	67
Cro'jack-bowline. (To any convenient pin in MR.)	—	—	—	—
Mizzen-lower-topsail. Bunt-lines & Clew-lines	BP.	P. & S.	PR.	84
Mizzen-lower-topsail. Sheets	,,	P. & S.	S-B.	108
Mizzen-lower-topsail. Brace	,,	P. & S.	MFR.	68
Mizzen-upper-topsail. Halliard	,,	P.	PR.	95
Mizzen-upper-topsail. Downhaul & Bunt-lines	,,	P. & S.	PR.	85
Mizzen-upper-topsail. Sheets. (Set up aloft)	—	—	—	—

TERMINOLOGICAL KEY TO BELAYING PIN LAYOUT.

Name of Gear	Type	Side	Position	No.
SQUARE SAILS—*Continued.*				
Mizzen-upper-topsail. Brace	BP.	P. & S.	MFR	69
Mizzen-lower-topgallant. Bunt-lines & Clew-lines	,,	P. & S.	PR.	87
Mizzen-lower-topgallant. Sheets	,,	P. & S.	PR.	86
Mizzen-lower-topgallant. Brace	,,	P. & S.	MFR.	71
Mizzen-upper-topgallant. Halliard	,,	S.	PR.	101
Mizzen-upper-topgallant. Downhaul & Bunt-lines	,,	P. & S.	PR.	90
Mizzen-upper-topgallant. Sheet. (Set up aloft)	—	—	—	—
Mizzen-upper-topgallant. Brace	BP.	P. & S.	MFR.	72
Mizzen-royal. Halliard	,,	P.	PR.	102
Mizzen-royal. Bunt-lines & Clew-lines	,,	P. & S.	PR.	92
Mizzen-royal. Sheets	,,	P. & S.	PR.	91
Mizzen-royal. Brace	,,	P. & S.	MFR	73

BP.	Indicates Belaying Pin	PR.	Indicates poop-rail
P.	Indicates port side	HFR.	Indicates Fife-rail on fo'castle-head
S.	Indicates Starboard side	FFR.	Indicates Fife-rail round fore-mast
S-B.	Indicates Spider-band	MFR.	Fife-rail round main-mast
MR.	Indicates Main-rail		

APPENDIX IV.

NUMERICAL INDEX TO FOLDING PLATE No. 51.—*Cont.*

No	Type	Position		Gear for which used.
		Side	Rail	
1	BP.	P.	HFR.	Flying-jib-downhaul
2	,,	P.	HFR.	Outer-jib-downhaul
3	,,	S.	HFR.	Inner-jib-downhaul
4	,,	S.	HFR.	Fore-topmast-staysail-downhaul
5	,,	P. & S.	MR.	Fore-lazy-tack.
6	,,	P. & S.	MR.	Flying-jib-sheets
7	,,	P. & S.	MR.	Outer-jib-sheets
8	,,	P. & S.	MR.	Inner-jib-sheets
9	Bitts	P. & S.	Deck	Fore-topmast-staysail-sheets
10	BP.	P& S.	MR.	Fore-sail. Leech-lines and Bunt-lines
11	,,	P. & S.	MR.	Fore-sail. Clew-garnets
12	,,	P. &S.	MR.	Fore-lower-topsail. Bunt-lines & Clew-lines
13	,,	P. & S.	MR.	Fore-upper-topsail. Dowhaul & Bunt-lines
14	,,	P. & S.	MR.	Fore-lower-topgallant. Sheets
15	,,	P. & S.	MR.	Fore-lower-topgallant. Bunt-lines & Clew-line
16	,,	P.	MR.	Fore-upper-topsail. Halliard
17	,,	P. & S.	MR.	Fore-upper-topgallant. Downhaul & Bunt-line
18	,,	P. & S.	MR.	Fore-royal. Sheets
19	,,	P. & S.	MR.	Fore-royal, Bunt-lines and Clew-lines
20	,,	S.	MR.	Fore-topmast-staysail-halliard
21	,,	P.	MR.	Inner-jib-halliard
22	,,	S.	MR.	Outer-jib-halliard
23	,,	S.	MR.	Fore-upper-topgallant-halliard
24	,,	P.	MR.	Flying-jib-halliard
25	,,	P.	MR.	
26	,,	P.	MR.	Fore-royal-halliard
27	,,		MR.	
28	,,	P. & S.	S-B.	Fore-lower-topsail-sheets
29	BE-Fd	P. & S.	Deck	Fore-lower-topsail-sheets
30	BP.	P.	FFR.	Main-bowline. (port)
31	,,	P.	FFR.	Main-royal-staysail-downhaul
32	,,	P.	FFR.	Main-topmast-staysail-downhaul
33	,,	P.	FFR.	Fore-lifts. (port)
34	,,	S.	FFR.	Main-bowline. (Starboard)
35	,,	S.	FFR.	Main-topgallant-staysail-downhaul
36	,,	S.	FFR.	
37	,,	S.	FFR.	Fore-lift. (Starboard)
38	Bitts	P. & S.	MR.	Fore-sheet
39	B.P.	P. & S.	MR.	Fore-lazy-sheet
40	,,	P. & S.	MR.	Main-topmast-staysail-sheet
41	,,	P. & S.	MR.	Fore-brace
42	,,	P. & S.	MR.	Fore-lower-topsail-brace
43	,,	P. & S.	MR.	Fore-upper-topsail-brace
44	,,	P. & S.	MR.	Main-topgallant-staysail-sheet
45	,,	P. & S.	MR.	Main-royal-staysail-sheet
46	,,	P. & S.	MR.	Main-sail. Leach-lines & Bunt-lines
47	,,	P. & S.	MR.	Main-sail. Clew-garnets
48	,,	P. & S.	MR.	Main-lower-topsail. Bunt-lines & Clew-lines
49	,,	P. & S.	MR.	Main-upper-topsail. Downhaul & Bunt-lines
50	,,	P. & S.	MR.	Main-lower-topgallant. Sheets
51	,,	P. & S.	MR.	Main-lower-topgallant. Bunt-lines & Clew-lines
52	,,	P. & S.	MR.	Main-upper-topgallant. Downhaul & Bunt-lines
53	,,	P. & S.	MR.	Main-royal-sheets

NUMERICAL INDEX TO FOLDING PLATE NO. 51.—*Contd.*

No.	Type	Position		Gear for which used.
		Side	Rail	
54	BP.	P. & S.	MR.	Main-royal. Bunt-lines & Clew-lines
55	,,	S.	MR.	Main-upper-topsail-halliard
56	,,	P.	MR.	Main-topmast-staysail-halliard
57	,,	P. & S.	MR.	Fore-lower-topgallant-brace
58	,,	P. & S.	MR.	Fore-upper-topgallant-brace
59	,,	P. & S.	MR.	Fore-royal-brace
60	,,	S.	MR.	Main-topgallant-staysail-halliard
61	,,	P.	MR.	Main-upper-topgallant. Halliard
62	,,	S.	MR.	Main-royal. Halliard
63	,,	P.	MR.	Main-royal-staysail-halliard
64	,,	P. & S.	MR.	Main-lifts
65	,,	P.	MFR.	Mizzen-topgallant-staysail-downhaul
66	,,	S.	MFR.	Mizzen-topmast-staysail-downhaul
67	,,	P. & S.	MFR.	Cro'jack-brace
68	,,	P. & S.	MFR.	Mizzen-lower-topsail-brace
69	,,	P. & S.	MFR.	Mizzen-upper-topsail-brace
70	,,	P. & S.	S-B.	Main-lower-topsail-sheets
71	,,	P. & S.	MFR.	Mizzen-lower-topgallant-brace
72	,,	P. & S.	MFR.	Mizzen-upper-topgallant-brace
73	,,	P. & S.	MFR.	Mizzen-royal-brace
74	Bitts	P. & S.	MR.	Main-sheet
75	BP.	P.	MR.	Cro'jack-lazy-tack (Port)
76	,,	S.	MR.	Cro'jack-lazy-tack (Starboard)
77	,,	P. & S.	MR.	Mizzen-topmast-staysail-sheet
78	,,	P. & S.	MR.	Main-brace
79	,,	P. & S.	MR.	Main-lower-topsail-brace
80	,,	P. & S.	MR.	Main-upper-topsail-brace
81	,,	P. & S.	MR.	Mizzen-topgallant-staysail-sheet
82	,,	P. & S.	MR.	Cro'jack. Leech-lines & Bunt-lines
83	,,	P. & S.	MR.	Cro'jack. Clew-garnets
84	,,	P. & S.	PR.	Mizzen-lower-topsail. Bunt-lines & Clew-lines
85	,,	P. & S.	PR.	Mizzen-upper-topsail. Downhaul & Bunt-lines
86	,,	P. & S.	PR.	Mizzen-lower-topgallant-sheets
87	,,	P. & S.	PR.	Mizzen-lower-topgallant Bunt-lines & Clew-lines
88	,,	P.	PR.	Spare
89	,,	S.	PR.	Spare
90	,,	P. & S.	PR.	Mizzen-upper-topgallant. Downhaul&Bunt-lines
91	,,	P. & S.	PR.	Mizzen-royal-sheets
92	,,	P. & S.	PR.	Mizzen-royal Bunt-lines & Clew-lines
93	,,	S.	PR.	Spare
94	,,	P.	PR.	Spanker-head-downhaul & outhaul
95	,,	P.	PR.	Mizzen-upper-topsail-halliard
96	,,	S.	PR.	Mizzen-topmast-staysail-halliard
97	,,	P. & S.	PR.	Main-lower-topgallant-brace
98	,,	P. & S.	PR.	Main-upper-topgallant-brace
99	,,	P. & S.	PR.	Main-royal-brace
100	,,	P.	PR.	Mizzen-topgallant-staysail-halliard
101	,,	S.	PR.	Mizzen-upper-topgallant-halliard
102	,,	P.	PR.	Mizzen-royal-halliard
103	,,	P. & S.	PR.	Spanker-vangs
104	Bitts	P. & S.	Deck	Cro'jack Sheets
105	BP.	P. & S.	PR.	Spanker-boom-guys
106	,,	P. & S.	PR.	Spanker-sheet
107	BE-Fd.	P. & S.	Deck	Mizzen-lower-topsail-sheet
108	BP.	P. & S.	S-B.	Mizzen-lower-topsail-sheet
109	Bitts	P. & S.	Deck	Fore-tack
110	EB.	P. & S.	Deck	Standing part of jib-sheet
111	BE-Fd.	P. & S.	Deck	Jib-sheet
112	EB.	P. & S.	Bulwk.	Standing part of fore-sheet
113	Fd.	P. & S.	Bulwk.	Fore-sheet
114	BE-Fd.	P. & S.	Deck	Main-lower-top sail-sheet

NUMERICAL INDEX TO FOLDING PLATE No. 51.

| No. | Type | Position | | Gear for which used. |
		Side	Rail	
115	EB.	P. & S.	Deck	For lead blocks
116	,,	P. & S.	Bulwk.	Standing part of main-sheet
117	Fd.	P. & S.	Bulwk.	Main-sheet
118	EB.	P. & S.	Bulwk.	Standing part of fore-braces
119	—	P. & S.	—	Flying-jib-sheet
120	—	P. & S.	—	Outer-jib-sheet
121	—	P. & S.	—	Inner-jib-sheet
122	—	P. & S.	—	Fore-topmast-staysail-sheet
123	—	P. & S.	—	Fore-upper-topsail-brace
124	—	P. & S.	—	Fore-lower-topsail-brace
125	—	P. & S.	—	Fore-brace
126	—	P. & S.	—	Main-upper-topsail-brace
127	—	P. & S.	—	Main-lower-topsail-brace
128	—	P. & S.	—	Main-brace
129	TSB.	P. & S.	MR.	Lower brace blocks
130	—	P. & S.	—	Bumkin for lower main-braces
131	—	P. & S.	—	Main-brace-purchase-block
132	BP.	P.	MR.	Two spare pins
133	,,	Mid	S-B	Spanker-foot-outhaul & inhaul
134	,,	P. & S.	S-B.	Spanker-brails
135	,,	P. & S.	S-B.	Cro'jack-lifts

A	Indicates Fore-shrouds	R	Indicates Mizzen royal-backstay
B	Indicates Fore-lower-capstay	BP.	Indicates Belaying pin
C	Indicates Fore-topmast-backstays	P.	Indicates Port side
D	Indicates Fore-topmast-capstay	S.	Indicates Starboard side
E	Indicates Fore-topgallant-backstays	S-B.	Indicates Spider-band
F	Indicates Fore-royal-backstay	MR.	Indicates Main-rail
G	Indicates Main-shrouds	PR.	Indicates poop-rail
H	Indicates Main-lower-capstay	HFR	Indicates fife-rail on fo'castle-head
I	Indicates Main-topmast-backstays	FFR	Indicates Fife-rail round fore-mast
J	Indicates Main-topmast-capstay	MFR.	Indicates Fife-rail round main-mast
K	Indicates Main-topgallant-backstays	Mid	Indicates Midships
L	Indicates Main-royal-backstay	EB.	Indicates Eye-bolt
M	Indicates Mizzen-shrouds	Fd.	Indicates Fairlead
N	Indicates Mizzen-lower-capstay	BE.	Indicates Bulls-eye
O	Indicates Mizzen-topmast-backstays	BE-Fd	Indicates Bulls-eye-fairlead
P	Indicates Mizzen-topmast-capstay	TSB.	Indicates Triple-sister-blocks
Q	Indicates Mizzen-topgallant-backstays		

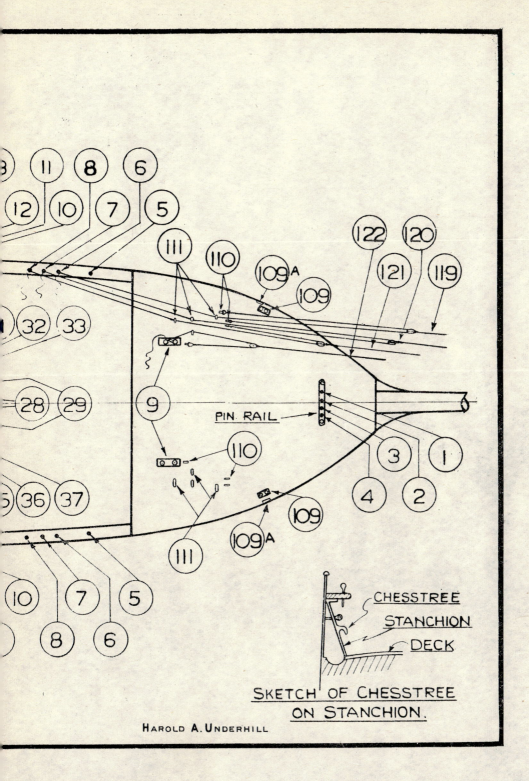

PIN RAIL

CHESSTREE

STANCHION

DECK

SKETCH OF CHESSTREE
ON STANCHION.

HAROLD A. UNDERHILL

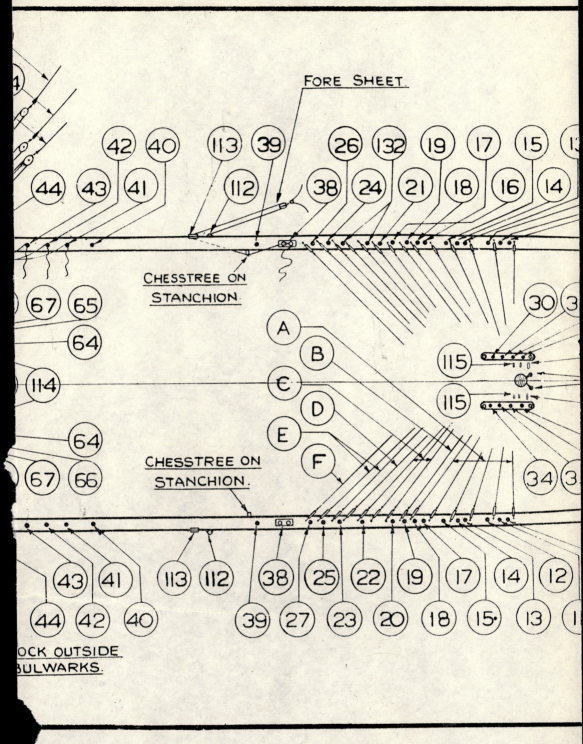

FORE SHEET.

CHESSTREE ON STANCHION.

CHESSTREE ON STANCHION.

OCK OUTSIDE
BULWARKS.

FOR FULL-RIGGED SHIP.

PAGES 281 TO 286.

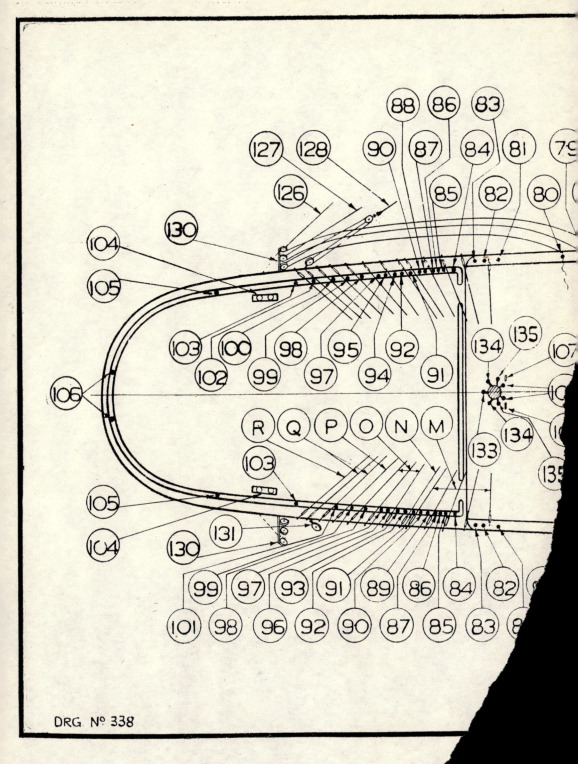

DRG. Nº 338

INDEX

INDEX